CRITICAL THEORY IN CRITICAL TIMES

NEW DIRECTIONS IN CRITICAL THEORY

NEW DIRECTIONS IN CRITICAL THEORY

Amy Allen, General Editor

New Directions in Critical Theory presents outstanding classic and contemporary texts in the tradition of critical social theory, broadly construed. The series aims to renew and advance the program of critical social theory, with a particular focus on theorizing contemporary struggles around gender, race, sexuality, class, and globalization and their complex interconnections.

Narrating Evil: A Postmetaphysical Theory of Reflective Judgment, María Pía Lara

The Politics of Our Selves: Power, Autonomy, and Gender in Contemporary Critical Theory, Amy Allen

Democracy and the Political Unconscious, Noëlle McAfee

The Force of the Example: Explorations in the Paradigm of Judgment, Alessandro Ferrara

Horrorism: Naming Contemporary Violence, Adriana Cavarero

Scales of Justice: Reimagining Political Space in a Globalizing World, Nancy Fraser

Pathologies of Reason: On the Legacy of Critical Theory, Axel Honneth

States Without Nations: Citizenship for Mortals, Jacqueline Stevens

The Racial Discourses of Life Philosophy: Négritude, Vitalism, and Modernity, Donna V. Jones

Democracy in What State?, Giorgio Agamben, Alain Badiou, Daniel Bensaïd, Wendy Brown, Jean-Luc Nancy, Jacques Rancière, Kristin Ross, Slavoj Žižek

Politics of Culture and the Spirit of Critique: Dialogues, edited by Gabriel Rockhill and Alfredo Gomez-Muller

Mute Speech: Literature, Critical Theory, and Politics, Jacques Rancière

The Right to Justification: Elements of Constructivist Theory of Justice, Rainer Forst

The Scandal of Reason: A Critical Theory of Political Judgment, Albena Azmanova

The Wrath of Capital: Neoliberalism and Climate Change Politics, Adrian Parr

Media of Reason: A Theory of Rationality, Matthias Vogel

Social Acceleration: The Transformation of Time in Modernity, Hartmut Rosa

The Disclosure of Politics: Struggles Over the Semantics of Secularization, María Pía Lara

Radical Cosmopolitics: The Ethics and Politics of Democratic Universalism, James Ingram

Freedom's Right: The Social Foundations of Democratic Life, Axel Honneth

Imaginal Politics: Images Beyond Imagination and the Imaginary, Chiara Bottici

Alienation, Rahel Jaeggi

The Power of Tolerance: A Debate, Wendy Brown and Rainer Forst, edited by Luca Di Blasi and Christoph F. E. Holzhey

Radical History and the Politics of Art, Gabriel Rockhill

The Highway of Despair: Critical Theory After Hegel, Robyn Marasco

A Political Economy of the Senses: Neoliberalism, Reification, Critique, Anita Chari

The End of Progress: Decolonizing the Normative Foundations of Critical Theory, Amy Allen

Recognition or Disagreement: A Critical Encounter on the Politics of Freedom, Equality, and Identity, Axel Honneth and Jacques Rancière, edited by Katia Genel and Jean-Philippe Deranty

What Is a People?, Alain Badiou, Pierre Bourdieu, Judith Butler, Georges Didi-Huberman, Sadri Khiari, and Jacques Rancière

Left-wing Melancholia: Marxism, History, and Memory, Enzo Traverso

CRITICAL THEORY IN CRITICAL TIMES

TRANSFORMING THE GLOBAL POLITICAL AND ECONOMIC ORDER

EDITED BY
PENELOPE DEUTSCHER
AND CRISTINA LAFONT

Columbia University Press
New York

Columbia University Press
Publishers Since 1893
New York   Chichester, West Sussex
cup.columbia.edu
Copyright © 2017 Columbia University Press
All rights reserved

Library of Congress Cataloging-in-Publication Data

Names: Deutscher, Penelope, 1966– author. | Lafont, Cristina, 1963– author.
Title: Critical theory in critical times : transforming the global political and economic order / edited by Penelope Deutscher and Cristina Lafont.
Description: New York : Columbia University Press, [2017] | Series: New directions in critical theory | Includes bibliographical references and index.
Identifiers: LCCN 2016044939| ISBN 9780231181501 (cloth : alk. paper) | ISBN 9780231181518 (pbk. : alk. paper) | ISBN 9780231543620 (e-book)
Subjects: LCSH: Critical theory.
Classification: LCC HM480 .C745 2017 | DDC 142—dc23
LC record available at https://lccn.loc.gov/2016044939

Columbia University Press books are printed on permanent and durable acid-free paper.

Printed in the United States of America

Cover design: Jordan Wannemacher

CONTENTS

Acknowledgments xi

Introduction: Critical Theory in Critical Times xiii

I. THE FUTURE OF DEMOCRACY

1. AN EXPLORATION OF THE MEANING OF TRANSNATIONALIZATION OF DEMOCRACY, USING THE EXAMPLE OF THE EUROPEAN UNION

JÜRGEN HABERMAS

3

II. HUMAN RIGHTS AND SOVEREIGNTY

2. DEMOCRATIC SOVEREIGNTY AND TRANSNATIONAL LAW: ON LEGAL UTOPIANISM AND DEMOCRATIC SKEPTICISM

SEYLA BENHABIB

21

3. HUMAN RIGHTS, SOVEREIGNTY, AND THE RESPONSIBILITY TO PROTECT

CRISTINA LAFONT

47

4. A CRITICAL THEORY OF HUMAN RIGHTS—SOME GROUNDWORK

RAINER FORST

74

III. POLITICAL RIGHTS IN NEOLIBERAL TIMES

5. NEOLIBERALISM AND THE ECONOMIZATION OF RIGHTS

WENDY BROWN

91

6. LAW AND DOMINATION

CHRISTOPH MENKE

117

IV. CRITICIZING CAPITALISM

7. BEHIND MARX'S HIDDEN ABODE: FOR AN EXPANDED CONCEPTION OF CAPITALISM

NANCY FRASER

141

8. A WIDE CONCEPT OF ECONOMY: ECONOMY AS A SOCIAL PRACTICE AND THE CRITIQUE OF CAPITALISM

RAHEL JAEGGI

160

V. THE END OF PROGRESS IN POSTCOLONIAL TIMES

9. ADORNO, FOUCAULT, AND THE END OF PROGRESS: CRITICAL THEORY IN POSTCOLONIAL TIMES

AMY ALLEN

183

10. "POST-FOUCAULT": THE CRITICAL TIME OF THE PRESENT

PENELOPE DEUTSCHER

207

11. CRITICIZING CRITICAL THEORY

CHARLES W. MILLS

233

Bibliography 251

About the Contributors 271

Index 277

ACKNOWLEDGMENTS

This collection of essays started its life as the conference "Critical Theory in Critical Times," held at Northwestern University, May 2–4, 2014. Neither the conference nor this volume would have been possible without the generous support of the Equality Development and Globalization Studies program at Northwestern's Buffett Institute for Global Studies. Additional support at Northwestern was provided by the departments of Communication Studies, Philosophy, Political Science, Religious Studies, and Sociology; the Alice Kaplan Institute for the Humanities; the Center for Global Culture and Communication; and the Weinberg College of Arts and Sciences' Edith Kreeger Wolf Endowment. Important support was also provided by the Goethe Institute of Chicago and the Excellence Cluster on the Formation of Normative Orders at Goethe University Frankfurt. We extend our warm thanks to these many partners, and to Jasmine Hatten, Ozge Kocak, Mara Weber, and, particularly, Tara Sadera for their extremely professional and engaged assistance. We are grateful also to our colleagues at Northwestern, especially those who acted as respondents and chairs, whose support was crucial to the success of the conference, and to an extraordinary audience, whose questions and comments generated a lively discussion throughout the sessions. We extend our gratitude also to the many graduate and undergraduate students, especially those affiliated with Northwestern's Critical Theory Cluster, who supported the conference. We are particularly grateful to Carlos Pereira

Di Salvo for his superb editing of this volume. Finally, our warm thanks to Wendy Lochner, Christine Dunbar, Amy Allen, Todd Manza, all those involved in the volume's acceptance and production at Columbia University Press, and, of course, to the volume's contributors for their participation and help in bringing this project to fruition.

INTRODUCTION

Critical Theory in Critical Times

PENELOPE DEUTSCHER AND CRISTINA LAFONT

We live in critical times. There is a widely shared sense of unease about the future. On the one hand, we face global crises—an overtaxed environment, a volatile global economy, mass migrations, new forms of war and terrorism. On the other hand, there is also a crisis of confidence in the capacity for political action to address such global problems.

Yet, there is also another, more positive sense in which we live in critical times. Since the end of the cold war, the global order has been in a state of constant flux. Perhaps this is a historic window of opportunity for new visions of the transnational and new political imaginaries to address current and future crises. These also are critical times for proposals aimed at transformation and improvement, and thus are propitious times for critical theory.

It is in this spirit that this collection gathers work by some of the most distinguished contemporary critical theorists, representing a number of traditions within critical theory, broadly conceived. These eleven essays offer new perspectives on issues such as the need and possibilities for transnational democracy, the justification and role of international human rights in strengthening democratic sovereignty against global neoliberalism, the neoliberal erosion of rights through the encroachment of the economic on all spheres of social and political life, the need to reconceptualize the critique of capitalism in the global era, and the need for critical theory to confront its Eurocentric heritage and respond to challenges from critical race theory and postcolonial studies. The essays reveal new ways of conceiving and connecting the diversity of explanatory paradigms across the different fields and disciplines encompassed in the tradition of critical theory, and of sharpening its conceptual tools. Those familiar with the tradition's prior generations will gain an overview of the many ways contemporary critical theory has responded to profound social, political, cultural, and economic transformations with new themes, approaches, sensitivities, and perspectives—even while the emancipatory ambitions of prior generations of critical theory endure.

The volume is centered around several pressing problems of contemporary politics, which provide a unifying reference point for the contributions included in each part. Parts 1 and 2 focus on the global order from a political-legal perspective. In the opening essay, Jürgen Habermas confronts a key political challenge of our times, namely, how transnational democratization might be possible in the absence of a world state. The challenge arises from a mismatch between the increased demand for global governance to tackle global problems and the limitation of democratic politics to the domestic level, leaving transnational political action without any form of genuinely democratic governance. There are two sides to this problem. On the one hand, improving the democratic institutions of states won't eliminate this democratic deficit. On the other hand, a weakening of state institutions by transnational measures could undermine the important historical achievements of democratic states (such as the commitment to equal protection of rights and freedoms or to equitable living conditions).

As a way out of this conundrum, Habermas offers a theoretical model for thinking of transnational democratization in a way that is sensitive to the need to preserve state sovereignty while enabling a constitutionalization of world society. He takes the European Union as a model for articulating this theoretical possibility. Although the democratic deficits of the EU are very different from those of a global political society, a fruitful connection between these cases can be established.

In order to overcome the democratic deficits within the EU, some model of transnational democratization is needed. The problem with the current political structure of the EU is not so much that its member states are not themselves democratic but rather that a form of political and, particularly, economic decision making has significantly migrated "up" to the transnational level, thus escaping the democratic controls that national political institutions could provide. But the model of transnational democratization suitable to the EU would not require it to transform into a European federal state. Thus, it may also serve as a model for the formation of transnational political communities in a future international order wherein global democratic politics could be possible without a world state. Habermas argues for a form of supranational constitutionalization that would not undermine national sovereignty and would enable political authority to meet the appropriate criteria for democratic legitimacy at each level: national, transnational, and supranational.

The compatibility between global constitutionalism and national sovereignty is also the focus of the contributions included in part 2 of the book. These three essays challenge, from different perspectives, the view that international human rights undermine democratic sovereignty. Against critics of legal cosmopolitanism, Seyla Benhabib argues that, far from being incompatible, human rights and democratic self-determination form a dialectic through an interdependent and productive process of norm enhancement and ongoing interpretation.

In pointing to the hermeneutic fact that human rights conventions are not self-interpreting documents, Benhabib contrasts their status as concepts and conceptions. They may provide a core concept of the rights they specify, but they cannot provide a specific conception of them or a full determination of the exact scope of application of each of these rights under all possible circumstances. Because such determination unavoidably leads to contextual variation over time and across regions, the legitimacy of the legal imposition of one or another interpretation of rights will depend on who has the legitimate authority to make such determinations. The fundamental incompleteness of rights, their permanent need for specification and contextualization, points to the conceptual interdependency between rights and democracy.

Moreover, Benhabib goes on to argue, without the right to self-government, the range of variation in the legal interpretation of the content of basic human rights cannot be justified. Thus, the right to self-government is not just a right alongside all other rights. It is the condition for enjoying any right as a right rather than as a privilege that some authority might give or take away at will. However, the very same incompleteness of rights, and the range of their legitimate variation, also can be turned against the statists' privileging of national sovereignty as the only legitimate domain for the specification of rights. Benhabib develops a cosmopolitan theory of their "democratic iterations" to emphasize the important struggle among local, national, and international levels of governance, as well as among various organizations, social movements, national and international nongovernmental organizations (NGOs), and others, in their interpretations of human rights. These are complex processes of public argument and deliberation through which universalist rights claims are contested and contextualized, invoked and revoked, posited and positioned, through national and transnational civil society and global public spheres, in diverse sites that are porous, permeable, and open to the kind of cross-cultural and transnational affiliations that contemporary legal cosmopolitanism aims to elucidate.

In the second essay of part 2, Cristina Lafont defends the claim that human rights strengthen rather than undermine national sovereignty, though from a different perspective than that of Benhabib. Instead of focusing on the determination of the content of specific human rights, Lafont challenges the alleged incompatibility between human rights and sovereignty by foregrounding the distribution of responsibilities for human rights protections.

She considers the recently endorsed Responsibility to Protect (R2P) doctrine, which contemplates the possibility of coercive international action against sovereign states in cases of gross violations of human rights. This possibility fuels the impression that principled commitments to human rights and to sovereignty are on a collision course. In reaction, statists propose to minimize and de-internationalize human rights standards in order to protect national sovereignty against coercive intervention by powerful states.

Against these proposals, Lafont argues that the international commitment to human rights standards can strengthen the sovereignty of weak states against forms of international action that undermine their ability to protect human rights within their jurisdiction. To show how this should work in practice, Lafont challenges the tendency to see states as primarily inclined to deny the human rights that the global community might seek to enforce. On the contrary, she reminds us that weak states come under pressure from global governance institutions such as the World

Trade Organization (WTO), the International Monetary Fund (IMF), or the World Bank—bodies not governed by human rights standards—to comply with the conditions of economic policies and regulations (from patent agreements to structural adjustment polices) that undermine those states' ability to protect the socioeconomic rights of their populations. In that context, the international human rights obligations of states can be understood as strengthening their claim to sovereignty. Lafont articulates a view of the international responsibility to protect human rights that is more demanding than current R2P doctrine and that calls for shoring up the sovereignty of states whose ability to protect the human rights of their populations has been undermined.

In the final essay of part 2, Rainer Forst also challenges the alleged conflict between human rights and democratic sovereignty, as well as the human rights minimalism that often is defended as the way out of that conflict. He defends a philosophical account of human rights in which human rights and democracy are conceptually interdependent, tracing both to a common ground in one basic moral right: the right to justification. According to Forst, we bear a right to be given adequate reasons for actions or norms that affect us in relevant ways. On this basis, we are entitled to basic human rights that secure this status. These include the essential personal, political, and social rights necessary to establish what Forst calls a "social structure of justification." They also include substantive rights that, within such a structure of justification, could not reasonably be denied to others without violating the demands of reciprocity and generality.

By emphasizing that human rights have long been claimed in social struggles against exploitation and oppression, Forst's critical theory of human rights aims to reconstruct their basic emancipatory claim, which seeks to make the moral right to justification socially effective. Human rights enshrine the basic right to live in a society in which social and political agents determine which rights they can claim and must recognize. Thus, human rights necessarily include the right to political participation. Forst repudiates the view that there is an intrinsic conflict between human rights and sovereignty. On the contrary, according to his argument, one cannot limit the human right to democracy by appealing to the principle of sovereignty or collective self-determination without contradiction. Anticipating the line of criticism that Amy Allen articulates in the final part of the book, Forst claims that his argument is immune to the charge of ethnocentrism, insofar as such a charge still presupposes a tacit claim to the principle he defends as universal: the right to justification.

Part 3 shifts the focus from recent contributions by critical theorists to the area of transnational law and democracy toward a discursively oriented critique of the contemporary and historical challenges to democracy, equality, and rights. Wendy Brown brings a different perspective to the erosion of powers discussed in parts 1 and 2. Her guiding question is whether states are still capable of ensuring popular sovereignty at all. She focuses on the means by which neoliberalism has steadily eroded democracy not only in the Global South but also in the Global North, albeit through more subtle means. For example, she describes the recent erosions of free speech, civil rights, the political process, labor unions, affirmative action, and the welfare state in the United States. Brown seeks to broaden contemporary critiques of the erosion of political sovereignty by bodies such as the World Bank, the IMF, and the eurozone. Such critiques must go further, to challenge the pervasive neoliberal rationality organizing not only economic policies but also, increasingly, all aspects of contemporary social, public, private, and political life.

But the question is how to avoid capitulating to an increasingly pervasive neoliberal common sense and its generalized marketization. Brown argues for closer analysis of exactly how this occurs. Exactly how is it, for example, that crucial aspects of the democratic political process, such as elections, come to be marketized and undermined by neoliberalism? Her precise account of the 2010 US Supreme Court's *Citizens United* ruling illustrates the type of analysis she advocates. She shows that the ruling did more than analogize political speech to a free marketplace, which is a common interpretation. Instead, she shows that the ruling really did effect the "economization" of political speech, threatening the very distinction between the political and the economic.

Without idealizing past forms of democracy, Brown nonetheless claims that neoliberalism has eroded a lever long vital to the process of ongoing critique, which she associates with democracy. We lose democracy's (always incomplete) aspirational meaning, its ideals and its imaginary, when we confuse the public sphere with a market of ideas. And, in combination with the convention of deeming market forces to be unavoidable, a further result is an erosion of confidence in our capacity to transform social and political futures.

Brown's close textual analysis of the *Citizens United* ruling is followed by a second contribution to critical theory's tradition of close textual analysis. In his reconstruction of Karl Marx's political critique of bourgeois law, Christoph Menke offers a detailed analysis of a blind spot that emerges in the course of Marx's distinction between social and political rights. Because Marx saw capitalism as requiring the private, bourgeois law that protected property rights, sustained class inequality, and concealed and enabled class domination, he considered the rise of "social" rights claims politically irrelevant.

Menke argues that Marx was right to distinguish between two different types of law and rights—private and social—but that he misunderstood and underestimated the significance of social rights. The critical analysis of private rights adds to our understanding of law as domination and as distributing and concealing inequality. However, because social rights concern the right to equal participation and communication in social and public life, Marx's analysis must be complemented with a different form of critique if we are to understand the role played by this form of law in structures of domination. A critical theory of law and rights will require multiple concepts of domination and power.

Accordingly, in his essay Menke turns to the work of Michel Foucault to retrieve an alternative analysis of the social rights disregarded by Marx. They are, he suggests, the "life rights" described in Foucault's *Volonté de savoir* as intertwined with discipline and biopower. In claiming "life rights," we participate unwittingly in forms of normalization and subjectification whose analysis requires the reformulation of how we understand domination. Although the analyses of Foucault and Marx are often taken to be opposed, given their different analytics of power and Foucault's well-known critique of Marx, Menke concludes that the corresponding modes of domination they describe—through their various analyses of private bourgeois law and of the normalization of social rights—should not be separated. Through this double concentration on its social and political dimensions, the law can be newly understood in terms of its constitutive double antagonism and ambiguity: normalization is expressed and made possible by social rights, while inequality is expressed and made possible by private rights, the former also relying on the latter.

The fourth part of the book focuses on the current economic order and, in particular, on the need to articulate an understanding and critique of capitalism that is appropriate to our time. Both essays in part 4 are based on the assumption that capitalism is much more than an economic system; the differences in their respective diagnoses are marked by how this "more" should be understood. Nancy Fraser aims to offer a critical theory of contemporary capitalism that revises traditional Marxist conceptions by incorporating the insights of feminism, postcolonialism, and ecological thought. As she argues, the remarkable recent revival of capitalism as a central category of analysis results from the growing intuition that the heterogeneous ills that surround us—financial, economic, ecological, political, and social—can be traced to a common root. Reforms that fail to engage with the deep structural underpinnings of these ills are doomed to fail. Consequently, only a unified analysis that includes capitalism as a central category can clarify the relations among the disparate social struggles of our time.

To provide a framework for such a unified analysis, Fraser follows and radicalizes what she sees as the key methodological strategy of Marx's analysis of capitalism. Marx was able to identify the four defining features of capitalism—private property in the means of production, a free labor market, capital accumulation, and the distinctive role of markets—by looking behind the sphere of exchange into the "hidden abode" of production. Employing a similar theoretical move, Fraser aims to identify additional key features of contemporary capitalism by looking behind the sphere of production into its even more hidden "conditions of possibility." She identifies the realms of social reproduction, ecology, and political power as necessary background conditions for commodity production, labor exploitation, and capital accumulation. If this is the case, then capitalist production is not self-sustaining but depends on social reproduction, nature, and political power. Yet capitalism's orientation toward capital accumulation threatens to destabilize the very conditions of its possibility. It undermines its own social-reproductive conditions: the sociocultural processes that supply solidary relations and affective dispositions, and the value horizons that underpin social cooperation. It undermines its ecological conditions: the natural processes that sustain life and provide the material inputs for social provisioning. And it undermines its political conditions: the public powers, both national and transnational, that guarantee property rights, enforce contracts, quell anticapitalist rebellions, and maintain the monetary supply.

As Fraser emphasizes, these background conditions enabling the capitalist system of production are themselves not features of a capitalist economy but of a capitalist *society*. However, she rejects the widespread view of capitalism as a reified form of ethical life, characterized by pervasive commodification and monetization. She argues that capitalist commodification depends for its very existence on zones of noncommodification that embody their own, distinctive normative and ontological grammars. Rejecting a purely functionalist analysis of capitalism, Fraser conceives of the "hidden abodes" of reproduction, ecology, and politics as reservoirs of "noneconomic" normativity that are pregnant with critical possibility, helping us to understand how a critique of capitalism is possible within it.

In the second essay of part 4, Rahel Jaeggi addresses explicitly the need for a "wider" understanding of capitalism. Her proposal connects with and differs from Fraser's in interesting ways. An important point of coincidence between both diagnoses is the rejection of what Jaeggi calls the inside/outside metaphor: the popular picture of capitalism as a self-enclosed economic system that follows a logic of its own, a threatening black box from which other spheres (cultural, social, personal) need to be protected. So long as we are captives of that picture, Jaeggi argues, so long as the *economy itself* is not seen as part of the social order, it cannot become the object of social critique. Therefore, developing a wider understanding of the economy is necessary to taking a critical look at the political economy of our times.

The key to Jaeggi's approach is to understand societies as forms of life in the specific sense of aggregate ensembles of various social practices that are subject to their own problem-solving dynamics. From that perspective, economic practices are social practices, a part of the sociocultural fabric of society. To view them critically is to see them as *failed* practices. Like all practices, economic practices are subject to normative criteria of appropriateness, and thus their ability or inability to solve predefined normative problems can be critically examined and subjected to a critique immanent to their normative content.

To defend this claim, Jaeggi questions the widespread view of the economy as a norm-free zone, a sphere disembedded from the normative fabric of society. She offers a detailed analysis of key features of social practices, which she then applies to paradigmatic practices and institutions of capitalism (such as regulation of property and distribution through market exchanges). Her analysis reveals that, in capitalism, economic practices are still practices, based on norms, aggregated into institutions, and involved in the larger practical context of a form of life. As Jaeggi argues, far from generating a norm-free zone, the capitalist economy replaces a prior (premodern) ethos with a new one. The ethos of abolishing substantial ethical relations and restrictions, such as those broken in the formation of "modern" or capitalist economic institutions, is still itself an ethos. Thus, we should not be duped by capitalism's tendency to make the normative character of economic institutions invisible.

The book's final part takes up the issue of possible ethnocentrism in critical theory, broached in part 2. Amy Allen questions the role played by narratives of progress presupposed by the second, third, and fourth generations of critical theory—thus, in the work of philosophers from Habermas to Forst. None would endorse overtly colonialist images of Europe as civilizing, yet Allen argues that Habermas's and Axel Honneth's reliance on the idea of historical progress continues a problematic tradition in which the peoples and forms of life identified as premodern are indirectly supposed to have lesser worth.

Allen proposes a return to the first generation of critical theory, given its greater skepticism about the state of historical progress, and its decoupling of this negative assessment from the more positive projection of progress as an ideal, as seen in the work of Theodor Adorno. This is Allen's first step toward supplementing the critical theory lineage running from Habermas to Forst with the resources of a countertradition within critical theory, a lineage that would extend from Adorno to Foucault, which has particularly favored forms of immanent critique.

Her further reasons for considering a more promising alternative for the project of decolonizing critical theory include its stronger account of reason's entanglement in power and history and its rejection of a privileged modern, European, or contemporary vantage point. This tradition offers a more ambiguous appraisal of the Enlightenment as connoting both domination and promise. It has tended to emphasize the ways in which freedom can also, simultaneously, be understood as a form of subjection. It can offer a more critical vantage point on our contemporary perspective, among whose "terminal truths" Allen would count modernity's enduring Eurocentrism.

Allen also revises a common view among some critical theorists that Adorno and Foucault negated modernity's normative inheritance. Instead, she finds in these writers' alternative concepts of freedom a commitment to modernity's central values. And, notwithstanding the inadequacy of Adorno's and Foucault's actual considerations of racial hierarchy and colonial and imperial power, she argues that their alternative conceptualizations of freedom, power, and history offer a more promising resource for the contemporary project of its decolonization.

In the first of two responses to Allen, Penelope Deutscher focuses on the turn to Foucault's work by a number of critical theorists. Some, including contributors Nancy Fraser and Wendy Brown, have argued that contemporary times have seen forms of political, social, and economic change not anticipated by Foucault, such that his models of power, particularly his disciplinary model, are less relevant today. Others understand today's pressing theoretical imperatives to constitute a post-Foucauldian time of theory and criticism. In the final chapter of this volume, Charles Mills urges critical theorists and philosophers to recognize the challenge slavery poses to philosophical accounts of recognition or alterity. He doubts that existing philosophical considerations of alterity—including Foucault's "unreason"—are adequate to the task.

Deutscher directs the same question to those who derive from Foucault abstract conceptions of freedom and normalization (Allen and Menke) and to those who situate Foucault's models as overly specific to their time: Don't these interpretations bypass or presuppose the status of Foucauldian time and timeliness, thereby bypassing the importance of this question to Foucault's understanding of critique, a temporality by means of which Mills's criticisms of Foucault on race could also be reconsidered?

Adding to those who have directed renewed interest at a Foucauldian understanding of the ambiguity of rights (Menke) and of freedom (Allen), Deutscher returns to the complex role of the "present" in Foucault's understanding of critical theory and of the "presence" of epistemes and formations of power. Foucauldian temporality is, she argues, fundamental to understanding the ambiguity of the Foucauldian freedom emphasized by Allen and the Foucauldian ambiguity of rights, emphasized by Menke. Deutscher defends the role of Foucauldian time as rendering more complex our assessment of the time in which we find ourselves, and our realization of its ruptures and impending transformations.

In the second response to Amy Allen, Charles Mills agrees with Allen that critical theory's own promotion of emancipation, freedom, justice, and respect for the other ought to provide a promising foundation for challenging its Eurocentrism. But he takes Allen's project to insufficiently distinguish between decolonization and deracialization, hindering its scope of critique. Moreover, he would question the sufficiency of any project to decolonize critical theory if it occludes the actual literature of critical race studies. Thus, Mills is wary of Allen's appeal to an alternative critical theory lineage extending from Adorno and Foucault as the more promising resource for critical theory's decolonization.

Moreover, Mills reminds us that not all forms of challenge to critical theory's Eurocentrism and imperialism are automatically aligned in sympathy. An attunement to its Eurocentrism does not automatically deliver a comprehensive understanding of critical theory's whiteness. In fact, postcolonial studies have tended to marginalize questions of race, failing to engage the literature of critical race studies, which, all the while, has been dominated by a largely American focus. Both fields, for instance, have neglected the theorization of race within Native American studies. Thus, Mills argues for more integrated and globally oriented forms of analysis, which would confront critical theory with at least five further conditions. These are, first, the need to address the actual presence and numbers of philosophers of color as more than a merely "demographic" question and, second, to dialogue with the literature of critical race studies and its different perspectives and analytic starting points. Third, the project to decolonize and deracialize critical theory requires a broader contextualization. This project is just as pressing for philosophy, and for political theory generally, which also have failed to appreciate the social significance of race and its role in structuring reality. Fourth, there is need for greater skepticism about well-meaning denunciations of race bias, because these may coincide with the systematic adoption of analytic categories and approaches that render the significance of race invisible. Fifth, Mills reminds us that the very geography and chronology of modernity, its space and time, in addition to its rationality, have come to be racially inflected. We tend to underestimate this phenomenon, and it can, he argues, be only insufficiently characterized by concepts such as second nature and ideology.

The contributions to this volume exemplify a variety of distinctive, sometimes competing approaches to critical theory. Far from solidifying a methodological orthodoxy, the tensions among different paradigms contribute to the internal dialogue among the various contributions. Whereas, for some, the legal-political paradigm offers the best entry point for understanding and transforming the current economic and political order, others question the limits of such paradigms. These methodological tensions become explicit in the final part of the book, in the self-reflective dialogue on the limits and pitfalls of some traditions of critical theory. Collectively, the book reflects critical theory's ongoing gains from the methodological diversity that has emerged in response to the profound transformations of the global order.

CRITICAL THEORY IN CRITICAL TIMES

I

THE FUTURE OF DEMOCRACY

1

AN EXPLORATION OF THE MEANING OF TRANSNATIONALIZATION OF DEMOCRACY, USING THE EXAMPLE OF THE EUROPEAN UNION

JÜRGEN HABERMAS

I use the term *transnationalization* to refer to the process that aims to create a "supranational" democracy, that is, one above the level of a state. Taking the European Union as a model, *supranational* is meant to express the idea that such a polity assumes a federal character but—unlike federal states—not the familiar characteristics of a state. This supranational construct is not supposed to enjoy either a monopoly on the legitimate use of force or ultimate decision-making authority. Instead, it should be based on the weak priority of applying federal law and leave the implementation of statutes, guidelines, and decrees to the governments of the member states. Can such a union satisfy the standards of democratic legitimacy that we are familiar with from nation-states? I think that this question is important not only when it comes to the future of the European Union but also when one considers the current threat to the democratic substance of all nation-states, the smaller more than the larger.

Our era is marked by a growing mismatch between a world society that is becoming increasingly interdependent at the systemic level and a world of states that remains fragmented. The states that are consciously integrated by their citizens are still the only collectives capable of acting effectively on the basis of democratic decisions and with the intention to protect and shape the social conditions of their populations. But they are becoming ever more deeply entangled in systemic relationships that permeate national boundaries. Above all, globalized markets make use of accelerated digital communication to create ever-denser networks and to bring these collective actors into completely new kinds of dependencies. In view of the politically undesirable side effects of systemic integration, a need for steering arises, which single nation-states are increasingly unable to cope with. Politicians and citizens sense this loss of political decision-making power and, in a psychologically understandable but paradoxical defensive reaction, cling even more firmly to the nation-state and its borders, which have long since become porous.

The national scope for action that has already been lost and is still shrinking can be made good only at the supranational level. Indeed, this is actually happening in the form of international cooperation. The rapidly increasing number of influential international organizations has given rise to various forms of governance beyond the nation-state. But these international treaty regimes escape proper democratic control.[1] An alternative would be to form supranational communities that, as I will show, can in principle satisfy democratic standards of legitimacy even when they do not assume the format of states writ large. One need not share Marxist background assumptions to recognize in the unleashing of financial markets and the "financialization" of capitalism one of the crucial reasons for this development[2]—and to conclude that we must first implement a promising re-regulation of the global banking sector within an economic region of at least the size and importance of the eurozone.[3] In Europe, these problems have come to a particularly drastic head as a result of the high level of economic integration we have achieved in the meantime.

I will first discuss the management of the crisis, which, although it has left the core of the problems untouched, has led to a self-empowerment of the European executive. The resulting shortfalls in legitimation, as much as the unsolved problem of structural economic imbalances, call for deeper integration, at least in the eurozone (1). Against the background of these current developments, I will then turn to the theoretical question of how a supranational polity can satisfy the principle of democracy that has hitherto been realized only in the nation-state format (2). Taking the example of how the United States arose, I will discuss the constitutional problem that must be solved in the process of European integration if the

EU, or at least a future Euro Union, is one day to measure up to its own aspirations (3). On the other hand, the most important resource—namely, mutual trust among the European peoples—is lacking, even if one disregards the national prejudices that were first stirred up during the crisis. At the same time, we must not fail to recognize that the fear of a superstate mainly betrays the desire to hold on to the democratic substance guaranteed by one's own nation-state. A democratically organized union could take this justified insistence on a normative achievement into account (4). Therefore, I will suggest a counterfactual scenario of constitution making, in which the European peoples would participate together with the European citizenry on an equal footing. This hypothetically assumed perspective reveals the innovative ways in which the European Union is already moving in the direction of a transnational democracy, as well as the reforms that would still have to be made in order to turn the existing union into a democracy (5). In conclusion, I will briefly examine some implications of the unfamiliar proposal of two subjects simultaneously engaging in the constitution of a transnational democracy (6).

1

First, some observations on a still unsolved problem that so far prevents a lasting stabilization of the eurozone. It was possible to avert the sovereign debt crisis only because the European Central Bank managed to present a credible simulation of joint liability—that is, a fiscal sovereignty that the union in fact lacks because of the ban on a bailout. Nevertheless, the lack of repayment responsibility is not the essential design flaw of the monetary union. Economists have been warning for a long time about the suboptimal conditions that the eurozone offers for a common currency area.[4] Because of the real economic differences in the current account balances of the different national economies, uniform interest rates send national governments the wrong signals. One size for all fits no one. The structural differences among the economies of the member states mean that their performance will drift further apart unless a joint economic government is established.

It is a well-known fact that the European Council has pursued an investor-friendly policy that, aside from necessary administrative and labor market reforms, confines itself to dictating austerity measures to the crisis-plagued countries—requirements that weigh exclusively on wages, social benefits, the civil service, and public infrastructure. The council imposes conditions on national governments that amount to treating the citizens of democratic polities like minors. Instead, the design flaw of a monetary union without a political union should have been tackled. Without the institutional framework for jointly coordinated fiscal and economic policies (with implications for a common social policy), the structural imbalances between the different economies are destined to increase. Therefore, the economic constraints speak in favor of a reform that would put the council and the European Parliament in a position to make joint decisions on federal guidelines for fiscal, economic, and social politics. But the governments of the donor countries, particularly the German government, lack the courage to canvass support for solidaristic measures among their electorates.

The pattern of off-loading problems onto pseudosovereign member states has an ironic reverse side—the power of the executive bodies has actually grown. The crisis management under German leadership has necessitated a self-empowerment of the governments assembled in the Eurogroup. In an alliance with the European executive branch—thus, the council, the commission, and the European Central Bank—they have extended their scope for action at the cost of the national parliaments, and in the process have greatly exacerbated the existing shortfalls in legitimacy.[5] The European Parliament did not have any share in the increase in competences generated by the momentous reform measures of recent years—the Fiscal Compact, the European Stability Mechanism, and the so-called six-pack—even when it participated in the legislative process. To this day, the European Parliament lacks a counterpart to the powerful Eurogroup in the council. Without a standing committee for the members from the eurozone, the parliament cannot even properly exercise its monitoring rights, which are in any case far too weak.

In this complicated situation, the theoretical question of the possibility of a transnationalization of democracy in the shape of a polity that is both federal and supranational acquires immediate political relevance. In the academic literature, one finds repeated attempts to solve this persistent problem through recourse to semantic cosmetics. There is no lack of proposals that cast the existing democratic deficits in a flattering light through a cunning reduction of democratic standards.[6] Therefore, I would first like to explain briefly the concept of democracy as it is properly understood.

2

With the self-empowerment of the National Assembly, the French Revolution facilitated the exemplary breakthrough of the principle of democracy in the shape of a unitary state. The Kingdom of France had long been a sovereign state. Within this national framework, the revolutionary constitutions were able to realize the principle of the self-legislation of a nation of free and equal citizens—in a different way than in federations. Democratic self-determination means that the addressees of coercive laws are subject only to the laws that they have enacted for themselves through a democratic process. This procedure owes its legitimizing force, on the one hand, to the inclusion of all citizens in political decision making (though this is mediated) and, on the other hand, to the linking of political decisions with a deliberative mode of public opinion formation and parliamentary deliberation.[7]

Legitimate state power proceeds from the "people" in such a way that the constitution is the result of a democratic procedure involving the entire future citizenry (or their representatives). Only in this constitution-building process do the people exercise their authority in an undivided way—this idea is expressed in the concept of popular sovereignty.[8] At the level of the constituted political authority, by contrast, the citizens exercise their sovereignty only through the channels of a division of powers; legislative power is supplemented by judicial and administrative powers. Within the constitutional state, popular sovereignty is dispersed and emerges from its latency only when it comes to changing the constitution.

The same principle of democracy was realized in a different way in the shape assumed by the United States since 1789, namely, within a federation of states. Here, a democratic federation emerged from a confederation of individual states that had seceded from the British Empire. Over the course of the nineteenth century, this federation—in a manner similar to Switzerland after its constitutional revolution in 1848—developed into a national federal state with features clearly distinct from the earlier forms of a confederation of states.

The problem that arises in every federal entity is the interpenetration of the international relations among the member states with the national organization of political will-formation within each of the states. International law and the concept of a contract, on the one side, and state law and the concept of a national constitution, on the other side, intermingle in all federations. But in the early modern confederations, the integration of the legal relations between the states and the national legal systems of the member states remained superficial. In the controversies recorded in the Federalist Papers, by contrast, one can trace the chief issue at stake in the development from a confederation into a democratic federal state—namely, how the democratic character of an alliance of member states, each of which has already been democratically constructed, can be preserved.[9] One result of that debate is especially relevant in our context: the debate revealed that the principle of democracy is realized in federal states in a way that is not open to federations of a supranational character.

3

An alliance of democratic states affects not only the relation between national governments and federal institutions, as was the case in the early federations. In addition, the peoples themselves must pool their "sovereignties." With the founding of the United States, the integration of states had crossed a historical threshold that led to an integration not only of governments but also of the participating "peoples." For this reason, the international legal principle of the equality of states, for the first time, served a different function: to ensure the equal status of the peoples of democratic member states. The principle of "state equality," hitherto a principle of international law, was, if you like, domesticated for the purpose of securing the equal representation of member states in a democratic federal state. In international law, this guarantees an equal standing of states and governments, but within a federal state it protects, together with the equal standing of member states, the democratic rights of the peoples of each of the states.

Insofar as the colonial states, which had just fought for their independence, regarded themselves as the subjects of the constitution-building process, it was only logical not to communalize the constitution-amending powers of the individual states completely but to reserve decisive veto positions for the states in the federation. On the other hand, insofar as the entire future citizenry of the union recruited from the individual states regarded itself as the true constitution-framing subject, there was no obstacle to the constitution of a federal state. From a legal point of view, this issue was ultimately decided in favor of the federation. As is well known, agreement was reached in Article V of the US Constitution. Instead of unanimity, only the approval of a majority of the legislatures of the individual states is required to change the Constitution. This provision can be understood, retrospectively at any rate, as a pointer in the direction of a federal state.[10]

We can learn two things from this development for the comparison with a supranational democracy composed of nation-states, such as the EU. Bringing the two competing principles of the equality of states and the equality of citizens into harmony within the framework of a nation-state was accomplished by the invention of a two-chamber system and a corresponding division of powers. The Senate, or the second chamber, can ensure a suitable form of participation in federal legislation through the competing legislation of the member states. The principle of democracy finds full application in such a federal state precisely by virtue of the fact that the principle of state equality is adequately embodied in the second chamber. Only in this way are the citizens of the member states, which are themselves democratically structured, invested with the right to a form of democratic participation that is indirect but of equal weight. However, it is not the case that each individual state can claim the last word on changing the Constitution.

Thus, the first thing that is needed for a proper federal state is the normative subordination of the states to the federal level. Second, that priority of the federal level over the individual states expresses the political identity of the people, from whom all political authority proceeds; in the end, it is the national citizenry as a whole that establishes and sustains a democratic federal state, not the governments of the several states or their citizens.

4

As it happens, the citizens of Europe do not want to fulfill either of these conditions. They don't want a large-scale federal state. The peoples who took part in the establishment of the United States comprised immigrants who had liberated themselves from the colonial rule of their common mother country; by contrast, the peoples who are playing a decisive role in the European project have been living in "old" nation-states for centuries. There are many reasons why the process of European unification is stalled. But the main one is the lack of mutual trust that the citizens of different nations would have to show one another as a precondition for their willingness to adopt a common perspective that transcends national boundaries when making political decisions on federal issues. Yet this lack of trust should not be located in the wrong place. Nationalism confuses two forms of solidarity that we must distinguish today. We should not confuse the informal solidarity that habitually develops in families and prepolitical communities with legally constituted civic solidarity.

In European states that emerged from national unification movements, a national consciousness fostered—indeed produced—by schools, the military, national historiography, and the press became superimposed on older dynastic and religious ties as well as on regional forms of life and loyalties. We see in many places today that, in times of crisis, conflicts continually flare up around these older regional and ethnic boundaries, conflicts that awaken older loyalties and can lead to the disintegration of national solidarity. But we should not be enticed into drawing hasty parallels between this sort of conflict and the awkward role that the nation-states are currently playing in blocking the European integration process.

Nations are composed of citizens, and these form political communities that did not develop spontaneously but instead were legally constructed. Contrary to the ethnonational ideologies that try to suppress this fact, the political level of civic integration acquires here a weight entirely its own, compared with the informal layers of sociocultural integration.[11] Unlike the loyalty to a territorial lord, which rests on existing forms of social integration, national consciousness, including the ascriptive characteristics attributed to it retrospectively, is the result of an organized form of political integration. The mass of the population was mobilized over the course of the nineteenth century and was included, step by step, in political will-formation.

Viewed historically, a relatively high level of political inclusion has been achieved in the meantime, and we have to keep this political level in mind if we want to explain the lack of reciprocal trust among national populations. The lack of trust that we presently observe among European nations is not primarily an expression of xenophobic self-isolation against foreign nations but instead reflects, in the first place, self-conscious citizens' insistence on the normative achievements of their respective nation-states. In present-day Europe, there is a widespread conviction that national citizens owe the fragile resource of free and relatively equitable living conditions to the democratic practices and liberal institutions of their states. Therefore, they have a well-founded interest in "their" nation-states remaining a guarantor of these achievements and in not being exposed to the risk of intrusions and encroachments by an unfamiliar supranational polity. Their suspicion is directed more against the supranational paternalism of a superstate than against the forms of life and mentalities of neighboring peoples who are rejected as foreign.

This is why the lack of a "European people" is not the allegedly insurmountable obstacle to joint political decision making. Indeed, translingual citizenship uniting such a numerous variety of different language communities is a novelty. But Europeans already share the principles and values of largely overlapping political cultures. What is required is a Europe-wide political communication. For that, we need a European public sphere—which, however, does not mean a new one. The existing national public spheres are sufficient for this purpose; they only have to become mutually open to one another. The existing national media are sufficient, too, provided they perform a complex task of translation: they must learn to report on the discussions being conducted in one another's countries about the issues of common concern to all citizens of the union.[12] Then, the trust among citizens that currently exists in the form of a nationally limited civic solidarity may well develop into an even more abstract form of trust that reaches across national borders.[13]

The "no demos" thesis obscures a factor that we must take seriously: the conviction that the normative achievements of the democratic state are worth preserving. This self-assertion of a democratic civil society is something different from the reactive clinging to naturalized characteristics of ethnonational origin that provides sustenance to right-wing populism. In addition, democratic self-assertion is not only an empirical motive but also a justifying reason that, under the given circumstances, speaks for the attempt to realize a supranational democracy. For it is not as if democracies shut up in nation-states could preserve their democratic substance, as though they were unaffected by involvement in the systemic dynamics of a global society—at any rate not, as indicated, in Europe.

Let me summarize. European citizens have good reasons to pursue two competing goals simultaneously: on the one hand, they want the union that has arisen from nation-states to assume the form of a supranational polity that can act effectively in a democratically legitimate way; on the other hand, they want to embark on this transnationalization of democracy only under the proviso that their nation-states, in the role as future member states, remain guarantors of their already achieved level of justice and freedom. In the supranational polity, the higher political level should not be able to overwhelm the lower one. The issue of ultimate decision-making authority should not be resolved through hierarchization, as it is in federal states. The supranational federation should instead be constructed in such a way that the heterarchical relationship between the member states and the federation remains intact.

5

To solve this problem, I propose a thought experiment. Let us imagine a democratically developed European Union as if its constitution had been brought into existence by a double sovereign.[14] The constituting authority should be composed of the entire citizenry of Europe, on the one hand,

and of the peoples of Europe, on the other. Already, during the constitution-framing process, one side should be able to address the other side, with the aim of achieving a balance between the corresponding interests. In that case, the heterarchical relationship between European citizens and European peoples would structure the founding process itself. The competition over interests between the two constitution-founding subjects would then be reflected, at the level of the constituted polity, in procedures that require agreements between two legislative bodies with equal rights—such as the European Parliament and the European Council.

In this scenario, the doubled sovereign can no longer decide in a really sovereign manner. The "leveling up" of the European citizens through the addition of the European peoples indicates that, from the outset, the sovereign must have already committed itself to recognizing the historical achievement of a level of justice embodied by the nation-states. "Higher-level" or "shared" sovereignty means that the constituting authority is limited by being under an obligation to conserve, within the larger frame of the future union, the substance of what national citizens claim as the emancipatory achievements of their respective national democracies from a revolutionary past.

If one asks, from this perspective of a "double" sovereign, which further reforms of the existing European treaties are necessary to eliminate the existing legitimation deficits of the European Union in its present state, then the answer is obvious. The European Parliament would also have to be able to introduce legislative initiatives, and the so-called "ordinary legislative procedure," which requires the approval of both chambers, would have to be extended to all policy fields. In addition, the European Council—thus, the assembly of heads of government, who to this day enjoy a semiconstitutional status—would have to be incorporated into the Council of Ministers. Finally, the European Commission would have to assume the functions of a government answerable to council and parliament in equal measure. With this transformation of the union into a supranational polity that satisfies democratic standards, the principles of equality of states and of citizens would be accorded equal consideration. The democratic will of the two constitution-framing subjects is reflected in the symmetrical participation of both "chambers" in the legislative process and in the symmetrical status of parliament and council with respect to the executive branch.

Such a radically reformed union would still deviate considerably from the model of a federal state. Interestingly enough, current EU law includes a range of important provisions that, on the assumption of a sovereignty shared by European citizens and peoples, can be understood as legitimate deviations from the model of the federal state:

- the requirement of consensus among member states for any ordinary change of the treaties;
- the right of member states to leave the union, in which the qualifications governing the process of exit throw an interesting light on how the original sovereignty of the accessing state was "divided" but not completely "forfeited";
- the right of review, to which the national constitutional courts lay claim in order to prevent European law from falling below the level achieved in the member states;
- the principle of limited conferral of powers, which ensures that European institutions do not gain ultimate decision-making authority;
- strong competences of the member states in implementing European decisions, which prevents the supranational polity from acquiring the character of a state;
- a primacy of European law over the national legal systems, which is justified only in functional terms and not by the general priority of federal over national competences; and
- the decentralized monopoly on the use of legitimate force, which remains with the member states.

These principles and provisions can be understood from a reconstructive perspective as a logical expression of democratic will-formation in a constituent assembly that has a heterogeneous composition in the sense outlined. To this extent, the European treaties already prefigure an at once federally and democratically constituted supranational polity.

6

With this step, the democratic legitimation of the constituted polity is shifted from the level of the constitution-building process to the meta-level justification for the peculiar composition of the constituting authority itself. What counts as a legitimating reason at this level is the assumption that, in the course of the founding process, the citizens of a future European Union as a whole are willing to share equal rights with the peoples of the future member states. According to the assumption, these peoples are willing to participate in the project, in turn, only on the condition that, in the supranational political community to be established, the integrity of their states, in their role as guarantors of the historically achieved levels of freedom and justice, is assured. Even though the totalities of "citizens" and "peoples" overlap exactly, so that they are composed of the same persons, the willingness on both sides to accept these terms does not fall from the sky—neither the concession made by the future European citizens to restrict their sovereignty in favor of the involvement of European peoples nor the reservation that the European peoples make by insisting on the normative substance of their respective national states. Seeping down from the abstract level of political theory to the rough waves of history, such an agreement, which Europeans must reach with themselves, can come about only as the result of a painful learning process.

From the perspective of democratic theory, which I have preferred to adopt in this chapter, the agreement by the two sides to cooperate in founding a constitution opens up a new dimension. Such a process, which precedes the actual process of constitution making, is reminiscent of the controversy recorded in the Federalist Papers. However, that discussion had a different outcome: the result of a long process was the first democratically legitimized federal state.

Today we are conducting a discussion in the European Union that is similar in some respects. To judge by the course of our present discussion, however, it does not seem possible to resolve the tension-laden relationship between the two subjects—the citizens of the separate states and the future citizens of the union—in favor of a hierarchical arrangement. The best that we can hope for is to throw light on two competing objectives that the respective proponents regard as nonnegotiable. The formation of a federation composed of nation-states is already de facto far advanced. Under the pressure of the problems of the banking and sovereign debt crisis, it is now a matter of how this project can be brought to a conclusion in such a way that the conflicting goals can be achieved simultaneously. The supranational polity that is empowered to act in important policy fields should, on the one hand, be allowed to exercise its jurisdiction only in democratically legitimate ways, without, on the other hand, depriving the member states of the measure of autonomy that allows them to keep watch, themselves, over the conservation of the normative substance that our national democracies embody today.

The best outcome that can be hoped for is that the citizens satisfy their two allegiances when they press ahead with the integration process, as if they had participated in the constitution-building process from the outset as equal subjects, in the dual role of future citizens of the union and current national citizens. In addition, if this shared intention of both parties could be reconstructed as if it were the result of a process of democratic opinion- and will-formation, then the last remaining gap in the chain of legitimation would be closed in our scenario.

From the viewpoint of political theory, this "higher-level" constitutional process differs from all that have gone before. Following in the footsteps of the two constitutional revolutions of the late eighteenth century, many more constitutional states have been founded, right up to the present day. All of these constitutional foundations can be understood (at the requisite level of abstraction) as a replication of the two original founding acts in Philadelphia and Paris. As we can now see, the creation of a supranational democracy, by contrast, cannot be understood on the model of a two-stage process, according to which the constitutional democracies are a product of one homogenous constitution-framing process. More suitable here is instead a three-stage model in which the existence of democratically constituted nation-states is already presupposed. With the citizens who want to defend the historical achievement of constitutional revolutions, a subject comes into play that now empowers itself to serve as another constituting authority.

Unlike the case of the revolutionary popular sovereign, this is, of course, not a case of self-empowerment in the strict sense. The empowerment of the already democratically constituted subjects to engage in constitution building at a higher level depends on the consent of a classical popular sovereign, which now comes on the scene in the guise of the European citizenry as a whole and must be willing to divide its constituent authority. With the prior constitution of a higher-level sovereignty itself—hence, with the agreement between the two designated constitution-building subjects—the classical picture of a constituting and a constituted level is supplemented by a further dimension that once again underlies the actual constitution-building process.

Translated by Ciaran Cronin

NOTES

1. For an account of this deficiency that focuses on the legal branch of the international governance network, see Armin Bogdandy and Ingo Venzke, *In wessen Namen? Internationale Gerichte in Zeiten des globalen Regierens* (Berlin: Suhrkamp, 2014). For a general account, see Jürgen Habermas, "Stichworte zu einer Diskurstheorie des Rechts und des demokratischen Rechtsstaates," in *Im Sog der Technokratie* (Berlin: Suhrkamp, 2013), 67–81; here 77–80.
2. Wolfgang Streeck, *Gekaufte Zeit: Die Krise des demokratischen Kapitalismus* (Berlin: Suhrkamp, 2013).
3. The startling decisions taken by the first G-20 in London, in November 2008, under the influence of the banking crisis that had just broken out, have predictably remained without consequences. International agreements among states are insufficient unless the coordination of divergent interests is also subjected to institutional regulation. Politics can take an effective stand against the imperatives of markets, which play the interests of different states against one another, only by establishing institutions that generalize interests, that is, by constructing supranational capacities for joint action.
4. Henrick Enderlein, *Nationale Wirtschaftspolitik in der europäischen Währungsunion* (Frankfurt: Campus, 2014); Fritz W. Scharpf, "Monetary Union, Fiscal Crisis and the Preemption of Democracy," *Zeitschrift für Staats- und Europawissenschaften* 2 (2011): 163–98; Scharpf, "The Costs of Non-Disintegration: The Case of the European Monetary Union," in *Zur Konzeptionalisierung europäischer Desintegration: Zug- und Gegenkräfte im europäischen Integrationsprozess*, ed. Annegret Eppler and Henrik Scheller (Baden-Baden: Nomos, 2013), 165–84; and Scharpf, "Die Finanzkrise als Krise der ökonomischen und rechtlichen Überintegration," in *Grenzen der europäischen Integration*, ed. Claudio Franzius, Franz C. Mayer, and Jürgen Neyer (Baden-Baden, 2014), 51–60.
5. Eppler and Scheller, eds., *Zur Konzeptionalisierung europäischer Desintegration*.
6. Recently, on the "shared sovereignty" line of argument, see Francis Chevenal, "The Case for Democracy in the European Union," *Journal of Common Market Studies* 51 (2013): 334–50. For critical accounts, see Daniel Gaus, "Demoi-kratie ohne

Demos-kratie: Welche Polity braucht eine demokratische EU?," in *Deliberative Kritik— Kritik der Deliberation: Festschrift für Rainer Schmalz-Bruns*, ed. Oliver Flügel-Martinsen, Daniel Gaus, Tanja Hitzel-Cassagnes, and Franziska Martinsen (Wiesbaden: VS-Verlag, 2014).

7. Jürgen Habermas, *Between Facts and Norms*, trans. William Rehg (Cambridge, MA: MIT Press, 1996).

8. Ingeborg Maus, *Zur Aufklärung der Demokratietheorie* (Frankfurt: Suhrkamp, 1992); Maus, *Volkssouveränität: Elemente einer Demokratietheorie* (Frankfurt: Suhrkamp, 2011).

9. The Federalist Papers are often used as a reference point in discussions of European law. See Christoph Schönberger, "Die Europäische Union als Bund," *Archiv des öffentlichen Rechts* 129 (2004): 81–120; Schönberger, "The European Union's Democratic Deficit Between Federal and State Prohibition," *Der Staat* 48 (2009); and Robert Schütze, "On 'Federal' Ground: The European Union as an (Inter)national Phenomenon," *Common Market Law Review* 46 (2009): 1069–105.

10. However, the centuries-old ambivalence about whether "We the people of the United States" in the preamble to the US Constitution must be interpreted, after all, in the sense of the totality of the "peoples" of the individual states suggests that, as an empirical matter, the alternative between the citizens of the American nation taking precedence over the citizens of the states and, conversely, the state peoples taking precedence over the heterogeneous nation of an immigrant society remains open.

11. Interestingly enough, migration research is currently discovering that citizenship status is the crucial dimension of social integration for immigrants. This status is the point of reference for the communication strategies of official naturalization policy. Daniel Naujolis shows this, using the integration of people from India into the United States as an example. Naujolis, *Migration, Citizenship, and Development* (New Delhi: Oxford University Press, 2013).

12. Jürgen Habermas, "Political Communication in Media Society: Does Democracy Still Have an Epistemic Dimension?," in *Europe: The Faltering Project*, trans. Ciaran Cronin (Cambridge: Polity, 2009), 181–3.

13. Drawing on Ulrich K. Preuss, Claudio Franzius develops the concept of a "transaction-we in the sense of a we of others" for supranational federations. See Preuss, "Europa als politische Gemeinschaft," in *Europawissenschaft*, ed. Gunnar Folke Schuppert, Ingolf Pernice, and Ulrich Haltern (Baden-Baden: Nomos, 2005), 489–539; and Franzius, "Europäisches Vertrauen? Eine Skizze," *Humboldt Forum Recht*, Aufsätze 12 (2010): 159–76.

14. I introduced the idea of a form of popular sovereignty split at the root in Jürgen Habermas, *The Crisis of the European Union: A Response*, trans. Ciaran Cronin (Cambridge: Polity, 2012), 28–53.

II

HUMAN RIGHTS AND SOVEREIGNTY

2

DEMOCRATIC SOVEREIGNTY AND TRANSNATIONAL LAW

On Legal Utopianism and Democratic Skepticism

SEYLA BENHABIB

INTERNATIONAL LAW AND AMERICAN COURTS: A CASE OF AMERICAN EXCEPTIONALISM

On April 17, 2013, the US Supreme Court issued its much-awaited decision regarding *Kiobel et al. v. Royal Dutch Petroleum*.[1] The Nigerian plaintiffs had sued three oil companies and the military dictatorship in Nigeria for attempting to silence protesters who were militating against environmental damage caused by the companies' actions. It is reported that scores were killed, and the plaintiffs themselves claimed to have been captured and beaten. Writing for the majority, Chief Justice John G. Roberts Jr. argued that "the ATS [Alien Tort Statute] covers actions by aliens for violations of the law of nations, but that does not imply extraterritorial reach—such violations affecting aliens can occur whether within or outside the United States" (III). He concluded, "Even where the claims touch and concern the territory of the United States, they must do so with sufficient force to displace the presumption against extraterritorial application" (IV). Invoking a traditional understanding of Westphalian territorial sovereignty and sovereign immunity, Justice Roberts and the majority in the court made it much more difficult, with this decision, to extend the reach of transnational human rights claims into US courts.

The matter of the citation of foreign law, whether the law of other nations or international law and treaties, has in the meantime become an American political *scandalon*. It now serves as a litmus test in the appointment of Supreme Court justices, who are asked whether or not they will interpret the US Constitution in the light of "foreign doctrine or influence." A group of scholars, intellectuals, and policy makers "who view the emerging international legal order and system of global governance with consternation" have now coalesced as the "new sovereigntists."[2]

For some, this court's sovereigntism is nothing new. They have called it "American exceptionalism," which has mutated into Michael Ignatieff's "American exemptionalism."[3] One of the most forceful early criticisms of the United States, with regard to its "exemptionalist" behavior vis-à-vis the law of nations, was formulated by Carl Schmitt. As he quite bitingly put it:

> Once the priority of the Monroe Doctrine—the traditional principle of Western Hemisphere isolation, with its wide-ranging interpretations—was asserted in Geneva, the League abandoned any serious attempt to solve the most important problem, namely, the relation between Europe and the Western Hemisphere. Of course, the practical interpretation of the ambiguous Monroe Doctrine—its application in concrete cases, its determination of war and peace, its consequences for the question of inter-allied debts, and the problem of reparations—was left solely to the United States.[4]

And, in a turn of phrase that could have flown from Jacques Derrida's pen, Schmitt concluded:

> The United States was, thus, formally and decisively *not present* in Geneva. But they were, as in all other matters, and hardly ineffectively and very intensely, *present* as well. There thus resulted an odd combination of *official absence* and *effective presence*, which defined the relationship of America to the Geneva Convention and to Europe.[5]

It is not only the historical attitude of US courts and lawmakers that should draw our renewed attention to the status of foreign law, whether international treaty law or transnational law.[6] A wide-ranging contemporary controversy has emerged that spans legal studies as well as political theory, jurisprudence as well as cultural studies. This controversy concerns, at its deepest level, the meaning of democratic sovereignty in a new age and under conditions of nascent legal cosmopolitanism. We can distinguish among several questions.

First, what is the status of foreign law, including the law of other nations and international treaties, in constitutional and statutory adjudication? As we know, great variations across countries exist in this regard. Although international law becomes part of the valid constitutional order in many countries of the world, such as the Netherlands and South Africa (referred to as "constitutional monism"), other constitutions are "dualist" with respect to treaty-based international law and require various forms of parliamentary and/or treaty ratification before these can become part of the law of the land.

A second question is whether recent developments in legal doctrine and practice can be seen as leading toward global constitutionalism, with or without the state.[7] Global constitutionalists point to increasing cooperation among constitutional court justices across the globe, their learning from one another, and, increasingly, their citing one another in considering similar cases, not as precedent but as significant evidence. Even some scholars, such as Jeremy Waldron, who find the concept of "global constitutionalism" exaggerated, nonetheless argue that there is increasing convergence around a "law for all nations."[8]

Others, who defend constitutionalization without the state, such as Günther Teubner, single out the spread of norms of *lex mercatoria* and many other "*lex*es," such as *lex sportiva*, to argue that processes of norm hierarchization, coordination, and cooperation beyond the purview of states have evolved into a self-regulating system.[9] Why shouldn't a system that exhibits so many features of constitutionalism also be honored with that title?[10]

In contemporary political philosophy, the utopian claims of legal cosmopolitans and global constitutionalists have been met with a reticence that at times borders on hostility. And here, strange bedfellows have emerged. Joining Chief Justice Roberts in his Westphalian understanding of sovereignty as territorially circumscribed jurisdictional sovereignty is a group of eminent political thinkers, ranging from communitarians such as Michael Walzer to liberals such as Thomas Nagel to progressive left thinkers such as Samuel Moyn and Jean Cohen.[11] These thinkers wish to defend the value of democratic self-determination, and they claim either (a) that recent developments in international law are ideals of cosmopolitan elites with little traction in the life of peoples (Walzer and Moyn); (b) that the principle of self-determination expresses an important value, and that "legal pluralism" may be the desirable middle ground between global cosmopolitanism and national sovereigntism (Walzer and Cohen); or (c) that international law is no more than the consensually undertaken contractual commitments among sovereign states that remain the central units of jurisdiction and enforcement (Nagel).

I take these objections, particularly (a) and (b), very seriously. My own questions in this essay are related to, but distinct from, both sets of issues named under (a) and (b). I am interested in legal cosmopolitanism as it bears on the moral individual as a legal person in the international community, and I wish to examine the alleged conflict between one class of international legal norms in particular—namely, those pertaining to human rights, broadly understood, and democratic sovereignty. I will argue that transnational human rights norms strengthen rather than weaken democratic sovereignty. My thesis is that this is a false juxtaposition, and that even though there are inevitable conflicts and tensions between the application of and compliance with human rights norms in domestic contexts and in international treaties and covenants, we need to develop a conceptual and empirical model for understanding these tensions not as a zero-sum game but rather as a process of dialectical norm-enhancement and interpretation. I am less interested in cases of blatant violations of human rights norms and more focused on the interpretation and evocation of these norms through democratic legislatures, nongovernmental actors, and social movements in quotidian politics as they lead to further norm articulation and interpretation. Distinguishing between a "concept" and a "conception" of human rights, I will claim that self-government in a free public sphere and free civil society is essential to the concretization and iteration of the necessarily abstract norms of human rights. I will further argue that, without the right to self-government, exercised through proper legal and political channels, we cannot justify the range of variation in the content of basic human rights across constitutional democracies as being legitimate. I name such processes "democratic iterations."

THE RESURGENCE OF COSMOPOLITANISM

It is now widely accepted that, since the Universal Declaration of Human Rights in 1948, we have entered a phase in the evolution of global civil society that is characterized by a transition from *international* to *cosmopolitan* norms of justice. Whereas norms of international law emerge either through what is recognized as customary international law or through treaty obligations to which states and their representatives are signatories, cosmopolitan norms accrue to individuals considered as moral and legal persons in a worldwide civil society. By "cosmopolitanism," I have in mind both a moral and a legal proposition. Morally, the cosmopolitan tradition is committed to viewing each individual as equally entitled to moral respect and concern; legally, cosmopolitanism considers each individual as a legal person entitled to the protection of his or her human rights by virtue of individual moral personality and not on account of citizenship or other membership status. Even if cosmopolitan norms also originate through treaty-like obligations, such as the UN Charter, the Universal Declaration of Human Rights, and various other human rights covenants, their peculiarity is that they bind signatory states and their representatives to treat their citizens and residents in accordance with certain norms, even if states later wish, as is often the case, to engage in actions that contradict these terms and violate the obligations generated by these treaties themselves. This is the uniqueness of the many human rights covenants concluded since World War II: through them, sovereign states undertake the self-limitation of their own prerogatives.

The best known of the human rights agreements that have been signed by a majority of the world's states since the 1948 Universal Declaration of Human Rights are as follows: the United Nations Convention on the Prevention and Punishment of the Crime of Genocide; the 1951 Convention on Refugees, which entered into force in 1954, with only 19 state signatories and 145 state parties, and its Protocol of 1967 (with 146 state parties); the International Covenant on Civil and Political Rights (signed in 1966 and entered into force in 1976, with 168 countries out of 195 being party to it as of 2015); the International Covenant on Economic, Social and Cultural Rights (ICESCR), entered into force the same year and with 164 member parties as of 2015; the Convention to Eliminate of All Forms of Discrimination Against Women (CEDAW), signed in 1979 and entered into force in 1981, with 99 signatories and 189 state parties as of 2015; the International Convention on the Elimination of All Forms of Racial Discrimination (entry into force on January 4, 1969, with 87 signatories and 177 parties as of 2015); the Convention Against Torture and Other Cruel, Inhuman or Degrading Treatment or Punishment (entry into force June 26, 1987, with 81 signatories and 158 state parties as of 2015).[12] These are some of the best known among many other treaties and conventions.[13]

The skeptic will ask, What does all this really mean? What possible significance can these multilateral human rights covenants have if states continuously and brazenly violate them, manipulate them to serve their own ends, etc.? Are they not mere words, at worst, or aspirational ideals, at best, that have little traction in influencing and limiting state conduct? Do these developments create a novel, enforceable, and justiciable legal world order? Doesn't the process of formulating reservations, understandings, and declarations take the bite out of the human rights treaties, in particular, and make them merely convenient smoke screens for states to hide behind?

Although skeptical doubts about state behavior and an international state system that remains beset by violence, civil wars, and proxy wars cannot be set aside, I remain convinced that something has changed profoundly in the grammar and syntax of the language of international law, sovereignty, and human rights.

Let me begin, then, with the question of whether legal cosmopolitanism is a form of constitutional monism and what degree of pluralism can be thought to be compatible with legal cosmopolitanism when it comes to the interpretation of human rights in different polities. Human rights constitute the core of legal cosmopolitanism; without clarifying the relationship of human rights treaties and international practices to the institutions and practices of states, much talk about legal cosmopolitanism hangs in thin air.[14]

HUMAN RIGHTS AND CONSTITUTIONAL RIGHTS

In recent debates, two quite distinct ways of considering human rights and their justification have emerged: the so-called traditional conception of Alan Gewirth and James Griffin, and Joseph Raz's and Charles Beitz's so-called political or functional conception of rights, inspired by John Rawls's work in *The Law of Peoples*. Whereas traditional human rights theories such as Gewirth's and Griffin's build human rights around a conception of human agency, the approach to human rights initiated by Rawls's project of developing "public reason" assumes that the late modern political world, characterized by an inevitable value pluralism and burdens of judgment, does not need to presuppose any such philosophical accounts.[15]

Admittedly, the philosophical discussion of human rights and the conversation among lawyers, jurists, and legal scholars do not run in tandem, but the philosophical debate does raise a legitimate question about the relationship between human rights norms and constitutional rights. In this essay, I do not provide my preferred strategy of philosophical justification for human rights, which proceeds from the value and norm of communicative freedom to a conception of "the right to have rights." I have done so elsewhere.[16] Briefly, in my view, human rights constitute a narrower group of claims than general moral rights. Human rights bear on human dignity and equality; they are protective of the *human status* as such. I agree with Griffin that human rights do not exhaust the *entirety* of our conceptions of justice, let alone of morality.[17] Human rights have their proper place in discourses of political legitimation. Such discourses presuppose moral principles, in the sense that the justification of human rights always leads back to some moral principle and some view of human agency. Human rights are most central to a public vocabulary of political justice; they designate a special and narrow class of moral rights.

Human rights covenants and declarations articulate general principles that need contextualization and specification in the form of legal norms. How is this legal content shaped? Basic human rights are rights that require justiciable form; that is, they require embodiment and instantiation in a specific legal framework. Human rights straddle the line between morality and legality; they enable us to judge the legitimacy of law.[18]

In negotiating the relationship between general human rights norms, as formulated in various human rights declarations, and their concretization in the multiple legal documents of various countries, we may invoke the distinction between a *concept* and a *conception*.[19] In *Political Liberalism*, Rawls clarifies this distinction as follows: "Roughly, the concept is the meaning of a term, while a particular conception includes as well the principles required to apply it... A conception includes... principles and criteria for deciding which distinctions are arbitrary and when a balance between competing claims is proper."[20] I will not follow Rawls in identifying "concept" with "meaning"; rather what is helpful in his elucidation is the articulation of how conceptions differ from concepts. For example, we can differentiate between moral *concepts*, such as fairness, equality and liberty, let us say, and *conceptions* of fairness, equality, and liberty, which would be fleshed out by introducing additional moral and political principles to supplement the original concept so as to be able to make necessary distinctions.[21]

The terms "principles" and "norms," as introduced by Robert Alexy, are more appropriate in this context. Alexy writes:

> The decisive point in distinguishing rules from principles is that principles are norms which require that something be realized to the greatest extent possible given their legal and factual possibilities. Principles are optimization requirements, characterized by the fact that they can be satisfied to varying degrees... [B]y contrast, rules are norms that are always either fulfilled or not.[22]

The binarism of concept/conception can now be read as one of principle/norm. A concept of human rights is a *principle* of human rights that permits "realization to the greatest extent possible," whereas *conceptions* of human rights require specific legal norms for their concretization and are subject to varying rules of application and interpretation.

Applied to the question of how we move from general normative principles of human rights, as enshrined in the various covenants, to specific conceptions of them as enacted in various legal documents, this would suggest that we can view these documents as formulating core concepts of human rights, which would form part of any conception of valid constitutional rights. How then is the legitimate range of rights to be determined across liberal democracies, or how can we transition from general concepts of rights to specific conceptions of them? Even as fundamental a principle as "the moral equality of persons" assumes a justiciable meaning as a human right, once it is posited and interpreted by a lawgiver. Here, a range of legitimate variations can always be the case.

For example, while equality before the law is a fundamental principle of all societies observing the rule of law, in many societies, such as Canada, Israel, and India, this is considered quite compatible with special immunities and entitlements that accrue to individuals by virtue of their belonging to different cultural, linguistic, or religious groups. In societies such as the United States and France, with their more universalistic understandings of citizenship, these multicultural arrangements would be completely unacceptable.[23] At the same time, in France and Germany, the principle of gender equality has led political parties to adopt various versions of the norm of *parité*—namely, that women ought to hold public offices on a fifty-fifty basis with men, and that, for electoral office, their names ought to be placed on party tickets on an equal footing with male candidates. In the United States, by contrast, gender equality is protected by Title VII and Title IX, which apply only to major public institutions that receive federal funding.[24] Political parties are excluded from this.

There is, in other words, a legally legitimate range of variation even in the interpretation and implementation of such a basic right as that of equality before the law.[25] But the legitimacy of this range of variation and interpretation is crucially dependent upon the principle of self-government. My thesis is that *without the right to self-government, which is exercised through proper legal and political channels, we cannot justify the range of variation in the content of basic human rights as being legally legitimate.* Unless a people can exercise self-government through some form of democratic channels, the translation of human rights norms into justiciable legal claims in a polity cannot be actualized. *So, the right to self-government is the condition for the possibility of the realization of a democratic schedule of rights.* Just as without the actualization of human rights themselves, self-government cannot be meaningfully exercised, so too, without the right to self-government, human rights cannot be contextualized as justiciable entitlements. They are coeval. That is, the liberal defense of human rights as placing limits on the publicly justifiable exercise of power needs to be complemented by the civic-republican vision of rights as constituents of a people's exercise of public autonomy. Without the basic rights of the person, republican sovereignty would be blind, and without the exercise of collective autonomy, the rights of the person would be empty.[26] Cosmopolitan citizenship is formed through such democratic iterations within and across *demoi*.

This strong thesis will provoke the objection that surely it is possible that a nondemocratic regime, say a monarchy or some other form of benevolent authoritarianism—maybe even a form of "constitutional theocracy," to use Ran Hirschl's term, or Rawls's Kazanistan—could respect human rights without accepting a human right to self-government.[27] I am willing to bite the bullet here and argue that such a limitation of human rights to minimal protections of the person, the rule of law, and guarantees of civic peace and property is fundamentally incomplete. Human rights cannot be separated from the right to self-government, because when they are, they no longer are rights but "privileges" granted to one by some higher authority. The people can claim rights to be their own only when they can recognize themselves, through the proper institutional channels, to be the author of those rights as well. Certainly, stability, some respect for the rule of law and property relations, civic peace among competing ethnic and religious groups, which many "decent hierarchical" regimes (as Rawls calls them) may achieve, are politically valuable and not to be dismissed. But they cannot satisfy a prime condition of political modernity, that legitimacy originates with respect for the capacity of persons to be the sources of reasonable consent or the "self-authenticating sources of valid claims."[28]

In *The Law of Peoples*, Rawls interpreted human rights as defining conditions of just membership for peoples in a world society of states. Since then, discussions of human rights have been linked to "*pro tanto* justifications" for limiting state sovereignty, including, when necessary, through military intervention.[29] Because of this restrictive understanding of the purpose of international human rights, both Raz and Beitz have adjusted their expectations of decent hierarchical peoples' compliance with human rights norms to what may be reasonable to ensure pluralism and peace in the world community alone.

The cosmopolitan theory of democratic iterations that I defend, by contrast, proceeds from individuals and not from peoples as subjects of transnational human rights law. Furthermore, I do not accept that human rights violations provide *pro tanto* justifications for intervention, except in the event of the most severe violations such as are also prohibited by the genocide convention and international human rights law—that is, genocide, slavery, mass extermination or ethnic cleansing, mass deportations, and crimes against humanity.[30]

Once we move beyond the options of military or economic intervention against or indifference toward human rights violations in other states and consider individuals in decent hierarchical societies as our "moral and legal contemporaries," the conversation and practice around international human rights take a different form. The question now becomes, What good reasons can we reciprocally provide each other, such that some accept certain forms of gender inequality, while others do not? Why do some of us recognize the curtailment of the rights of religious minorities and others do not? Reasonable pluralism among peoples' interpretation of human rights must not be understood as a static reality, sealed off from contention with other human groups at the borders of the state; rather, we must understand reasonable pluralism as an evolving and contentious conversation among individuals, groups, and peoples of different nationalities, faiths, and cultures. If we are *moral contemporaries* in a conversation that spans the same coordinates of space and time, and if, in some cases, we share the same lifeworld with individuals from decent hierarchical societies, who might be our observant Muslim, Jewish, or Sikh neighbors, we need good reasons to convince one another that we may accept radically different normative sources of justification for human rights and their content. The issue has been misleadingly stated by Rawlsians, insofar as the conversation has always been assumed to occur *elsewhere* and *at other times*, across imaginary borders and boundaries, thus ignoring the challenge of moral contemporaneity.[31]

Historically, human rights evolved well in advance of democratic struggles. T. H. Marshall's famous trilogy of civil, political, and socioeconomic rights still has something instructive to teach us.[32] Insofar as the evolution of human rights in Western European societies is concerned, this account, despite some historical flaws, is still quite illuminating. Clearly, the civil rights of property and contract, and some privacy rights, such as freedom of marriage and the right to freedom of conscience, evolved out of struggles in the course of the sixteenth and seventeenth centuries. With the American and French revolutions, political rights over equal suffrage, freedom of association and the press, freedom of assembly, and democratic voice gained prominence. Socioeconomic rights, such as the right to unemployment compensation, old-age and disability pensions, health care, and the like, are the last to have been attained through democratic struggles and show the most variation across democracies. My claims about the interdependence of democracy and human rights do not concern this historical legacy. Rather, I am concerned to account for the "unity and diversity" in the interpretation of human rights across democracies, or in their *legitimate range of legal variation* across different societies.

A careful reader will note, however, that I am using the somewhat awkward locution "legitimate range of legal variation" rather than "legitimacy" *simpliciter*. Why? Because there needs to remain a "normative gap" between concepts of human rights as enshrined in various documents, treaties, and covenants and the specific articulations of them—or legally legitimate conceptions of them—as posited by the legislators of various peoples. This "normative gap" enables the struggle among the national, local, and the international levels, as well as among various organizations, social movements, national and international nongovernmental organizations, and others, in their interpretation of human rights. Concepts of human rights cannot be *reduced* to their specific conceptions, and they may be and usually are invoked with a moral force that transcends the legally legitimate will of the demos. The meaning of a term is not exhausted by its multiple instantiations; likewise, the force of a principle is not exhausted by the number of norms said to concretize the principle. And so it is with general human rights principles as well. They enframe and are enframed by democratic iterations, but the sum total of democratic iterations does not exhaust their meaning or their normative force.[33]

The model of democratic legitimacy presented above may also be named "the authorship model of democratic legitimacy." The democratic people are said to be the "authors" as well as the "addressees" of human rights and constitutional rights. But this normative model seems to presuppose a centered form of Westphalian authority with a clearly demarcated demos, thus flying in the face of post-Westphalian transformations of state sovereignty, both sociologically and in international law. Maybe one should accept the sociological force of the post-Westphalian diagnosis and admit that democratic authorship and popular sovereignty remain captive to a historically defunct model of territorially bounded sovereignty, and thus forfeit them normatively?[34] It may be that we need to conceptualize democratic authorship in less unitary and more heterarchical terms and instead approach it through a different model of sovereignty and the public sphere. Maybe we should all embrace "postdemocracy"?[35] Or should one insist that these normative criteria of legitimacy remain necessary even in view of new global arrangements, and that, in fact, they may be in a healthy tension with these arrangements? Such tensions may enable further institutional reform.[36] So instead of forfeiting the ideal of popular sovereignty, the task ahead may be to re-embed this ideal in new transnational institutions through processes of what Turkuler Isiksel calls "reflective adjustment."[37]

Let me review the course of the argument so far. The examination of the relationship between human rights embedded in international covenants and treaties and constitutional norms has led me to distinguish between a *concept* and a *conception* of human rights. I have further argued that whereas international human rights treaties can be viewed as formulating general principles of human rights, constitutional rights can be considered their further concretization, now in the form of justiciable norms. To judge the range of divergence between these two, one must introduce the principle of self-determination, because I maintain that the right to self-government is the condition for the possibility of the realization of a democratic schedule of rights. I have further named this claim a model of "democratic authorship." How can such a strong normative criterion of democratic authorship make any sense of the heterarchical practices of transnational law of the present?[38]

DEMOCRATIC LEGITIMACY AND INTERNATIONAL HUMAN RIGHTS PRINCIPLES

A normative model of democratic authorship is particularly inappropriate, it appears, in the context of international norms whose legitimacy *cannot* be traced back to the united will of a sovereign people. Such norms originate either in declarations and covenants formulated by expert bodies in international organizations, such as the United Nations or other treaty-producing organizations, or they originate through customary international law as upheld by national and international courts and shared practice. But it is not the genesis of the norm alone that should determine its legitimacy. Just as the major human rights declarations of the international community have taken the constitutions of the world's liberal democracies as a model for articulation, so too can these international rights norms enter the democratic conversation of citizens through various venues and thus become "contextualized"—or, to use Peggy Levitt and Sally Engle Merry's felicitous word, "vernacularized."[39]

In a number of works over the past decade, I have proposed "democratic iterations" as a possible normative model with empirical implications to think through some of these dilemmas. By democratic iterations, I mean complex processes of public argument, deliberation, and exchange through which universalist rights claims are contested and contextualized, invoked and revoked, posited and positioned, throughout legal and political institutions as well as in the associations of civil society. In the process of repeating a term or a concept, we never simply produce a replica of the first intended usage or its original meaning; rather, every repetition is a form of variation. Every iteration transforms meaning, adds to it, enriches it in ever-so-subtle ways. Every act of iteration involves making sense of an authoritative original in a new and different context, through interpretation. The antecedent is thereby reposited and resignified via subsequent usages and references. Meaning is enhanced and transformed. Conversely, when the creative appropriation of that authoritative original ceases or stops making sense, then the original loses its authority over us as well.

Democratic citizens and stakeholders must reinterpret and reappropriate human rights principles in order to give them shape as constitutional rights and, if and when necessary, must suffuse constitutional rights with *new* content. Nor is it to be precluded that such constitutional iterations may themselves provide feedback loops in rendering more precise the intent and language of international human rights declarations and treaties.[40]

Democratic iterations occur throughout national and transnational civil society and global public spheres, in diverse sites. In constitutional democracies, the courts are the primary authoritative sites of norm iteration through judicial interpretation—although not of their democratic iteration, since *per definitionem* they operate according to different criteria of legitimacy. Yet the interaction between domestic norms and transnational ones does not take place only in courts. Increasingly, intervening in these processes are the contributions of other organizations, such as national and international nongovernmental organizations like Amnesty International or Human Rights Watch, which can produce expert reports and mobilize public opinion around controversial norm interpretation and norm implementation issues. A third site of iteration emerges through the interaction of domestic-judicial and transnational sources of norm interpretation and the political opinion-formation of ordinary citizens and residents. In formulating the concept of democratic iterations, it is this latter process that I had most in mind, though the other two processes were not excluded. Robert Post captures this tension between the legal and political very well:

> Politics and law are thus two distinct ways of managing the inevitable social facts of agreement and disagreement. As social practices, politics and law are both independent and interdependent. They are independent in the sense that they are incompatible. To submit a political controversy to legal resolution is to remove it from the political domain; to submit a legal controversy to political resolution is to undermine the law. Yet they are interdependent in the sense that law requires politics to produce the shared norms that law enforces, whereas politics requires law to stabilize and entrench the shared values the politics strives to achieve.[41]

If democratic iterations are necessary in order for us to judge the legitimacy of a range of variation in the interpretation of a rights claim, how can we assess whether democratic iterations have taken place, rather than demagogic processes of manipulation or authoritarian indoctrination? Do not democratic iterations themselves presuppose some standards of rights to be properly evaluated? Furthermore, aren't democratic iterations conceding too much to, or maybe even idealizing, democratic processes that are inevitably messy, are often ill informed, and, more significantly, may result in the trampling of the rights of unwanted others and minorities? I am very aware of this conflict, and yet I would insist on the necessary interaction between the liberal discourse of rights protection and the democratic processes of opinion- and will-formation.[42]

Democratic iterations do not idealize populist politics, but they have some formal discourse conditions built into them that would exclude the most egregious rights violations.

Democratic legitimacy reaches back to principles of normative justification. Democratic iterations do not alter the validity conditions of moral discourses of justification that are established independently of them. The "normative gap" remains. As is well known, this discourse model of justification, much like John Rawls's model of the two principles of justice, is a counterfactual one. It leads us to judge as "legitimate" or "illegitimate," in a preliminary and formal sense, processes of opinion- and will-formation through which rights claims are contested and contextualized, expanded and debated, in actual institutions of civil and political society. Such criteria minimally distinguish a de facto consensus from a rationally motivated one. Such criteria are not guidelines for building institutions, any more than Rawls's second principle of justice—the "difference principle"—tells us how to organize the economy! They are counterfactual criteria that can lead participants to challenge the legitimacy of a decision reached or a norm advocated. They provide moral agents with what Rainer Forst terms a "veto right."[43]

Some will note that there may be some kind of circularity here. I am talking about the right of participants to equal say, to agenda setting, and so forth, and the objection will be voiced: Weren't such norms supposed to result from a practical discourse in the first place? The answer to this objection is as follows. Since Aristotle, we know that, in reasoning about matters of ethics and politics, we are "always already situated" in medias res—we never begin the conversation without some presupposition and, in this case, without some shared understanding of what equality of participation in the conversation, challenging the agenda, and the like, may mean. Discourses are reflexive processes through which much of what we always already take for granted is challenged, questioned, "bracketed," if you wish, until these presuppositions are reestablished at the end of the conversation—a conversation that itself is always open to a future challenge.

This hermeneutic model of iteration is a recursive one, based on the same principles of nonfoundationalism that Neil Walker recently articulated.[44] There is an empirical and normative incompleteness to the interpretation of the rules that frame the discourses themselves, which then need to be reposited and rearticulated through the conversation. This recursive model of justification, based on the force of iterations, is related to many discussions in contemporary nonfoundationalist epistemology as well.[45]

When deployed with respect to international law and democratic sovereignty, democratic iterations help us understand a process that Judith Resnik has documented. Treaty ratification processes now no longer center upon "a singular formal moment of ratification through a monovocal nation-state." Increasingly, cities, states, counties, and municipalities are themselves incorporating major human rights treaties into their own charters. The city of San Francisco and San Paolo, Brazil, have adopted CEDAW; Portland, Oregon, has incorporated the Universal Declaration of Human Rights.[46] These processes of "legal seepage" at levels below the centralized judicial authority of the state testify to disaggregation processes of the national that Saskia Sassen is also concerned with.[47] However, one cannot naively assume that all local iterations will enhance democratic processes and values; they will not and do not. Nevertheless, such affiliations multiply the sites at which transjudicial conversations can occur, and they show how, even in the face of national recalcitrance and resistance to some human rights organs, such as CEDAW, for example, a human rights discourse can take place across national and local boundaries.

Resnik's innovative contribution is to suggest that reservations, understandings, and declarations themselves can be viewed in analogy to doctrines such as "margin of appreciation" or types of legal pluralism permitted by a variety of federalist arrangements (such as, for example, India's Muslim Family Law).[48] Yet, whereas the local and regional incorporation of rights treaties suggest their expansion across borders, these other processes suggest the limitation and blunting of their normative reach. Resnik cites how Bangladesh in 1997 withdrew reservations to CEDAW, which were earlier based on the conflict between Sharia law and the convention; Jordan withdrew a similar objection to a woman's right to independent residence and domicile outside that of her husband, in 2009. Sex-based differences in the military had led countries such as Australia, Austria, Germany, New Zealand, Switzerland, and Thailand to place reservations on CEDAW; many of these nations have subsequently withdrawn their caveats.

Resnik is not oblivious, either, to the limiting effect of reservations, understandings, and declarations, nor to the potentially opportunistic uses European courts make of the doctrine of "margin of appreciation." Yet she sees these models of "mediated participation" as offering a "cosmopolitical" vision to "capture the idea of polities joining in commitments that both acknowledge their independent identities while imposing reciprocal obligations."[49]

As this final discussion indicates, although I do not share the skepticism of realist state-theorists, I also am unable to share in the enthusiasm of global constitutionalists. It is within and across *bounded* polities (which may or may not be nation-states—they can be multiethnic or multicultural democracies, binational federations, or constitutional postnational polities such as the EU) that democratic iterations can occur. Empires have frontiers; democracies have boundaries. These boundaries are porous, permeable, and active sites of transnational conversations and interactions. It is this radical fact of interdependence and transnational affiliation that contemporary legal cosmopolitanism ought to seek to elucidate.

Let me conclude by returning to the objections, outlined at the beginning of this essay, of those thinkers who wish to defend the value of democratic self-determination and who claim (a) that recent developments in international law are ideals of cosmopolitan elites with little traction in the life of peoples (Walzer and Moyn); (b) that the principle of self-determination expresses an important value, and that "legal pluralism" may be the desirable middle ground between global cosmopolitanism and national sovereigntism (Walzer and Cohen); and finally, (c) that international law is no more than the consensually undertaken contractual commitments among sovereign states that remain the central units of jurisdiction and enforcement (Nagel). I hope to have shown that (a) and (c) are empirically false. The normative reach of international and transnational law is not limited by their conditions of origin; they are not merely fancy documents drawn by remote elites but actually have consequences for the empowerment of peoples around the world. Nor can they be viewed as contractual treaty obligations undertaken by sovereign states alone. They certainly are that, at least, but they also are much more than that, in that they bind states to a new sovereignty regime.

My struggle in this chapter has been to do justice to the values of self-determination and democratic sovereignty, on the one hand, and of legal cosmopolitanism and transnational solidarities on the other. "Legal pluralism" certainly captures a truth, but it does not go far enough, because the most difficult questions today emerge around the tug-of-war between the demands of international human rights norms and the sovereignty claims of constitutional democracies. Legal pluralism does not tell us how we ought to think about such conflicts and move beyond the zero-sum approach entertained by many. For example, what is the legitimate range of variation in the interpretation and implementation of human rights norms across democracies? How do we account for the force of the "normative gap" between concepts and conceptions of human rights?

I have suggested that there are some plausible theoretical answers to these dilemmas, all of which operate along the shared moral and political intuition that the democratic and the transnational, the local and the cosmopolitan are not opposed but may be seen, through contentious interpretation and conflict, as enhancing one another.

NOTES

An expanded and slightly revised version of this essay appeared as "The New Sovereigntism and Transnational Law: Legal Utopianism, Democratic Skepticism and Statist Realism," *Global Constitutionalism*, 5, no. 1 (March 2016), 109–44.

I am grateful to Joseph Weiler for his hospitality during my stay at NYU's Straus Institute for the Advanced Study of Law and Justice, under the auspices of a Guggenheim Fellowship in spring 2012. I am equally thankful to Judith Resnik for her extensive feedback as this essay has assumed final form, and to Robert Post, Neil Walker, Alec Stone Sweet, and Bruce Ackerman for helpful conversations. Participants in the "Justification Beyond the State" conference at NYU's Straus Center, on November 15, 2013—Rainer Forst, Jean Cohen, Mattias Kumm, Turkuler Isiksel, Lea Ypi, and, in particular, Stefan Gosepath—provided very sharp comments on another draft of this essay. Thanks also to my American Political Science Association co-panelists of August 2014, Max Pensky and Cristina Lafont, for their engagement with these themes.

1. Kiobel et al. v. Royal Dutch Petroleum, 569 U.S. (2013), No. 10–1491.
2. Michael Goodhart and Stacy Bondanella Tanichev, "The New Sovereigntist Challenge for Global Governance: Democracy Without Sovereignty," *International Quarterly Studies* 55, no. 4 (2011), 1047.
3. Michael Ignatieff, "Human Rights as Politics," in *Human Rights as Politics and Idolatry* (Princeton: Princeton University Press, 2001), 12–14.
4. Carl Schmitt, *Der Nomos der Erde im Voelkerrecht des Jus Publicum Europaeum*, 4th ed. (Berlin: Duncker and Humblot, 1997), 224; Schmitt, *The Nomos of the Earth in the International Law of the* Jus Publicum Europaeum, trans. G. L. Ulmen (New York: Telos, 2003), 254–5. I have consulted, but have not always used, the English translation.
5. Schmitt, *Nomos der Erde*, 224–5. My emphasis. I used my own translation here because the English has been somewhat abbreviated.
6. I am using the term "transnational law" in the sense described by Harold Koh, as international law that moves through public and private institutions and engages not only states but also nongovernmental organizations and commercial corporations. See Koh, "Transnational Legal Process," *Nebraska Law Review* 75, no. 1 (1996): 181–208; and Koh, "Transnational Public Law Litigation," *Yale Law Journal* 100 (1991): 2347–402. See also Oren Perez's statement: "This expanding network of transnational 'legalities' is not based on a coherent set of normative or institutional hierarchies. Rather, it represents a highly pluralistic mixture of legal regimes, with variable organizational and thematic structures: from state-oriented systems—such as the dispute settlement of the WTO, or the adjudicative system of the Law of the Sea Convention—to hybrid or private regimes." Perez, "Normative Creativity and Global Legal Pluralism: Reflections on the Democratic Critique of Transnational Law," *Indiana Journal of Global Legal Studies* 10, no. 2 (2003): 25. By "hybrid regimes," Perez also means "the cooperation between public and private bodies."
7. Among the literature discussing "global constitutionalization," see Bardo Fassbender, "The United Nations Charter as Constitution of the International Community," *Columbia Journal of Transnational Law* 36, no. 3 (1998): 529–619; Fassbender, " 'We the Peoples of the United Nations': Constituent Power and Constitutional Form," in *The Paradox of Constitutionalism*, ed. Martin Loughlin and Neil Walker (Oxford: Oxford University Press, 2007), 269–90; Arnim von Bogdandy, "Constitutionalism in International Law: Comment on a Proposal from Germany," *Harvard International Law Journal* 47, no. 1 (2006): 223–42; Brun-Otto Bryde, "Konstitutionalisierung des Voelkerrechts und Internationalisierung des Verfassungsbegriffs," *Der Staat* 1 (2003): 61–75; and Hauke Brunkhorst, "Globalizing Democracy Without a State: Weak Public, Strong Public, Global Constitutionalism," *Millenium: Journal of International Studies* 31, no. 3 (2002): 675–90.

    For historical antecedents, see Hans Kelsen, *Das Problem der Souveränität und die Theorie des Völkerrechts: Beitrag zu einer reinen Rechtslehre* (1928; repr. Vienna: Scientia Allen, 1960); Alfred Verdross, *Die Verfassung der Völkerrechtsgemeinschaft* (Vienna: J. Springer, 1926). There are parallel discussions with regard to constitutionalization in the EU, the World Trade Organization, and the International Monetary Fund. See Alec Stone Sweet, "Constitutionalism, Legal Pluralism, and International Regimes," *Indiana Journal of Global Legal Studies* 16, no. 2 (2009): 621–45.

8. Jeremy Waldron, *"Partly Laws Common to All Mankind": Foreign Law in American Courts* (New Haven, CT: Yale University Press, 2012). See also Jeremy Waldron, "The Supreme Court, 2004 Term-Comment: Foreign Law and the Modern *Ius Gentium*," *Harvard Law Review* 119, no. 1 (2005): 129–47.

9. See Günther Teubner, "Global Bukovina," in *Global Law Without a State*, ed. Günther Teubner (Aldershot, VT: Dartmouth, 1997), 3–28; and Teubner, "Societal Constitutionalism: Alternatives to State-Centered Constitutional Theory," in *Transnational Governance and Constitutionalism*, ed. Christian Joerges, Inger-Johanne Sand, and Günther Teubner (Oxford: Hart, 2004), 3–29.

10. Mark Tushnet argues that the "globalization of constitutional law" is unavoidable. For him, the driving mechanisms are economic; he leaves aside the question of the globalization of human rights norms insofar as they constitute the core of constitutional law. Tushnet, "The Inevitable Globalization of Constitutional Law," *Virginia Journal of International Law* 49 (2009): 985–1006.

11. Michael Walzer, *Spheres of Justice: A Defense of Pluralism and Equality* (New York: Basic Books, 1983); Thomas Nagel, "The Problem of Global Justice," *Philosophy and Public Affairs* 33, no. 2 (2005): 113–47; Samuel Moyn, *The Last Utopia: Human Rights in History* (Cambridge, MA: Belknap Press of Harvard University Press, 2010); Jean Cohen, *Globalization and Sovereignty: Rethinking Legality, Legitimacy and Constitutionalism* (Cambridge: Cambridge University Press, 2012).

Theorists such as Quentin Skinner and Michael Sandel also are skeptical about the force of the international. See Skinner, "The Sovereign State: A Genealogy," in *Sovereignty in Fragments: The Past, Present and Future of a Contested Concept*, ed. Hent Kalmo and Quentin Skinner (Cambridge: Cambridge University Press: 2010), 26–46; and Sandel, *Democracy's Discontent: America in Search of a Public Philosophy* (Cambridge, MA: Belknap Press of Harvard University Press, 1996). Sandel states, "If the global character of the economic suggests the need for transnational forms of governance, however, it remains to be seen whether such political units can inspire the identification and allegiance—the moral and civic culture—on which democratic authority ultimately depends" (399).

12. See Universal Declaration of Human Rights, G.A. Res. 217A (III) (Dec. 10, 1948); United Nations Convention on the Prevention and Punishment of the Crime of Genocide, G.A. Res. 260 (III)A (chapter 2) (Dec. 9, 1948); Convention Relating to the Status of Refugees, G.A. Res. 429 (V) (entered into force Apr. 22, 1954); International Covenant on Civil and Political Rights, G.A. Res. 2200A (XXI), 21 U.N. GAOR Supp. (no. 16) at 52, U.N. Doc. A/6316 (1966), 999 U.N.T.S. 171 (entered into force Mar. 23, 1976); International Covenant on Economic, Social and Cultural Rights, G.A. Res. 2200A (XXI), 21 U.N.GAOR Supp. (No. 16) at 49, U.N. Doc. A/6316 (1966), 993 U.N.T.S. 3 (entered into force Jan. 3, 1976); The Convention to Eliminate All Forms of Discrimination Against Women, G.A. Res. 34/180, Dec. 18, 1979 (entered into force

Sept. 3, 1981); International Convention on the Elimination of All Forms of Racial Discrimination, G.A. Res. 2106 (XX) (Dec. 21, 1965); and Convention Against Torture and other Cruel, Inhuman or Degrading Treatment or Punishment, G.A. Res. 39/46 (Dec. 10, 1984).

13. These provisions are, of course, augmented by many others. See, for example, Declaration on the Human Rights of Individuals Who are not Nationals of the Country in Which They Live, G.A. Res. 40/144, Annex, 40 U.N. GAOR Supp. (No. 53) at 252, U.N. Doc. A/40/53 (1985), providing such "aliens" with rights to leave, liberty of movement within a country, the right to have spouses and minor children admitted to join and stay with them, and protection from expulsion by requiring opportunities for hearings and for decision making not predicated on discrimination based on "race, colour, religion, culture, descent or national or ethnic origin"; Convention on the Reduction of Statelessness, 989 U.N.T.S. 175 (Dec. 13, 1975), requiring that nations grant nationality rights, under certain conditions, to "persons born in its territory who would otherwise be stateless"; Migration for Employment (Revised) (ILO no. 97), 120 U.N.T.S. 70 (Jan. 22, 1952), providing that members of the International Labour Organization make work policy and migration policies known, and treat fairly "migrants for employment"; and Declaration on Territorial Asylum, G.A. Res. 2312 (XXII), 22 U.N. GAOR Supp. (no. 16) at 81, U.N. Doc. A/6716 (1967).

14. In recent years, the historiography of human rights has commanded the attention of many historians, as well, and it is as if each historian has his or her heroes and heroines in telling the tale of the Universal Declaration of Human Rights, in particular. For Mary Ann Glendon, *A World Made New: Eleanor Roosevelt and the Universal Declaration of Human Rights* (New York: Random House, 2001), this is Eleanor Roosevelt; for Samantha Powers, *"A Problem from Hell": America and the Age of Genocide* (New York: Basic Books, 2002), it is Ralph Lemkin; for Jay Winter, *Dreams of Peace and Freedom: Utopian Movements in the Twentieth Century* (New Haven, CT: Yale University Press, 2006), it is the French jurist René Cassin; for Mark Mazower, *No Enchanted Palace: The End of Empire and the Ideological Origins of the United Nations* (Princeton: Princeton University Press, 2009), it is South African Prime Minister Smuts, whose efforts, ironically, resulted in the condemnation of his own South Africa for its treatment of "colored" peoples. Johannes Morsink's extremely instructive and more philosophical reconstruction of the debates resulting in the Universal Declaration takes the Canadian jurist Humphreys as its hero. Morsink, *The Universal Declaration of Human Rights: Origins, Drafting, and Intent* (Philadelphia: University of Pennsylvania Press, 1999). In contrast to these works, Samuel Moyn's much-discussed narrative in *The Last Utopia* is less reverent and explicitly antiteleological and antihagiographic. Joining Marc Bloch in criticizing the "idol of origins" (we can also think here of Walter Benjamin), Moyn refuses to see history as the tracing of antecedents and argues that human rights are something new that has transformed old currents beyond recognition. The "true key to the broken history of human rights, then, is the move from the politics of the state to the morality of the globe which now defines contemporary aspirations" (Moyn, *Last Utopia*, 42). In this

provocative work, Moyn goes wrong in his simplistic juxtaposition of human rights and democratic self-determination, and in misconstruing the interaction between the ethical and political dimensions of human rights. See my critique, in Seyla Benhabib, "Moving Beyond False Binarisms: On Samuel Moyn's *The Last Utopia*," *Qui Parle?* 22, no. 1 (Fall/Winter 2013): 81–93.

15. See Alan Gewirth, *Human Rights: Essays on Justification and Applications* (Chicago: University of Chicago Press, 1982); Gewirth, *The Community of Rights* (Chicago: University of Chicago Press, 1996); James Griffin, *On Human Rights* (Oxford: Oxford University Press, 2008); John Rawls, *The Law of Peoples with "The Idea of Public Reason Revisited"* (Cambridge, MA: Harvard University Press, 1999); Charles Beitz, *The Idea of Human Rights* (Oxford: Oxford University Press, 2009), 13; and Joseph Raz, "Human Rights Without Foundations," in *The Philosophy of International Law*, ed. Samantha Besson and John Tasioulas (Oxford: Oxford University Press, 2010), 321–39. Pablo Gilabert names the traditional conception the "humanistic" view. See Gilabert, "Humanist and Political Perspectives on Human Rights," *Political Theory* 39, no. 4 (May 2011): 439–67. I discuss these differences in Seyla Benhabib, "Reason-Giving and Rights-Bearing: Constructing the Subject of Rights," *Constellations: An International Journal of Critical and Democratic Theory* 20, no. 1 (2013): 38–51.

16. See Seyla Benhabib, "Another Universalism: On the Unity and Diversity of Human Rights," in *Dignity in Adversity: Human Rights in Troubled Times* (Cambridge: Polity, 2011), 57–77; and Benhabib, "Reason-Giving and Rights-Bearing," 38–51.

17. James Griffin, "Human Rights: Questions of Aim and Approach," *Ethics* 120, no. 4 (July 2010): 745.

18. See the classic essay by Ronald Dworkin, "Taking Rights Seriously" (1970), in *Taking Rights Seriously* (Cambridge, MA: Harvard University Press, 1978), 184–205.

19. John Rawls invokes H. L. A. Hart's discussion to introduce this distinction. See Rawls, *A Theory of Justice* (Cambridge, MA: Harvard University Press, 1971), 5; and H. L. A. Hart, *The Concept of Law* (1961; repr. Oxford: Clarendon, 1975), 155–9. Many thanks to the late Ed Baker for clarifying some of the intertextual issues involved here.

20. John Rawls, *Political Liberalism* (New York: Columbia University Press, 1993), 14, note 15.

21. Dworkin, "Constitutional Cases," in *Taking Rights Seriously*, 131–49.

22. Robert Alexy, *A Theory of Constitutional Rights* (Oxford: Oxford University Press, 2002), 47–48.

23. Seyla Benhabib, *The Claims of Culture: Equality and Diversity in the Global Era* (Princeton: Princeton University Press, 2002), 154–68.

24. Title IX, Education Amendments of 1972, 20 U.S.C. §§ 1681–1688 (1972); Title VII, 42 U.S.C. §§ 2000e to 2000e-15 (1970), as amended, 42 U.S.C. §§ 2000e to 2000e-17 (supp. II, 1972).

25. There is an epistemic parallel between what I am calling "range of variation" and jurisprudential principles such as "margin of appreciation" and "proportionality," used frequently by courts in their interpretation and application of human rights

norms. But sometimes these principles are also invoked to eviscerate the normative power of international human rights. Particularly disappointing in this respect have been many judgments of the European Court of Human Rights, which have clearly upheld state sovereignty over and against human and civil rights claims with regards to the so-called "scarf affair." For a discussion of the position of the European Court of Human Rights in the Leyla Sahin case, see Seyla Benhabib, "Human Rights, International Law and the Transatlantic Rift," in *The Democratic Disconnect: Citizenship and Accountability in the Transatlantic Community*, by Benhabib et al. (Washington, DC: Transatlantic Academy, 2013), 89–96. http://www.transatlanticacademy.org/sites/default/files/publications/TA%2020123report_May13_complete_web.pdf.

26. I owe this formulation to Jürgen Habermas's thesis of the cooriginality of public and private autonomy. Habermas, *Between Facts and Norms*, trans. William Rehg (Cambridge, MA: MIT Press, 1996), 84–104. The final sentence here ("Without the basic rights of the person . . .") refers, of course, to Immanuel Kant's famous formulation, "Thoughts without concepts are empty; intuitions without concepts are blind." Kant, *Critique of Pure Reason*, unabridged ed., trans. Norman Kemp Smith (New York: St. Martin's, 1965), 93. Although I am indebted to Habermas's general discussions of the relationship between public and private autonomy and his analysis of the discursive legitimation of law, I do not follow his "discourse-theoretic deduction of basic rights." See Seyla Benhabib, review of Habermas's *Between Facts and Norms*, in *American Political Science Review* 91, no. 3 (1997): 725–6.

27. Ran Hirschl, *Constitutional Theocracy* (Cambridge, MA: Harvard University Press, 2010); Rawls, *Law of Peoples*, 79–80.

28. Rawls, *Political Liberalism*, 32. There is a substantial shift in Rawls's understanding of the concept of the person between *Political Liberalism* and *Law of Peoples*, and this is behind the turn to Joshua Cohen's "minimalism" in the defense of human rights among Rawlsians. I explore some of these issues in Seyla Benhabib, "Is There a Human Right to Democracy? Beyond Interventionism and Indifference," in *Philosophical Dimensions of Human Rights: Some Contemporary Views*, ed. Claudio Corradetti (New York: Springer, 2011), 190–213.

29. See Raz, "Human Rights Without Foundations," 321–39. For a defense of the "political conception" of rights, which goes beyond the limitations formulated by Raz, see Cristina Lafont, "Human Rights, Sovereignty and the Responsibility to Protect," *Constellations* 22, no. 1 (2015): 68–78.

30. For a judicious analysis, see Cohen, *Globalization and Sovereignty*, 196–203.

31. For further reflections on these issues, see my exchange with Saladin Meckled-Garcia, in Seyla Benhabib, "Defending a Cosmopolitanism Without Illusions: Reply to My Critics," *Critical Review of International Social and Political Philosophy* 17, no. 6 (2014): 697–715; and Saladin Meckled-Garcia, "What Comes First: Democracy or Human Rights?" in the same issue, 681–88.

32. T. H. Marshall, *Citizenship and Social Class and Other Essays* (Cambridge: Cambridge University Press, 1950).

33. I am grateful to the participants at the "Justification Beyond the State" conference at NYU's Straus Center, held in November 2013, and in particular to Stefan Goosepath, Rainer Forst, and Chris McCrudden, for helping me see the difficulties of this point.
34. For a compelling recent statement of this objection, see Nancy Fraser, "Transnationalizing the Public Sphere: On the Legitimacy and Efficacy of Public Opinion in a Post-Westphalian World," in *Transnationalizing the Public Sphere*, ed. Kate Nash (Cambridge: Polity, 2014), 8–42.
35. See the much-discussed book by Colin Crouch, *Post-Democracy* (Cambridge: Polity, 2004).
36. "We argued above," write Goodhart and Taninchev, "that popular sovereignty represents the reconciliation of sovereignty . . . with the democratic principles of freedom and equality . . . Freedom and equality do not require popular sovereignty; they require that if there is sovereignty it must be popular . . . The challenge, then, is to decouple democratic freedom and equality from the notion of popular control, to develop new democratic criteria more appropriate for making sense of and evaluating global governance arrangements" (Goodhart and Taninchev, "New Sovereigntist Challenge," 1060). My central argument in this essay is that the "decoupling" of democratic authorship from freedom and rights makes no sense conceptually and is hardly possible institutionally. Rather, we need to recognize the *multiplicity* of national, international, and transnational political arrangements and their messy interlinkages through various iterations, all the while subjecting such arrangements to democratic accountability and scrutiny.
37. Turkuler Isiksel, *Europe's Functional Constitution* (Oxford: Oxford University Press, 2016).
38. See Neil Walker, "Constitutionalism and the Incompleteness of Democracy: An Iterative Relationship," *Rechtsfilosofie & Rechtstheorie* 39, no. 3 (2010): 206–33.
39. Peggy Levitt and Sally Engle Merry, "Vernacularization on the Ground: Local Uses of Global Women's Rights in Peru, China, India and the United States," *Global Networks* 9, no. 4 (2009): 441–61.
40. I have discussed in more detail the role of global social movements in claiming rights across borders and generating cosmopolitan citizenship in Seyla Benhabib, "Claiming Rights Across Borders: International Human Rights and Democratic Sovereignty," in *Dignity in Adversity*, 117–38. This was originally published in *American Political Science Review* 103, no. 4 (November 2009): 691–704.
41. Robert Post, "Theorizing Disagreement: Re-conceiving the Relationship Between Law and Politics," *California Law Review* 98, no. 4 (2010): 1319–50. See also the concept of "democratic constitutionalism" developed in Robert Post and Reva B. Siegel, "Roe Rage: Democratic Constitutionalism and Backlash," *Harvard Civil Rights and Civil Liberties Review* 42, no. 2 (2007): 373–434.
42. For further elucidation, see Seyla Benhabib, "The New Sovereigntism and Transnational Law: Legal Utopianism, Democratic Skepticism and Statist Realism," *Global Constitutionalism* 5, no. 1 (March 2016): 109–44.

43. Rainer Forst, *The Right to Justification: Elements of a Constructivist Theory of Justice*, trans. Jeffrey Flynn (New York: Columbia University Press, 2012), 183, 265.
44. Neil Walker, "Constitutionalism and the Incompleteness of Democracy"; and Walker, "Constitutionalism and the Incompleteness of Democracy: A Reply to Four Critics," *Rechtsfilosofie & Rechtstheorie* 39, no. 3 (2010): 276–88. Walker is discussing democracy in these articles and not rules of discourse per se, but rules of discourse are the most abstract norms that undergird democratic practices, and the principle of "incompleteness" holds for both. Although he does not accept the prospect of "postnational constitutionalism without democracy," Walker shows the inadequacy of the sovereign nation-centric model by elucidating how constitutionalism and democracy define and "complete" each other (Walker, "Constitutionalism and the Incompleteness of Democracy: An Iterative Relationship," 228–33).
45. See, for example, Robert Brandom's statement: "Saying 'we' in this sense is placing ourselves and each other in the space of reasons, by giving and asking for reasons for our attitudes and performances . . . Our attitudes and acts exhibit an intelligible content, a content that can be grasped or understood, by being caught up in a web of reasons, by being inferentially articulated." Brandom, *Making It Explicit: Reasoning, Representing and Discursive Commitment* (Cambridge, MA: Harvard University Press, 1994), 5.
46. Judith Resnik, "Comparative (in)equalities: CEDAW, the jurisdiction of gender, and the heterogeneity of transnational law production," *I.CON* 10, no. 2 (2012): 531–50, 546.
47. Saskia Sassen, *Territory, Authority, Rights: From Medieval to Global Assemblages* (Princeton: Princeton University Press, 2006).
48. See Benhabib, *The Claims of Culture*, 91–94.
49. Resnik, "Comparative (in)equalities," 549.

3

HUMAN RIGHTS, SOVEREIGNTY, AND THE RESPONSIBILITY TO PROTECT

CRISTINA LAFONT

At the 2005 High-Level Plenary Meeting of the General Assembly, world leaders reached consensus on the responsibility to protect vulnerable populations from genocide, war crimes, ethnic cleansing, and crimes against humanity.[1] The basis for this development was the 2001 *Report of the International Commission on Intervention and State Sovereignty*, in which the innovative concept of the "responsibility to protect" was first introduced, its elements articulated, and its scope of application delimited.[2] Without denying the path-breaking character of this development, the international community's explicit acknowledgement of a responsibility to protect human rights seems like a natural step in the development of contemporary human rights practice. Human rights were conceived, from the beginning, as part of an international regime whose aim—as explicitly stated in the Universal Declaration of Human Rights and the UN Charter—was to secure the protection of human rights worldwide.[3] In contrast to declarations of rights such as the 1789 French Declaration of the Rights of Man and the Citizen, the main innovation brought about by the post–World War II human rights regime is precisely that it framed human rights as international norms whose violation is a matter of international concern.[4] Nonetheless, the fact that the Responsibility to Protect (R2P) principle was unanimously endorsed by the UN General Assembly indicates that the international community's responsibility to protect human rights is no longer merely an aspiration but an emergent norm of customary international law.[5]

Because this is a recent development, the precise nature, scope, and implications of this emergent norm are still quite unclear. However, the same cannot be said of the reactions that it has generated so far. These tend to be clearly divided between those who strongly support this development and those who are skeptical or even deeply concerned by it.[6] Within the latter camp, the main worry among those who have principled reasons against the idea of international intervention is that it is a direct threat to the sovereignty and equality of states.[7] Their fear is that the linkage of human rights law with humanitarian intervention, which began after the end of the cold war, may open the door to (neo-imperialist) invasions of weak states by powerful ones for any reason whatsoever.[8] A quick look at the demanding list of rights included in international human rights conventions and treaties reinforces this fear. If, as Article 25 of the International Covenant on Civil and Political Rights suggests, there is a human right to democracy, for instance, then the international community's responsibility to protect human rights may seem to open the door for not just humanitarian but also "prodemocratic" interventions, that is, military interventions to promote or to bring about democracy in other countries.[9] The same basic concern could arise with respect to any of the noble goals that are contained in the core human rights conventions.

This worry leads many authors to embrace human rights "minimalism." If a distinctive function of human rights norms is to justify coercive intervention, then restricting the scope of human rights seems to be the only viable option to avoid providing powerful states with illegitimate excuses for intervention against sovereign states. A prominent example of a functionalist approach to human rights that leads to minimalism is offered by Rawls in *The Law of Peoples*. According to Rawls, a distinctive function of human rights norms is to "specify limits to a regime's internal autonomy," such that the regime's fulfillment of the rights of its citizens "is sufficient to exclude justified and forceful intervention by other peoples, for example, by diplomatic and economic sanctions or . . . by military force."[10] Given that Rawls interprets human rights as (defeasible) triggers for coercive intervention,[11] it is unsurprising that he proposes a severely truncated list of rights that bears little resemblance to the list of rights actually contained in the core human rights conventions and treaties that have been ratified by a majority of states.[12] According to Rawls, the "proper subset" of genuine human rights is limited to rights such as the right to life, to liberty, to property, and to formal equality, whereas rights to political participation, to an education, or to full equality and nondiscrimination are conspicuously absent.[13]

Against this revisionary approach, many authors have pointed out just how implausible it is to interpret the distinctive function of contemporary human rights practice as being the justification of coercive intervention against sovereign states. Obviously, the main function of human rights norms is the protection of individual persons. Insofar as they serve that function, they provide normative standards that empower individuals (as well as nongovernmental organizations [NGOs] and many other agents who act in their name) to denounce, contest, and defend themselves and others from abuses at the hands of not only their own governments but also transnational corporations, international organizations, and so on. As James Nickel points out, quite apart from justifying coercive intervention, human rights norms fulfill a variety of critical and aspirational functions.[14] Seen from this perspective, the rationale behind the international community's R2P principle is the "protection of the person, rooted in universal human rights standards, and not a military doctrine aimed at justifying intervention."[15] Although this is a very plausible response to the revisionary approach, it nevertheless appears to be insufficient as it stands. Merely pointing out that the main function of human rights norms is to protect individual persons does nothing to address the suspicion that such protection may come at the price of undermining the sovereignty and equality of states. As long as both sides of the debate fail to examine the assumption that human rights and state sovereignty are mutually exclusive values, *the normative credentials of the international community's default responsibility to protect human rights remain questionable in principle.*

In what follows, I would like to explore the scope and implications of the international community's responsibility to protect human rights under current conditions of globalization. Taking the main purposes and normative principles that underlie contemporary human rights practice as a guide, I defend a much broader and more demanding interpretation of the international community's R2P principle than is currently acknowledged. However, as I will try to show, even under such an ambitious interpretation, the international protection of human rights and the sovereign equality of states do not have to be seen as antithetical but rather can and should be seen to be mutually reinforcing principles of international law.

SOVEREIGNTY AND HUMAN RIGHTS: CAN THE CIRCLE BE SQUARED?

As I have suggested, the attempt to harmonize human rights and state sovereignty as equally valid principles of international law seems to lead to a dilemma. In order to give an account of the international function of human rights that is compatible with respecting state sovereignty, it seems that the content of human rights needs to be restricted so that it fits within the scope of legitimate intervention by external agents against sovereign states. This strategy exerts pressure toward narrowing the list of human rights to rights to life and bodily integrity, so that only interventions to prevent grave rights violations through criminal acts such as genocide or ethnic cleansing show up as legitimate. However, once the content of human rights is reduced to such a minimum, respecting human rights becomes too easy to provide a meaningful "standard of achievement."[16] As a consequence, human rights norms can no longer fulfill any of their other functions. They would become useless as standards for criticism and political struggle against any form of rights violation that does not involve mass killings—from abuses of power, to discrimination, to a lack of political representation, freedom of speech, and so on. Yet the converse of this approach also seems to have problems. The principle of equal sovereignty of states seems seriously threatened if, in order to give a plausible account of the critical and aspirational function of human rights, one accepts the demanding list of rights contained in current human rights conventions. Respecting human rights would now become too difficult. It also could be claimed that any insufficiency or deviation in meeting such demanding human rights standards would provide a justified excuse for external intervention against sovereign states.

As a way out of this dilemma, some authors propose to follow a strategy of bifurcation. In her book *Globalization and Sovereignty*, Jean

Cohen follows this strategy and argues that, instead of minimizing the set of "human rights proper," as Rawls proposes, human rights should be divided into two separate categories with clearly differentiated functions. On the one hand, we have the set of what Cohen calls "human security rights," the violation of which could warrant international action, even coercive intervention against a state. Those are the rights violated by criminal acts such as genocide or ethnic cleansing. On the other hand, we have the full catalog of rights contained in the core human rights conventions, the function of which should be seen as merely domestic. Indeed, to ensure that the full catalog of rights does not become a set of potential triggers of the international community's R2P, as "human security rights do," they must be removed from the proper subset of "institutionalized and enforceable international human rights" and reinterpreted as standards that are entirely internal to a domestic political practice and that are, therefore, primarily directed to a domestic audience.[17] As Cohen indicates:

> While international human rights have been articulated as global public standards and aspirations, their main function is not to serve as norms to which the international community of states hold each country's government accountable through reciprocity mechanisms. Rather, they function as public standards of critique to which citizens and residents, domestic rights activists, and social movement actors can refer *in order to hold their own governments accountable*.[18]

Consequently, "*rights advocates should shift the focus back to the domestic arena* and the empowering and emancipatory role that human rights discourses still have to play *therein* when invoked by local actors, i.e., those whose rights are at issue, even though today these discourses reference international norms."[19]

This strategy of bifurcating and de-internationalizing human rights seems problematic in several respects.[20] First, without further clarification and justification regarding the conceptual and normative grounds for the proposed bifurcation within human rights, the proposal seems arbitrary. According to Jean Cohen's proposal, the bifurcation tracks the threshold below which a state loses all legitimacy by denying some sector of its population the right to political membership. Following Joshua

Cohen's proposal, she interprets human rights "as entitlements that ensure the bases of membership, or inclusion into organized political society."[21] However, she finds his interpretation of the principle too demanding, in that it includes political rights such as meaningful political participation, freedom of speech, and so forth. Accordingly, she claims that the substantive criterion for identifying the proper subset of "human security rights"—those that can trigger the international community's responsibility to protect—is "not the absence of political participation, dissent, or concern and respect, but rather absolute nonbelonging." A state that engages in criminal practices such as mass extermination, expulsion, ethnic cleansing, or enslavement is not simply violating some moral rights of its victims but is destroying the very conditions of possibility for the political agency of the targeted groups. In so doing, it "forfeits the claim to be representing the groups it oppresses in these radical ways and thus violates the membership principle."[22]

Now, even if one assumes, for the sake of argument, that the membership principle provides the right substantive criterion for identifying the "proper subset" of human rights whose violation should trigger the international community's responsibility to protect, and even if, also for the sake of argument, one agrees with an ultraminimalist interpretation of the membership principle, it is still not clear why massive starvation due merely to state neglect, as opposed to the same starvation caused by a deliberate criminal intent (that is, the deliberate attempt to bring about what she calls "the political death of a segment of the political community"), should not count as a violation of the principle.[23] Even less clear is why such massive starvation would not count as a threat to human security that appropriately triggers the international community's responsibility to protect.[24]

Seen from this perspective, the cogency of the proposed bifurcation among human rights norms would seem to depend on the truth of a quite implausible empirical claim: what Cohen refers to as "the four E's" (mass extermination, expulsion, ethnic cleansing, and enslavement) are the only current threats to the security of the person. Responding that they are the only threats that can legitimately trigger external intervention would simply beg the question. Thus, in order to dispel the impression that this is all rather ad hoc, the distinction would need to be justified against plausible alternative views, such as the UN human security approach, which explicitly emphasizes the multidimensional nature of threats to human security and the need for integrated responses that take into account all the relevant structural conditions at the local, national, and international levels. Restrictively reinterpreting the relevant threats to human security rights as the four E's would be clearly retrogressive vis-à-vis current UN doctrine, which is based on recognition of the fact that "the lives of millions of people [are] being threatened not only by international war and internal conflicts but also by chronic and persistent poverty, climate-related disasters, organized crime, human trafficking, health pandemics, and sudden economic and financial downturns."[25]

But whether one accepts a multidimensional view of human security threats or sticks with the narrower set of the four E's favored by Cohen, the problems associated with attempts to bifurcate human rights into two separate categories still remain. Cohen seems to assume that the specific subset of rights that belong to the category of "human security rights" can be discerned from the rights that are threatened in situations such as the four E's. However, as she herself indicates, these are not situations wherein some specific rights are violated. Instead, these are situations in which the very right to have rights is violated. Indeed, populations under the threat of genocide or ethnic cleansing do not lack secure access to some narrow set of rights; they lack secure access to *any rights at all*. Thus, focusing on threats like genocide or ethnic cleansing is not particularly helpful for demarcating a specific subset of human rights, because this would require drawing a line between the rights that are threatened in such situations and the rights that are not.[26] It is precisely because victims in such situations lack protection for any of their rights that coercive interventions to prevent or mitigate them can garner support among human rights minimalists and nonminimalists alike, for this support neither requires nor depends upon drawing a categorical distinction among types of human rights.[27]

Beyond the questionability of the proposal to bifurcate human rights, the proposal to de-internationalize them also seems retrogressive from the point of view of its practical consequences for the responsibilities of the international community. Removing from the list of enforceable international rights the bulk of human rights that fall outside the putative subset of "human security rights" not only would rule out military interventions against sovereign states in response to their violation but also, presumably, would rule out all other forms of external action, such as legal interventions by international courts (e.g., the International Court of Justice), those undertaken by regional human rights bodies (e.g., the European Court of Human Rights [ECHR] or the Inter-American Court of Human Rights), and the activities of the UN treaty-monitoring bodies that supervise the main human rights conventions. Certainly, the rulings of such supranational institutions limit the "margin of appreciation" of state parties and thereby infringe upon their sovereignty. In fact, the potential for infringing upon not just state but also popular sovereignty is unavoidable, since—as Cohen acknowledges—"human rights conventions tend to take on autonomous international meaning and weight that is not simply at the disposal of individual signatory states."[28]

Needless to say, it is precisely because the interpretation of the international human rights treaties is not at the disposal of individual states that their enforcement by supranational courts can provide potential victims some effective legal remedy against violations by their own states. From this perspective, removing the quite demanding political, social, and economic rights included in the core human rights conventions from the proper subset of "institutionalized and enforceable international rights" would be a clear retrogression in the legal development of the international human rights regime. Indeed, the widespread recognition that human rights are interdependent has led to the expansion rather than the narrowing of the list of "enforceable international rights." As recently as May 2013, the Optional Protocol to the International Covenant on Economic, Social and Cultural Rights entered into force. It includes an individual complaint mechanism that allows the UN Committee on Economic, Social and Cultural Rights to consider complaints from individuals or groups who claim their rights under the covenant have been violated. It also contains an inquiry mechanism that allows the committee to investigate, report upon, and make recommendations regarding "grave or systematic violations" of the convention. This is a slow but steady trend in the legal development of the international human rights regime. In fact, an individual complaint mechanism has already entered into force for seven of the nine core international human rights treaties.[29]

Now, this may suggest that we are once again facing a tragic conflict between the incompatible values of state sovereignty and individual human rights. Interestingly, Cohen's own discussion of the development of the international human rights regime throughout the twentieth century provides some cues that question this diagnosis. As Cohen rightly indicates, in contrast to the 1948 Universal Declaration of Human Rights, the regional ECHR that was established under the auspices of the Council of Europe was designed to be enforceable from the beginning. This convention includes a demanding set of civil and political rights for all persons within the jurisdiction of its member states, and it established a commission that could investigate a case, attempt a settlement, or refer it to the ECHR, the decisions of which are binding upon member states. Against this backdrop, Cohen raises the obvious question:

> But why would executives of democratic states delegate some of their sovereign powers to a strong regional regime and court (which acquired compulsory jurisdiction)? The answer is that they were executives of newly (re-)established democracies who sought to create supranational mechanisms to help lock in domestic constitutionalist and democratic institutions against the re-emergence of anti-democratic political threats... The possible enforcement of human rights by the ECHR could serve as a mechanism helping to strengthen domestic courts and institutions of judicial review, parliamentary legislation, and public action. Indeed the idea of signing on to a strong regional human rights regime was a way to *supplement and reinforce*, not substitute for, *the domestic institutions of constitutional democracy*.[30]

Now, if Cohen is right and a supranational human rights regime with binding authority to adjudicate on civil and political rights can reinforce rather than undermine sovereignty, then it is not at all clear why excluding those rights from the subset of "institutionalized and enforceable international rights" would be a welcome development of the international human rights regime. It would certainly leave the victims of violations of such rights without any protection. But, even more importantly, leaving citizens without protection from violations of their political rights at the hands of their own state would undermine rather than strengthen sovereignty—at least if we understand sovereignty in a normatively demanding sense, as Cohen does.[31] It seems to me that the citizens of any country in the world have just as good reasons today as the Europeans of fifty years ago to try to "lock in domestic constitutionalist and democratic institutions against the re-emergence of anti-democratic political threats" by maintaining international mechanisms for strengthening their constitutional rights. If so, they would have good reasons to resist the exclusion of the full range of human rights (from civil rights to political, social, and economic rights) from the domain of "institutionalized and enforceable international rights."

Still, this answer does not address the main worry that motivates Cohen's proposal. Taking into account the power differentials among states, any international enforcement of the full range of human rights contained in the core human rights conventions is damned to be bent toward the self-serving interests of the powerful states and thus to undermine the equal sovereignty of states as a fundamental organizing principle of international law. It is this worry that motivates proposals to *deflate* the international community's responsibility to protect human rights, so as to restrict it to the protection against egregious violations such as genocide or ethnic cleansing. Here, we finally face the central issue, namely, whether human rights and sovereign equality are necessarily in conflict.

HUMAN RIGHTS AND SOVEREIGNTY REVISITED

Although Jean Cohen herself warns of the danger of constructing state sovereignty and human rights as antithetical principles, in the end, her proposal succumbs to that very danger. Limiting the domain of "institutionalized and enforceable international human rights" to the subset of so-called human security rights can count as an improvement upon the status quo only if the international enforcement of human rights is seen as a process that necessarily weakens the sovereignty and equality of states. International action to enforce human rights, at its best, is undertaken for the sake of protecting vulnerable individuals and, at its worst, is pursued as a pretext for actions that serve the self-serving purposes of powerful states. Either way, sovereignty is the price we pay.

If this is right, then any attempt to promote the human rights project faces a dilemma. We can have international enforcement of minimal standards, and we also can have demanding standards that are merely domestic aspirations, but we cannot have international enforcement of demanding standards without simultaneously undermining the sovereignty and equality of states. However, as I will show, what is missing from this picture are the many ways in which "institutionalized and enforceable international human rights" can be a crucial tool for *strengthening* the sovereignty and equality of states against the undue influence of powerful actors in the international arena.[32] Let's take a look at some examples.

GLOBAL GOVERNANCE INSTITUTIONS AND HUMAN RIGHTS

Global governance institutions such as the World Trade Organization (WTO), the International Monetary Fund (IMF), and the World Bank are particularly relevant institutional contexts in which the power differentials among member states can have a very negative impact upon the sovereignty of weak states, not to mention upon the protection of human rights in these states. A recent case that has drawn a lot of public attention concerns WTO regulations on patents for pharmaceuticals and their impact upon access to essential medicines.

In 1995, members of the WTO signed the Agreement on Trade-Related Aspects of Intellectual Property Rights (TRIPS).[33] Among other things, this agreement grants pharmaceutical companies patent protection for a period of twenty years, during which they have the exclusive rights to market and sell their products. Prior to the TRIPS agreement, each country had its own legislation on intellectual property; in many cases, patents were exclusively applied to processes but not to products, or they did not apply to pharmaceuticals at all. It was therefore possible to produce cheaper, generic versions of expensive medications. However, the TRIPS agreement introduced drastic changes by significantly increasing the property rights privileges of pharmaceutical companies and shielding them from competition from companies that produce generic versions. Since ratification of the TRIPS agreement is a compulsory requirement for membership in the WTO, countries such as Brazil, India, South Africa, or Thailand were required to change their domestic legislation accordingly. This was problematic because such countries had previously been the main producers of generic pharmaceutical products and had supplied affordable, essential medicines to most of the developing world.

The issue gained public attention in light of the severe negative impact of this agreement upon the access that citizens of poor countries had to essential medicines, particularly their access to antiretroviral treatments for HIV/AIDS. Taking into account the pandemic proportions of the HIV/AIDS crisis in sub-Saharan Africa, it is not surprising that the implementation of the TRIPS agreement produced public outrage.[34] Two interesting cases in this fight were Brazil and South Africa. The constitutions of both countries explicitly recognize the right to health, the right to access essential medicines, and the obligation of the state to guarantee those rights. In the case of Brazil, its legislation also provides access to essential medicines free of charge. So the changes in domestic legislation required by the TRIPS agreement would have made it impossible for those states to protect an essential component of the right to health that their citizens were already supposed to have. This in turn would have been in direct breach of their international human rights obligations. All states that have ratified the International Covenant on Economic, Social and Cultural Rights (ICESCR) have accepted the principle of nonretrogression, which prohibits "deliberately retrogressive measures" through law or policy, that is, legislative measures that jeopardize existing achievements in the enjoyment of social and economic rights.

In October 2001, a group of more than twenty developing countries, which included Brazil, India, South Africa, and Thailand, prepared a draft ministerial declaration to be discussed at the Doha round of trade negotiations. In that declaration, they explicitly appealed to the member states' international obligation to protect the human rights of their populations as a justification for the need to amend the TRIPS agreement. In particular, they appealed to their obligation to protect and promote the fundamental human rights to life and the enjoyment of the highest attainable standard of physical and mental health, including the prevention, treatment, and control of epidemic, endemic, occupational, and other diseases and the creation of conditions that would ensure universal access to medical services and medical attention in the event of sickness, as affirmed in the ICESCR.[35]

In December 2001, the UN Committee on Economic, Social and Cultural Rights, which supervises the implementation of the ICESCR by state parties, issued a statement on "human rights and intellectual property," affirming that national and international intellectual property regimes must be consistent with the human rights obligations of states.[36] The final Doha declaration did not directly mention human rights to justify the amendment. Instead, the international legal obligation of states to protect their citizens' right to health was rendered as "the WTO members' right to protect public health and, in particular, to promote access to medicines for all."[37]

Several features of this development are of interest. Regarding the potential conflict between international human rights law and trade law, it is very significant that, for the first time, an amendment to a WTO trade regulation was introduced that explicitly recognized the priority of protecting fundamental rights (such as the right to health and to access essential medicines) over other trade goals and agreements. As for the sovereignty and equality of the states participating in global governance institutions, this was a clear case in which an appeal to international human rights law by weak states—with the decisive additional support of NGOs, global public opinion, and the UN human rights machinery—actually strengthened the sovereignty and equality of weak, developing countries against the strong economic interests of the most powerful states. It did so in spite of the disproportionate bargaining power of the powerful states within global governance institutions. The issue is far from resolved, and there are many reasons to be pessimistic about the whole process.[38] But what I find interesting about this development is that it calls into question the claim that the distinctive international function of human rights norms is to *limit the sovereignty of states*.

This claim might be true in cases in which human rights violations are due to the fact that states are unable or unwilling to protect the human rights of their populations. However, this example presents a totally different case. What we have in cases like the TRIPS agreement are states that are able and willing to protect the human rights in question but are prevented from doing so by economic obligations imposed by global governance institutions. In these cases, the appropriate form of international action (such as the amendment of the TRIPS agreement), far from limiting sovereignty, consists precisely in *strengthening the sovereignty of the states in question*. Because global economic regulations such as the TRIPS agreement threaten to limit the sovereignty of member states—that is, their authority to decide how to best meet their obligations to protect the basic rights of their populations—the 2005 amendment needed to explicitly affirm "the members' right to protect public health and promote access to essential medicines for all." This problem is not an isolated case but one of the major challenges confronting contemporary human rights practice.

Global economic institutions such as the WTO, the IMF, or the World Bank establish regulations, policies, and agreements based on the rationale and principles underlying their respective legal mandates (trade liberalization, financial stability, and so on). Protecting human rights is not part of their legal mandates, so their regulations, policies, and agreements are guided by economic considerations rather than by human rights. However, regulations and agreements on trade, investment, patents, and so forth may require changes in domestic law that can have a tremendous effect on the ability of states to protect the human rights of their members. This can lead to conflicts among the international obligations of member states, such as pitting their human rights obligations against their trade obligations.

However, member states are not at liberty to unilaterally decide how to best resolve potential conflicts among their international obligations. In the case of the WTO, for example, this is due to its "single undertaking" structure, which means that (1) all WTO members must participate in all WTO treaty regimes; (2) by default, all WTO rules apply to all members; and (3) individual WTO members may not reverse or adjust their obligations. Moreover, if they breach their agreements, member states are subject to enforceable sanctions imposed by these global economic institutions. Withdrawing from the agreements is not a feasible option for most states; it would only worsen their situation. Thus, it is clear that, unless these institutions develop legal mechanisms to ensure that conflicts between the economic obligations they impose on member states and the international human rights obligations of those states can be avoided, states may be forced to breach the latter in order to fulfill the former.

HUMAN RIGHTS: DEMANDING AND INTERNATIONAL

The articulation and defense of an appropriate international response to this structural problem lies behind the long-standing efforts of UN human rights agencies and other transnational actors—from NGOs to organizations of legal scholars, and even some countries—to entrench international human rights law in the operational mechanisms of international organizations such as the World Bank, the IMF or the WTO. The aim is to provide legal standards of operation as well as remedies in cases where such standards are violated, so that the actions of these institutions do not infringe upon human rights and do not constrain the ability of governments to protect the human rights of their populations.[39]

In recent years, specific proposals have been worked out by Special Rapporteurs commissioned by the Human Rights Council and the UN High Commissioner for Human Rights. Many of these rely on the "human rights due diligence standard" developed by John Ruggie to specify the scope and content of the responsibilities of transnational corporations to respect human rights. In his report to the Human Rights Council, in April 2009, this responsibility is interpreted as requiring "an ongoing process of human rights due diligence, whereby companies become aware of, prevent, and mitigate adverse human rights impacts." This process should include four elements: "adopting a human rights policy; undertaking—and acting upon—a human rights impact assessment; integrating the human rights policy throughout the company, across all functions; and tracking human rights performance by monitoring and auditing processes to ensure continuous improvement."[40] These four ways of operationalizing the standard of due diligence seem easily applicable to global economic institutions. An interesting development in that direction is the Maastricht Principles, adopted in 2011 by a group of leading experts in international law and human rights.[41]

Admittedly, efforts to make international human rights norms legally binding upon the actions of global governance institutions still have a long way to go before they succeed. However, it is hard to see how minimizing and de-internationalizing human rights could be a helpful approach to addressing these problems. Suppose that the protection of some basic human rights within a state is hampered by some trade regulation imposed by the WTO or some policies imposed by the IMF or the World Bank. It seems that the appropriate action for member states would be to change such policies or regulations. But this sensible course of action seems hard to fit within the framework of Cohen's proposals. Once social, economic, and political rights are excluded from the set of "institutionalized and enforceable international human rights," the normative basis to justify an international responsibility for undertaking such action would be eliminated. Shifting the focus of rights activists "back to the domestic arena" not only would leave these violations in place but also would divert international attention from the actual lack of state sovereignty and equality within global governance institutions. Inciting citizens to "hold their own governments accountable" for policies that are imposed on them by global governance institutions would simply add insult to injury. These difficulties bring us back to our initial question: Under current conditions of globalization, how should the international community conceptualize the appropriate scope, content, and implications of the R2P principle as an emergent norm of international law?

A DEMANDING INTERPRETATION OF R2P

Because the international community's default responsibility for human rights protections is only triggered when states are unable or unwilling to discharge their primary responsibilities, analyzing the scope and content of the responsibilities held by states should be helpful in determining those held by the international community. Following the standard tripartite model of human rights obligations, states are required to respect, protect, and fulfill human rights within their jurisdiction.[42] The duty to *respect* human rights is an obligation under which states must refrain from actions, carried out through the organs of the state, that would infringe upon the rights of individuals or groups. The duty to *protect* human rights extends beyond the state's own conduct to include an obligation to exercise the state's jurisdiction to prevent violations by third parties. The state must prevent violations even if they originate in the actions of other states that fail to respect the human rights of persons outside their jurisdiction. States must also prevent violations of rights by private actors, such as, for example, by passing legislation to prevent, prosecute, and punish domestic violence against women or to prevent corporations from putting the health and safety of their workers at risk.[43] In addition, states have the obligation to *fulfill* human rights by providing the institutional means and arrangements needed for the effective enjoyment of human rights.

If we take the threefold structure of state human rights obligations as a starting point, we can analyze the various ways in which states can fail to discharge their primary responsibilities under current conditions, and thereby discern the scope and content of the international community's default responsibility to protect human rights whenever states are unable or unwilling to do so. Because the international R2P principle aims at restoring the ability of states to discharge their primary responsibility, international action must address all salient threats to human rights protection at any given time, namely:

1. states that fail to *respect* human rights within their jurisdiction;
2. states that fail to *protect* human rights from violations by third parties that escape their effective control, such as
   a. private actors (e.g., individuals or transnational corporations),
   b. states that fail to respect the human rights of persons outside their jurisdiction, or
   c. international organizations (e.g., the WTO, IMF, or World Bank); and
3. states that fail to *fulfill* human rights within their jurisdiction.

The standard interpretation of the international community's human rights responsibilities limits international action to cases (1) and (3) and neglects (2). Thus, it is assumed that the international community's responsibility to protect must be discharged either in the form of coercive actions—such as, for example, economic sanctions or military intervention—against states that are *unwilling* to *respect* human rights, or in the form of humanitarian assistance, if states are *unable* to *fulfill* the rights of their populations, perhaps, for example, due to a lack of resources. But what is mostly neglected is cases of states that are *unable to prevent* human rights violations by third parties that escape their effective control. Conceiving the R2P principle in this way leaves the actions of global economic institutions and transnational corporations free from scrutiny of the negative impact they might have upon the ability of states to protect the human rights of their populations. Therefore, if we take the aim of securing the protection of human rights worldwide seriously, there is no reason why we should adopt a restrictive interpretation under which international action can only consist in interventions against the states whose members suffer human rights violations. Moreover, extending the international community's responsibility to protect, from the narrow domain of international criminal law to other domains of international human rights law, seems also a logical consequence of the practice's own aim.

Although this process is in its early stages, some legal scholars cite the UN General Assembly Declaration on the Right to Development, from 1986, as evidence that human rights practice is evolving in that direction. Among the many salient features of this human rights declaration, the most interesting feature, for present purposes, is that it involves adopting a *structural* approach to human rights protections.[44] In addition, the declaration establishes a direct link between the right to development and the existence of an international economic order in which all human rights can be fully realized. On this basis, the structural approach to human rights protections is not limited to the specification of actions that states must take in order to discharge their primary responsibility to protect the human rights of their populations. The structural approach is also taken in order to specify the kinds of actions that members of the international community must undertake to discharge their own responsibility toward human rights protections, which, in this declaration, is designated as a "duty to cooperate" in order to ensure development and eliminate obstacles to development. Although the declaration clearly falls short of more precisely specifying the kinds of actions that would be required to do so, it does indicate that the duty to cooperate includes direct assistance from developed to developing countries (Article 4.2). In addition, members of the international community are required to establish a new international economic order "based on sovereign equality, interdependence, mutual interest, and co-operation among all states" (Article 3.3).

Needless to say, the seriousness of members of the international community in discharging any of the self-imposed obligations expressed in this declaration is questionable, to put it mildly. However, the question we are addressing here is not how realistic it is to expect that members of the international community will discharge any of their obligations but, rather, whether the most plausible reconstruction of the norms underlying contemporary human rights practice reveals an inherent tension between human rights and the sovereign equality of states. Since the Declaration on the Right to Development *explicitly affirms the opposite*, reconstructing its rationale can be helpful for answering that question.

If the international community's default responsibility to protect is triggered whenever states are unable or unwilling to protect human rights, it seems obvious that international action geared toward enabling states to fulfill their primary responsibility for human rights protections must be seen as essential to properly discharging the responsibility to protect. However, it is not possible to enable states to discharge their responsibility to protect human rights without strengthening their ability to meet that responsibility—by strengthening their ability to prevent violations by third parties, for example. Since one of the standard circumstances in which international action is called for is precisely when states are not able to effectively prevent such violations on their own, two salient cases that call for international action under current conditions of globalization are the actions of global economic institutions and of powerful private entities, such as transnational corporations, that are in fact beyond the control of states, especially of weak states.[45] As mentioned above, many international efforts have been developed in recent years to address these problems: from the UN Global Compact initiative,[46] which encourages transnational corporations to integrate corporate social responsibility into their business models, to the Maastricht Principles, which specify the obligations of states, as members of international organizations, to refrain from actions that impair the ability of other states to protect the human rights of their populations.[47]

Whether or not these efforts are likely to succeed, what matters in our context is that this type of international action does not seem to present us with a dilemma between the values of state sovereignty and the international protection of human rights. In fact, it is just the opposite. Strengthening the power of the state vis-à-vis the actions of transnational corporations is not a by-product of the international efforts to protect human rights but a necessary condition for *enabling the state to discharge its primary responsibility for human rights protections*. Similarly, international action geared toward entrenching human rights standards within the operational mechanisms of global economic institutions would enhance the sovereign equality of weak states precisely in order to enable them to meet their human rights obligations. Strengthening the sovereign equality of states that are willing to protect the human rights of their populations is not simply an independently valuable political goal that may or may not be compatible with pursuing the goal of protecting human rights. Rather, it is a necessary condition for enabling states to discharge their primary responsibility of protecting the human rights of their populations.

COERCIVE INTERVENTION REVISITED

As long as the international community expects states to bear the very demanding primary responsibility of protecting the human rights of their populations, it must see to it that states are in fact able to bear such responsibility. This is a straightforward reason why human rights protection and state sovereignty cannot be seen as antithetical to each other but instead must be understood as mutually reinforcing political values. It also indicates an additional reason, internal to human rights practice, to be deeply concerned by coercive interventions against sovereign states.

Beyond the fact that such interventions themselves lead to additional human rights violations and are often unable to effectively prevent violations by third parties,[48] a major additional problem with coercive interventions against sovereign states, from a point of view internal to human rights practice, is that they disable the agent that has the primary responsibility to protect and fulfill the human rights of its population without providing an alternative agent that is able and willing to perform this crucial function. Indeed, after recent experiences with the aftermath of military interventions, it is becoming increasingly clear that when international agents intervene militarily against a state, they might do so in the name of the international community's default R2P principle, but by disabling the actor who has the primary responsibility to protect and to fulfill human rights, they inherit that *primary responsibility* in the occupied areas for as long as they exercise effective control over them.[49] This is a very demanding responsibility that few states (or "coalitions of the willing") are likely to be willing to bear. In the context of justifying a limited military strike in Syria, President Obama made this point crystal clear when he said, "I don't think we should remove another dictator with force—we learned from Iraq that doing so makes us responsible for all that comes next."[50]

Perhaps, in light of the disastrous results of recent "transformative" military occupations, the danger that keeping human rights standards both demanding and internationally binding might lead to a lot of "prodemocratic" military interventions against sovereign states is no longer as high as it might have been before those experiences. Regardless of how high or low that danger may be at any given time, however, it is still important to see why lowering human rights standards and minimizing the international community's responsibility to protect are not the right strategies to address such a danger. On the one hand, there is simply no need to lower human rights standards in order to have a very strong reason to restrict coercive intervention against sovereign states to situations of gross and systematic violations of human rights. But the reason is not that the rights violated in such cases exhaust some putative set of human rights proper, or that they are the only rights that are a matter of international concern and that, therefore, should trigger the international community's default responsibility to protect. Indeed, one needs to change the focus from the *object* of the rights in question to the allocation of the *obligations to protect* them, in order to identify the strongest reason. As I have suggested, the crucial problem, from a human rights perspective, is that forceful interventions against sovereign states disable the actor who bears the primary responsibility to protect and fulfill human rights without having any effective replacement to offer. Thus, because this type of international action is a very poor means of effectively protecting the human rights of the affected populations, it should be used only as a last resort, when other means of preventing imminent and massive human rights violations have failed.

On the other hand, because the sovereignty and equality of states is increasingly threatened by globalization, we actually need to increase rather than decrease the international community's default responsibility to protect. As we have seen in the examples analyzed, discharging this responsibility effectively requires, among other things, finding ways to strengthen the sovereignty of those states that are willing to protect the human rights of their populations but might be unable to do so as a consequence of actions that are beyond their control—such as those undertaken by transnational corporations or global economic institutions. What is hard to see, in light of this situation, is how proposals to lower the demanding and internationally binding standards contained in the core human rights conventions and treaties could help strengthen the sovereignty and equality of those states, let alone the protection of human rights within them.

NOTES

1. United Nations, 2005 World Summit Outcome, G.A. Res. 60/1 (Oct. 24, 2005), paras. 138–40.
2. International Commission on Intervention and State Sovereignty (ICISS), *The Responsibility to Protect: Report of the International Commission on Intervention and State Sovereignty* (Ottawa: International Development Research Centre, 2001), http//www.iciss.ca/pdf/Commission-Report.pdf.
3. See Article 1.3 of Charter of the United Nations, 1 UNTS XVI (Oct. 24, 1945); and the preamble of the Universal Declaration of Human Rights, G.A. Res. 217A (III) (Dec. 10, 1948).
4. On this crucial difference between contemporary human rights practice and prior declarations of rights, see Samuel Moyn, *The Last Utopia: Human Rights in History* (Cambridge, MA: Belknap Press of Harvard University Press, 2010).
5. See United Nations High-Level Panel on Threats, Challenges and Change, *A More Secure World: Our Shared Responsibility*, UN Doc. A/59/565 (Dec. 2, 2004), para. 203. For more skeptical analyses, see Carsten Stahn, "Responsibility to Protect: Political Rhetoric or Emerging Legal Norm?" *American Journal of International Law* 101, no. 1 (2007): 99–120; Nicholas Wheeler and Frazer Egerton, "The Responsibility to Protect: 'Precious Commitment' or a Promise Unfulfilled?," *Global Responsibility to Protect* 1, no. 1 (2009): 114–132. For an excellent historical reconstruction of the emerging Responsibility to Protect (R2P) doctrine as an expression of existing practices, see Anne Orford, *International Authority and the Responsibility to Protect* (Cambridge: Cambridge University Press, 2011).
6. Among those who welcome this development, there is nonetheless also widespread concern about the current institutional structure of the UN and, in particular, the Security Council, which in most cases leads to gridlock and prevents international action. For an example, see Allen Buchanan and Robert Keohane, "Precommitment Regimes for Intervention: Supplementing the Security Council," *Ethics & International Affairs* 25, no. 1 (2011): 41–63.
7. See Noam Chomsky, "Statement to the United Nations General Assembly Thematic Dialogue on the Responsibility to Protect," speech at the United Nations, New York, July 23, 2009, www.un.org/ga/president/63/interactive/protect/noam.pdf. For a more recent example, see Jean Cohen, *Globalization and Sovereignty* (Cambridge: Cam-

bridge University Press, 2012). I discuss Cohen's claims and proposals in the next section. For a defense of the contrary view of R2P as an international tool that can undermine unilateral (self-serving) interventions, see Orford, *International Authority*.

8. As Philip Alston aptly puts it, the concern is that "the Responsibility to Protect doctrine is merely a twenty-first-century version of earlier imperial interventions in the Global South." Alston, "Does the Past Matter? On the Origins of Human Rights," *Harvard Law Review* 126, no. 7 (2013): 2061.

9. See also Universal Declaration of Human Rights, Article 21; Council of Europe, *European Convention for the Protection of Human Rights and Fundamental Freedoms*, ETS 5 (Nov. 4, 1950), Protocol I, Article 3; and Organization of American States, *American Convention on Human Rights* (Nov. 22, 1969), Article 23. For an overview of this debate see Gregory Fox and Brad Roth, eds., *Democratic Governance and International Law* (Cambridge: Cambridge University Press, 2000). For recent defenses of a human right to democracy, see Seyla Benhabib, "Is There a Human Right to Democracy? Beyond Interventionism and Indifference," in *Dignity in Adversity: Human Rights in Troubled Times* (Cambridge: Polity, 2011), 77–93; and Thomas Christiano, "An Instrumental Argument for a Human Right to Democracy," *Philosophy & Public Affairs* 39, no. 2 (2011): 142–76. For arguments against the existence of a human right to democracy, see Jean Cohen, "Rethinking Human Rights, Democracy, and Sovereignty in the Age of Globalization," *Political Theory* 36, no. 4 (2008): 578–606; Joshua Cohen, "Is There a Human Right to Democracy?" in *The Egalitarian Conscience*, ed. Christine Sypnowich (Oxford: Oxford University Press, 2006), 226–48; and John Rawls, *The Law of Peoples with "The Idea of Public Reason Revisited"* (Cambridge, MA: Harvard University Press, 1999).

10. Rawls, *Law of Peoples*, 79–80.

11. I take this formulation from John Tasioulas, "Are Human Rights Essentially Triggers for Intervention?" *Philosophy Compass* 4, no. 6 (2009): 938–50.

12. For a complete collection of human rights documents, see Ian Brownlie and Guy Goodwin-Gill, eds., *Basic Documents on Human Rights* (Oxford: Oxford University Press, 2010).

13. See Rawls, *Law of Peoples*, 65. However, if Rawls is right in claiming that one of the distinctive functions of human rights is that they trigger coercive intervention against states, then his list may actually be too expansive. As many critics have pointed out, the main problem with Rawls's approach is that it tries to identify a single subset of rights that is supposed to serve too many disparate functions: drawing the limits of acceptable pluralism, acting as a trigger for coercive intervention, setting necessary conditions for the legitimacy of any government, determining the upper limit of international assistance to burdened societies, and so on. There is no obvious reason to assume that one and the same list of rights may plausibly fulfill all of these disparate functions. As I will argue, it is a mistake to think that we could specify triggers for different kinds of international actions simply by looking at the objects of various rights. Instead, it is essential to look at the proper allocation of (primary and default) obligations for their protection among different actors.

14. See James Nickel, "Are Human Rights Mainly Implemented by Intervention?" in *Rawls's Law of Peoples: A Realistic Utopia?*, ed. Rex Martin and David Reidy (Oxford: Blackwell, 2006), 270; and Charles Beitz, "Human Rights as a Common Concern," *American Political Science Review* 95, no. 2 (2001): 269–82.
15. Dorota Gierycz, "The Responsibility to Protect: A Legal and Rights-Based Perspective," *Global Responsibility to Protect* 2, no. 3 (2010): 252.
16. In its preamble, the Universal Declaration of Human Rights is categorized as "a common standard of achievement for all peoples and all nations."
17. Jean Cohen, *Globalization and Sovereignty*, 221.
18. Jean Cohen, *Globalization and Sovereignty*, 216. My italics.
19. Jean Cohen, *Globalization and Sovereignty*, 165. My italics.
20. Jürgen Habermas follows a similar strategy in his proposal for a new international order. He circumscribes the international protection of human rights (by a reformed world organization) to cases of violations of international criminal law, such as genocide, crimes against humanity, and so forth, and ascribes the protection of all other human rights standards exclusively to the national level. See Habermas, "A Political Constitution for the Pluralist World Society?" in *Between Naturalism and Religion*, trans. Ciaran Cronin (Cambridge, MA: MIT Press, 2008), 312–52. However, in his most recent writings, he seems to have abandoned that strategy. See Habermas, "From the International to the Cosmopolitan Community" in *The Crisis of the European Union: A Response*, trans. Ciaran Cronin (Cambridge: Polity, 2012), 53–70, especially 60, 65, and 69.
21. Jean Cohen, *Globalization and Sovereignty*, 187. See Joshua Cohen, "Minimalism About Human Rights: The Most We Can Hope For?," *The Journal of Political Philosophy* 12, no. 2 (2004): 197.
22. Jean Cohen, "Rethinking Human Rights," 587.
23. If we took massive starvation through state neglect to be a violation of the membership principle, this would suggest that the subset of "human security rights" includes rights to food, health, and so forth. Since Cohen does not offer a list of human security rights, it is hard to know the precise rights she has in mind. On the one hand, it is unlikely that she wants to include all the rights that are usually taken to be part of the right to security of the person, such as the right to a fair trial or to reproductive control. Including these rights would imply that the lack of secure access to them could justify coercive intervention. On the other hand, she cannot justify their exclusion by claiming that these rights are not threatened when the membership principle is violated. For it is obviously false that populations threatened by "the four E's" (mass extermination, expulsion, ethnic cleansing, and enslavement) can nonetheless enjoy secure access to these rights. Later, I will address the difficulties of trying to single out a specific subset of rights on the basis of the four E's.
24. The international outrage produced by the refusal of Myanmar's military junta to accept international relief aid to help the victims of Cyclone Nargis offers some strong evidence against this view.

25. See United Nations Trust Fund for Human Security, "Human Security Approach," accessed June 23, 2016, http://www.un.org/humansecurity/human-security-unit/human-security-approach.
26. Rawls's argumentative strategy in *The Law of Peoples* is instructive in this context. In order to demarcate the subset of "human rights proper," the violation of which might trigger coercive intervention by external agents, he does not appeal to situations of massive human rights violations such as genocide or ethnic cleansing. Instead, he appeals to his hypothetical thought experiment of "decent hierarchical societies," and he contends that subjects within such societies could have their human rights proper effectively protected, even if other rights he targets for exclusion (such as rights to democratic participation or to an education) were not. Jean Cohen rejects this argumentative strategy but does not offer an alternative upon which to base the bifurcation she proposes.
27. It is worth noting that the R2P doctrine does not postulate any bifurcation among types of human rights, nor does it call their interdependence into question. See ICISS, *The Responsibility to Protect*; and 2005 World Summit Outcome.
28. Jean Cohen, *Globalization and Sovereignty*, 161.
29. The individual complaint mechanisms have not yet entered into force for the Committee on Migrant Workers and the Committee on the Rights of the Child. For up-to-date information, see Office of the United Nations Office of the High Commissioner for Human Rights, "Human Rights Bodies—Complaints Procedures," accessed June 23, 2016, http://www.ohchr.org/EN/HRBodies/TBPetitions/Pages/HRTBPetitions.aspx.
30. Jean Cohen, *Globalization and Sovereignty*, 168; my italics. She follows here the interpretation offered by Andrew Moravcsik, "The Origins of Human Rights Regimes: Democratic Delegation in Postwar Europe," *International Organization* 54, no. 2 (2003): 217–52.
31. See Jean Cohen, "Rethinking Human Rights," 593; and Cohen, *Globalization and Sovereignty*, 15, 163, 205.
32. In what follows, I focus on cases in which the appeal to international human rights law by weak states may strengthen their sovereignty and equality as participants in global economic institutions. For examples of how the use of international law by national courts can similarly strengthen state sovereignty, see Eyal Benvenisti, "Reclaiming Democracy: The Strategic Uses of Foreign and International Law by National Courts," *The American Journal of International Law* 102, no. 2 (2008): 241–74. For an argument based on historical examples of how the enforcement of social and economic rights by national courts can strengthen the sovereignty of weak states, as against internationally determined austerity measures, structural adjustment, or developmental conditionality, see Kim Scheppele, "A Realpolitik Defense of Social Rights," *Texas Law Review* 82, no. 7 (2004): 1921–61. For a similar line of argument, see also Katharine Young, *Constituting Economic and Social Rights* (Oxford: Oxford University Press, 2012), 192–222.

33. The TRIPS agreement is Annex 1C of the Marrakesh Agreement Establishing the World Trade Organization, 1869 U.N.T.S. 299; 33 I.L.M. 1197 (Apr. 15, 1994), http://www.wto.org/english/docs_e/legal_e/legal_e.htm#TRIPs.
34. For an overview of the events leading to the 2005 amendment to the TRIPS agreement, see Holger Herstermeyer, *Human Rights and the WTO: The Case of Patents and Access to Medicines* (Oxford: Oxford University Press, 2007), 1–18.
35. See World Trade Organization, "Draft Ministerial Declaration: Proposal from a Group of Developing Countries," October 4, 2001, http://www.wto.org/english/tratop_e/trips_e/mindecdraft_w312_e.htm.
36. See United Nations Committee on Economic, Social and Cultural Rights, *Substantive Issues Arising in the Implementation of the International Covenant on Economic, Social and Cultural Rights*, E/C.12/2001/15, December 14, 2001.
37. See World Trade Organization, "Doha Declaration on the TRIPS Agreement and Public Health," WT/MIN(01)/DEC/2, November 20, 2001, http://www.wto.org/english/thewto_e/minist_e/min01_e/mindecl_trips_e.htm.
38. For an excellent analysis of the difficulties, see Herstermeyer, *Human Rights and the WTO*.
39. See Adam McBeth, "What Do Human Rights Require of the Global Economy? Beyond a Narrow Legal View," in *Human Rights: The Hard Questions*, ed. Cindy Holder and David Reidy (Cambridge: Cambridge University Press, 2010), 162.
40. See United Nations Human Rights Council, *Promotion of All Human Rights, Civil, Political, Economic, Social and Cultural Rights, Including the Right to Development*, A/HRC/11/13, April 22, 2009, http://www2.ohchr.org/english/bodies/hrcouncil/docs/11session/A.HRC.11.13.pdf. The official text of the final resolution adopted by the Human Rights Council in July 2011 is available at http://www.business-humanrights.org/media/documents/un-human-rights-council-resolution-re-human-rights-transnational-corps-eng-6-jul-2011.pdf. See also United Nations Office of the High Commissioner for Human Rights, *Guiding Principles on Business and Human Rights: Implementing the United Nations "Protect, Respect and Remedy" Framework* (New York: United Nations, 2011), http://www.ohchr.org/Documents/Publications/GuidingPrinciplesBusinessHR_EN.pdf.
41. See ETO Consortium, *Maastricht Principles on the Extraterritorial Obligations of States in the Area of Economic, Social and Cultural Rights*, February 29, 2012, http://www.etoconsortium.org/en/main-navigation/library/maastricht-principles.
42. See International Commission of Jurists, *Maastricht Guidelines on Violations of Economic, Social and Cultural Rights*, January 26, 1997, http://www.refworld.org/docid/48abd5730.html.
43. The concept of "due diligence" regarding state responsibility for nonstate acts was first developed in Velasquez Rodriguez v. Honduras, a case heard by the Inter-American Court of Human Rights. See Inter-Am.Ct.H.R. (Ser. C) No. 4 (1988). Since then, it has been applied by other regional human rights courts and has been extended to cover human rights violations committed by private actors, such as cases of domestic violence against women. For a good overview of this development, see Lee

Hasselbacher, "State Obligations Regarding Domestic Violence: The European Court of Human Rights, Due Diligence, and International Legal Minimums of Protection," *Northwestern Journal of International Human Rights* 8, no. 2 (2010): 190–215. See also Monica Hakimi, "State Bystander Responsibility," *The European Journal of International Law* 21, no. 2 (2010): 341–85.

44. See Margot E. Salomon, *Global Responsibility for Human Rights* (Oxford: Oxford University Press, 2007), 50–64.
45. For some in-depth analyses of the problem, see Andrew Clapham, *Human Rights Obligations of Non-State Actors* (Oxford: Oxford University Press, 2006); Salomon, *Global Responsibility*; James Harrison, *The Human Rights Impact of the World Trade Organization* (Oxford: Hart, 2007); and McBeth, "What Do Human Rights Require of the Global Economy?."
46. See United Nations Global Compact, http://www.unglobalcompact.org.
47. See ETO Consortium, *Maastricht Principles*.
48. This is why such interventions are constrained by stringent precautionary normative criteria, such as seriousness of threat, proper purpose, last resort, proportional means, balance of consequences, reasonable prospects, proper authority, etc. See ICISS, *Responsibility to Protect*.
49. On this central element of the R2P doctrine, see "Post-Intervention Obligations," in ICISS, *Responsibility to Protect*, 39–45. See also Hugh King, "The Extraterritorial Human Rights Obligations of States," *Human Rights Law Review* 9, no. 4 (2009): 521–56.
50. See transcript in Jon Campbell, "President Obama Syria Speech Transcript Text September 10, 2013: Obama Makes Case for Military Strike on Syria," *Christian Post*, September 10, 2013, http://www.christianpost.com/news/president-obama-syria-speech-transcript-text-september-10-2013-obama-makes-case-for-military-strike-on-syria-104254/#vLqg9HMJsWAszGxG.99.

4

A CRITICAL THEORY OF HUMAN RIGHTS—SOME GROUNDWORK

RAINER FORST

1

The concept of human rights comprises an array of different aspects. They have a *moral* life, expressing urgent human concerns and claims that must not be violated or ignored, anywhere on the globe; they also have a *legal* life, being enshrined in national constitutions and in lists of basic rights, as well as in international declarations, covenants, and treaties; and they have a *political* life, expressing standards of basic political legitimacy.

For a comprehensive philosophical account of human rights, all of these aspects are essential and need to be integrated in the right way. Yet, when doing so, one must not overlook the central *social* aspect of human rights, namely, that when and where they have been claimed, it has been because the individuals concerned suffered from and protested against forms of domination that they believed disregarded their dignity as human beings. They viewed the acts or institutions that they opposed as violations of the basic respect owed to human beings. Human rights are, first and foremost, weapons in combating certain evils that human beings inflict upon one another; they emphasize a status of nondomination that no human being could justifiably deny to others and that should be secured in a legitimate social order.

My thesis in what follows is that if it is true that human rights are meant to ensure that no human being is treated in a way that could not be justified to him or her as a person equal to others, then this implies—reflexively speaking—that one claim underlies all human rights, namely, human beings' claim to be respected as autonomous agents who have the right not to be subjected to certain actions or institutional norms that cannot be adequately justified to them. That kind of subjection I call domination.[1] The reflexive argument has three dimensions. First, human rights have a common ground in one basic moral right, the *right to justification*. Second, the legal and political function of human rights is to make this right socially effective, both substantively and procedurally. The substantive aspect consists in formulating rights that express adequate forms of mutual respect the violation of which cannot be properly justified between free and equal persons; and the procedural aspect highlights the essential condition that no one should be subjected to a set of rights and duties—to a political-legal rights regime—the determination of which he or she cannot participate in as an autonomous agent of justification. Thus, human rights do not just protect the autonomy and agency of persons; they also *express* their autonomy politically. Third, the reflexive argument claims that this way of grounding human rights is not open to the charge of ethnocentrism haunting so many justifications of human rights, for that charge itself demands a right to adequate justifications that do not exclude those subjected. I call that approach to human rights one of *critical theory*, because it starts from the participant's perspective in social struggles and reconstructs the basic emancipatory claim of human rights.

2

In philosophical debates, we encounter a plurality of perspectives on human rights that accord priority to one of the above-mentioned aspects.

(a) A primarily *ethical* justification of human rights focuses on the importance of the human interests they are meant to protect. There are some, like James Griffin in his recent book *On Human Rights*, who argue that core values such as autonomy and liberty are essential to what it means to be a "functioning human agent," and that rights can be derived from the basic interests persons have in realizing these values.[2] There are others, such as James Nickel and John Tasioulas, who defend a pluralistic conception of such essential human interests.[3] What these ethical justifications of human rights share, however, is their focus on substantive notions of well-being or the "good life" and their view of human rights as the means of guaranteeing essential minimal conditions for such forms of human life. The "human being" here is one who has an interest in leading a good life, and "rights" are the means to make this possible for everyone.

There have been numerous debates over such ethical justifications, over whether their notion of the good life is inextricably context-bound, so that it cannot be universalized, or whether it might be too "thin" rather than too "thick," and thus lacking in sufficient content. In addition, there are worries about the derivation of normative rights claims from basic human interests. There are many such interests in the first place—think of the interest in being loved—but how do we single out those that qualify for grounding human rights? Furthermore, how does a claim of subjective importance translate into a binding general claim to rights? What is the mediating factor that generates that kind of normativity?[4]

(b) In recent discussions, a radical alternative to ethical views has been developed that stresses the *political-legal* aspect or function of human rights, though in a very specific sense. According to such accounts, the main function of human rights is the role that they play in the area of international law, the basis being, as in John Rawls, a philosophical account of "the law of peoples" or, as in Joseph Raz's or Charles Beitz's view, international legal and political practice. And that role is, in Rawls's formulations, "to provide a suitable definition of, and limits on, a government's internal sovereignty" or "to restrict the justifying reasons for war and its conduct" and to "specify limits to a regime's internal autonomy." Furthermore, according to Rawls, a conception of human rights can be justified only as "intrinsic" to a conception of the law of peoples that is acceptable to liberal as well as "decent hierarchical peoples."[5] For Rawls, this is based on a reflection on the "reasonable pluralism" of peoples in the international arena. It suggests that there is not a single normative ground for a conception of human rights but that there are liberal grounds for liberal conceptions of human rights and other grounds for other conceptions, and because the role of human rights is such that their violation places sovereignty in question and justifies an intervention, the result of that construction is a minimal list of human rights as part of an "ecumenical" account of a law of peoples for an international order of peace.

Others have followed and radicalized this approach, which, as I will explain, introduced a major shift of perspective in political philosophy. Favoring a "practical" conception of human rights over an "orthodox" one, which holds that "human rights have an existence in the moral order that is independent of their expression in international doctrine," Beitz's view "takes the doctrine and discourse of human rights as we find them in international political practice as basic."[6] Whereas Rawls relies on a philosophical "political" conception of the law of peoples, Beitz takes current doctrine as well as practice to be authoritative. He follows Rawls, however, in defining the function of human rights as "justifying grounds of interference by the international community in the internal affairs of states."[7] Although he takes a broad view of the forms that such interference may take (and of the agents of such interference), Beitz shares Rawls's idea that the content of human rights is determined by their role as grounds for external interference.[8]

(c) Alternative approaches search for *political-moral* justifications that can be the focus of an international "overlapping consensus." Thus, a contest of modesty, so to speak, has developed about the most "minimal" but nevertheless sufficient normative justification for human rights. Some, like Michael Ignatieff, focus on rights that protect bodily security and personal liberty as the minimal core of human rights,[9] and they presuppose only a "minimalist anthropology" that provides reasons for the avoidance of grave evils. Others fear that such a "lowest common denominator" approach[10] runs the risk of mixing, in Joshua Cohen's words, "justificatory minimalism" with "substantive minimalism."[11] Whereas the former form of minimalism is seen as a justified "acknowledgement of pluralism and embrace of toleration" in the international realm, the latter form is to be avoided, for, according to Cohen, "human rights norms are best thought of as norms associated with an idea of *membership* or *inclusion* in an organized political society." And that kind of inclusion requires, first and foremost, having the right "to be treated as a member," i.e., to "have one's interests given due consideration" politically.[12] Human rights claims, then, are essential for securing social and political membership, whereas the moral agnosticism—or "unfoundational[ism]"[13]—that Cohen proposes leaves open the normative reasons for the claim to membership. The hope is that such a conception of rights can win support "from a range of ethical and religious outlooks" in "global public reason."[14] From that angle, Cohen argues, no human right to democracy will be seen as justifiable, for an "acceptable political society" needs to respect certain membership rights, though not a right to democracy in a fuller sense.[15]

3

How is it possible to navigate among these different ways of highlighting particular aspects of human rights, namely, their normative core as protecting basic human interests, their role in international law and political practice, and their claim to be universally justifiable across cultures and ethical ways of life? No doubt, human rights have a certain substance, function, and justification, but have the three views addressed them in the correct way? I think not.

For, in a nutshell, using the distinction between morality and ethics, I believe that a conception of human rights needs to have an independent and sufficient *moral substance* and justification, though not one of an *ethical* kind that relies on a conception of the good life. The moral basis for human rights, as I reconstruct it, is the respect for the human person as an autonomous agent who possesses a right to justification—a right to be recognized as a subject who can demand acceptable reasons for any action that claims to be morally justified and for any social or political structure or law that claims to be binding upon him or her. Human rights secure the equal standing of persons as nondominated equals in the legal, political, and social world, based on a fundamental moral demand of respect. This demand does not depend on the claim that it contributes to the good life of either the person showing or the person receiving respect; rather, mutual respect is owed independently of that.

From this, it follows that the main function of human rights is to guarantee, secure, and express each person's status as a nondominated equal, given his or her right to justification. The political meaning of human rights locates their legal and political role in that protection and in the grounding of political autonomy.

A moral justification for human rights has to be a universally valid and, as I argue, reflexive one. "Reflexive" here means that the very idea of justification itself is reconstructed with respect to its normative and practical implications. The argument states that, because any moral justification of the rights of human beings must be able to redeem discursively the claim to general and reciprocal validity raised by such rights, such a justification presupposes the right to justification of those whose rights are in question. They have a qualified "veto right" against any justification that fails the criteria of reciprocity and generality and that can be criticized as one-sided, narrow, or paternalistic, as the case may be. "Reciprocity" means that no one may make a normative claim (such as a rights claim) that he or she denies to others (call that "reciprocity of content"), and that no one may simply project one's own perspective, values, interests, or needs onto others such that one claims to speak in their "true" interests or in the name of some truth beyond mutual justification ("reciprocity of reasons"). "Generality" means that the reasons that are used to ground general normative validity have to be shareable by all affected persons, given their (reciprocally) legitimate interests and claims.

Thus, the reflexive approach manages to build the logic of the arguments against "false" (for example, ethnocentric) universalizations, as well as against false critiques of false universalizability, into its own structure. The very basis for the first critique—which says that ethnocentric definitions of human rights violate the rights of participants to live in a social structure they see as legitimate—as well as the basis for identifying illegitimate forms of such criticism, which might veil authoritarian cultural arguments, is taken up and identified as *the right to justification*.

4

I leave out at this point a discussion of the ethical justification of human rights and turn to the functionalist approaches. As it seems to me, it is generally misleading to emphasize the political-legal function of such rights within international law (or political practice) of providing reasons for a politics of legitimate intervention, for this is to put the cart before the horse. We first need to construct a justifiable set of human rights that a legitimate political authority has to respect and guarantee, and *then* we will ask what kinds of legal structures are required at the international level to oversee this and to help ensure that political authority is exercised in that way. Only *after* we have taken that step will it become necessary to think about and set up legitimate institutions of possible intervention (as measures of last resort). The first question of human rights is not how to limit sovereignty from the outside; it is about the essential conditions of the possibility of establishing legitimate political authority. International law and a politics of intervention have to *follow* a particular logic of human rights, not the converse. Such a logic is not a simple one, one must add, for a number of additional factors need to be taken into account when it comes to the issue of legitimate intervention.[16]

Human rights do not serve primarily to limit internal "autonomy" or "sovereignty" (Rawls uses both terms) but to ground internal legitimacy. The claim to external respect depends on internal respect based on justified acceptance; however, that does not mean, to repeat, that one can infer the legitimacy of intervention—or the lack of "external legitimacy"[17] or international "recognitional legitimacy"[18]—directly from a lack of internal acceptance. Violations of human rights place the *internal legitimacy* of a social and political structure in question, but they do not automatically dissolve the independent *standing* of that state in the international arena. To be sure, violations of human rights can provide a strong reason for taking external action, and Beitz is right to point out that this can take several forms,[19] but this does not mean that the point of human rights can be defined as that of generating interference-justifying reasons, as Beitz and Raz argue. Rather, human rights provide reasons for arranging a basic social and political structure in the right way; hence, the primary perspective of human rights is *from the inside*. Otherwise, their moral point of not just protecting but also expressing the autonomy of free and equal persons is not sufficiently taken into account. The main perspective is not that of the *outsider* who observes a political structure and asks whether there are grounds for intervention. In thinking about human rights and their justification, one must be careful not to assume the role of an international lawyer or judge who presides over certain cases of human rights violations and who, at the same time, wields global executive power.

In particular, because one important worry that drives "political-legal" views of human rights is to avoid a broad list of human rights that could serve to justify a wide range of interventions, reducing the list of core human rights accordingly is not the right conclusion.[20] Rather, the right conclusion is to devise legitimate international institutions with justifiable procedures for assessing and deciding cases of necessary external action.

5

A similar mistake of misplaced perspective is made in "minimalist" normative justifications for human rights. The most obvious one is a "lowest common denominator" approach, which would run the risk of being, to use a phrase Rawls coined in a different context, "political in the wrong way."[21] In looking for a possible universal consensus on human rights, one opts for a minimal justification and, all too often, a minimalist conception of human rights. And even if Rawls, in *The Law of Peoples*, was not guilty of locating the justification of human rights in a presumably existing or possible universal consensus, he was willing to restrict the list of human rights so that certain important rights, such as equal liberties for persons of different faiths or a right to equal political participation, were not included.[22] One reason for this is the assumed connection between human rights and intervention just criticized, and another is the aim to respect nonliberal but "decent" peoples as worthy of being agents of justification when it comes to a common law of peoples (and to avoiding Western ethnocentrism). But the question of whether "decent hierarchical peoples" can or should be expected to conform to a "liberal" conception of human rights that is foreign to their cultural self-understanding, if asked from the perspective of the "ideals and principles of the *foreign policy* of a reasonably just *liberal* people,"[23] is misguided. For the essential question, from a perspective that puts human rights first, would be whether such peoples—or their governments—had legitimate reasons to deny their members equal liberties or the claim to political participation.

This is what it means to say that we need to take "their" point of view properly into account in "our" perspective, assuming that we want to speak in this way.

Joshua Cohen's argument for the "toleration" of nondemocratic societies in the international sphere, as long as they exhibit a certain level of political self-determination, which allows for the assignment of special weight to "some social groups," attempts to do justice to the problem of reasonable pluralism in a global society and to avoid overly strict standards for "external reproach," which may take the form of sanctions and intervention.[24] But it shares the problems of Rawls's view. Cohen rightly stresses that the primary reason to argue against a narrow-minded "liberal" way of judging the legitimacy of a society's basic structure, and possibly to infer external permission to intervene, is the respect for the collective self-determination of such a society. But to then express that respect by narrowing the human right to political self-determination (as expressed, for example, in the Universal Declaration of Human Rights), such that, if some of the politically marginalized groups in such a society were to claim a human right to equal representation, "we"—and not just those who are in power there—would say that they have no such right, seems to run the danger of contradiction. It is right to "resist the idea that the political society should be held to a standard of justice that is rejected by its own members"[25]—but only if that rejection is not the result of political pressure and domination. It is thus unwarranted to infer from this that these members do not have a human *right* to resist unequal and undemocratic forms of organizing political government. As with every other human being or collective, a political community can decide to settle for different forms of political organization, but the point of human rights is to strengthen those who dissent from certain "decisions" for unequal representation that have not been and cannot be reciprocally justified. One cannot limit the right to democracy by appealing to the principle of collective self-determination, for that is a recursive principle, with a built-in dynamic of justification that favors those who criticize exclusions and asymmetries. The right to democracy, as I conclude, is an undeniable right to full membership in a society, but it need not be claimed in a "liberal" sense if "liberal" means conformity to current social orders in the West.[26]

6

At this point, I should at least sketch what a comprehensive picture of human rights would look like, given their many dimensions as stressed at the outset, namely, moral (rather than ethical), legal, social, and political dimensions. The normative basis for a conception of human rights is the right of every moral person to be respected as someone who has a moral and political right to justification, such that any action or norm that claims to be morally justified, as well as any social order or institution that claims to be legitimate, has to be justifiable in an adequate way. This means that moral actions or norms have to be justifiable with moral reasons in moral discourse (free from coercion or delusion) and that political or social structures or laws have to be justifiable within appropriate legal and political structures (and practices) of justification. The criteria of justification for moral norms are those of reciprocity and generality in a strict sense, for, recursively speaking, such norms claim to be strictly mutually and universally binding. The criteria for legal norms are those of reciprocity and generality within political structures of justification, thereby presupposing the possibility of free and equal participation and adherence to proper procedures of deliberation and decision making.[27]

Hence, the notion of "dignity" that lies at the heart of such a conception of human rights is not a metaphysical or an ethical one, combined with a doctrine about the good life. Rather, dignity means that a person is to be respected as someone who is worthy of being given adequate reasons for actions or norms that affect him or her in a relevant way. And this kind of respect requires us to regard others as autonomous sources of normative claims within a justificatory practice. Each person is an equal normative "authority" in the space of reasons, so to speak.[28] Dignity is thus a relational term; its concrete implications can be ascertained only by way of discursive justification.

With respect to human rights, we need to distinguish between what I call "moral constructivism" and "political constructivism" (using Rawls's terminology in a different way).[29] Both are forms of discursive constructivism, in contrast to the idea of "deriving" rights from the basic right to justification. Every content of human rights is to be justified discursively, yet one needs to be aware of the twofold nature of human rights as general *moral* rights and as concrete *legal* rights. At the moral level, the construction leads to a list of those basic rights that persons who respect one another as equals with rights to justification cannot properly deny each other. It is important to emphasize that the basic right to justification is not only conducive to rights that secure the political standing of persons as citizens in a narrow sense; it is also the basis of rights to bodily security, personal liberties, and secure equal social status. To put it in negative terms, human rights are those rights that cannot be rejected with reciprocally and generally valid reasons, and this requirement opens up the normative space for claims that secure a person's status as a nondominated agent with equal social standing. This implies rights against the violation of physical or psychological integrity as well as rights against social discrimination and exploitation. The right to justification is not just a right to political justification; rather, it is a right to be respected as an independent social agent who, at the same time, codetermines the social structure of which he or she is a part.

Using the right to justification as an anchor does not involve any narrowing of focus of human rights, as one may fear, for there are two ways to substantiate human rights on that basis: first, by spelling out the requirements—and powers, so to speak—attached to the status of a socially and politically recognized agent of justification; and second, via a consideration of the aspects of human life to be protected or enabled by basic rights that no person can morally deny to equal others with good reasons. At this point, claims about the importance of certain goods and about basic social interests reappear, though not as ethical values or interests from which certain rights claims can be derived but as *discursively justifiable* claims to *reciprocal* respect among persons who recognize one another as autonomous and, at the same time, vulnerable and needy social beings. Human rights materialize and protect that status, and it is by way of procedures of reciprocal and general justification that claims based on human interests can be transformed into rights claims.

Hence, the political point of the right to justification is especially important, for there is a particular institutional implication of this moral argument for human rights. They are moral rights of a specific kind, which are directed to a political-legal authority and have to be secured in a *legally* binding form; hence, they are an important part of what I call "fundamental justice." A fundamentally just basic political and legal structure is a "basic structure of justification" in which the members have the means to deliberate and decide in common about the social institutions that apply to them and about the interpretation and concrete realization of their rights. Human rights, in that sense, have a reflexive nature; they are basic rights to be part of the processes in which the basic rights of citizens are given concrete and legally binding shape. They are rights of a higher order, namely, rights not to be subjected to social institutions or legal norms that cannot be properly justified to those affected, and rights to be equal participants in such procedures of justification. *Political* constructivism thus has *moral* constructivism as its core, for there can be no legitimate interpretation and institutionalization of basic human rights that violates their moral core, as explained above, but it is also an autonomous discursive *practice* of citizens who are engaged in establishing a legitimate social and political order. There are certain core rights presupposed by that political construction—hence the idea of *fundamental justice* in a "basic structure of justification." But an essential point of the construction is to establish a contextualized structure of rights and institutions worthy of acceptance by a political community. The ultimate aim, ideally speaking, is *maximal justice*, that is, a "fully justified basic structure."

It must be added that human rights are more wedded to fundamental than to maximal justice; the task of establishing a justified—and just—basic structure is more comprehensive and complex than that of establishing an acceptable and legitimate structure of basic human rights. Human rights are an essential part of the full picture of social and political justice, but they are only a part. As the realm of moral rights is larger than that of moral human rights, so too is the realm of political and social justice larger than that of legally established human rights. It is important to stress in this connection that political constructivism is not simply a "realization" of fixed moral human rights; rather, it is a discursive exercise within proper procedures of justification.

Human rights, to sum up, are those basic rights without which the status of a being with a right to justification is not socially secured. They entail the essential personal, political, and social legal rights necessary to establish what I call a social structure of justification, and, second, they entail those substantive rights that no one within such a structure of justification can reasonably deny to others without violating the demands of reciprocity and generality. Recursively speaking, and that is my central idea, the point of human rights is that persons have the basic right to live in a society where they themselves are the social and political agents who determine which rights they can claim and have to recognize as nondominated equals. This is the autonomous agency highlighted by human rights, today as well as in earlier times.[30] To put the double, reflexive character of human rights in a nutshell: they are rights that protect against an array of social harms the infliction of which no one can justify to others who are moral and social equals, thus presupposing the basic right to justification. But, above that, such rights protect against the harm of not being part of the political determination of what counts as such harms.

NOTES

This paper is partly based on Rainer Forst, "The Justification of Human Rights and the Basic Right to Justification: A Reflexive Approach," *Ethics* 120, no. 4 (2010): 711–40. I develop my views further in Forst, "The Point and Ground of Human Rights: A Kantian Constructivist View," in *Global Political Theory*, ed. David Held and Pietro Maffettone (Cambridge: Polity, forthcoming).

1. I explain the difference between my view and that of Philip Pettit in Rainer Forst, "Transnational Justice and Non-Domination: A Discourse-Theoretical Approach," in *Domination and Global Political Justice: Conceptual, Historical, and Institutional Perspectives*, ed. Barbara Buckinx, Jonathan Trejo-Mathys, and Timothy Waligore (New York: Routledge, 2015), 88–110.
2. James Griffin, *On Human Rights* (Oxford: Oxford University Press, 2008), 35.
3. James Nickel, *Making Sense of Human Rights*, 2nd ed. (Oxford: Blackwell, 2006). See also John Tasioulas, "The Moral Reality of Human Rights," in *Freedom from Poverty as a Human Right*, ed. Thomas Pogge (Oxford: Oxford University Press, 2007), 75–101; Tasioulas, "Taking Rights Out of Human Rights," *Ethics* 120, no. 4 (2010); and William Talbott, *Human Rights and Human Well-Being* (Oxford: Oxford University Press, 2010).
4. I develop this further in Rainer Forst, "The Justification of Basic Rights: A Discourse-Theoretical Approach," *Netherlands Journal of Legal Philosophy*, forthcoming.
5. John Rawls, *The Law of Peoples* (Cambridge, MA.: Harvard University Press, 1999), 27, 62, 79.
6. Charles Beitz, "Human Rights and the Law of Peoples," in *The Ethics of Assistance. Morality and the Distant Needy*, ed. Deen K. Chatterjee (Cambridge: Cambridge University Press, 2004), 196–7. See also Beitz, *The Idea of Human Rights* (Oxford: Oxford University Press, 2009), 7–12 and 102–6, where the idea of a "practical conception" is laid out in detail.

7. Beitz, "Human Rights and the Law of Peoples," 202ff. See also Beitz, *Idea of Human Rights*, 41ff., 65, and 143.
8. See Beitz, *Idea of Human Rights*, 33–40.
9. Michael Ignatieff, *Human Rights as Politics and Idolatry* (Princeton: Princeton University Press, 2001).
10. R. J. Vincent, *Human Rights and International Relations* (Cambridge: Cambridge University Press, 1986), 48ff.
11. Joshua Cohen, "Minimalism About Human Rights: The Most We Can Hope For?," *The Journal of Political Philosophy* 12, no. 2 (2004), 190–213, 192.
12. Joshua Cohen, "Minimalism," 197; emphasis in original.
13. Joshua Cohen, "Minimalism," 199
14. Joshua Cohen, "Minimalism," 210.
15. Joshua Cohen, "Is There a Human Right to Democracy?," in *The Egalitarian Conscience: Essays in Honour of G. A. Cohen*, ed. Christine Sypnowich (Oxford: Oxford University Press, 2006), 226–48.
16. For a comprehensive treatment of these issues, see Allen Buchanan, *Justice, Legitimacy, and Self-Determination: Moral Foundations for International Law* (Oxford: Oxford University Press, 2004). A more skeptical view is expressed in Jean Cohen, "Whose Sovereignty? Empire Versus International Law," *Ethics & International Affairs* 18, no. 3 (2004), 1–24.
17. Jean Cohen, "Rethinking Human Rights, Democracy and Sovereignty in the Age of Globalization," *Political Theory* 36, no. 4 (2008): 578–606, 591, following Michael Walzer, "The Moral Standing of States: A Response to Four Critics," *Philosophy & Public Affairs* 9, no. 3 (1980), 209–29, 214.
18. Buchanan, *Justice, Legitimacy, and Self-Determination*, chapter 6.
19. Beitz, "Human Rights and the Law of Peoples," 203. See also Beitz, *The Idea of Human Rights*, 33–40.
20. Even though Beitz criticizes minimalist views of human rights (see Beitz, *The Idea of Human Rights*, 106, 142), his own critique of the human right to democratic institutions (185) attests to the reductivist tendency in "practical" approaches.
21. John Rawls, "The Domain of the Political and Overlapping Consensus," in *Collected Papers*, ed. Samuel Freeman (Cambridge, MA: Harvard University Press, 1999), 491.
22. Rawls, *Law of Peoples*, 65, 71.
23. Rawls, *Law of Peoples*, 10; italics in original.
24. Joshua Cohen, "Is There a Human Right to Democracy?," 233–34.
25. Joshua Cohen, "Minimalism," 211.
26. On this point, see also Seyla Benhabib's argument based on the idea of a "right to have rights." Benhabib, "Is There a Human Right to Democracy? Beyond Interventionism and Indifference," in *Dignity in Adversity: Human Rights in Troubled Times* (Cambridge: Polity, 2011), 77–93.
27. On the notion of democracy implied here, see Rainer Forst, "The Rule of Reasons: Three Models of Deliberative Democracy," *Ratio Juris* 14, no. 4 (2001), 345–78.

28. This also holds true for persons who cannot use their right to justification in an active sense, such as (to some extent) children or mentally disabled persons; the passive status of having that right does not depend on its active exercise.
29. In making this distinction between moral and political constructivism, I differ from Benhabib, *Dignity in Adversity*, chapters 4 and 5.
30. In an important sense, I share Habermas's idea of the "equiprimordiality" of personal and political autonomy as well as of human rights and popular sovereignty, as explained in Jürgen Habermas, *Between Facts and Norms: Contributions to a Discourse Theory of Law and Democracy*, trans. William Rehg (Cambridge, MA: MIT Press, 1996), especially chapter 3. In another sense, however, I diverge from it, for my notion of equiprimordiality sees the right to justification as *one* source for both, whereas Habermas sees different sources at work. In addition, none of these has the moral status of the right to justification for which I argue. For a discussion of this, see Rainer Forst, "The Justification of Justice: Rawls's Political Liberalism and Habermas's Discourse Theory in Dialogue," in *The Right to Justification: Elements of a Constructivist Theory of Justice*, trans. Jeffrey Flynn (New York: Columbia University Press, 2012).

III

POLITICAL RIGHTS IN NEOLIBERAL TIMES

5

NEOLIBERALISM AND THE ECONOMIZATION OF RIGHTS

WENDY BROWN

As is well known, Karl Marx identified law in bourgeois society as the effluent of the material conditions of life. Law primarily secures conditions (such as private property) and expresses dominant powers and interests within any mode of production, even as certain struggles, such as struggles over labor conditions, are appropriately fought out in the legal domain.[1] By contrast, Michel Foucault, in *The Birth of Biopolitics*, argues that "the juridical brings form to the economic" in neoliberal rationality, a remark some have cast as his Weberian challenge to a Marxist historiography in which law is presumed to derive from and mirror modes of production. However, this formulation also reflects Foucault's own deep appreciation of the politically constructivist dimension of neoliberal governmentality, the importance of the state in organizing competition and facilitating capital accumulation in a putatively free market. It is particularly the ordoliberals, Foucault notes, who recognize that every instantiation of capitalism is an economic-juridical complex. Law does not merely secure capitalist conditions or respond to its putatively natural laws of accumulation and crisis; rather, law gives capitalism its specific shape in any time and place.[2] Indeed, appreciation of capitalism as an "economico-juridical complex" disrupts the very idea of a single capitalism in favor of multiplicity and malleability.[3] It is also precisely what brings neoliberalism into being: far from being a mere unleashing of the market, the state, law, and institutions are mobilized (and radically reconfigured) to bring about a new order.

Both the Marxist and Foucauldian formulations are indispensable, yet neither is sufficient for understanding the distinctive mobilization of law in neoliberal transformations today. Together, the Marxist and Foucauldian perspectives capture dimensions of law's role in deregulating and empowering capital and in defanging or dismantling labor, consumer, welfare, and other popular solidarities. Foucault's emphasis also illuminates the specific deployment of law in inaugurating and sustaining neoliberal regimes and in managing crises such as the 2008 finance capital meltdown or the more recent fiscal crisis in southern Europe. Marx reminds us that, even in the heyday of Keynesianism, law never radically challenges or undermines capital—even as it may demand concessions from it—and Foucault reminds us that neoliberalism is not an extension of capitalism, or only a reprogramming of liberalism, but a fundamental remaking of both through law as well as through other institutions and, of course, through political rationality.

Paradoxically, however, Foucault's emphasis on capitalism as an "economico-juridical complex" does not enable him to see what neoliberal rationality itself might do to law. He treats law as an instrument for structuring or enabling economic organization, not as a domain that itself might be transformed by the rationality governing that organization. Put another way, in formulating law's relationship to capitalism, and its role in bringing about neoliberalism, Foucault brackets his own deep insight into one of neoliberal rationality's signature dynamics: its extension of economic principles and metrics to every realm; its transformation of formerly noneconomic venues, activities, and identities by the specific form of the economic advanced by neoliberal reason.

If this insight into economization were appended to an understanding of law as structuring and abetting neoliberalization, it also would have to bend back to illuminate the neoliberalizing of law itself. Here, law would appear not only as an instrument to neoliberalize economy and society, securing that process (Marx) or giving form to it (Foucault). Instead, what would come into relief is neoliberal rationality's economization of legal interpretation, legal reasoning, and judgments. Law itself would appear remade by this neoliberalization; not simply legal enactments but also legal reasoning and jurisprudence would be at stake. And more: because law is a crucial venue for iterating, circulating, and limiting the meanings of democracy's constitutive elements, neoliberalized law will necessarily have its way with these meanings, and indeed with the meaning of democracy itself. Legal reasoning in a neoliberalized modality will necessarily transform liberal democratic formulations of popular sovereignty, rights of speech and assembly, the organization of deliberation and voting, as well as the very meaning of "public," "political," and "democratic." That is, it will transform from a liberal democratic to a neoliberal register all those legal formulations delimiting the spaces, practices, and powers through which democracy takes shape. It will thus supply new meaning to how democracy is imagined . . . or becomes unimaginable.

Thus, in this chapter, I develop a Foucauldian insight for purposes that exceed Foucault's own, and I do so in order to consider the remaking of democracy by neoliberalized legal reasoning. I do not offer a general theory of law and neoliberalism—which would be a misbegotten enterprise in any event—and the chapter is not an analysis of the "law and economics" wing of legal scholarship and jurisprudence, a project only tangentially related to my concerns. Rather, I consider how, through a specific economization of the terms of the political in legal reasoning, liberal democratic constitutional law may contribute to de-democratization. Thus, this chapter takes Foucault's point about law's role in neoliberalization further than he did: not only do law and legal reasoning give form to the economic but also the economic gives new form to the law, and the two processes together economize new spheres and practices. In this way, law becomes a medium for disseminating neoliberal rationality beyond the economy, including to constitutive elements of democratic life. More than simply securing the rights of capital and structuring competition, neoliberal juridical reason recasts political rights, citizenship, and the field of democracy itself in an economic register; in doing so, it disintegrates the very idea of the demos. Legal reasoning thus contributes a means by which democratic political life and imaginaries are undone.

Let me begin by saying a bit more about what is meant by the process of economization entailed in the dissemination of neoliberal rationality.[4] In contrast with an understanding of neoliberalism as a set of economic policies, a phase of capitalism, or an ideology that set loose the market to restore profitability for a capitalist class, it is important to grasp neoliberalism as an order of normative reason, which, when it becomes ascendant, takes shape as a governing rationality that, among other things, extends a specific formulation of economic values, practices, and metrics to every dimension of human life—from the state to the family, from warfare to the arts, from thinking to desiring.[5] At its very simplest, this governing rationality involves remaking, in economic terms, the form, content, and conduct of heretofore noneconomic domains. However, importantly, such economization does not always involve monetization.[6] That is, we may (and neoliberalism interpellates us as subjects who do) think and act like contemporary market subjects even when wealth generation is not the immediate issue. So the relentless and ubiquitous economization of all features of life by neoliberalism doesn't mean neoliberalism literally *marketizes* all spheres, even as such marketization is one important effect of neoliberalism. Rather, the point is that neoliberal rationality disseminates the *model* of the market to all domains and activities and configures human beings exhaustively as market actors, everywhere and only *homo oeconomicus*.

So, widespread economization, not necessarily marketization, of heretofore noneconomic domains, activities, and subjects is the distinctive signature of neoliberal rationality. But economization in what sense? Contemporary neoliberal rationality does not mobilize a timeless figure of economic man and simply enlarge its purview; that is, *homo oeconomicus* does not have a constant shape and bearing across the centuries. Several hundred years ago, the figure was one of truck, barter and exchange, a merchant or trader who relentlessly pursued his own interests . . . the figure famously drawn by Adam Smith. One hundred years ago, the figure was that of the Benthamite utilitarian minimizing pain and maximizing pleasure through careful cost–benefit calculations. Thirty years ago, at the dawn of the neoliberal era, *homo oeconomicus* was still oriented by interest and profit seeking, but it now entrepreneurialized *itself*—its aims and assets—at every turn.[7] Today, *homo oeconomicus* maintains aspects of that entrepreneurialism but has been significantly reshaped as financialized human capital: its project is to self-invest and attract investors in ways that enhance its actual or figurative credit rating, whether through social media followers, "likes," and retweets, through rankings and ratings for every activity and domain, or through more directly monetized practices.

The contemporary "economization" of subjects by neoliberal rationality is thus distinctive in at least three ways. First, in contrast with classical economic liberalism, we are only and everywhere *homo oeconomicus*—this is one of the oft-noted novelties that neoliberalism introduces into political and social thought and practice, and is among its most subversive elements. Second, neoliberal *homo oeconomicus* takes its shape as human capital (whose imperative is to strengthen its competitive positioning and appreciate its value) rather than as a figure of exchange or interest. This, too, is novel, and it distinguishes the neoliberal subject from the subject drawn by classical or neoclassical economists and by Jeremy Bentham, Karl Marx, Karl Polanyi, or Albert O. Hirschman. Third, today, the specific model for human capital and its spheres of activity is increasingly that of financial or investment capital and not only productive capital. Marketeering based on profitable exchange and entrepreneurializing one's assets and endeavors has not entirely vanished and remains part of what contemporary human capital is and does. Increasingly, however, as Michel Feher argues, *homo oeconomicus* as human capital is concerned with enhancing its portfolio value in all domains of its life, an activity undertaken through practices of self-investment and attracting investors.[8] Consumption, education, training, leisure, mate selection, and more are configured as decisions about self-investment related to enhancing its future value. This also makes both the project and the appropriate ethos and conduct of human capital relatively indistinguishable from that of all financialized capitals today—which is to say, all capitals.

When the construction of human beings and human conduct as *homo oeconomicus* spreads to every sphere, including that of political life itself, it radically transforms not merely the organization but also the purpose and character of each sphere and the relations among them. In political life, neoliberalization transposes democratic political principles of justice into an economic idiom, transforms the state itself into a manager of the nation on the model of a firm, and hollows out much of the substance of democratic citizenship and even popular sovereignty as it reduces all to *homo oeconomicus*. Thus, one important effect of neoliberalization is the vanquishing of liberal democracy's already anemic *homo politicus*, a vanquishing with enormous consequences for democracy itself.

The remaking of political life by neoliberalism (and the specific platform of this remaking in the legal domain) is not simply the result of corruption by corporate power or corporate values, or of the explicit application of economic models to law and politics. Rather, this remaking is occurring through a form of reason that has, during the past several decades, taken shape as a political rationality (a "governmentality" in Foucault's idiom). Among other things, this rationality is remaking legal reasoning and judgments; it is transforming as it "economizes" constitutional interpretation. Increasingly circulating as common (legal) sense, it is abetting the transmogrification of fundamental elements of political life and meaning.

To return to where we began: along with explicit neoliberal deployments of law to underwrite the empowerment of capital and disempowerment of the demos through reforms in tax, corporate, property, labor, and welfare law, there is another operation to track in the de-democratization performed by neoliberal rationality. This is the part played by legal reasoning itself in disseminating that rationality, transforming what it touches in consequential ways that exceed facilitating unequal wealth distribution, removing safety nets, unleashing capital, or yoking popular power. This distinctive framing of fields of conduct, interpretations of precedent, and construal of subjects, rights, dangers, or benefits is evident in the infamous US Supreme Court decision, *Citizens United v. Federal Election Commission* (2010), to which we now turn.[9]

Building on two Supreme Court decisions from the 1970s—*Buckley v. Valeo* and *First National Bank of Boston v. Bellotti*—*Citizens United* is often taken to emblematize the radical neoliberal turn of the Roberts Court.[10] As is well known, the majority opinion in *Citizens United*, authored by Justice Anthony Kennedy, permits corporate money to flood the American electoral process as it lifts restrictions on corporate expenditures for all types of electoral communications. *Citizens United* overturns previous regulations concerning the time, place, and amount of corporate spending in elections, arguing that these regulations unconstitutionally restrict free speech rights to which corporations are entitled and from which the citizenry also benefits.

Certainly, the *Citizens United* decision expresses neoliberal values in an obvious way. It erases the distinction between fictitious (corporate) and natural (human) persons in allocating free speech rights, it subverts legislative and popular efforts at limiting corporate influence in politics, and it overturns a century of previous court rulings aimed at modestly restricting the power of money in politics. *Citizens United*, however, represents more than the ideological favoring of wealth, deregulation, and corporations by the court. And it represents more than the unleashing of market forces in politics or the elimination of a crucial membrane between politics and markets.[11] Rather, it is a chapter in the far-reaching neoliberalization of politics, mobilizing law and even the constitution for the relentless remaking of political life as a market with market rules. It "economizes" politics at the level of reason, norms, and subjects. It recasts *homo politicus* as *homo oeconomicus* and replaces the distinctively (and distinctively fragile) political valences of rights, equality, liberty, access, autonomy, fairness, the state, and the public with economic valences of these terms. Thus, more than merely unleashing market forces in what remains of democracy, embedding and advancing a pro-corporate and antipopular viewpoint, or even applying neoclassical economic principles to rights interpretation and the space of politics, the majority opinion in *Citizens United* represents neoliberal rationality's signature economization of law and politics. Like the more recent *McCutcheon v. Federal Election Commission* decision, *Citizens United* is a force in the deep and wide remaking of democracy.

Let us reprise the decision. In the majority opinion, Justice Kennedy argues that campaign finance regulations concerning corporate electioneering bear upon a First Amendment right that ought to be neither limited to natural persons nor apportioned differently among them. "All speakers," he declares simply, "use money amassed from the economic marketplace to fund their speech, and the First Amendment protects the resulting speech."[12] Restrictions on speech ought not to pertain to differential resources or differential capacity for influence, he adds, and First

Amendment standards must always prioritize "protecting rather than stifling speech."[13] Hence, Justice Kennedy concludes, there is no justification for limiting spending on campaign ads by corporations; such restrictions represent both inappropriate governmental intervention in the free market of ideas and discrimination against certain speakers on the basis of status or content.

That is the reasoning, at once simple and radical in its jettisoning of more than a century of law aimed at mitigating the potentially overwhelming power of corporate wealth in electoral politics. But what makes this reasoning possible? What new common sense does it draw upon, and what transformations of the constitution and political life does it enact?

DEREGULATING SPEECH, WHICH IS LIKE CAPITAL . . .

Writing for the majority, Justice Kennedy sets out to emancipate speech from the webs of regulation and censorship by which he claims it is currently discouraged or worse. "First Amendment freedoms need breathing space to survive," he quotes approvingly from Chief Justice Roberts's opinion in an earlier case.[14] "As additional rules are created for regulating political speech," Kennedy adds, "any speech arguably within their reach is chilled." Depicting the Federal Election Commission as generating "onerous restrictions [that] function as the equivalent of prior restraint," and largely reducing it to the business of censorship, Kennedy underscores the danger represented by this government agency, which it is the task of the court to hold off:

> When the FEC [Federal Election Commission] issues advisory opinions that prohibit speech, "[m]any persons, rather than undertake the considerable burden (and sometimes risk) of vindicating their rights through case-by-case litigation, will choose simply to abstain from protected speech—harming not only themselves but society as a whole, which is deprived of an uninhibited marketplace of ideas." *Virginia v. Hicks*, 539 U.S. 113, 119 (citation omitted). Consequently, "the censor's determination may in practice be final." *Freedman, supra*, at 58.[15]

At times, Kennedy raises the pitch in *Citizens United* to depict limits on corporate funding of political action committee (PAC) ads as "an outright ban on speech"; at other times he casts them merely as inappropriate government intervention and bureaucratic weightiness.[16] But beneath all the hyperbole about government chilling of corporate speech is a crucial rhetorical move: the figuring of speech as analogous to capital in what Kennedy terms "the political marketplace." On the one hand, government intervention is featured throughout the opinion as harmful to the marketplace of ideas that speech generates.[17] Government restrictions damage freedom of speech just as they damage all freedoms. On the other hand, the unfettered *accumulation and circulation* of speech is cast as an unqualified good, essential to "the right of citizens to inquire … hear … speak … and use information to reach consensus, [itself] a precondition to enlightened self-government and a necessary means to protect it."[18] Not merely corporate rights, then, but democracy as a whole is at stake in the move to deregulate speech. Importantly, however, democracy is here conceived as a marketplace whose goods—ideas, opinions, and ultimately, votes—are generated by speech, just as the economic market features goods generated by capital. In other words, at the very moment that Justice Kennedy deems disproportionate wealth irrelevant to the equal rights exercised in this marketplace and the utilitarian maximization these rights generate, speech itself acquires the status of capital and a premium is placed on its unrestricted sources and unimpeded flow.

What is significant about rendering speech as capital? Economization of the political occurs not through the mere *application* of market principles to nonmarket fields but through the *conversion* of political processes, subjects, categories, and principles to economic ones. This is the conversion that occurs on every page of the Kennedy opinion. If everything in the world is a market, and neoliberal markets consist only of competing capitals, large and small, and speech is the capital of the electoral market, then speech will necessarily share capital's crucial attributes: it appreciates through calculated investment and its purpose is to advance the position of its bearer. Put the other way around, once speech is rendered as the capital of the electoral marketplace, it is appropriately unrestricted and unregulated, fungible across actors and venues, and exists solely for the advancement or enhancement of its bearer's interests. The classic associations of political speech with freedom, conscience, deliberation, and persuasion *among the demos* are nowhere in sight.

How, precisely, is speech capital in the Kennedy opinion? How does it come to be figured in economic terms, where its regulation or restriction appears as bad for its particular marketplace and where its monopolization by corporations appears as proliferating growth good for all? The transmogrification of speech into capital occurs on a number of levels in Kennedy's account. First, speech is like capital in its tendency to proliferate and circulate, to push past barriers, to circumvent laws and other restrictions, indeed, to spite efforts at intervention or suppression.[19] Speech is thus rendered as a force both natural and good, which can be wrongly impeded and encumbered but never quashed.

Second, persons are not merely producers but consumers of speech, and government interference is a menace—wrong in principle and harmful in effect—at both ends. The marketplace of ideas, Kennedy repeats tirelessly, is what decides the value of speech claims. Every citizen must judge the content of speech for him- or herself; it cannot be a matter for government determination, just as government should not usurp other consumer choices. In this discussion, Kennedy makes no mention of shared deliberation or judgment in politics, or of voices that are unfunded and relatively powerless. His focus is on the wrong of government *"command[ing]* where a person may get his or her information or what distrusted source he or she may not hear, [using] censorship to control thought." If speech generates goods consumed according to individual choice, government distorts this market by "banning the political speech of millions of associations of citizens" (i.e., corporations) and by paternalistically limiting what consumers may know or consider.[20] Again, if speech is the capital of the political marketplace, then we are politically free when it circulates freely. And it circulates freely only when corporations are not restricted in what speech they may fund.

Third, Kennedy casts speech not as a medium for expression or dialogue but rather as innovative and productive, just as capital is. There is "a creative dynamic inherent in the concept of free expression" that intersects in a lively way with "rapid changes in technology" to generate the public good. This aspect of speech, Kennedy argues, specifically "counsel[s] against upholding a law that restricts political speech in certain media or by certain speakers."[21] Again, the dynamism, innovativeness, and generativity of speech, like that of all capital, is dampened by government intervention.

Fourth, and perhaps most important in establishing speech as the capital of the electoral marketplace, Kennedy sets the power of speech and the power of government in direct and zero-sum opposition to one another. Repeatedly across the lengthy opinion for the majority, he identifies speech with freedom and government with control, censorship, paternalism, and repression. When free speech and government meet, it is to contest one another; the right of speech enshrined in the First Amendment, he argues, is "premised on mistrust of governmental power" and is "an essential mechanism of democracy [because] it is the means to hold officials accountable to the people." Here are other variations on this theme in the opinion:

> The First Amendment was certainly not understood [by the Framers] to condone the suppression of political speech in society's most salient media. It was understood as a response to the repression of speech... When Government seeks to use its full power, including criminal law, to command where a person may get his or her information or what distrusted source he or she may not hear, it uses censorship to control thought... The First Amendment confirms the freedom to think for ourselves.[22]

This reading of the First Amendment and of the purpose of political speech positions government and speech as warring forces parallel to those of government and capital—always opposed, always requiring deference of the former to the latter.

In short, Justice Kennedy's opinion construes the First Amendment not as a human or civil right but as a capital right. He aims to secure from regulation or interference not ideas, deliberation, or the integrity of the democratic political sphere but an unimpeded flow of speech. While retaining the language of rights and persons, he has effectively detached speech and speech rights from individuals, which facilitates the move to protect corporate speech rights. Thus, the problem with *Citizens United* is not (as critics of this decision often declare) that corporations have been awarded the rights of individuals but that individuals as rights-bearing participants in popular sovereignty disappear when speech flows obtain the status of capital flows and all actors are seeking to enhance the value of their capital.

Rendering government as the fundamental enemy of speech also links all members of society and economy, from the poorest citizen to the richest corporation, as potential victims of government interference or censorship. When persons and corporations are thus allied—even identified with one another in the perils they face—the distinctive power of corporate speech, more than glossed, is converted into a cause. What must be fought are conditions in which "certain disfavored associations of citizens—those that have taken on the corporate form—are penalized" and prevented "from presenting both facts and opinions to the public," which is deprived of "knowledge and opinion vital to its function."[23] Put differently, in a rhetorically structured field in which there is only speech and its endangerment by government, and in which the unimpeded flow of speech benefits all, while government intervention invariably targets and discriminates, significant differences among speakers disappear. Whether the speaker is a homeless woman or Exxon, speech is speech, just as capital is capital.

This disavowal of stratification and power differentials in the field of analysis and action is a crucial feature of neoliberal rationality, precisely the feature that discursively erases distinctions between capital and labor, owners and producers, landlord and tenant, rich and poor. There is only capital, and whether it is human, corporate, financial, or derivative, whether it is tiny or giant, is irrelevant to both its normative conduct and its right to be free of interference. Similarly, in *Citizens United*, there is only speech, all of which has the same right, the same capacity to enrich the marketplace of ideas, the same capacity to be judged by the citizenry, and the same vulnerability to restriction or repression by government.

In sum, in Justice Kennedy's formulation, speech is capital-like in its natural, irrepressible, dynamic, and creative nature, its market field of operations and circulation, its undifferentiated standing across diverse social agents, its generation of freedom through producer and consumer choice, and its absolute antagonism to government regulation. This transformation of the meaning, character, purpose, and value of speech from a political to an economic register quite precisely expresses the unfolding of neoliberal rationality in a political and ethical sphere. It also facilitates arguments to lift restrictions on entering the speech marketplace, to eliminate regulations on operating within it, and to quash concerns about its internal distributions of power and effect. Once this economization is secured, subjecting the marketplace in which speech operates to manufactured equality or redistribution is simply a Keynesian moral and technical error. If all markets are domains of natural equality, founded on and fostered by unimpeded competition, then government may facilitate entry and foster competition but is otherwise an unwarranted intruder. Thus, Justice Kennedy opines, previous Supreme Court decisions that place limits on corporate speech interfere with the "open marketplace" of ideas protected by the First Amendment.[24]

MARKETS MULTIPLIED

If the figuration of speech as capital is one index of the economization of law and politics achieved by *Citizens United*, the decision's multiplication of marketplaces is another. In addition to discussing marketplaces of speech and ideas, Kennedy, drawing from *Bellotti*, depicts electoral contests themselves as "political marketplaces." According to Kennedy, the question before the court is whether winners in the economic marketplace may operate unimpeded in "the political marketplace."[25] This is how he construes the relevant precedents:

> Political speech is "indispensable to decision making in a democracy and this is no less true because the speech comes from a corporation rather than an individual." *Bellotti*, 435 U.S., at 777 . . . *Austin* sought to defend the antidistortion rationale as a means to prevent corporations from obtaining "an unfair advantage in the political marketplace" by using "resources amassed in the economic marketplace." 494 U.S., at 659 . . . But *Buckley* rejected the premise that the Government has an interest "in equalizing the relative ability of individuals and groups to influence the outcome of elections." . . . *Buckley* was specific in stating that "the skyrocketing cost of political campaigns" could not sustain the governmental prohibition. 424 U.S., at 26. The First Amendment's

protections do not depend on the speaker's "financial ability to engage in public discussion."[26]

Justice Kennedy acknowledges that, if everything is a marketplace, those dominant in one marketplace will likely bring some of that power to another. Yet this does not justify government intervention to equalize marketplace positioning. Even if amassed wealth can be mobilized to influence election outcomes qua marketplaces, each must be left free of government interference and practices of equalization. Markets, no matter how they overlap and affect one another, must all be left to work on their own.

What has happened here? Democratic political speech, far from being a delicate and corruptible medium for public persuasion, which must be protected from monopolization, becomes, in and as a marketplace, an unhindered property right. Similarly, the political, far from being a field of highly specific powers through which common existence is negotiated, protected, or transformed, becomes, as a market, a field for advancing every kind of capital—human, corporate, financial, cultural. Both of these moves make perfect sense insofar as neoliberal rationality recognizes market conduct as the sole principle of action and market metrics as the sole measure in every sphere of human action.

STRICT SCRUTINY FOR CORPORATIONS

While Justice Kennedy's opinion involves a relentless economization of political life, it also braids key strands of civil rights discourse into the opinion to bolster the argument for deregulating corporate speech in the political sphere. Here is how this goes:

First, Kennedy argues that, construed as a person (or as an aggregate or association of persons), corporations straightforwardly share with all persons the right to speak in the political sphere. A corporation's potentially greater power to finance the broadcast of its speech is no more relevant to this right than are the greater buying capacities of the rich to their private property rights. Equality, for neoliberals as for liberals, pertains to rights' distribution, not to the effects of rights' exercise.

Second, Kennedy formulates corporate rights to political speech as bearing directly on citizen information gathering and hence on popular sovereignty: "The right of citizens to inquire, to hear, to speak and to use information to reach consensus is a precondition to enlightened self-government and a necessary means to protect it . . . For these reasons, political speech must prevail against laws that would suppress it, whether by design or inadvertence."[27] Thus, Kennedy aims to protect both corporate rights to speak and citizen rights to know; both are abridged when government intervenes in the speech marketplace. Speech restrictions aimed at preventing the "distorting effects of immense aggregations of wealth" deprive, rather than protect, citizens.[28] A viewpoint is suppressed, and voices from an essential quarter of society are lost:

> The censorship we now confront is vast in its reach. The Government has "muffle[d] the voices that best represent the most significant segments of the economy." *McConnell, supra*, at 257–258. . . . And "the electorate [has been] deprived of information, knowledge and opinion vital to its function." *CIO*, 335 U.S., at 144. . . . By suppressing the speech of manifold corporations, both for-profit and nonprofit, the Government prevents their voices and viewpoints from reaching the public and advising voters on which persons or entities are hostile to their interests.[29]

Here is the added fillip: although corporate political speech may be especially valuable, it is, according to Justice Kennedy, the least likely to be protected. Muzzled by previous Supreme Court decisions, burdened by government bureaucracy, and suffering prejudice in ordinary political discourse, corporations emerge in the Kennedy opinion as beleaguered and victimized in their speech rights, hovering close to a suspect class. "Speech restrictions based on the identity of the speaker," he intones, "are all too often simply a means to control content." And worse:

> Quite apart from the purpose or effect of regulating content, moreover, the Government may commit a constitutional wrong when by law it identifies certain preferred speakers. By taking the right to speak from some and giving it to others, *the Government deprives the disadvantaged person or class* of the right to use speech to strive to establish worth, standing and respect for the speaker's voice. The Government may not

by these means deprive the public and privilege to determine for itself what speech and speakers are worthy of consideration. The First Amendment protects speech and speaker, and the ideas that flow from each.[30]

In sum, government privileging of any speaking subject over any other is discrimination of the classic sort, making the deprivileged subject (corporations!) into a disadvantaged person or class. Such discrimination is wrong on its face, but it also curtails the ability to use speech to articulate one's value in the world of speaking creatures. Thus a cycle of prejudice is perpetuated: corporations denied speech rights because of prejudice against them are in turn deprived of a means for overturning this prejudice and advancing their public worth. And again, when the government chooses "which speech is safe for public consumption," the public, too, is deprived of its right to exercise its judgment.[31] More than merely protecting speech, in this reading, the First Amendment protects the *integrity* of all parties—corporations, citizens, publics—and the value of speaking, listening, and judging.

We are now in a position to grasp how the civil rights language works as a supplement to the marketplace language. Corporations share with all persons free speech rights in the political sphere. The decision in *Citizens United* aims to secure these rights for a historically disenfranchised class of persons so that this class of persons may become equal and free competitors in the political marketplace and so that all may benefit from this enriched competition. Two different strands from two different eras of minority discourse are mobilized on behalf of deregulating corporate electoral speech: the classic liberal equal rights argument and the more recent "all are enriched by diversity" argument. Drawing on both to advance what Justice Stevens, in his dissent, notes the public has never clamored for more of, namely, corporate influence in politics, Justice Kennedy positions the court as enfranchising not the powerful but the disliked, unwanted, and historically excluded.[32] Removing the boot from the necks of this class of persons simultaneously advances the cause of universal rights and enriches the political marketplace of democracy.

RIGHTS V. MARKETS

One effect of deploying rights discourse in this way is that the unimpeachable virtue of civil and political rights as instruments of resistance against discrimination and against state power obscures their own subversion by economization. The inclusive and egalitarian promise of rights shrouds the most fundamental dynamic of the marketplace: competition, in which the strong extinguish the weak. Corporate speech rights do not technically cancel the right of others to speak, but as Justice Stevens notes in his dissent, when corporations eat up the airwaves and drive up the price of media ads, views backed by less funding are driven out.[33] And here is where rights and markets cross-thread: there is no limit to how many may enjoy speech rights, but there are limits to how much speech may be bought and sold in a given venue at a given time. Submission of democratic politics to the market thus subverts equal rights to participation, or, put the other way around, when rights to political participation are marketized, political equality is the first casualty.

In his dissent, Justice Stevens refers to this development as trammeling the long-held constitutional principle of restricting "the speech of some in order to prevent a few from drowning out the many."[34] He rereads the very cases on which Kennedy rests his judgment—*Austin v. Michigan Chamber of Commerce*, *Bellotti*, *Buckley*, and *McConnell v. Federal Election Commission*—to draw opposite conclusions. "Over the course of the past century, Congress has demonstrated a recurrent need to regulate corporate participation in candidate elections," and the Supreme Court has appropriately vindicated this need. Both branches of government limited and regulated "corporate electoral advocacy" to "preserve the integrity of the electoral process, prevent corruption, sustain the active, alert responsibility of the individual citizen, protect the expressive interests of shareholders and preserve . . . the individual citizen's confidence in government."[35]

Preventing the many from being drowned out by the few is precisely what legislatures and courts do to preserve democracy. Such prevention, however, is squarely at odds with the economization of politics. It has no place in a market, where the most innovative, ambitious, and aggressive prevail and where this prevalence also equates the "voices" with "valuable expertise" in interpreting and shaping political life.³⁶ The majority opinion Stevens is struggling against in *Citizens United* not only saturates political life with economic power but also transforms it via the normative principles and measures of neoliberalized markets. It is a textbook case of the neoliberal economization of the political.

CORRUPTION AND INFLUENCE

The thoroughgoing character of this economization is evident in Justice Kennedy's discussion of corruption in *Citizens United*.³⁷ He raises the issue in order to dismiss its relevance to limiting corporate spending in elections: "Influence over or access to elected officials does not mean that these officials are corrupt." How is this remarkable sentence possible? Citing *Buckley*, Kennedy limits the meaning and existence of corruption to explicit quid pro quo arrangements—"dollars for political favors."³⁸ The classical definition of political corruption refers to the sustained bending of public to private interest, the overtaking of res publica by private concerns. Republican theorists identify it as a disease almost impossible to cure once it has settled into the body politic.³⁹ Such a meaning is impossible to feature in neoliberal rationality, where there are only private interests, contracts, and deals and no such thing as a body politic, public good, or political culture. Thus, although corporations will obviously wield their financial might in the political sphere in pursuit of their own ends (consider, for example, banks writing the new regulations for the financial sector),⁴⁰ this does not qualify as bending public to private interest because, on the one hand, neoliberalism eliminates the very idea of the public interest and, on the other, corporations now have standing as persons whose speech is public and "all can judge its content and purpose."⁴¹

Justice Kennedy also cites his own previous opinion in *McConnell* for this point, a passage that further illuminates the way neoliberal rationality transforms the meaning and operation of democratic terms. Here is Kennedy in *McConnell*:

> Favoritism and influence are not . . . avoidable in representative politics. It is in the nature of an elected representative to favor certain policies, and

by necessary corollary, to favor the voters and contributors who support those policies. It is well understood that a substantial and legitimate reason, if not the only reason, to cast a vote for or to make a contribution to, one candidate over another is that the candidate will respond by producing those political outcomes the supporter favors. Democracy is premised on responsiveness.[42]

What exactly is Kennedy is claiming about political influence in *McConnell* and reaffirming in *Citizens United*? He argues, first, that elected representatives naturally favor voters and contributors who support the policies the representative favors; thus, the politician is not representing a district or constituency but rather "responds to" and "favors" the people and money corresponding to the positions she or he holds. He argues, second, that the "only" reason to vote for or give money to a candidate is that the candidate "will respond" by producing the outcomes the voter or contributor desires. The verb and its tense are both crucial here, their importance underlined by Kennedy's concluding statement that "democracy is premised on responsiveness." Kennedy sets aside the conventional view that voters or contributors support candidates whose political positions align with their own to argue that political "representatives" *will respond* to support by producing the political outcomes supporters expect. Public service thus gains a new meaning as representatives literally stand to deliver the outcomes their supporters purchase with votes and dollars.

As he equates voters with financial contributors, including corporate contributors, Kennedy may seem to be finessing a point that would be more tendentious if he spoke only of contributors. But the equation is actually crucial to the transformation of democracy his words perform, the shift from a representative to a purely market form. In his economic contractarian account of political representation premised on responsiveness, we all expect to get something from our investment, whether a campaign contribution or a vote. Elected officials are for making deals with, not for securing justice or national welfare and not for addressing contemporary common challenges or preventing future common predicaments. If votes and money are the available currencies for these deals, big capital can enhance its own value and positioning by delivering votes—exactly what *Citizens United* facilitates.

There are still more inversions of meaning in Kennedy's discussion of corruption and influence. Here is his formulation of the chain of influence from money to votes to political office: "The fact that a corporation, or any other speaker, is willing to spend money to try to persuade voters presupposes that the people have the ultimate influence over public officials." Again, how is this sentence possible and what could it mean? Here is the full passage from which it is extracted:

> The appearance of influence or access . . . will not cause the electorate to lose faith in our democracy. By definition, an independent expenditure is political speech presented to the electorate that is not coordinated with a candidate . . . The fact that a corporation, or any other speaker, is willing to spend money to try to persuade voters presupposes that the people have the ultimate influence over elected officials.[43]

Clearly, Justice Kennedy is flailing a bit. The first declarative is wild, especially insofar as it depends on the second, which repeats the formal conceit of independence in PACs that no one believes. And the lack of logical entailment from one sentence to the next is almost painful. However, these strange stipulations and leaps of logic can also be explained by the radically new set of meanings for which the justice is reaching and for which a new idiom must be crafted. Influence has now been redefined as responsiveness, narrowly stipulated as following the money. Corporately financed super PACs have been redefined as speech. Super PACs are, by definition, independent political speech because they are not the direct voice of corporations or the political campaign; the super PAC is independent of each by virtue of its distinct corporate persona. And if the purpose of super PACs is to enable corporate speech to persuade voters, it stands to (neoliberal economic) reason that voters must have the greatest influence over elected officials—otherwise, why would corporations bother persuading them rather than moving to influence politicians directly? Thus, Justice Kennedy comforts himself that, even with unlimited corporate funds working over the electorate, democracy remains intact, because the point of the super PACs is not to directly influence the candidate but to deliver votes, the source of "ultimate influence."

But in what sense is a vote identical with influence, especially as it has just been defined? That is, how do we square this passage with the previous one? It would seem that Kennedy is now making a distinction between votes and financial contributions, a distinction he elided in the discussion of democracy as a system of responsiveness to both. If voters have the "ultimate influence," but corporations seek to persuade them via super PACs, has he not effectively confessed that voters are but a medium through which corporations wield their political influence? Has democracy become more than a shield of legitimation for corporate domination?

Justice Kennedy, of course, spins the matter differently, returning us to the importance of corporate speech as an indispensable contribution to the democratic process, the people's deliberations and sovereignty. He cites at length from a three-justice dissent in the 1957 decision to remand in *United States v. Automobile Workers*:

> Under our Constitution it is We The People who are sovereign. The people have the final say. The legislators are their spokesmen. The people determine through their votes the destiny of the nation. It is therefore important—vitally important—that all channels of communications be open to them during every election, that no point of view be restrained or barred, and that the people have access to the views of every group in the community ... [Deeming] a particular group too powerful [is not a] justification for withholding First Amendment rights from any group—labor or corporate.[44]

So while corporations "speak" to persuade voters through whom they will influence politics, this persuasion is construed as voter information essential to popular sovereignty. A ruse? Or, again, a new way of conceiving democracy, in which voters depend upon corporate points of view, corporations share free speech rights because speech itself is a form of capital, elections are political marketplaces where resource inequities are a given, political advertising is detached from either objective value or public interest, and the game of influence and even quid pro quo is one in which everyone plays a part?

The many inversions of democratic meaning in *Citizens United* suggest that this decision does far more than permit corporate funds to flood the electoral process. In its insistence that the corporation must share in the rights of man, its heralding of corporate speech as vital to democracy, and its jettisoning of concerns with equality in access to or effects of political speech, the court certainly licenses and legitimates unlimited corporate power in politics. But, more, as it submits politics, rights, representation, and speech to economization, it subverts key components of liberal democracy—popular sovereignty, free elections, political freedom, and equality. Casting every actor and activity in market terms, it vanquishes the political meaning of citizenship and erases the crucial distinction between economic and political orders essential to the most modest version of popular sovereignty. It aggressively abandons the distinctively political valence and venue of democracy, and turns its back on the fragility of democratic conditions and cultures. It supplants democratic political deliberation and voice with a formulation of speech as capital and free speech as an unhindered property right. It reduces political knowledge and political participation to practices of individual or corporate capital enhancement achieved through broadcasting one's economic position as a political one. Rendering government regulation or limits as the enemy of freedom everywhere, the court blends flows of capital and speech into a single stream, sharing characteristics and rights against a common enemy: the regulatory state.

Each of these moves is novel in the history of democratic thought and practice. Each hollows out the practices and institutions of liberal democracy and scorches the ground of any other democratic form. Together, they extinguish a conception of democracy in which this would matter.

NOTES

1. For Marx's argument that law reflects the power of the dominant classes, see Karl Marx, *The German Ideology*, in *The Marx-Engels Reader*, 2nd ed., ed. Robert C. Tucker (New York: Norton, 1978), 146–201; and "On the Jewish Question," in *The Marx-Engels Reader*, 26–52. For appreciation of legal struggles (especially about the length of the working day and child labor) as class struggles, see Marx, *Capital*, vol. 1, trans. Ben Fowkes (London: Penguin Classics, 1990); and Marx, *Capital*, vols. 2–3, trans. David Fernbach (London: Penguin Classics, 1993).
2. Michel Foucault, *The Birth of Biopolitics: Lectures at the Collège de France, 1978–79*, ed. Michel Senellart, trans. Graham Burchell (New York: Picador, 2004), 162–4.
3. Pierre Dardot and Christian Laval, *The New Way of the World: On Neoliberal Society*, trans. Gregory Elliott (London: Verso, 2013), 10–11.

4. This section of the chapter draws from chapter 1 of Wendy Brown, *Undoing the Demos: Neoliberalism's Stealth Revolution* (Brooklyn, NY: Zone, 2015).
5. This argument is elaborated at length in Brown, *Undoing the Demos*. My earlier efforts at developing Foucault's account of neoliberalism as political rationality appear in Wendy Brown, "Neoliberalism and the End of Liberal Democracy," in *Edgework: Critical Essays on Knowledge and Politics* (Princeton: Princeton University Press, 2005), 37–59, previously published in *Theory and Event* 7, no. 1 (Fall 2003); and Brown, "American Nightmare: Neoconservatism, Neoliberalism, and De-Democratization," *Political Theory* 34, no. 6 (2006): 690–714. I stand by some but not all of those earlier formulations now.
6. Koray Caliskan and Michel Callon, "Economization, Part 1: Shifting Attention from the Economy Towards Processes of Economization," *Economy and Society* 38, no. 3 (2009): 369–98.
7. Foucault, *Birth of Biopolitics*, 148.
8. See Michel Feher, *Rated Agencies: Political Engagements with Our Invested Selves* (Brooklyn, NY: Zone, forthcoming); and Feher, "Self-Appreciation; or, the Aspirations of Human Capital," *Public Culture* 21, no. 1 (2009): 21–41.
9. The remainder of the chapter is drawn from "Law and Legal Reason," in Brown, *Undoing the Demos*, chapter 5.
10. See, for example, Timothy K. Kuhner, "*Citizens United* as Neoliberal Jurisprudence: The Resurgence of Economic Theory," *Virginia Journal of Social Policy and the Law* 18, no. 3 (Spring 2011): 395–468; and Kuhner, *Capitalism v. Democracy: Money in Politics and the Free Market Constitution* (Stanford, CA: Stanford University Press, 2014).
11. Kuhner, "*Citizens United* as Neoliberal Jurisprudence," 460, 468.
12. Citizens United v. Federal Election Commission, 130 S. Ct. 876, 558 U.S. 310, 175 L. Ed. 2d 753 (2010) at 314.
13. *Citizens United*, 558 U.S. at 327, citing Federal Election Commission v. Wisconsin Right to Life, Inc., 551 U.S. 449 (2007) at 469, citing New York Times Co. v. Sullivan, 376 U.S. 254, 269070 (1964).
14. *Citizens United*, 558 U.S. at 329, citing *Wisconsin Right to Life*, 551 U.S. 449 at 468–69, quoting National Association for the Advancement of Colored People v. Button, 371 U.S. 415 (1963) at 433.
15. *Citizens United*, 558 U.S. at 334–36.
16. *Citizens United*, 558 U.S. at 312 and 339. Following one lengthy account of all the record keeping, accounting, and reporting that political action committees (PACs) must do "just to speak," Kennedy concludes that "given the onerous restrictions, a corporation may not be able to establish a PAC in time to make its views known" in an election. Such a "ban on speech," he continues, injures not only the would-be speaker but also the public, insofar as it "necessarily reduces the quantity of expression by restricting the number of issues discussed, the depth of their exploration, and the size of the audience reached." *Citizens United*, 558 U.S. at 339, quoting *Buckley v. Valeo*, 424 U.S. 1 (1976).

17. No one has offered a better set of discussions about the problematic of the marketplace metaphor in interpreting and adjudicating First Amendment cases than Steven Shiffrin. In a series of articles and books, as well as in his casebook, Shiffrin decisively cuts asserted connections between an imagined marketplace of ideas and truth, fairness, dissent, deliberation, or even genuine choice. See, for example, Shiffrin, *The First Amendment, Democracy, and Romance* (Princeton: Princeton University Press, 1990), where he argues:

> A . . . commitment to sponsoring dissent does not require a belief that what emerges in the "market" is usually right or that the "market" is the best test of truth. Quite the contrary, the commitment to sponsor dissent assumes that societal pressures to conform are strong and that incentives to keep quiet are often great. If the marketplace metaphor encourages the view that an invisible hand or voluntaristic arrangements have guided us patiently, but slowly, to Burkean harmony, the commitment to sponsoring dissent encourages us to believe that the cozy arrangements of the status quo have settled on something less than the true or the just. If the marketplace metaphor encourages the view that conventions, habits, and traditions have emerged as our best sense of the truth from the rigorous testing ground of the marketplace of ideas, the commitment to sponsoring dissent encourages the view that conventions, habits, and traditions are compromises open to challenge. If the marketplace metaphor counsels us that the market's version of truth is more worthy of trust than any that the government might dictate, a commitment to sponsoring dissent counsels us to be suspicious of both. If the marketplace metaphor encourages a sloppy form of relativism (whatever has emerged in the marketplace is right for now), the commitment to sponsoring dissent emphasizes that truth is not decided in public opinion polls.

Cited in Steven Shiffrin and Jesse Chopper, *First Amendment: Cases, Comments, Questions*, 3rd ed. (St. Paul, MN: West Academic Publishing, 2001), 15–16. See also, Shiffrin, "The First Amendment and Economic Regulation: Away From a General Theory of the First Amendment," *Northwestern University Law Review* 78, no. 5 (1983): 1212–83.
18. *Citizens United*, 558 U.S. at 339.
19. *Citizens United*, 558 U.S. at 364.
20. *Citizens United*, 558 U.S. at 349–50, 356; italics added.
21. *Citizens United*, 558 U.S. at 354, 364.
22. See *Citizens United*, 558 U.S. at 339–40, 349–50, 353, 356.
23. *Citizens United*, 558 U.S. at 354–356.
24. *Citizens United*, 558 U.S. at 354.
25. *Citizens United*, 558 U.S. at 313, 369.
26. *Citizens United*, 558 U.S. at 313.
27. *Citizens United*, 558 U.S. at 339–40.
28. *Citizens United*, 558 U.S. at 354, citing Austin v. Michigan Chamber of Comm., 494 U.S. 652 (1990) at 660.

29. *Citizens United*, 558 U.S. at 354.
30. *Citizens United*, 558 U.S. at 340–41; italics added.
31. *Citizens United*, 558 U.S. at 336.
32. *Citizens United*, 558 U.S. at 469–71.
33. *Citizens United*, 558 U.S. at 472.
34. *Citizens United*, 558 U.S. at 441.
35. *Citizens United*, 558 U.S. at 446.
36. *Citizens United*, 558 U.S. at 364.
37. The 2014 successor to *Buckley v. Valeo* and *Citizens United*, McCutcheon v. Federal Election Commission, 572 U.S. _ (2014), was decided after this chapter was written. *McCutcheon* overturns limits on total electoral spending ($123,000) for any individual contributor, while maintaining limits on how much a contributor may give to any one candidate ($5,200). The reasoning is that if a $5,200 contribution from one donor to one candidate does not qualify as potentially corrupting that candidate, then $5,200 from one donor to an indefinite number of candidates is not corruption. If no candidate can be bought for a mere $5,200, then it does not matter how much money a single individual dedicates to political campaigns. Thus, instead of having to wash large political contributions through super PACs, donors can now write a $3.6 million–dollar check directly to a party, or to a "joint fundraising committee" supporting a number of candidates.

    Left and liberal legal pundits decrying the decision have blasted the Supreme Court majority for its sustained dismantling of election regulations through mobilizing a highly restricted definition of corruption and through sustaining the reasoning about political speech contained in *Buckley v. Valeo* and *Citizen United*, where limits on spending were equated with restrictions on speech, and "leveling the playing field" and all other equality concerns were construed as government interference with both speech and elections.

    To these points, I would add the following: As I have argued in this chapter, confinement of the meaning of corruption to quid pro quo is itself an effect of the neoliberal economization of political terms and processes. Quid pro quo corruption marks a contractual arrangement through which a political representative would be paid to serve the interests of a particular individual or group rather than its whole constituency. As we saw in *Citizens United*, a version of quid pro quo is actually how Justice Kennedy believes all political representation works, because, for him, there is no politics outside the model of economization. Thus, all that designates quid pro quo as corruption is making the payment of dollars for outcomes explicit. Most importantly, however, the classic definition of political corruption—not merely inappropriate dependence or influence but the sustained bending of public to private interest, the undoing of res publica by private interests—is literally unintelligible in neoliberal reasoning. This is so both because of the narrowing of the public interest to economic indicators and because economization of political life makes this sustained bending at once normal and invisible—normal because all private interests necessarily seek to enhance their power in every domain; invisible because res publica itself is stripped of all political or popular signification when political language is economized. In short, within neoliberal reason, the language of corruption ceases to be able to signify the commandeering or destruction of public by private interests.

38. *Citizens United*, 558 U.S. at 359.
39. See Niccolo Machiavelli, *The Prince*, ed. Quentin Skinner and Russell Price (Cambridge: Cambridge University Press, 1988); and Jean-Jacques Rousseau, *"The Social Contract" and Other Late Political Writings*, ed. Victor Gourevitch (Cambridge: Cambridge University Press, 1997).
40. See Eric Lipton and Ben Protess, "Banks' Lobbyists Help in Drafting Bills on Finance," *New York Times*, May 24, 2013, http://dealbook.nytimes.com/2013/05/23/banks-lobbyists-help-in-drafting-financial-bills; "Wall St. Lobbyists and Financial Regulation," *New York Times*, October 28, 2013, http://www.nytimes.com/interactive/2013/10/29/business/dealbook/29lobbyistsdocuments.html; and Ailsa Chang, "When Lobbyists Literally Write the Bill," *All Things Considered*, November 11, 2013, http://www.npr.org/blogs/itsallpolitics/2013/11/11/243973620/when-lobbyists-literally-write-the-bill.
41. *Citizens United*, 558 U.S. at 355.
42. McConnell v. Federal Election Commission, 540 U.S. 93 (2003) at 297 (opinion of Kennedy, J.), cited in *Citizens United*, 558 U.S. at 359.
43. *Citizens United*, 558 U.S. at 360.
44. United States v. Automobile Workers, 352 U.S. 567 (1957) at 593, 597 (Dissenting opinion of Douglas, J. joined by Warren, C. J. and Black, J.), cited partially in *Citizens United*, 558 U.S. at 344.

6

LAW AND DOMINATION

CHRISTOPH MENKE

In the preface to his *Contribution to the Critique of Political Economy*, Karl Marx states the agenda of his critical theory of law in the claim that legal relations "originate in the material conditions of life" (or "arise out of" them), "the totality of which Hegel . . . embraces within the term 'civil [or bourgeois] society.' "[1] This is the hypothesis that defines the program of a *social critique of law*: its objective is to reveal the social logic of law, the structural nexus between its normative content and the basic forms of social domination.

In this chapter, I will try to sketch a critique of the social critique of law. A critique of this social critique must accomplish two things: it must both justify the social critique of law and delimit it. I will begin with the first component, with an exposition of Marx's program of the social critique of law, in which I will seek to recall the originality, consistency, productivity, and radicalness of this program; there can be no critical theory of law without its social critique (sections 1–2). I will then show why Marx's critical revelation of the social logic of law is insufficient, in a twofold sense: it cannot comprehend the double existence of the law in bourgeois society as private and social law (sections 3–4), and so it also cannot comprehend the political logic of law (section 5). In recent years, however, the program of a political critique of law has largely supplanted that of its social critique (in all those forms of theory that have sought to replace the critique of society with a theory of democracy). I will argue that both critical programs must be conceived in their contradictory union (section 6), because of the contradictory union of the two fundamentally different versions in which the one fundamental form of bourgeois law, the form of subjective rights, is realized (section 7).

1. THE LAW AS "DIFFERENT FORM"

In his draft for an introduction to his *Contribution to the Critique of Political Economy*, Marx sums up the program of a social critique of law in a deceptively simple figure that is intrinsically double and, indeed, self-conflicting. Marx writes that the conventional arguments for the legitimacy of the bourgeois constitutional state or state of law, which are mostly based on natural law, ultimately amount to the trivial point that "production proceeds more smoothly with modern police than, e.g., under club-law [*Faustrecht*: law of the fist]. They forget, however, that club-law too is law, and that the law of the stronger, only in a different form [*unter andrer Form*], still survives in their 'constitutional State.' "[2] The progression from club-law to the bourgeois constitutional state does nothing to change the fact that the law of the stronger persists. The bourgeois constitutional state is the law of the stronger "in a different form." In other words, the legal relations of equal recognition are the social relations of domination, oppression, exploitation, and violence in a different form.

So the form of the bourgeois constitutional state is "different" not only in the historical sense—it not only differs from the older club-law—but also in a structural sense: it is "different" vis-à-vis its own content. The "form" and "content" of law, as Marx emphasizes on several occasions,[3] differ; they correspond to each other only in the sense that they conflict with each other. The law contradicts itself, yet it does so not because it possesses a normative content that, unfortunately, is not (yet) entirely realized but because it has its material basis as well as its content in social domination, and a "form" that is "different" vis-à-vis this basis and content: the form of relations of equal recognition. The social logic of law is a double logic: the content of law is social domination, while the law is at once the inversion of this social content into a different form.

With this claim, Marx, on the one hand, assigns the law to the field of ideology; it makes social relations of domination appear as relations of legal equality. On the other hand, law is the "condition of the existence" of social domination.[4] Social domination requires the different form of law not just because it seeks to conceal itself. Rather, it *functions* only *by virtue of* the form of law. It is not just the ideology but the *reality* of legal relations of equal recognition that is required for relations of social domination and oppression to exist. The law serves a "necessary function" for social domination, and so has a "necessary presence."[5] The inversion into the "different form" of law enables social domination in a twofold way: it both conceals *and* engenders it. The law is necessary and semblance—necessary semblance.

2. BOURGEOIS PRIVATE LAW AND CAPITALISM

Marx's critical hypothesis of the law as the inversion of social domination into a "different form" concerns a historically as well as a socially specific object and scene. The *object* of this hypothesis is bourgeois private law; the *scene* of the inversion of social domination into legal equality is the interrelation between the capitalist mode of production and the contractual relations of exchange in the sphere of circulation.

Bourgeois private law is the only legal formation Marx analyzed and criticized. That is because, for Marx, bourgeois private law is the only functionally necessary legal formation of bourgeois society. So the law that comes into consideration for Marx, the student of Friedrich Savigny and G. W. F. Hegel, is "modern Roman law" (Savigny) or "abstract law" (Hegel). Marx shared Savigny's and Hegel's conviction that the Roman law of antiquity provided the model for the modern development of this legal formation by defining the legal person by his or her ability to acquire through exchange. Yet bourgeois private law, Marx further recapitulates his teachers, reframes the Roman concept of the legal person in such a way that it comes to express "exactly the opposite" of the classical legal idea, which was based not only on the inequality between freemen and serfs but also on the premise that the exercise of rights is regulated by a shared ethos.[6] Bourgeois private law reinterprets the figures of Roman law, which turn on the contracting person, as media of the equal freedom to engage in the arbitrary acquisition and disposal of things. The bourgeois revolutions claim this freedom of arbitrary disposal to be equally enjoyed by all citizens and guaranteed by private law as an inalienable human or basic right vis-à-vis the politically constituted commonwealth (the "state").

There can thus be no social relation in bourgeois society that would not meet this condition. As a society constituted by private law, bourgeois society is the realm of freedom and equality. These principles apply no less to its basic economic transaction: the purchase and sale of labor power as a commodity. Considered in terms of private law, the sale of the commodity of labor power is not special in any way. It is a transaction in which equal freemen trade their commodity, exchanging it with other equal freemen for the commodity the latter offer, or the sum of money corresponding to its value. In so doing, as in any contractual act of exchange, they abstract from the use value the commodity being exchanged has for either of them. The realization of equal freedom in exchange is premised on the "indifference" of this use value.[7]

Marx's central argument homes in on this point by insisting that the use value of the commodity of labor power the capitalist purchases is of a particular nature. Crucially, the capitalist, in legally purchasing the commodity of labor power, also acquires, as in the purchase of any commodity, the right to the use of this commodity; that is part of the meaning of the contractual acquisition of property as defined by private law. Yet the use of the commodity of labor power is qualitatively distinct from that of other commodities. The use of labor power consists in the exercise of that power, which is to say, in labor. So, if the purchase of the commodity of labor power includes the right to its use, this implies the right to use its use: one person's right to the other person's exercise of his labor power. This severs the right to use from the execution of that use. The laborer uses his labor power by working, and the capitalist who has bought his labor power has the right to this use (or more precisely, a right to the use of this use).

The purchase of the commodity of labor power, in other words, is the acquisition of a peculiar commodity because it implies the acquisition of a right *over* the person who is solely capable of exercising this labor power. The purchase of the commodity of labor power establishes a right to domination of the laborer. The equal freedom enjoyed by both sides in the exchange of the commodity of labor power, guaranteed by bourgeois private law, is thus revealed to be merely a "surface process, beneath which, however, in the depths, entirely different processes go on, in which this apparent individual equality and liberty disappear"[8]—processes of *unilateral* appropriation, of the domination and exploitation of one party by the other. As labor power becomes a commodity that can be exchanged in accordance with the rules of private law, like any other commodity, and then freely used at the purchaser's discretion, bourgeois private law turns from a normative order of equal freedom into a mechanism that serves both to conceal and to enable social domination.

Thus, the dialectical nexus between circulation (where legal equality and freedom prevail) and production (in which one class rules over the other) has two implications. First, there is no capitalist production, and hence no capitalist domination, without legal equality and freedom in the purchase and sale of labor power.[9] Second, when labor power becomes a commodity, the equality and freedom of bourgeois private law engender the relations of domination in capitalist production.

3. BOURGEOIS PRIVATE LAW AND "SOCIALIST BASIC RIGHTS"

Bourgeois private law is not merely the particular object for which Marx elaborated his hypothesis regarding the social logic of law in bourgeois society; it is the only such object. Marx's hypothesis regarding the law of bourgeois society is that it is bourgeois private law because only bourgeois private law constitutes the "different form" of the capitalist relations of production.

This claim follows from the conjunction of two premises; the first is a conceptual premise, while the second is an empirical one. According to the first premise, there is no law whose purpose is not to enable social domination; according to the second premise, the forms of social domination in bourgeois society are rooted in the capitalist relations of production. Therefore, bourgeois law can only be one whose purpose is to enable the capitalist relations of production. This law, Marx argues (as noted in section 2), is bourgeois property and contractual law; bourgeois society neither needs nor has room for more law.

Yet the hypothesis concerning the law of bourgeois society, which follows necessarily from the two premises of Marx's theory, is incorrect. The law of bourgeois society is not only bourgeois private law. Rather, the law of bourgeois society is always already codetermined by a second, coequal legal concept: the concept of "social rights" or, more properly, of "social law." The term "social law" indicates that this is not merely another class of rights than those of bourgeois private law but also is a different conception of law vis-à-vis (and *antagonistic to*) bourgeois private law. Bourgeois society knows two equiprimordial and fundamentally different legal formations: private and social law. Both legal formations are conceptions of the basic bourgeois idea of equal legal freedom, which they interpret in opposite ways: as the equality of owners of (private) property enjoying the freedom to use and dispose of their property, and as the equality of (social) participants enjoying the freedom to develop and exercise their abilities.

In his reflections on the law of bourgeois society, Marx systematically misapprehended the reality and logic of social law. That is not because Marx did not yet know the social law of bourgeois society, let alone because he could not have known it. On the contrary, social law as the equal right to free participation develops concurrently with bourgeois society and constitutes a central element of the "state of the understanding" (*Verstandesstaat*, from Hegel) or "state of providence" (*l'état providence*, from François Ewald), which begins to emerge in the eighteenth century. Such a state undertakes not only to administer (private law) justice but also to comprehensively secure the *"possibility of sharing* in the universal assets" of bourgeois society.[10] This initially "authoritarian" conception of social law becomes a point of reference for "progressive" demands as the socialists, from François-Noël Babeuf and Pierre-Joseph Proudhon to Ferdinand Lassalle and the German social democrats, take up the idea of human rights, and (as Engels and Karl Kautsky summarize the matter in 1887, in their critique of this interpretation of social law) develop them into "socialist basic rights."[11] In the welfare state of the twentieth century, some of these socialist legal demands eventually became a defining legal reality.

Marx dismissed the socialist conception of social law, and rights, as the "foolishness of those socialists."[12] According to the reading of Marx's critical theory of law that I have sketched, this is not just a political or strategic claim. It follows consistently from the two premises of Marx's argument. Marx calls the socialist idea of social law "foolish" because it runs counter to the conditions required for a discourse of "law" to be meaningful. The social logic of law consists in its being the "different form" of social domination. Social domination is defined by the relations of production. The idea of a law that, like social law, does *not* relate to the social domination defined by the relations of production—whether in authoritarian or socialistic fashion, whether it expresses, enables, or seeks to change these relations—is meaningless and so is indeed "foolish."

As Marx's dismissal of the socialist conception of social law is not a political/strategic question, neither is the rejection of this claim. It is a matter, first and foremost, of legal theory; it concerns the question of how the law of bourgeois society must be *understood*. In the following, I will sketch the counterhypothesis to Marx's, that, if private law has a "necessary presence" in bourgeois society, due to its "necessary function" (in the words of Étienne Balibar) for this society, so does social law.[13] I am thus interested here not in the question of the legitimacy of social law, not in its justice, but in its necessity, which is to say, in its functionality for the form of social domination that constitutes bourgeois society. Furthermore, I am interested in the consequences that the insight into the existence of social law has for our understanding of the structure and functioning of law in modern, bourgeois society in general.

4. SOCIAL LAW AND NORMALIZATION

According to Marx's methodological premise, all law is a "different form" of domination. It is obvious—and this is why Marx dismisses its idea and thus existence—that social law is not a different form of the specifically capitalist form of domination. If social law, too, is a different form of social relations of domination, these relations are not economically determined relations of production. To understand the social relations of domination that find their expression in social law, we may look to that legal formation itself. The idea of social law does not at all consist, as Marx and Engels's critique of the socialist-progressive reframing of the idea of social law maintains, in the demand for an equal distribution of the means of consumption. Its pretensions go much further and, more importantly, are fundamentally different *in kind*, as even the form in which it was articulated by its nineteenth-century proponents makes plain. As socialist demands for rights to, say, education (which Marx also mentions) or labor regulations show, social law has never been only about equal distribution; it is about the ability to participate equally in social life. Social law proclaims the right to (a social) life or, as the programmatic writings of (neo-)Kantian socialism put it, the "right to existence."[14] In short, social law is concerned with relations of social *participation*—including relations of social discipline, formation, and normalization, without which there is no social participation. The relations of domination, of which social law must be understood as a "different form," are relations of participation.

Michel Foucault's interpretation of the socialist demand for a right to participation, a right for "existence" or "life," can help us describe social law in this perspective:

> Since the last century, the great struggles that have challenged the general system of power were not guided by the belief in a return to former rights, or by the age-old dream of a cycle of time or a Golden Age. One no longer aspired toward the coming of the emperor of the poor, or the kingdom of the latter days, or even the restoration of our imagined ancestral rights; what was demanded and what served as an objective was life, understood as the basic needs, man's concrete essence, the realization of his potential, a plenitude of the possible ... The "right" to life, to one's body, to health, to happiness, to the satisfaction of needs, and beyond all the oppressions of "alienation," the "right" to rediscover what one is and all that one can be, this "right"—which the classical juridical system was utterly incapable of comprehending—was the political response to all these new procedures of power which did not derive, either, from the traditional right of sovereignty.[15]

The final sentence of this analysis reframes Marx's program of the social critique of law, of revealing its social logic. It links the new category of social law—the right to social participation, to social existence or life—to the "new procedures of power" that have evolved since the eighteenth century, procedures Foucault describes as normalization. These procedures of power aim to ensure and enhance the possibilities of social life, to engender, organize, and promote participation in social processes. This normalizing form of social domination is distinct from—not antagonistic to—the capitalist form, not least importantly in that it is essentially in the purview of the state. Normalizing domination concerns the relation between the state and the populace, not the relation between owners of private property, governed by private law, or the socioeconomic relation between the classes. The normalizing form of social domination consists in defining and enforcing the conditions of social participation.

So, the fact that the social rights demanded by socialists are, as Foucault puts it, the "political response" to this formation of social domination does not imply that they attack it from outside, from a conceptually and normatively independent basis. The social rights demanded by socialists (and, a fortiori, their realization in the welfare state) quite emphatically relate to this new formation of social domination as what Marx would have called its "different form." Social rights *express* the social domination of normalization in the legal formation of equal recognition—and, in expressing it, make it possible in the first place. The domination of normalization is realized *through* the demands of equality, supported by social law, of those who are subjected to this domination. This means that what Marx showed for the relation between private law and the capitalist mode of production is also true of the relation between social law and normalization: the "different form" of social rights is the "condition of the existence" (according to Nicos Poulantzas) of normalizing domination—just as private law is the condition of the existence of capitalist domination. The critical revelation of the social logic of social law consists in the demonstration that—regardless of whether that social law is enforced by authoritarian power, called for by socialists, or realized in the welfare state—it is the "mere semblance" of normalization.

5. THE STRUGGLE FOR LAW

Marx writes that the idea of a social law that is distinct from bourgeois private law, and, indeed, its (authoritarian or critical) antagonist, is "foolish" because it cannot have any social function. By implication, he disputes its practical role in the class struggle as well. When workers fighting over the length of the workday invoke their "right," Marx argues, they, too, understand this "right" in the sense it has in bourgeois private law. The struggle between the classes over the normalization of the workday pits "right against right, *both equally* bearing the seal of the law of exchanges"[16]—in other words, it pits the title under private law of the owner of the commodity of labor power against the title under private law of the owner of the means of production.

Empirically, this interpretation—that the struggle between the classes is waged solely in the conceptual framework of bourgeois private law—is hardly persuasive. The counterhypothesis concerning the "presence" and "function" of social law in bourgeois society, sketched in the preceding section, enables us to abandon this interpretation as well. What my counterhypothesis proposes, instead, is that we interpret the struggle of "right against right" between workers and capitalists as being also a "struggle *for* law,"[17] a struggle over how to understand the *concept* of law—a struggle of the socialist legal idea of equal participation against the bourgeois legal idea of equal ownership. It is this struggle for law—between the bourgeois-liberal legal idea and one that is now authoritarian, now socialist, between private and social law—that constitutes the reality of law in bourgeois society. The law in bourgeois society is not just the "different form" of social domination but the object, medium, and scene of a struggle, of antagonistic relations of power.

We begin to recognize the consequence that the insight into the positive existence of social law, and hence into the double formation of law in bourgeois society as both private *and* social law, has for the conceptual premise of Marx's legal theory. This premise consists in the hypothesis of the "social logic" of law. It asserts that the law is *defined* by the fact that it is the "different form" of social domination; it is the social logic of the legal form that has relations of social domination as its content. The struggle between private and social law that is the reality of law in bourgeois society shows that we must speak of "laws" rather than a single "law," and it shows, moreover, that each legal formation not only corresponds to social domination but also is antithetical to—wages a struggle against—the other. If this relation of struggle is constitutive of law, then it is in this regard at once also subject to a logic other than the logic of the social;

it is subject to a *political* logic (since political logic concerns relations of struggle or power).

The central theorem of Marx's theory of law is that social domination generates legal equality as its "different form," so that legal equality enables or expresses social domination. Contrary to appearances, this theorem is not implicitly a form of reductionism; it does not deny the normative content of law. On the contrary, it is only the normative content of law that makes social domination possible.

Yet normative content does not come into being of itself. Normative content is generated in acts and processes; specific normative contents flow from acts of normative determination. Being generated in such acts, particular normative contents may change, divide, combat, overlap, rewrite one another. The "development" of normative content is "the succession of the more or less far-reaching, more or less independent processes of overpowering which affect it—including also in each case the resistance marshaled against these processes, the changes of form attempted with a view to defense and reaction, and the results of these successful counteractions. The form is fluid, but the 'meaning' even more so."[18]

This brings the problem of Marx's social theory of law to the fore: it can refer only to *specific*, already determinate and fixed legal content and must accordingly both presuppose the conclusion of the process of the determining generation of that content and abstract from the process of its ongoing redetermination. The social logic of law applies only to definable, which is to say, to ahistorical,[19] or more precisely, to apolitical law. This is the constraint that limits the conceptual premise in which Marx's legal theory frames the hypothesis of the social logic of law: it can address the law only as independent or *dissociated* from the political process in which it is engendered and subject to change.

6. THE CIRCLE OF LAW IN BOURGEOIS SOCIETY

What are the consequences of this methodological critique of Marx's social theory of law for the critical examination of the law of bourgeois society? This law, I have argued (see section 3), exists in twofold form, as social and as private law. Following the methodology of Marx's social critique of law, but going beyond the limitations of his own realization of this method, we can say that each of these two kinds of law is the "different form" of each of two kinds of social domination in bourgeois societies: social domination in capitalist production and social domination in normalization by the welfare state. At the same time, each kind of law is political in having been made. Moreover, their relation is political, as a relation of struggle—a struggle for (about) law. This political logic of law is structurally different from its social logic (the functionality of its normative content for social domination). At the same time, the critical insight into the social logic of law plays a fundamental role in the political struggle between the two basic forms of bourgeois law.

The relation between the two legal formations in bourgeois society is defined by the fact that their political struggle manifests itself as a mutual critique in which each reveals the social logic of the other. Private law criticizes social law as the "different form" of normalizing domination; social law criticizes private law as the "different form" of capitalist domination. Both legal formations of bourgeois society are not only functional for domination, each the "different form" of a formation of social domination—private law for capitalist, social law for normalizing domination. They also are functional in such fashion that they are at once also *critical* of domination; each is the critique of the other formation of social domination.

In the arguments proffered in the struggle for law to vindicate private as well as social law, each side avers that the other side's legal equality is revealed, in the process of critical experience, to be the mere semblance of social domination—that it undergoes a dialectical reversal into domination. Both legal formations are subject to the same dialectical reversal of the critique of domination into functionality for domination. Private law critiques normalizing domination in the name of individuality and undergoes reversal into the privatization of the basic means of production; social law critiques capitalist domination in the name of social participation and undergoes reversal into the normalization of the basic conditions of life (see figure 6.1). The reversal of law into domination, then, is here no longer observed by a critical theorist standing outside the law; it is an observation asserted in the *struggle* (between the classes and ideological camps) for law. The social critique of law, the critical revelation of its so-

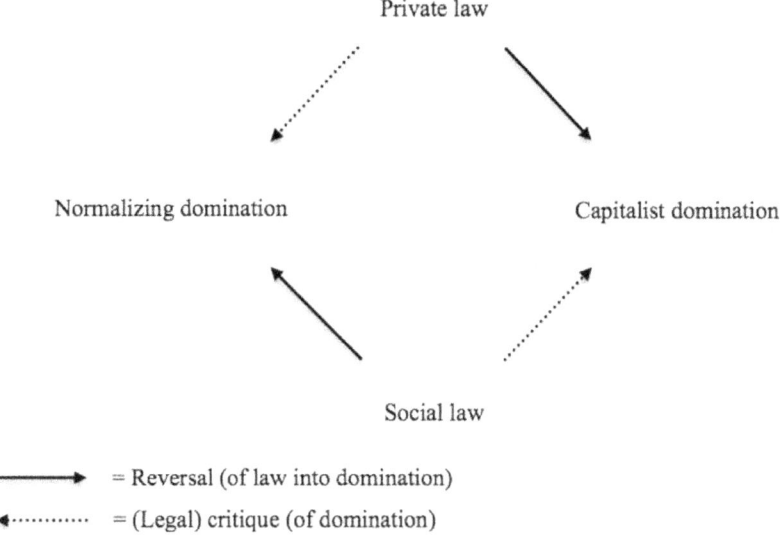

FIGURE 6.1. The struggle for law in bourgeois society.

cial logic, is a strategy in the political struggle for power, as both sides seek to vindicate themselves in this struggle by invoking the dialectical reversal into domination of the other, opposing, legal formation.

7. THE DIALECTICAL UNITY OF BOURGEOIS LAW

The claim of the preceding argument is that the critique of law that reveals its social logic as the "different form" of domination is already implicit in (and thus complicit with) the struggle that defines the existence of law in bourgeois society. In this way, the critique of law is limited. It can only look from one side at the other; it can only take sides *in* the struggle of bourgeois law and thus remains unable to understand the internal entanglement of the opposite legal formations, which reproduce themselves precisely by struggling against each other. Marx distinguishes this internal and thus limited form of critique from a "truly philosophical critique," which "not only shows the contradictions as existing, but explains them, grasps their genesis and necessity." True critique is genealogical: it "shows the internal genesis . . . It describes the act of [the] birth [of its object]."[20] True critique reveals the necessity that binds the two opposite formations of bourgeois law together by revealing the common ground of the two conceptions of bourgeois law that charge each other with reverting into social domination. True critique is genealogical in leading these opposite legal formations back to their ground.

This ground is the new basic form of bourgeois law; it is the form of subjective rights. The turn to the form of subjective rights, as the basic form of bourgeois law, thus allows us to offer *one* answer to the question concerning *both* legal formations; it enables us to conceive the unity of bourgeois law behind or beneath the struggle between its formations.

Max Weber has defined the basic purpose of subjective rights as the "empowerment" of the subject.[21] Subjective rights subjectivate; they confer power, and to have power means to be able to do something or to be a subject. Weber explains this subjectivating empowerment conferred by rights as giving a subject the power to engage, or fail to engage, in certain conduct, as it pleases. This is the specific innovation of the bourgeois form of subjective rights. They are rights to the subject's own willing, and actions without "interference," which is to say, unhampered—not only, and not even primarily, by the intervention of some other; this was already the traditional function of rights. Rather, subjective rights in the specifically modern or bourgeois sense empower the subject to will and act beyond the interference, also, of the Other, unrestricted by any ethical, political, or legal regulations.

Furthermore, unlike in the theories of private law since Thomas Hobbes, Weber conceives of such empowerment not just in a negative sense—that *nothing specific* is prescribed in certain respects and domains. Rather, Weber conceives the permission of private law in positive terms, as the acquisition of an ability. That I have rights does not just mean that I am unimpeded and permitted to do as I please; instead, rights, by permitting, *give* me the ability or power to do as I please in the first place. To conceive of rights as empowerment is to understand what law entitles me to do—to do as I please—as the exercise of a faculty or power that I only have *by virtue* of my rights. This faculty engendered by law is the will of the individual: subjective rights empower the subject to have its own will.

Empowerment by subjective rights means *empowerment of the subject's own* or *empowerment of the subject to have its own*—the constitution of the unethical, apolitical, nonmoral private will of the individual. The empowerment of subjective rights engenders a new subject: the subject of "its own will [*Eigenwille*]." This is the sense in which subjective rights can be said to implement a proprietary logic; the subjective right is "*ius proprium*."[22]

This fundamental trait of subjective rights has two implications. First of all, it allows us to trace back the two different shapes of subjective rights—the rights of private law and of social law—to one single source; this source or ground is the bourgeois empowerment of the subject's "own will" (A). Second, in accordance with Marx's idea of genealogical critique, by tracing back the formations of bourgeois law to their ground, we also can identify the error that they share (B).

A. THE DUALISM OF SUBJECTIVE RIGHTS

The form of subjective rights exists only as intrinsically double and divided within itself. The exemplary manifestation of this dualism is the bourgeois concept of private property. The traditional definition of private property is that the owner is entitled, to the exclusion of all others, to determine the use he or she will make of the property. Bourgeois private property lends a radically new meaning to the privacy of decision making; it is the exercise of the individual subject's own will. Thus, the basic liberal definition of bourgeois private property is that it is the "province of the independent mastery of the individual will."[23] Bourgeois private property is the *private sphere* in which the subject can decide "without interference" and solely according to its own will. Unauthorized infringement of my property by another is thus no longer merely an encroachment on my power (*dominium*) but now a violation of myself (or my self); it is something that "would injure [*lädieren*] me."[24]

This bourgeois redefinition of property implies a radical transformation of society. It "release[s] the individual property right from the limitations of the law of nature"[25] by unshackling it from all limitations—except for other property. The proprietary principle of bourgeois property—its conception as *ius proprium*—undoes the constraints limiting the possessive power of disposal. On the one hand, this has implications for the question of what can become property. Quite simply, anything that can fall within the private "province of the independent mastery of the individual will." This makes bourgeois property the juridical instrument for the expansion of the category of the commodity to include labor, land, and money, which marks the inception of bourgeois society.[26] On the other hand, the proprietary unshackling affects ways in which the subject can dispose of its property. It can do so, quite simply, in any way it pleases—including, in particular, by allowing others to make use of its property in a quid pro quo arrangement. The very exclusion of the other from the decision concerning the subject's own property "internalizes" him into the province of the private property owner's mastery; it effects an "absorption of his 'sphere of rights' into the sphere of property." Bourgeois property enables the subject to use its power of exclusive disposal in order to exercise "inclusive domination" over others.[27]

The formal structure of bourgeois property is this: protection and security for the subject's own will. In the formation I have considered until now, these protections are provided by the warranty of a private sphere within which the subject freely disposes of its own. This presupposes an understanding of the subject's will as discretion: the legal warranty of a private sphere secures the subject's own will *as discretion*. Discretion is the ability or power of will to set itself objectives as it pleases. It does so by making a choice. Exercising its discretion, the subject sets itself objectives by choosing among the different impulses it finds within itself and thus "incorporat[ing]" them "into [its] maxims."[28] By power of its discretion, the subject *confers* on an impulse the form of a maxim, an objective it does not have but has set itself.

But subjects do not merely choose objectives; to will these objectives is to will their realization. To this end, they select appropriate means as the conditions of the realization of their objectives. To choose objectives is to will means, and to will means is to assess or evaluate them. This evaluative attention to means constitutes the subject's "interests": interests are interests in abilities, expedients, or resources. Thus, if discretion is the willing of objectives, interest is the willing of means. The subject's own will is both: choice and evaluation, discretion and interest, the willing of objectives and of means. That is why, furthermore, the bourgeois property that secures the subject's own will takes not only the form of an own or private *sphere* but also the form of own or private *assets*. Property as the private sphere secures the exercise of discretion; in its private sphere, the subject is free to choose objectives as it pleases. Property as the subject's own asset, by contrast, secures the subject's interests, its will to have abilities, resources, expedients. Contrary to the ideology of liberal private law, the subject of subjective rights cannot be reduced to its discretion. As an agent, it has interests, it wills means or resources, and this is the basis for a second formation of bourgeois property: property as asset.

The definition of property as the private sphere of arbitrary decision concerning the individual's own objectives is the foundation of liberal private law. The concept of the asset—which secures the *realization* of the individual's own will that is the object of the subject's interest—marks the first and crucial step beyond the confines of liberal private law. The second step consists in the insight that the subject's assets, contrary to what liberal ideology wishes it to believe, are of course not the subject's own. The subject, this critique of liberalism notes, has assets that are its own only by appropriating socially generated and existing assets; the subject has its "*particular* assets" only by "*sharing* in the universal assets" of society.[29] All particular assets are appropriated social assets. That is why the property right as an asset is nothing but a right to social participation or access.[30] To define property as privately appropriated social assets is to see "that the concept of property [must] be broadened—that it [must] no longer be confined to the individual right to exclude others, but be extended to include each individual's right not to be excluded from the use or benefit of things, and productive powers, that can be said to have been created by the joint efforts of the whole society."[31] Property as asset is the right to social participation, because social participation here means participation in a social asset—acquisition of individual assets through the appropriation of social assets.

Social rights to participation, too, are subjective rights founded on the subject's own private will; *that, how,* and *to which end* the subject wills assets through social participation is no less a matter of its own will than the arbitrary choice of its objectives. Social rights to participation are rights to social participation *in the subject's own interest*; social rights to participation are rights *to* private assets *by way of* social participation. That is what social participation here is about: acquiring particular assets through sharing in the universal assets. The right to social participation is no less the legalization of the fact that the subject wills this, takes an interest in this. It is not a break with the form of subjective rights but the expansion of this legal form to include social content.

The form of subjective rights, which is based on or legalizes the subject's own will, exists in two irreducible and equiprimordial formations:[32] as the legalization of discretion and of interest, the first through property as the private sphere of arbitrary decisions and the second through property as the private asset of social participation. These two formations of bourgeois (property) right are fundamentally different because they are rooted in two no less divergent conceptions of the will—as the faculty of arbitrary choice and of interested evaluation. Hence the antithetical relation, in legal practice as much as in legal policy, between the two conceptions of property. They are the parties in the "struggle for law" in bourgeois society—the struggle, in legal practice, between private and social law, and in legal policy, between liberalism and socialism (or between liberal democracy and social democracy). Yet it is precisely because the two formations of bourgeois property are rooted in different conceptions of the will as discretion and interest, as choice and evaluation, that they are not mutually exclusive in the perspective of the logic or theory of law; both are aspects of the subject's own will. That is why the struggle between the two formations of bourgeois (property) law cannot be resolved. Bourgeois law *consists* in this struggle.

B. THE EMPIRICISM, OR POSITIVISM, OF SUBJECTIVE RIGHTS

Empiricism is the "myth of the given." It ascribes unquestionable "authority" to something merely given, demanding its passive acceptance by declaring it to be the "ultimate court of appeal" for all normative questions.[33] In epistemological empiricism, what is given are sensory data; they are the noninferential basis capable of determining the truth of propositions. Similarly, bourgeois law is empiricistic or positivistic in presupposing the subject's own will as given and hence as the ultimate court of appeal. The fact that juridical empiricism invokes as its unquestionable authority is thus an act: the act of willing. Bourgeois law treats the subject's will as (or as though it were) a fact; it constructs, presupposes, and authorizes a will that "does not refer to any judgment, reasoning, or calculation."[34] The bourgeois subject, the subject of subjective rights, wills—without a view to judgment, reasoning, or grounds. The subject of rights is a subject without grounds, or more precisely, a subject whose willing, as mere fact, counts as ground, that is to say, whose willing needs no ground, no good reason, in order to legally count. The subject's own will is a category of law and hence a category of validity; the subject's own will *is valid*—without a view to whether its will has good or bad reasons, whether it is autonomous or heteronomous in its formation.

The form of subjective rights empowers the subject's own will. In the form of subjective rights, the law legalizes the pure fact that something is a subject's own will; subjective rights lend force to the fact that the subject wills something. All subjective rights presuppose this fact; it is their prerequisite. True, another step is necessary to turn this prerequisite—the individual subject's own will—into a legally binding title: the fact must be converted into a right. But, crucially, this conversion into a right does not require a transformation of the will. It is not an intrinsic conversion, a transformation of the substance, but an extrinsic one, a quantitative modification. The step from a subject's will to its right does not consist in an evaluation of the content or manner of its will. If it did, the subject would have the mere right to an ethical or autonomous will. Yet the subject's will becomes a subjective right not by virtue of the ethical quality of its content or the autonomy of its genesis but solely by virtue of its extrinsic delimitation in accordance with a universal law of equality. The equality of everyone's subjective wills is the *only* normative consideration in the evaluation—which is to say, the merely extrinsic delimitation—of each individual will. That is why the basic principle of subjective right is this: each subject's will, whatever it may be, is legitimate when it remains within the bounds drawn by the law of equality.

The thesis thus is that subjective rights operate in a mythical way. They produce a myth not in the sense of an ideological misrepresentation but, on the contrary, by effectively granting the subject's will the status of a given—something presupposed, valid in itself, beyond ethical and political evaluation, and hence also immune to ethical and political transformation. I want to suggest that this is the fundamental role that law, the law in the form of subjective rights, fulfills in bourgeois society. It is the mechanism by which the bourgeois state presupposes bourgeois society as its natural "basis."[35] The fundamental trait of the relation between "civil society and the state" is the assumption that "society . . . is already given," and so the politics of bourgeois society is "much more a naturalism than liberalism."[36] More precisely, liberalism *is* in reality a naturalism, because the form of subjective rights that liberalism makes the foundation of law lends force to the subject's own will and thus *makes* it a fact. The form of subjective rights is myth put into practice, the inversion of something that is made into a given.

NOTES

1. See also his "Critique of the Gotha Programme," where Karl Marx claims that "legal relations arise out of economic ones." Marx, "Kritik des Gothaer Programms," in *Werke*, by Karl Marx and Friedrich Engels, 43 vols. (Berlin: Dietz, 1956–90), 19:18. Translated as Marx, "Critique of the Gotha Programme" (Moscow: Progress, 1970), https://www.marxists.org/archive/marx/works/1875/gotha/ch01.htm; and Marx, *Zur Kritik der Politischen Ökonomie*, in Marx and Engels, *Werke*, 13:8. Translated by S. W. Ryazanskaya as Marx, *A Contribution to the Critique of Political Economy* (Moscow: Progress, 1970), https://www.marxists.org/archive/marx/works/1859/critique-pol-economy/preface.htm.
2. Karl Marx, "Einleitung zur Kritik der Politischen Ökonomie," in Marx and Engels, *Werke*, 13:620. Translated by S. W. Ryazanskaya as Marx, "Introduction to a Contribution to the Critique of Political Economy," in *A Contribution to the Critique of Political Economy*, appendix 1, https://www.marxists.org/archive/marx/works/1859/critique-pol-economy/appx1.htm.
3. See Karl Marx, *Das Kapital*, vol. 1, in Marx and Engels, *Werke*, 23:99 and 23:609; and Marx, *Das Kapital*, vol. 3, in Marx and Engels, *Werke*, 25:352.
4. Nicos Poulantzas, "A propos de la théorie marxiste du Droit," *Archives de philosophie du droit* 12 (1967): 145–62.
5. Étienne Balibar, "The Basic Concepts of Historical Materialism," in *Reading Capital*, by Louis Althusser and Étienne Balibar, trans. Ben Brewster (New York: New Left Books, 1970), https://www.marxists.org/reference/archive/althusser/1968/reading-capital.
6. Karl Marx, *Grundrisse der Kritik der Politischen Ökonomie 1857–1858*, 2nd ed. (Berlin: Dietz, 1974), 156. Translated by Martin Nicolaus as *Grundrisse: Foundations of the Critique of Political Economy (Rough Draft)* (New York: Penguin Books, 1973), https://www.marxists.org/archive/marx/works/1857/grundrisse/ch05.htm.
7. "Thus indifference and equal worthiness are expressly contained in the form of the thing. The particular natural difference which was contained in the commodity is extinguished, and constantly becomes extinguished by circulation." Marx, *Grundrisse*, 158.

8. Marx, *Grundrisse*, 159; translation modified.
9. See Oskar Negt, "10 Thesen zur marxistischen Rechtstheorie," in *Probleme der marxistischen Rechtstheorie*, ed. Hubert Rottleuthner (Frankfurt: Suhrkamp, 1975), 46–54.
10. Georg Wilhelm Friedrich Hegel, *Elements of the Philosophy of Right*, ed. Allen W. Wood, trans. H. B. Nisbet (Cambridge: Cambridge University Press, 1991), § 200, 233; translation modified.
11. Friedrich Engels and Karl Kautsky, "Juristensozialismus," in *Marxistische und sozialistische Rechtstheorie*, ed. Norbert Reich (Frankfurt: Athenäum, 1972), 58. The idea of equal social participation is already an essential element of the French declarations of human rights in their Jacobin version. See Maximilien Robespierre, "Draft Declaration of the Rights of Man and of the Citizen," in *Robespierre: Virtue and Terror*, ed. Slavoj Žižek (New York: Verso, 2007), 66–72.
12. Marx, *Grundrisse*, 160. In this instance, Marx's scorn is directed at Pierre-Joseph Proudhon.
13. Étienne Balibar, "Basic Concepts of Historical Materialism."
14. Quoted in Engels and Kautsky, "Juristensozialismus," 58. See the texts collected in Hans Jörg Sandkühler and Rafael de la Vega, eds., *Marxismus und Ethik: Texte zum neukantianischen Sozialismus* (Frankfurt: Suhrkamp, 1974). The clearest articulation of this idea by a contemporary writer can be found in Amartya Sen, *Inequality Reexamined* (Cambridge, MA: Harvard University Press, 1992).
15. Michel Foucault, *The History of Sexuality*, vol. 1, *An Introduction*, trans. Robert Hurley (New York: Knopf Doubleday, 1986), 144–45. For the following, see also the suggestions on the paradox of juridification in the welfare state in Jürgen Habermas, *Theorie des kommunikativen Handelns*, vol. 2 (Frankfurt: Suhrkamp, 1981), 522–47.
16. Marx, *Das Kapital*, vol. 1, 249; my emphasis. Marx's analyses of revolutionary movements like the Paris Commune, however, deviate from this rigorous explication of his legal-theoretical premises in *Capital*.
17. Rudolf von Ihering, *The Struggle for Law*, trans. John J. Lalor (Chicago: Callaghan, 1915).
18. Friedrich Nietzsche, *On the Genealogy of Morals*, trans. Douglas Smith (Oxford: Oxford University Press: 1996), II.12, 58.
19. "Only that which is without history can be defined." Nietzsche, *On the Genealogy of Morals*, II.13, 60.
20. Karl Marx, *Critique of Hegel's "Philosophy of Right,"* ed. Joseph O'Malley, trans. Annette Jolin and Joseph O'Malley (Cambridge: Cambridge University Press, 1977), 92; translation modified.
21. Max Weber, *Economy and Society: An Outline of Interpretive Sociology*, ed. Guenther Roth and Claus Wittich (Berkeley: University of California Press, 1978), 667.
22. Roberto Esposito, *Immunitas: The Protection and Negation of Life*, trans. Zakiya Hanafi (Cambridge: Polity, 2011), 21–28.
23. Friedrich Karl von Savigny, *System of the Modern Roman Law*, vol. 1, trans. William Holloway (Madras: J. Higginbotham, 1867), 271.

24. Immanuel Kant, *The Metaphysics of Morals*, ed. and trans. Mary Gregor (Cambridge: Cambridge University Press, 1996), 37; translation modified.
25. C. B. Macpherson, "Locke on Capitalist Appropriation," *The Western Political Quarterly* 4, no. 4 (December 1951): 550–66.
26. Karl Polanyi, *The Great Transformation: The Political and Economic Origins of Our Time*, 2nd ed. (Boston: Beacon, 2001), 68–76.
27. Ulrich K. Preuß, *Die Internalisierung des Subjekts: Zur Kritik der Funktionsweise des subjektiven Rechts* (Frankfurt: Suhrkamp, 1979), 43.
28. Immanuel Kant, *Religion Within the Boundaries of Mere Reason, and Other Writings*, ed. Allen Wood and George di Giovanni (Cambridge: Cambridge University Press, 1998), 65.
29. Hegel, *Philosophy of Right*, § 200, 233; translation modified.
30. Étienne Balibar, " 'Possessive Individualism' Reversed: From Locke to Derrida," *Constellations* 9, no. 3 (2002): 299–317.
31. C. B. Macpherson, *Democratic Theory: Essays in Retrieval* (Oxford: Clarendon, 1973), 136.
32. The formation that the classical periodizing schema of Thomas H. Marshall or the typological schema of Georg Jellinek list as the final in a series of three formations—political rights—is actually located on a different categorical plane; it concerns the act that engenders the (form of) rights.
33. Wilfried Sellars, *Empiricism and the Philosophy of Mind* (Cambridge, MA: Harvard University Press, 1997), 68–79; for "authority," see 71.
34. Foucault, *The Birth of Biopolitics: Lectures at the Collège de France, 1978–79*, ed. Michel Senellart, trans. Graham Burchell (New York: Palgrave Macmillan, 2008), 272.
35. Marx, "Zur Judenfrage," in Marx and Engels, *Werke*, vol. 1, 369.
36. Foucault, *Birth of Biopolitics*, 61, 309.

IV

CRITICIZING CAPITALISM

7

BEHIND MARX'S HIDDEN ABODE: FOR AN EXPANDED CONCEPTION OF CAPITALISM

NANCY FRASER

Capitalism is back! After decades in which the term could scarcely be found outside the writings of Marxian thinkers, commentators of varying stripes now worry openly about its sustainability, scholars from every school scramble to systematize criticisms of it, and activists throughout the world mobilize in opposition to its practices. Certainly, the return of "capitalism" is a welcome development, a crystal clear marker, if any were needed, of the depth of the present crisis—and of the pervasive hunger for a systematic account of it. What all the talk about capitalism indicates, symptomatically, is a growing intuition that the heterogeneous ills that surround us—financial, economic, ecological, political, and social—can be traced to a common root, and that reforms that fail to engage with the deep structural underpinnings of these ills are doomed to fail. Equally, the term's renaissance signals the wish in many quarters for an analysis that could clarify the relations among the disparate social struggles of our time, and that could foster the close cooperation, if not the full unification, of their most advanced, progressive currents in a countersystemic bloc. The hunch that capitalism could supply the central category of such an analysis is on the mark.

Nevertheless, the current boom in capitalism talk remains largely rhetorical—more a symptom of the desire for systematic critique than a substantive contribution to it. Thanks to decades of social amnesia, whole generations of younger activists and scholars have become sophisticated practitioners of discourse analysis while remaining utterly innocent of the traditions of *Kapitalkritik*. They are only now beginning to ask how it could be practiced today to clarify the current conjuncture. Their "elders," veterans of previous eras of anticapitalist ferment who might have provided some guidance, are burdened with blinders of their own. They have largely failed, despite professed good intentions, to incorporate the insights of feminism, postcolonialism, and ecological thought systematically into their understandings of capitalism.

The upshot is that we are living through a capitalist crisis of great severity without a critical theory that could adequately clarify it. Certainly, today's crisis does not fit the standard models that we have inherited. It is multidimensional, encompassing not only the official economy, including finance, but also such "noneconomic" phenomena as global warming, "care deficits," and the hollowing out of public power at every scale. Yet our received models of crisis tend to focus exclusively on the economic aspects, which they isolate from, and privilege over, the other factors. Equally important, today's crisis is generating novel political configurations and grammars of social conflict. Struggles over nature, social reproduction, and public power are central to this constellation, implicating multiple axes of inequality, including nationality/race-ethnicity, religion, sexuality, and class. In this respect, too, however, our received theoretical models fail us, as they continue to privilege labor struggles at the point of production.

In general, then, we lack conceptions of capitalism and capitalist crisis that are adequate to our time. My objective in this essay is to suggest a path that could remedy this lacuna. The path leads through the thought of Karl Marx, whose understanding of capitalism I propose to reexamine with that aim in mind. Marx's thought has much to offer in the way of general conceptual resources, and it is, in principle, open to these broader concerns. Yet it fails to reckon systematically with gender, ecology, and political power as structuring principles and axes of inequality in capitalist societies—let alone as stakes and premises of social struggle. Thus, its best insights need to be reconstructed from these perspectives. My strategy, then, is to look first at Marx, and then to look *behind* him, in the hope of shedding some new light on some old questions: What exactly is capitalism? How is it best conceptualized? Should we think of it as an economic system, a form of ethical life, or an institutionalized social order? How should we characterize its "crisis tendencies," and where should we locate them?

DEFINING FEATURES

To address these questions, I shall begin by recalling what Marx took to be capitalism's four core features. Thus, my approach will appear at first sight to be very orthodox, but I intend to "deorthodoxize" it by showing how these presuppose other features, which in fact constitute their background conditions of possibility. Whereas Marx looked behind the sphere of exchange, into the "hidden abode" of production, in order to discover capitalism's secrets, I shall seek production's conditions of possibility behind that sphere, in realms that are more hidden still. For Marx, the first defining feature of capitalism is private property in the means of production, which presupposes a class division between the owners and the producers. This division arises as a result of the breakup of a previous social world in which most people, however differently situated, had access to the means of subsistence and means of production—access, in other words, to food, shelter, and clothing, and to tools, land, and work—without having to go through labor markets. Capitalism decisively overturned such arrangements. It enclosed the commons, abrogated the customary use rights of the majority, and transformed shared resources into the private property of a small minority.

This leads directly to Marx's second core feature, the free labor market, because the others—that is, the vast majority—now have to go through a very peculiar song and dance in order to work and get what they need to continue living and to raise their children. It is worth stressing just how bizarre, how "unnatural," how historically anomalous and specific this free labor market institution is. Labor is "free" here in a double sense. First, it is free in terms of legal status—not enslaved, enserfed, entailed, or otherwise bound to a given place or particular master, and hence mobile and able to enter into a labor contract. But second, it also is free from access to means of subsistence and means of production, including from customary use rights in land and tools, and hence bereft of the resources and entitlements that could permit one to abstain from the labor market.

Next is the equally strange song and dance of self-expanding value, which is Marx's third core feature. Capitalism is peculiar in having an objective systemic thrust or directionality, namely, the accumulation of capital. In principle, accordingly, everything the owners do qua capitalists is aimed at expanding their capital. Like the producers, they, too, stand under a peculiar systemic compulsion. And everyone's efforts to satisfy their needs are indirect, harnessed to something else that assumes priority—an overriding imperative inscribed in an impersonal system, capital's own drive to unending self-expansion. Marx is brilliant on this point. In a capitalist society, he says, capital itself becomes the subject. Human beings are its pawns, reduced to figuring out how they can get what they need in the interstices, by feeding the beast.

The fourth feature specifies the distinctive role of markets in capitalist society. Markets have existed throughout human history, including in noncapitalist societies. Their functioning under capitalism, however, is distinguished by two further characteristics. First, markets serve in capitalist society to allocate the major inputs to commodity production. Understood by bourgeois political economy as "factors of production," these inputs were originally identified as land, labor, and capital. In addition to utilizing markets to allocate labor, capitalism also uses them to allocate real estate, capital goods, raw materials, and credit. Insofar as it allocates these productive inputs through market mechanisms, capitalism transforms them into commodities. It is, in Piero Sraffa's arresting phrase, a system for the "production of commodities by means of commodities," albeit one that also relies, as we shall see, on a background of noncommodities.[1]

But there is also a second key function that markets assume in a capitalist society: they determine how society's *surplus* will be invested. By surplus, Marx meant the collective fund of social energies exceeding those required to reproduce a given form of life and to replenish what is used up in the course of living it. How a society uses its surplus capacities is absolutely central, raising fundamental questions about how people want to live—where they choose to invest their collective energies, how they propose to balance "productive work" vis-à-vis family life, leisure, and other activities—as well as how they aspire to relate to nonhuman nature and what they aim to leave to future generations. Capitalist societies tend to leave such decisions to "market forces." This is perhaps their most consequential and perverse characteristic, this handing over of the most important matters to an apparatus for reckoning monetized value. It is closely related to our third core feature, capital's inherent but blind directionality, the self-expansionary process through which it constitutes itself as the subject of history, displacing the human beings who have made it and turning them into its servants.

By stressing these two roles of markets, I aim to counter the widely held view that capitalism propels the ever-increasing commodification of life as such. That view leads down a blind alley, I think, to dystopian fantasies of a totally commodified world. Such fantasies not only neglect the emancipatory aspects of markets but also overlook the fact, stressed by Immanuel Wallerstein, that capitalism has often operated on the basis of "semiproletarianized" households. Under these arrangements, which allow owners to pay workers less, many households derive a significant portion of their sustenance from sources other than cash wages, including self-provisioning (such as the garden plot or sewing), informal reciprocity (such as mutual aid or in-kind transactions), or state transfers (including welfare benefits, social services, or public goods).[2] Such arrangements leave a significant portion of activities and goods outside the purview of the market. They are not mere residual holdovers from precapitalist times, nor are they on their way out. They were intrinsic to Fordism, which was able to promote working-class consumerism in the industrialized countries of the capitalist core only by way of semiproletarianized households that combined male employment with female homemaking, as well as by inhibiting the development of commodity consumption in the periphery. Semiproletarianization is even more pronounced in neoliberalism, which has built an entire accumulation strategy by expelling billions of people from the official economy into informal gray zones, from which capital siphons off value. As we shall see, this sort of "primitive accumulation" is an ongoing process from which capital profits and on which it relies.

The point, then, is that marketized aspects of capitalist societies coexist with nonmarketized aspects. This is no fluke or empirical contingency but a feature built into capitalism's DNA. In fact, "coexistence" is too weak a term to capture the relation between marketized and nonmarketized aspects of a capitalist society. A better term would be "functional imbrication" or, stronger still and more simply, "dependence."[3] Markets depend for their very existence on nonmarketized social relations, which supply their background conditions of possibility.

BACKGROUND CONDITIONS

So far, I have been elaborating a fairly orthodox definition of capitalism, based on four core features that seem to be "economic." I have effectively followed Marx in looking behind the commonsense perspective, which focuses on market exchange, to the "hidden abode" of production. Now, however, I want to look behind that hidden abode, to see what is more hidden still. Marx's account of capitalist production only makes sense when we start to fill in its background conditions of possibility. So the next question will be, What must exist behind these core features in order for them to be possible?

Marx himself broaches a question of this sort near the end of volume 1 of *Capital*, in the chapter on so-called "primitive" or original accumulation.[4] Where did capital come from? he asks. How did private property in the means of production come to exist, and how did the producers become separated from them? In the preceding chapters, Marx had laid bare capitalism's economic logic in abstraction from its background conditions of possibility, which were assumed as simply given. But it turned out that there was a whole backstory about where capital itself comes from—a rather violent story of dispossession and expropriation. Moreover, as David Harvey has stressed, this backstory is not located only in the past, at the "origins" of capitalism.[5] Expropriation is an ongoing, albeit unofficial, mechanism of accumulation, which continues alongside the official mechanism of exploitation—Marx's "front story," so to speak.

This move, from the front story of exploitation to the backstory of expropriation, constitutes a major epistemic shift, which casts everything that went before in a different light. It is analogous to the move Marx makes earlier, near the beginning of volume 1, when he invites us to leave behind the sphere of market exchange, and the perspective of bourgeois common sense associated with it, for the hidden abode of production, which affords a more critical perspective. As a result of that first move, we discover a dirty secret: accumulation proceeds via exploitation. Capital expands, in other words, not via the exchange of equivalents, as the market perspective suggests, but precisely through its opposite—via the noncompensation of a portion of workers' labor time. Similarly, when we move, at the volume's end, from exploitation to expropriation, we discover an even dirtier secret: behind the sublimated coercion of wage labor lie overt violence and outright theft. In other words, the long elaboration of capitalism's economic logic, which constitutes most of volume 1, is not the last word. It is followed by a move to another perspective, the dispossession perspective. This move to what is behind the "hidden abode" is also a move to history—and to what I have been calling the background "conditions of possibility" for exploitation.

Arguably, however, there are other, equally momentous epistemic shifts that are implied in Marx's account of capitalism but are not developed by him. These moves, to abodes that are even more hidden, are still in need of conceptualization. They need to be written up in new volumes of *Capital*, if you like, if we are to develop an adequate understanding of twenty-first-century capitalism. One is the epistemic shift from production to social *re*production—the forms of provisioning, caregiving, and interaction that produce and maintain social bonds. Variously called "care," "affective labor" or "subjectivation," this activity forms capitalism's human subjects, sustaining them as embodied natural beings, while also constituting them as social beings, forming their habitus and the socio-ethical substance, or *Sittlichkeit*, in which they move.

Central here is the work of socializing the young, building communities, and producing and reproducing the shared meanings, affective dispositions, and horizons of value that underpin social cooperation. In capitalist societies, much, though not all, of this activity goes on outside the market, in households, neighborhoods, and a host of public institutions, including schools and child-care centers, and much of it, though not all, does not take the form of wage labor. Yet social-reproductive activity is absolutely necessary to the existence of waged work, the accumulation of surplus value, and the functioning of capitalism as such. Wage labor could not exist in the absence of housework, child raising, schooling, affective care, and a host of other activities that help to produce new generations of workers and to replenish existing ones as well as to maintain social bonds and shared understandings. Much like "original accumulation," therefore, social reproduction is an indispensable background condition for the possibility of capitalist production.

Structurally, moreover, the division between social reproduction and commodity production is central to capitalism—indeed, is an artifact of it. As scores of feminist theorists have stressed, the distinction is deeply gendered, with reproduction associated with women and production with men. Historically, the split between "productive" waged work and unwaged "reproductive" labor has underpinned modern capitalist forms of women's subordination. Like the division between owners and workers, this division, too, rests on the breakup of a previous world. In this case, what was shattered was a world in which women's work, although distinguished from men's, was nevertheless visible and publicly acknowledged, an integral part of the social universe. With capitalism, by contrast, reproductive labor is split off, relegated to a separate, "private" domestic sphere, where its social importance is obscured. And, in this new world, where money is a primary medium of power, the fact of its being unpaid seals the matter: those who do this work are structurally subordinate to those who earn cash wages, even as their work also supplies necessary preconditions for wage labor.

Far from being universal, then, the division between production and reproduction arose historically, with capitalism. But it was not simply given once and for all. On the contrary, the division mutated historically, taking different forms in different phases of capitalist development. During the twentieth century, some aspects of social reproduction were transformed into public services and public goods, deprivatized but not commodified. Today, the division is mutating again, as neoliberalism (re) privatizes and (re)commodifies some of these services, while also commodifying other aspects of social reproduction for the first time. Moreover, by demanding retrenchment of public provision while at the same time massively recruiting women into low-wage service work, it is remapping the institutional boundaries that previously separated commodity production from social reproduction, reconfiguring the gender order in the process. Equally important, by mounting a major assault on social reproduction, it is turning this background condition for capital accumulation into a major flash point of capitalist crisis.

NATURE AND POWER

But we should also consider two further, equally momentous shifts in epistemic perspective, which direct us to other hidden abodes. The first is best embodied in the work of ecosocialist thinkers, who are now writing another backstory about capitalism's free ride on nature. This story concerns capital's annexation—its *Landnahme*—of nature, both as a source of "inputs" to production and as a "sink" to absorb production's waste. Nature, here, is made into a resource for capital, one whose value is both presupposed and disavowed. Treated as costless in capital's accounts, it is expropriated without compensation or replenishment and is implicitly assumed to be infinite. Thus, nature's capacity to support life and renew itself constitutes another necessary background condition for commodity production and capital accumulation.

Structurally, capitalism assumes—indeed, inaugurates—a sharp division between a natural realm, conceived as offering a free, unproduced supply of "raw material" that is available for appropriation, and an economic realm, conceived as a sphere of value, produced by and for human beings. Along with this goes the hardening of a preexisting distinction between human—seen as spiritual, sociocultural, and historical—and nonhuman nature—seen as material, objectively given, and ahistorical. The sharpening of this distinction, too, rests on the breakup of a previous world, in which the rhythms of social life were in many respects adapted to those of nonhuman nature. Capitalism brutally separated human beings from natural, seasonal rhythms, conscripting them into industrial manufacturing, powered by fossil fuels, and profit-driven agriculture, bulked up by chemical fertilizers. Introducing what Marx called a "metabolic rift," it inaugurated what has now been dubbed the Anthropocene, an entirely new geologic era in which human activity has a decisive impact on Earth's ecosystems and atmosphere.[6]

Arising with capitalism, this division, too, has mutated in the course of capitalist development. The current neoliberal phase has inaugurated a new round of enclosures—the commodification of water, for example—which are bringing "more of nature" (if one can speak that way) into the economic foreground. At the same time, neoliberalism promises to blur the nature/human boundary—witness new reproductive technologies and Donna Haraway's "cyborgs."[7] Far from offering a "reconciliation" with nature, however, these developments intensify capitalism's commodification-cum-annexation of it. Unlike the land enclosures Marx and Polanyi wrote about, which "merely" marketized already existing natural phenomena, the new enclosures penetrate deep "inside" nature, altering its internal grammar. Ultimately, neoliberalism is marketizing environmentalism—witness the brisk trade in carbon permits and offsets and in "environmental derivatives," which draw capital away from the long-term, large-scale investment needed to transform unsustainable forms of life premised on fossil fuels. Against the background of global warming, this assault on what remains of the ecological commons is turning the natural condition of capital accumulation into another central node of capitalist crisis.

Finally, let us consider one last major epistemic shift, which points to capitalism's *political* conditions of possibility—its reliance on public powers to establish and enforce its constitutive norms. Capitalism is inconceivable, after all, in the absence of a legal framework underpinning private enterprise and market exchange. Its front story depends crucially on public powers to guarantee property rights, enforce contracts, adjudicate disputes, quell anticapitalist rebellions, and maintain, in the language of the US Constitution, "the full faith and credit" of the money supply that constitutes capital's lifeblood. Historically, the public powers in question, for the most part, have been lodged in territorial states, including those that operated as colonial powers. It was the legal systems of such states that established the contours of seemingly depoliticized arenas within which private actors could pursue their "economic" interests, free from overt "political" interference, on the one hand, and from patronage obligations derived from kinship, on the other. Likewise, it was territorial states that mobilized "legitimate force" to put down resistance to the expropriations through which capitalist property relations were originated and sustained. Finally, it was such states that nationalized and underwrote money.[8] Historically, we might say, the state "constituted" the capitalist economy.

Here we encounter another major structural division that is constitutive of capitalist society: that between polity and economy. With this division comes the institutional differentiation of public from private power, of political from economic coercion. Like the other core divisions we have discussed, this one, too, arises as a result of the breakup of a previous world. In this case, what was dismantled was a social world in which economic and political power were effectively fused—as, for example, in feudal society, where control over labor, land, and military force was vested in the single institution of lordship and vassalage. In capitalist society, by contrast, as Ellen Wood has elegantly shown, economic power and political power are split apart; each is assigned its own sphere, its own medium and modus operandi.[9]

Yet capitalism's front story also has political conditions of possibility at the geopolitical level. What is at issue here is the organization of the broader space in which territorial states are embedded. This is a space in which capital moves quite easily, given its expansionist thrust. But its ability to operate across borders depends on international law, brokered arrangements among the Great Powers, and supranational regimes, which partially pacify (in a capital-friendly way) a realm that is often imagined as a state of nature. Throughout its history, capitalism's front story has depended on the military and organizational capacities of a succession of global hegemons, which, as Giovanni Arrighi has argued, have sought to foster accumulation on a progressively expanding scale within the framework of a multistate system.[10]

Here we find further structural divisions that are constitutive of capitalist society: the "Westphalian" division between the "domestic" and the "international," on the one hand, and the imperialist division between core and periphery, on the other. Both divisions are premised on the more fundamental division between an increasingly global capitalist economy organized as a "world system" and a political world organized as an international system of territorial states. These divisions are currently mutating as well, as neoliberalism hollows out the political capacities on which capital has historically relied, at both the state and geopolitical levels. As a result of this hollowing out, capitalism's political conditions of possibility are also now a major site and flash point of capitalist crisis.

Much more could be said on each of these points, but the general thrust of my argument should be clear. In filling out my initial account of capitalism, I have shown that its "economic," foreground features depend on "noneconomic" background conditions. An economic system defined by private property, the accumulation of self-expanding value, markets in free labor and in other major inputs to commodity production, and the market allocation of social surplus is rendered possible by three crucial background conditions, concerned with social reproduction, Earth's ecology, and political power. To understand capitalism, therefore, we need to relate its front story to these three backstories. We must connect the Marxian perspective to feminist, ecological, and political-theoretical perspectives—state-theoretical, colonial/postcolonial, and transnational.

AN INSTITUTIONALIZED SOCIAL ORDER

What sort of animal is capitalism, in this account? The picture I have elaborated here differs importantly from the familiar idea that capitalism is an economic system. Granted, it may have looked, at first sight, as if the core features we identified are "economic." But that appearance is misleading. One of the peculiarities of capitalism is that it treats its structuring social relations as if they were economic, but, in fact, we quickly found it necessary to talk about the "noneconomic" background conditions that enable such an "economic system" to exist. These are features not of a capitalist economy but of a capitalist *society*, and we concluded that those background conditions must not be airbrushed out of the picture but must be conceptualized and theorized as part of our understanding of capitalism. Therefore, capitalism is something larger than an economy.

Likewise, the picture I have sketched differs from the view of capitalism as a reified form of ethical life, characterized by pervasive commodification and monetization. In that view, as articulated in Georg Lukács's celebrated essay on "Reification and the Consciousness of the Proletariat," the commodity form colonizes all of life, stamping its mark on such diverse phenomena as law, science, morality, art, and culture.[11] In my view, commodification is far from universal in capitalist society. On the contrary, where it is present, it depends for its very existence on zones of noncommodification. Social, ecological, and political, these noncommodified zones do not simply mirror the commodity logic but embody distinctive normative and ontological grammars of their own. For example, social practices oriented to reproduction (as opposed to production) tend to engender ideals of care, mutual responsibility, and solidarity, however hierarchical and parochial these may be.[12] Likewise, practices oriented to polity, as opposed to economy, often refer to principles of democracy, public autonomy, and collective self-determination, however restricted or exclusionary these may be. Finally, practices associated with capitalism's background conditions in nonhuman nature tend to foster such values as ecological stewardship, nondomination of nature, and justice among generations, however romantic and sectarian these may be. Of course, my point is not to idealize these "noneconomic" normativities but to register their divergence from the values associated with capitalism's foreground—above all, growth, efficiency, equal exchange, individual choice, negative liberty, and meritocratic advancement.

This divergence makes all the difference to how we conceptualize capitalism. Far from generating a single, all-pervasive logic of reification, capitalist society is normatively differentiated, encompassing a determinate plurality of distinct but interrelated social ontologies. What happens when these collide remains to be seen. But the structure that underpins them is already clear: capitalism's distinctive normative topography arises from the foreground–background relations we have identified. If we aim to develop a critical theory of it, we must replace the view of capitalism as a reified form of ethical life with a more differentiated, structural view.

If capitalism is neither an economic system nor a reified form of ethical life, then what is it? My answer is that it is best conceived as an institutionalized social order, on a par with, for example, feudalism. Understanding capitalism in this way underscores its structural divisions, especially the institutional separations that I have identified. Constitutive of capitalism, we have seen, is the institutional separation of "economic production" from "social reproduction," a gendered separation that grounds specifically capitalist forms of male domination even as it also enables capitalist exploitation of labor power and, through that, its officially sanctioned mode of accumulation. Also definitive of capitalism is the institutional separation of "economy" from "polity," a separation that expels matters defined as "economic" from the political agenda of territorial states, freeing capital to roam in a transnational no-man's-land, where it reaps the benefits of hegemonic ordering while escaping political control. Equally fundamental to capitalism, finally, is the ontological division, preexisting but massively intensified, between its (nonhuman) "natural" background and its (apparently nonnatural) "human" foreground.

Therefore, to speak of capitalism as an institutionalized social order, premised on such separations, is to suggest its nonaccidental, structural imbrication with gender oppression, political domination—both national and transnational, colonial and postcolonial—and ecological degradation, in conjunction, of course, with its equally structural, nonaccidental foreground dynamic of labor exploitation.

This is not to suggest, however, that capitalism's institutional divisions are simply given once and for all. On the contrary, as we saw, precisely *where* and *how* capitalist societies draw the line between production and reproduction, economy and polity, human and nonhuman nature varies historically, according to the regime of accumulation. In fact, we can conceptualize competitive laissez-faire capitalism, state-managed monopoly capitalism, and globalizing neoliberal capitalism in precisely these terms, as three historically specific ways of demarcating economy from polity, production from reproduction, and human from nonhuman nature.

BOUNDARY STRUGGLES

Equally important, the precise configuration of the capitalist order at any place and time depends on politics—on the balance of social power and on the outcome of social struggles. Far from being simply given, capitalism's institutional divisions often become foci of conflict, as actors mobilize to challenge or defend the established boundaries separating economy from polity, production from reproduction, human from nonhuman nature. Insofar as they aim to relocate contested processes on capitalism's institutional map, capitalism's subjects draw on the normative perspectives associated with the various zones that we have identified.

We can see this happening today. For example, some opponents of neoliberalism draw on ideals of care, solidarity, and mutual responsibility, associated with reproduction, in order to oppose efforts to commodify education. Others summon notions of stewardship of nature and justice among generations, associated with ecology, to militate for a shift to renewable energy. Still others invoke ideals of public autonomy, associated with polity, to advocate international capital controls and to extend democratic accountability beyond the state. Such claims, along with the counterclaims they inevitably incite, are the very stuff of social struggle in capitalist societies—as fundamental as the class struggles over control of commodity production and distribution of surplus value that Marx privileged. These boundary struggles, as I shall call them, decisively shape the structure of capitalist societies.[13] They play a constitutive role in the view of capitalism as an institutionalized social order.

The focus on boundary struggles should forestall any misimpression that the view I have been sketching is functionalist. Granted, I began by characterizing reproduction, ecology, and political power as necessary background conditions for capitalism's economic front story, stressing their functionality for commodity production, labor exploitation, and capital accumulation. But this structural moment does not capture the full story of capitalism's foreground–background relations. It coexists, rather, with another "moment," already hinted at, which is equally central and which emerges from the characterization of the social, political, and ecological as reservoirs of "noneconomic" normativity. This implies that, even as these "noneconomic" orders make commodity production possible, they are not reducible to that enabling function. Far from being wholly exhausted by, or entirely subservient to, the dynamics of accumulation, each of these hidden abodes harbors distinctive ontologies of social practice and normative ideals.

Moreover, these "noneconomic" ideals are pregnant with critical-political possibility. Especially in times of crisis, they can be turned against core economic practices associated with capital accumulation. In such times, the structural divisions that normally serve to segregate the various normativities within their own institutional spheres tend to weaken. When the separations fail to hold, capitalism's subjects—who live, after all, in more than one sphere—experience normative conflict. Far from bringing in ideas from the "outside," they draw on capitalism's own complex normativity to criticize it, mobilizing against the grain the multiplicity of ideals that coexist, at times uneasily, in an institutionalized social order premised on foreground–background divisions. Thus, the view of capitalism as an institutionalized social order helps us understand how a critique of capitalism is possible from within it.

Yet this view also suggests that it would be wrong to construe society, polity, and nature romantically, as "outside" capitalism and as inherently opposed to it. That romantic view is held today by a fair number of anticapitalist thinkers and left-wing activists, including cultural feminists, deep ecologists, and neo-anarchists, as well as by many proponents of "plural," "postgrowth," "solidary," and "popular" economies. Too often, these currents treat "care," "nature," "direct action," or "commoning" as intrinsically anticapitalist. As a result, they overlook the fact that their favorite practices not only are sources of critique but also are integral parts of the capitalist order.

Rather, the argument here is that society, polity, and nature arose concurrently with economy and developed in symbiosis with it. They are effectively the latter's "others" and only acquire their specific character in contrast to it. Thus, reproduction and production make a pair, with each term co-defined by way of the other. Neither makes any sense apart from the other. The same is true of polity/economy and nature/human. Part and parcel of the capitalist order, none of the "noneconomic" realms affords a wholly external standpoint that could underwrite an absolutely pure and fully radical form of critique. On the contrary, political projects that appeal to what they imagine to be capitalism's "outside" usually end up recycling capitalist stereotypes, as they counterpose female nurturance to male aggression, spontaneous cooperation to economic calculation, nature's holistic organicism to anthropocentric individualism. To premise one's struggles on these oppositions is not to challenge but to unwittingly reflect the institutionalized social order of capitalist society.

CONTRADICTIONS

It follows from this that a proper account of capitalism's foreground–background relations must hold together three distinct ideas. First, capitalism's "noneconomic" realms serve as enabling background conditions for its economy; the economy depends for its very existence on values and inputs from the "noneconomic." Second, however, capitalism's "noneconomic" realms have a weight and character of their own, which can, under certain circumstances, provide resources for anticapitalist struggle. Nevertheless, and this is the third point, these realms are part and parcel of capitalist society, historically coconstituted in tandem with its economy and marked by their symbiosis with it.

There is also a fourth idea, which returns us to the problem of crisis with which I began. Capitalism's foreground–background relations harbor built-in sources of social instability. As we have seen, capitalist production is not self-sustaining; it free rides on social reproduction, nature, and political power. Yet its orientation to endless accumulation threatens to destabilize these very conditions of its possibility. In the case of its ecological conditions, what is at risk are the natural processes that sustain life and provide the material inputs for social provisioning. In the case of its social-reproduction conditions, what is imperiled are the sociocultural processes that supply the solidary relations, affective dispositions, and value horizons that underpin social cooperation while also furnishing the appropriately socialized and skilled human beings who constitute "labor." In the case of its political conditions, what is compromised are the public powers, both national and transnational, that guarantee property rights, enforce contracts, adjudicate disputes, quell anticapitalist rebellions, and maintain the money supply.

Here, in Marx's language, are three "contradictions of capitalism," the ecological, the social, and the political, which correspond to three "crisis tendencies." Unlike the crisis tendencies stressed by Marx, however, these do not stem from contradictions internal to the capitalist economy. They are grounded, rather, in contradictions between the economic system and its background conditions of possibility—between economy and society, economy and nature, economy and polity.[14] Their effect, as noted before, is to incite a broad range of social struggles in capitalist society—not only class struggles at the point of production but also boundary struggles over ecology, social reproduction, and political power. As responses to the crisis tendencies inherent in capitalist society, those struggles are endemic to our expanded view of capitalism as an institutionalized social order.

What sort of critique of capitalism follows from the conception sketched here? The view of capitalism as institutionalized social order calls for a multistranded form of critical reflection, much like that developed by Marx in *Capital*. As I read him, Marx interweaves a systems critique of capitalism's inherent tendency to (economic) crisis, a normative critique of its built-in dynamics of (class) domination, and a political critique of the potential for emancipatory social transformation inherent in its characteristic form of (class) struggle. The view I have outlined entails an analogous interweaving of critical strands, but the weave here is more complex because each strand is internally multiple. The systemic-crisis critique includes not only the economic contradictions discussed by Marx but also the three interrealm contradictions discussed here, which destabilize the necessary background conditions for capital accumulation by jeopardizing social reproduction, ecology, and political power. Likewise, the domination critique encompasses not only the relations of class domination analyzed by Marx but also those of gender domination, political domination, and the domination of nature. Finally, the political critique encompasses multiple sets of actors—classes, genders, status groups, nations, *demoi*, possibly even species—and vectors of struggle—not only class struggles but also boundary struggles over the separations of society, polity, and nature from economy.

What counts as an anticapitalist struggle is thus much broader than Marxists have traditionally supposed. As soon as we look behind the front story to the backstory, all the indispensable background conditions for the exploitation of labor become foci of conflict in capitalist society—not just struggles between labor and capital at the point of production but also boundary struggles over gender domination, ecology, imperialism, and democracy. But, equally important, the latter now appear in another light—as struggles in, around, and, in some cases, against capitalism itself. Should they come to understand themselves in these terms, participants in these struggles could conceivably cooperate or unite.

NOTES

These arguments were worked out in conversation with Rahel Jaeggi and will appear in our *Crisis, Critique, Capitalism*, forthcoming from Polity. Thanks to Blair Taylor for research assistance and to the Centre for Gender Studies (Cambridge), the Collège d'études mondiales, the Forschungskolleg Humanwissenschaften, and the Centre for Advanced Studies "Justitia Amplificata" for their support.

1. Piero Sraffa, *Production of Commodities by Means of Commodities: Prelude to a Critique of Economic Theory* (Cambridge: Cambridge University Press, 1960).
2. Immanuel Wallerstein, *Historical Capitalism* (London: Verso, 1983), 39.
3. See Karl Polanyi, *The Great Transformation* (New York: Farrar and Rinehart, 1944); and Nancy Fraser, "Can Society Be Commodities All the Way Down?" *Economy and Society* 43, no. 4 (2014): 541–58.
4. Karl Marx, *Capital*, vol. 1 (London: Penguin Harmondsworth, 1976), 873–76.

5. David Harvey, *The New Imperialism* (Oxford: Oxford University Press, 2003), 137–82.
6. See Karl Marx, *Capital*, vol. 3 (New York: Random House, 1981), 949–50; and John Bellamy Foster, "Marx's Theory of Metabolic Rift: Classical Foundations for Environmental Sociology," *American Journal of Sociology* 105, no. 2 (1999): 366–405.
7. Donna Haraway, "A Cyborg Manifesto: Science, Technology, and Socialist-Feminism in the Late Twentieth Century," in *Simians, Cyborgs, and Women: The Reinvention of Nature* (New York: Routledge, 1991), 149–81.
8. See Geoffrey Ingham, *The Nature of Money* (Cambridge: Polity, 2004); and David Graeber, *Debt: The First 5,000 Years* (New York: Melville House, 2011).
9. Ellen Meiksins Wood, *Empire of Capital* (London: Verso, 2003).
10. Giovanni Arrighi, *The Long Twentieth Century: Money, Power and the Origins of Our Times* (London and New York: Verso, 1994).
11. Georg Lukács, "Reification and the Consciousness of the Proletariat," in *History and Class Consciousness: Studies in Marxist Dialectics*, trans. Rodney Livingstone (Cambridge: MIT Press, 1971), 83–222.
12. See Sara Ruddick, *Maternal Thinking: Towards a Politics of Peace* (London: The Women's Press, 1990); and Joan Tronto, *Moral Boundaries: A Political Argument for an Ethic of Care* (New York: Routledge, 1993).
13. See Nancy Fraser, "Struggle over Needs: Outline of a Socialist-Feminist Critical Theory of Late-Capitalist Political Culture," in *Unruly Practices: Power, Discourse and Gender in Contemporary Social Theory* (Minneapolis: University of Minnesota Press, 1989), 161–87.
14. See James O'Connor, "Capitalism, Nature, Socialism: A Theoretical Introduction," *Capitalism, Nature, Socialism* 1, no. 1 (1988): 1–22.

8

A WIDE CONCEPT OF ECONOMY

Economy as a Social Practice and the Critique of Capitalism

RAHEL JAEGGI

A NARROW CONCEPT OF ECONOMY

In a postscript to his programmatic text, "Traditional and Critical Theory," Max Horkheimer makes the following remark: "Economism, to which the critical theory is often reduced, does not consist in giving too much importance to the economy, but in giving it *too narrow a scope*."[1] Starting out from this observation and this distinction between a "wide" and "narrow" understanding of economy, we can briefly sketch the history of critical theory and, more specifically, the history of its relation to the economy in the following way: The "old" critical theory gave itself the task of tracking the intrusion of the "commodity form" into all social relations, including individual self-relations. This was done to point out that the influence of the economy or the commodity form extends far beyond the sphere of economics into cultural preferences and worldviews.

Inspired by Lukács's theory of reification,[2] they thus understood the economy, in fact, very *widely*. According to this thesis, economic preferences in mature capitalism encompass and corrupt all spheres of life. The economic—understood as a specific mode of intercourse with things and people—is therefore made responsible for the characteristic pathologies of capitalist societies: exploitation, oppression, instrumentalization, reification, alienation, and, generally speaking, its irrationality. By tracing and criticizing the diffusion or even invasion of the commodity form into formerly or constitutively "noneconomic" spheres, Horkheimer and others have, without a doubt, contributed to freeing Marxist-inspired social critique from "economism." However, despite this kind of "widening" of perspective in the early days of critical theory, surprisingly little attention was paid to the sphere of the economy proper—with some exceptions in the very early phase of the Institute for Social Research.[3]

Because of this, critical theory as a critique of capitalism finds itself in a slightly paradoxical situation. On the one hand, early critical theory, *as a whole*, is the critique of capitalism. It is thus, in a certain sense, *nothing but* the critique of capitalism, insofar as everything it deals with—including the most elaborate thoughts on aesthetic phenomena—is addressed in terms of the effects and character of capitalist socialization. On the other hand, however, the question arises as to what extent such a theory is actually a critique of capitalism *at all*, since, in fact, it deals very little with the analysis and critique of actual economic practices specific to capitalist societies.

There are complex reasons for this, some of them connected to the difficulties of actually implementing the original interdisciplinary program. The result of this development, however, is that no approach really emerged from this period of critical theory[4] that would allow it to give a "wider" meaning, as Horkheimer demanded, to the field of economic practices and institutions *themselves*. In other words, this conception of the economic is "wide" only because it attests to the wide *influence* of the economic. Yet behind it still stands a *narrow* view of the economy, which in a certain way misses the above-cited claim from Horkheimer.

The enormous differences between early critical theory and what has been labeled the "second" generation of critical theory should, of course, not be underestimated. But, ironically enough, with respect to the point in question, little has actually changed in the follow-up to early critical theory. Jürgen Habermas's theory of the colonization of the lifeworld,[5] even if it could successfully overcome the totalizing grip of older critical theory and establish its normative foundations, has solidified a view according to which one must pay critical attention, above all, to the invasion of the economic into other areas of life, while the economic sphere *itself* is removed from the realm of criticism. In the widest sense, the conception of the economy in a differentiation-theoretical approach, which Habermas (among others) follows, grasps the economy as a sphere that is to some extent autonomous with respect to other social spheres. It is understood as a nonnormative sphere driven by its own logic.[6] The economy, as a result, was treated as a "black box." Wherever critical theory now deals with the economic formation of capitalist societies, it thinks in the metaphor of politically or democratically taming the tiger that is capitalism. (The economy, then, is based on the rational pursuit of self-interest; politics represents the public good and uses this to challenge such self-interest.) This makes it not only impossible but also unnecessary to rethink the economy itself, and, as it were, to grasp it *widely*.

CRITICAL THEORY IN CRITICAL TIMES: OPENING THE BLACK BOX

I don't want to rehash the old debate about the alternative of reformist *transformation* versus the radical *overcoming* of capitalism. Whether a capitalism tamed into a house cat corresponds to its concept is an "academic" question, in the bad sense of the word. And one also should not underestimate how much of this discussion depends on the availability of an economic alternative to capitalism. However, we are today (both as critical theorists and citizens) confronted with what many of us, in one way or another, experience as "excesses" and threats posed by contemporary capitalism. For many, this raises the suspicion that the theory of "taming capitalism" is inadequate—not only because of our current, real powerlessness in the face of economic imperatives but also for already-existing systematic reasons. At issue, then, is what kind of animal is actually being "tamed," whether it even can be tamed, and, finally, whether the domestication metaphor is itself adequate at all.

In a situation in which Habermas's "historical connection between democracy and capitalism,"[7] a *liaison dangereuse* all along, has become untenable, a new take on economic issues begins to develop. And it is not only within critical theory that we witness a renewed interest in the critique of capitalism—and a renewed interest in conceptualizing the economy. Whether one takes issue with recent developments within the field of a critical economy[8] or with the insights into the "normative character of the market" (as Axel Honneth addresses it),[9] the very question of how to conceptualize the economy and how to understand economic practices and institutions in the context of our societies has become persistent. We might have to open up the black box in order to bring into view the internal state and constitution of economic practices and institutions that shape our lives as such. The object of critique might then (again) become the economy itself, instead of only looking at its effects in certain respects.

Such a project immediately raises difficult questions on the basic conceptual level, a level that one might call the "social ontology of the economic." My attempt, in this essay, is not to give an outright or exhaustive answer to the questions involved. In this first attempt to come to grips with them, I will only try to understand what it might look like to understand the economy as "part of the social order," as Jens Beckert puts it, and not as its "other."[10] I take it that this understanding is required to open up the conceptual space for thinking the economy in a wide sense.

A WIDE CONCEPT OF ECONOMY: ECONOMY AS SOCIAL PRACTICE

What does it now mean to conceive of the economy in a wide instead of a narrow sense? What does this wide scope entail, if it is not only meant to bring our attention to the *effects* of economic orientations on our lives?

A first, tentative, answer would be that a narrow conception can be limited in scope with respect to *content*, insofar as it conceives of the economic as the sphere of material reproduction in a narrow sense; it can also be narrow with respect to the *attitude* that is taken to be the economic approach—a certain kind of rationality that is focused on utility maximization and the rational pursuit of self-interest.

My thesis is as follows: In order to understand the economy in a wider sense, we should conceive of it as a set of social practices—of *economic social practices*, to be precise. To put it differently, I will suggest a practice-theoretical approach, a practice-oriented foundation for our thinking about economy and its institutions.[11] Economic practices, then, are a subset of social practices in general and share the features of "practices" that I will go into below. As such, they are interrelated with other practices in a variety of ways and (together with them) form part of the sociocultural fabric of society.

Taking up such a perspective should enable a critique of the layout of economic contexts of practice, a critique immanent to their normative content, that is, to the normative conditions of fulfillment underlying these practices. To view them critically is to conceive of them as *failed economic practices* themselves. It would then no longer be the invasion of the economy into the social but *defects* in the shape and content of economic practices and institutions themselves that come into view (again).

To make my argument, several steps need to be taken. To begin with, I will briefly explain what I mean by "social practices" and will develop the idea of "forms of life" as "inert bundles of social practices." Then I'll describe in which sense the field of economics is a field of social practices and how to think of the connection of economic practices with other practices—as a form of life. Finally, I will draw some conclusions with respect to the "wide" concept of economy for which I am aiming and will tentatively point toward the prospects for a critique of capitalism that could be drawn from my approach.

SOCIAL PRACTICES AND FORMS OF LIFE

What then are social practices (according to the specific understanding that I suggest), what are forms of life, and in what way are economic practices social practices that aggregate with other social practices to constitute forms of life?

PRACTICES

The term "social practice" refers to practices concerning oneself, others, and the material world. To attend a dinner party or to play hide-and-seek are practices. So are taking an exam, shopping in a grocery store, or, more generally, exchanging commodities in a market. Practices are sequences of single actions (or deeds) that can be more or less complex and comprehensive and that have a (more or less) repetitive or habitual character. These practices are "social" not in the sense that they necessarily concern/relate to interpersonal relations or the coordination of social relationships. Rather, they are "social" because they can only exist and be understood against the background of a socially constituted realm of meaning.

Let me now highlight a couple of aspects regarding the very concept of a practice.

First, practices are not just intentional actions. Due to their repetitive and habitual character, they might be based on implicit rather than explicit knowledge, to a certain extent, as long as they are not interrupted or confronted with problems. They are patterns in which we act, patterns that allow us to act even if they are constituted by our actions. It is possible to describe them, therefore, as both *results* of our actions and as their *precondition*.

Second, practices are not "brute facts." They have to be interpreted and understood *as* something. They are constituted *as practices* only through interpretations. I should be able to understand your hiding behind the tree as part of a game of hide-and-seek (as opposed to hiding from the police). And, by understanding it as hide-and-seek, I implicitly understand its link to a set of other practices and interpretations, such as, for instance, to other games and to the interpretative concept of "game," but, even more comprehensively, to the concept of childhood as opposed to adulthood, and so on. To someone who cannot correctly interpret the practice of shopping in a supermarket—and everything that goes with it—the piling of items in a shopping cart may seem like a kind of robbery.

Third, practices are regulated by norms. They are organized around an essential idea of what it means to "fulfill" this practice at all, that is, to act according to the normative expectations involved in a certain practice. (If you don't at least *try* to hide, we are certainly not playing hide-and-seek.) But there also are norms that regulate what counts as a good way to fulfill a practice. (If you don't examine your patients thoroughly, you are not a good doctor.)

Finally, practices have an inherent telos. They are directed at some aim that might be realized through engaging in them, even if we might find a multiplicity of aims coming together in a single practice. (I go shopping because I need to buy food for dinner, but also because I want to talk to the shopkeeper or because I'm bored at home.)

FORMS OF LIFE

Now, practices are typically connected to other practices. This is particularly tangible when practices are connected in a material sense. For example, the practice of standing in line at the cash register and paying clearly depends on a whole host of other practices that first make this one possible. But the interconnectivity of individual practices also occurs on another level: practices are connected with one another via a common horizon of interpretation, a horizon that alone makes these practices intelligible and functional. Our ability to pay at the register to acquire an item by purchase does not depend only on others producing the corresponding goods beforehand and carrying them to the shelf, or even on someone designing a cash register that others bought and placed in their shop. The functioning of this practical context also depends on the "institutional fact" that a certain piece of paper is understood and recognized as money, that the act of purchase and exchange is institutionalized and interpreted in a specific way.[12] Without the social constitution of meanings like "this bill is valid in country A as money," without the understanding and practice of using money as a general equivalent, and without the corresponding act of exchange as a specific variant of reciprocity, the exchange of printed bills for a loaf of bread appears as a very odd transaction.

What comes into view now are *sets* or *ensembles* of practices that are connected to and inform one another—and those are what I would like to call "forms of life." (Forms of life in this sense can be more or less encompassing.) Stated the other way around, forms of life are to be understood as inert sets, ensembles, or bundles of social practices. They are ensembles of social practices because they encompass a diversity of practices that, while dependent on one another, do not exist as an impenetrable and closed totality. They are *inert* to a certain extent, because they maintain "sedimentary elements," that is, praxis components that are not always open to change, explicit, or transparent. That is to say, the practices involved can have states of aggregation ranging from more fluid to inert ones. As a result, forms of life (as it holds for single practices) are not always engaged in deliberately or even reflected upon; we might participate in them without planning, intending, or even knowing exactly what we are doing.

We also have to take into account that social practices and forms of life are "materialized" in institutions and, even more "materially," in architecture, tools, and material structures that (even if a result of our own actions) *make us act*. Therefore, they set limits to what we can do as well as enable us to do things in a certain way. Practices and forms of life, in short, are *given* as well as *created*. And they might develop a certain dynamic of their own. Nevertheless, they are something that human beings *do* and therefore *could do otherwise*. This becomes clear as soon as a certain set of practices and self-understandings hits its limit—when things no longer run smoothly. When a set of practices is interrupted, it doesn't go unnoticed anymore. The moment of crisis forces reflection on and adjustments of practices—a re-creation of practices—that were previously taken for granted.

Now, if all of this is true, then practices individually and in their connection to each other constitute a shape that is not intentionally structured as a whole. They emerge (and maintain themselves), as opposed to being drafted at the drawing table from scratch, so to speak. In its concatenation with other practices, this shape brings about consequences that might not, or even could not, have been intended or imagined by the participants involved in those practices and forms of life. Adam Ferguson's remark fits well here: "History is the result of human action, but not the execution of any human design."[13]

ECONOMIC PRACTICES

To what extent, then, and in which respect, are economic practices social practices, practices that aggregate with other kinds of social practices into a form of life (and share the aforementioned characteristics)? What does it mean and what does it imply to conceive of the "economic realm" as a realm of practices?

Let's consider the domain of the economic as that which, roughly speaking, is concerned with the satisfaction of the reproductive needs of society, the production and distribution of goods and services. It is easy to see, then, that each element that comes into play here—property, market exchange, and labor, to name only some—can be seen as a configuration of social practices and institutions (or practices that have become an institution). Seen from this perspective, practices addressing economic concerns (or, as it were, fulfilling "economic" aims in the narrower sense) are connected or even entangled with other, noneconomic practices and interpretations. They are part of what I have called an "ensemble" of social practices and their respective interpretations, which mutually inform and establish one other.

I want to illustrate this by brief reference to a few examples (without claiming any completeness).

PROPERTY

Let's consider an institution like property as part of a complex, always socially interpreted and normatively infused set of practices—that is, let's consider it as part of a form of life. Understandings of property, along with the corresponding practices of handling it, are parts of and fundamental to very different economic formations; economic regimes are always also property regimes. In this case, different understandings of the legal title to property are accompanied by different practices of acquisition, preservation, and disposal of that which is understood as property within a social order. One can alienate it more or less without limit, or not; one appropriates it in different ways, and certain ways of appropriation count as property creating, or not. Property is therefore not only a "bundle of rights" but also a bundle of social practices recognized and interpreted as something, which are guided by and (the other way around) expressed in legal norms.[14] These norms are deeply bound up with underlying interpretations and partially "faded" cosmologies in which the world (among other things) divides itself not only into animate and inanimate but also into possessable and unpossessable things, qualities, or goods.[15]

Different social orders can thus be characterized, among other ways, by means of the following criteria: which objects in general can be owned (or not), and what kinds of disposal go along with the possession of objects. For example, in every social formation there are things that cannot be considered property: taboos, sacred objects, persons, or personal things. There also are limits to disposing of what one possesses—even in our society, in which property appears largely unrestricted. One may not sell a gun to a minor; some things—certain artworks for instance—may not be destroyed or even exported, although they may belong to someone. For other entities—such as body organs or patent rights—it is debatable to what extent the right to sell is tied to having property in them.[16] But there also are classifications in regards to the question, What may be owned by whom? It is a relatively new achievement of some modern political systems that (with some exceptions) whatever can be property at all can be owned by all in the same manner. And, as with the other characteristics mentioned, this achievement is deeply embedded in comprehensive interpretations of what it means to be a person and is entrenched with normative understandings of our being in the world and our relations with one another.

MARKET AND EXCHANGE

When we turn to the act of *exchange*, we will confront a similar situation: it can be carried out by independent private property owners confronting each other in the marketplace, or not; it can be based on the idea of reciprocity or based on ideas of gift exchange, without an explicit agreement for immediate or future rewards. Practices of exchange are based on norms and rules characteristic of those particular forms of exchange, and thus these forms must be understood altogether within a context of practices and interpretations. To be a "commodity" and to be able to be exchanged is an ascribed status (like a "goal" in a soccer game). For the process of exchanging money for goods to work, the *principle* of exchange must be established, that is, the principle that qualitatively unlike objects can be exchanged with each other through the medium of money under the assumption of their quantitative equivalence.

None of this can be taken for granted. As the extensive anthropological discussions about gift exchange and potlatch practices show, the very ideas of symmetry and reciprocity (not to mention basic conceptions of alienability and indifference connected with the exchange of commodities) are bound up with a whole bunch of broader social meanings and understandings.[17] Market exchange itself is a quite complex and little understood social operation based on other social practices and interpretations—which it also affects. Contrary to mainstream approaches to thinking about the market, much more than "maximizing preferences" is necessary for the institution of the market to function, and some quite basic understandings/social paradigms are at stake before the ideas and practices implied can even be thought of.

LABOR AND PRODUCTION

Another social practice crucial for fulfilling the economic needs of society is labor or work. Labor is not simply a preinterpretively given, "raw" activity but rather is a practice that exists within a social and normative structure of recognition. It is not the activity, as such, that constitutes "work" but the social recognition of the activity as work and the role that the respective activity has in the social process of cooperation. Cooking or playing piano can be seen as work, or not, depending on whether it is practiced by the chef or the homemaker, by the pianist or the layperson. Work confronts us not only as an "eternal natural necessity," as Karl Marx has it, in service of the human "metabolism with nature,"[18] but always and already as a socially and culturally determined factor in the context of social cooperation and the division of labor. In this sense, work is guided by norms and interpretations and is formed within specific social institutions.

First, work activities assume definite sociocultural forms insofar as they are made possible by and shaped from the available skills, techniques, and resources of a given society in a specific historical time. And the other way around: those skills are brought into being by techniques and tools that have been historically achieved. (Producing a clay brick by hand requires and makes possible abilities and modes of behavior different from those necessary for electronically supervising a manufacturing plant; communication via the Internet requires and creates different abilities and behaviors than direct interaction.) It is not just the individual activities and modes of behavior that change here but a whole context of practice in which something means something, where standard procedures and habits take shape, right down to their sedimentation in the physical abilities and sensory skills of the workers or their relation to time. Work is, secondly, a social activity that gains a determinate form through the modes of cooperation in which it is brought about—from the simplest division of labor to the more complex social and internal division of labor in modern societies. Third, there are legal sets of norms that constitute labor relations by means of the relevant institutions (such as the modern civil employment contract or, alternatively, the system of feudal rights for protection and obedience), which provide, for example, the legal framework for free or, alternatively, dependent labor.

While these sets of norms constitute labor in a specifically legal and institutional way, there also are less comprehensive and rigid customary social norms that must be understood as central to giving labor its structure. Labor thus can be brought about only if certain social preconditions are given, and can be identified *as such* only in the framework of a particular interpretation and in its connection with other practices and interpretations. As a result, if it would be a reductive take on the economic institution of the market to understand market activities as merely "maximizing preferences" of purely rational agents, it also would be a mistake to reduce labor to "instrumental action." Labor is a far richer activity, composed of a variety of attitudes and symbolic and communicative skills, and marked by habits, customs, and embodiments, and is to be understood only within a broader social context.[19]

THE PRACTICE CHARACTER OF PROPERTY, EXCHANGE, AND LABOR

These are just some preliminary hints and first bits of evidence; it certainly would be vital to elaborate and specify these examples. The crucial result for my argument, though, is the following: in each of the cases discussed, we find indications of what I have called the practice character of the relevant economic activities.

First, they are socially constituted, established in a distinctive social and historical framework, "under an interpretation" that is always also normatively infused. This holds even if many of the practices, interpretations, and (legal) norms that express such a view of property, exchange, and labor are so self-evident to us—so seamlessly embedded in the interpretative framework of our form of life—that we barely notice their existence or effects at all. The process of exchanging goods for money at the grocery store or paying rent for an apartment is such an ordinary practice that we rarely take note of the peculiarity of it. Looked at the other way around, the fact that we cannot buy children in the same way that we buy an apartment or grocery item is so taken for granted that we don't perceive it as a prohibition. But then, when we buy food at the grocery store, electronic devices at the shopping mall, or cars at the auto dealer, these transactions all are based on implicit understandings of the meaning of ownership and the status of commodities and exchange that are related to far-reaching and comprehensive normative assumptions and encompassing practices.

That these conceptions and accompanying practices are not self-evident only becomes clear once we realize, for example, how historically recent is the ban on human trafficking (and also how incompletely enforced it is), or that some indigenous peoples consider the land on which they live, including its flora and fauna, as in some sense unsalable, as we consider our children unsalable. Accordingly, there are crises and conflicts that mark the borders between what can and can't be a commodity or what should and should not be considered labor—and it is in the context of those debates that the normative character and the fact that these entities are socially constituted becomes visible. If this social and constituted character seems likely to disappear or to fade away, and processes of naturalization or reification of practical social contexts are widespread—thus blurring or rendering unrecognizable the social origins of the institutions and understandings in question—then this seems to be an important characteristic of practices. Although they are human-made, instances of second nature, the aspect of nature—of the given—seems to overtake them.

Second, economic practices have proved to rely on and be connected with a whole set of "neighboring" practices, a nexus of practices of a broader (noneconomic) concern. These practices inform one another, rely on one another, and are in some cases mutually dependent on one another. As a result, a distinct and determinate form of life and its respective (normative) understanding is involved, once we single out a certain economic practice.

SOME PRELIMINARY RESULTS

Let's briefly summarize what results from conceiving of the economy as a social practice, before addressing the criticizability of it so conceived. In my further reflections, a "practice-account" of the economy, which sees it as a part of a broader form of life, has the following consequences.

The first consequence can be drawn in relation to the question of the *normativity* of economic practices. The thesis that the market and even economic institutions, as such, are a "norm-free sphere" has in recent times been intensely countered with the argument that economic actors are not free from moral considerations, and even more so, are not free from ethical considerations, habits, and dispositions, that is, from their "ethical life" (*Sittlichkeit*).[20] My account of the economy as a social practice agrees with these diagnoses but goes even further. Normativity or the ethical background/embeddedness of the economy don't come into the picture from the outside, let's say, because the economic agents are in fact not free from moral considerations or ethical orientations. If practices are (internally) constituted by norms, then economic practices also have *inherent normative conditions of success*, or ethical-functional norms that are indispensable for their proper functioning.

Second, and to very briefly come back to my first comments about Habermas and the differentiation between "system" and "lifeworld," where the capitalist economy belongs to the system, I believe that, with a practice-theoretic approach, the alternative between an action- and a system-theoretic approach to the economy can be overcome in a meaningful way. One of the advantages of a systemic view of the economy seems to be that it can grasp "mechanisms of social integration" that "do not necessarily coordinate actions via the intentions of participants, but objectively, '*behind the backs*' of participants." The "invisible hand" of the market, then, is the paradigm case of this type of regulation.[21]

But to conceive of the economy as and in a context of social practices doesn't mean that it arises from actions and intentions, or from the results of such. Practices are, as I have said, only partially intentional, only partially explicit, and only partially due to the will and actions of people. They are not planned for in advance but emerge. And when practices "congeal" into institutions (which I think of as states of aggregate practices), they can achieve their own dynamic and take on a life of their own, a phenomenon that is difficult for the parties involved to see. It might then be fruitful to readdress the "systemic" phenomena in a practice and institutional theoretical framework, thereby avoiding the unwanted side effects of an understanding of economics as a nonnormative sphere.

Third, if it follows from the described character of economic activities that, as social practices, they are interrelated with other social practices and aggregate or bundle with them into a form of life, this context must be understood as an open one. The question of which practices are essential for what and which practices are dependent on one another cannot be clearly or conclusively answered a priori. We might think of a variety of different relations among these practices—functional dependencies of some sort, but also cases in which the relation is looser, mutual, or reciprocal. Even if, in some cases, one practice is more authoritative or "steers" more than another, it shouldn't be taken for granted a priori that, for instance, cultural practices would be premised upon economic practices or vice versa. We might, therefore, get rid of a simplistic "base/superstructure" model without losing sight of the mutual dependencies among different practices and norms.

Fourth, in each of the cases I've outlined (even if only sketched), I would argue that the extraeconomic aspects are not just *preconditions* for the economic activities and institutions in the narrower or "proper" sense—that is, for maximizing utilities in the market, for bringing about results in an instrumental fashion through labor, for being able to divide the world along property relations.[22] These far-reaching preconditions cannot easily be taken for granted. In addition, to conceive of economic attitudes as practices that are related to other (economic and noneconomic) practices, and thus as an ensemble within an ensemble, implies that the very distinction between economics and its preconditions, and the inside/outside dichotomy itself, turns out to be less informative and less helpful than we have thought. According to the practice-oriented description of the economic, then, it makes little sense to speak of rescuing a particular class of practices from the context of a form of life.

Among the basic orientations that we might have to reexamine, then, is the widespread concentration of critical efforts—within critical theory as well as within other discourses critical of capitalism—to protect certain spheres (cultural, social, personal) from "contamination" by the supposedly separate economic sphere. Economic practices, according to this view, are not merely reliant on or "embedded" in a surrounding or enabling ethical form of life; they are, rather, *part of the form of life* itself and its respective dynamic.

We are now in a position to readdress Horkheimer's remark. With a concept of the economic as a nexus of practices, we should be able to overcome the narrow concept of the economy criticized by him in two interrelated regards. First, the economy itself is understood in a wider sense, because it is no longer reduced to the (as it is, narrow) attitudes of purpose-oriented, utility-maximizing behavior that seeks to fulfill narrowly defined interests. Second, and further, the relation between economic and other social practices is understood in a wider sense than an economistic determinism allows for.

CAPITALISM AS A FORM OF LIFE?

But then, does this situatedness of economic practices still hold for capitalist societies? Isn't it a defining feature of a capitalist society that "the economy" (and economic rationality) has disentangled itself from the web of social practices in which it was involved—or, as Karl Polanyi has it, isn't the process of "disembedding" the economy from its social context the peculiar (and threatening) characteristic of capitalist societies?[23] Capitalism would then not be a "form of life"; it would, so to speak, not actually "live" but would threaten all forms of life with its dominance (and the domination of abstract and "dead" labor).

As a matter of fact, economic practices and institutions in capitalism take on a certain determinate and determining shape, such as private property in the means of production, the existence of a "free" labor market, and an accumulation of capital oriented toward "gain" instead of "need"—that is, toward the cultivation of capital instead of the consumption of it or subsistence on it. Economic relations seem not only to overtake other aspects of life but also to develop dynamics of their own that "exceed the subjective ends and the control of its participants and that, moreover, cannot be affirmed by them collectively." Here the social is transformed into "social forces."[24]

This is what one might want to refer to as the "systemic" character of a capitalist economy. But then, my (yet to be developed) hypothesis is that the activities involved are still *practices*, based on norms, aggregated into institutions, and involved in the larger practical context of a form of life—even if they might turn out to be "failed" practices in a certain respect.[25] The capitalist organization of the economy only *presents* itself as "disembedding" or "denormativizing," insofar as its dynamic consists in dissolving traditional ethical limits as they expressed themselves institutionally—for example, in premodern guild-like regulations and limitations on economic activity. But, I argue, it also constitutes its own, new normativity. What is being designated here is only the absence of a *specific* ethos and the replacement of a norm and its institutional framework with another one—one that presents itself as ethically "neutral" and based on rational preferences and utility maximization.

Here, one should not be fooled by capitalism's tendency to make the normative and the dense ethical character of economic institutions invisible, something that underlies neoclassical economics, for instance. Even the idea of universal exchangeability, as I have indicated, presupposes as well as constitutes a form of life. Even the practice that conceals its "practice character" is still a practice. And even dissolving the bonds to other practices is still characterized by entanglements, even if those are based upon "false abstraction" (from the entanglement with other practices) and are working behind our backs, without being (as one might have it with Hegel) self-consciously embraced. To put it in a way congenial to Marx's characterization of civil society: the "context of contextlessness" (*Zusammenhang der Zusammenhanglosigkeit*) is still a context. And the ethos of abolishing substantial ethical relations and restrictions, like the ones that were broken in the course of "modern" or capitalist economic institutions (which are both a presupposition and effect of such relations), is still itself an ethos—the *ethos of capitalism*. But then the capitalist form of life itself and its economic practices come into view—and thereby the prospect of a debate about and a critique of capitalism *as* a form of life.

Here, I would like to get one possible misunderstanding out of the way. When I speak of a "critique of capitalism as a form of life," given what has been said, this should not be equated with the so-called "ethical critique" of capitalism, such as the thematization of the ethically detrimental effects of what Max Weber calls the "economic mentality" of capitalism or the "culture of capitalism" on our ways of life.[26] At stake here is not critically judging capitalism against a standard of critique based on a theory of the good life. Rather, if economic practices are conceptualized *as practices* within a wider context of practices, as part of the sociocultural fabric of society, and if even the seemingly inaccessible and self-moving dynamics of economic processes should—in principle—be able to be thought of as results, in any case, of a complex chain of practices, what comes into view, rather, is the prospect of renewing a critique of capitalism as an *irrational* social order in a certain sense.

What, then, is wrong with capitalism (as a form of life)? It is both easy and, arguably, complicated to spell out what exactly is intrinsically wrong with capitalism.[27]

In my discussion, at least one meta-criterion for criticism evolves that might set the stage for further inquiry, building on the topic of "failed" practices and the supposed ethical neutrality of a capitalist economics. There seems to be something wrong with a social order that relies on an ethics that it, at the same time, conceals and universalizes as "neutral." And there seems to be something wrong with practices that we don't see as practices and that are constituted in such a way that the fact of their artificiality (of their "being made") is concealed, as is the case with the economic forces that drive our lives in capitalism.

NOTES

Thanks to Bastian Ronge, Lea Prix, and Benjamin Streim for comments on an earlier draft of this chapter. Most of all, thanks to Anna Katsman for her invaluable comments and revisions, without which I would not have been able to finish this chapter for publication.

1. Max Horkheimer, *Critical Theory: Selected Essays* (New York: Continuum, 1972), 249. Italics added.
2. Georg Lukàcs, "Reification and the Consciousness of the Proletariat," in *History and Class Consciousness: Studies in Marxist Dialectics*, trans. Rodney Livingstone (Cambridge: MIT Press, 1971), 83–222.

3. Bastian Ronge, "How to Think Critically About the Economy? Friedrich Pollock and Jürgen Habermas," conference presentation at Theorizing Crisis: The Economic Thought of the Frankfurt School, Minneapolis, March 28, 2014.
4. I am talking here about critical theory in the narrower or specific sense of the so-called Frankfurt School.
5. Jürgen Habermas, *Theory of Communicative Action*, vol. 2, trans. Thomas McCarthy (Cambridge: Polity, 1987).
6. Habermas, *Theory of Communicative Action*. For a thoughtful discussion of this, see Timo Jütten, "Habermas and Markets," *Constellations* 20, no. 4 (2013): 587–603.
7. Jürgen Habermas, "Demokratie oder Kapitalismus? Vom Elend der nationalstaatlichen Fragmentierung in einer kapitalistisch integrierten Weltgesellschaft," review of *Die gekaufte Zeit*, by Wolfgang Streeck, *Blätter für deutsche und internationale Politik* 5 (May 2013): 59–70. Translated by Ciaran Cronin as "Democracy or Capitalism," http://www.india-seminar.com/2013/649/649_jurgen_habermas.htm.
8. See, for example, J. K. Gibson-Graham, *The End of Capitalism (As We Knew It): A Feminist Critique of Political Economy* (Cambridge: Blackwell, 1996).
9. Axel Honneth, *Freedom's Right: The Social Foundations of Democratic Life* (New York: Columbia University Press, 2014).
10. See Jens Beckert, "Die sittliche Einbettung der Wirtschaft: Von der Effizienz und Differenzierungstheorie zu einer Theorie wirtschaftlicher Felder," *Berliner Journal für Soziologie* 22, no. 2 (2012): 247–66.
11. For a very informative overview of practice theory in its various forms, see Andreas Reckwitz, "Toward a Theory of Social Practices: A Development in Culturalist Theorizing," *European Journal of Social Theory* 5, no. 2 (2001): 243–63. For an extended version of my own understanding, see Rahel Jaeggi, *Kritik von Lebensformen* (Berlin: Suhrkamp, 2014). An English translation is forthcoming from Harvard University Press.
12. See John Searle's famous account of "social" or "institutional" facts of this kind in Searle, *The Construction of Social Reality* (New York: Free Press, 1995).
13. Adam Ferguson, *An Essay on the History of Civil Society* (1767), ed. Fania Oz-Salzberger (Cambridge: Cambridge University Press, 1995).
14. The understanding of property as a "bundle of rights" is a widely used metaphor that has informed much of the theorizing about property. For an early usage of the metaphor, see John R. Commons, *The Distribution of Wealth* (New York: A. M. Kelley, 1963). For a comprehensive discussion of property, see Jeremy Waldron, *The Right to Private Property* (Oxford: Clarendon, 1988).
15. I talk about "faded cosmologies" in analogy to what has been termed "faded metaphors," that is, words whose metaphorical origins have been forgotten.
16. For an extensive discussion of the ethical limits of property and market relations, see, among others, Elisabeth Anderson, *Value in Ethics and Economics* (Cambridge, MA: Harvard University Press, 1993); Margaret Jane Radin, *Contested Commodities* (Cambridge, MA: Harvard University Press, 1996); Debra Satz, *Why Some Things Should Not Be for Sale: The Limits of Markets* (Oxford: Oxford University Press,

2010); and Michael Sandel, *What Money Can't Buy: The Moral Limits of Markets* (New York: Farrar, Straus and Giroux, 2012).
17. See, most famously, Marcel Mauss, *Essai sur le don: Forme et raison de l'échange dans les sociétés archaïques* (Paris: Presses universitaires de France, 2007). See also Bronisław Malinowski, *The Argonauts of the Western Pacific: An Account of Native Enterprise and Adventure in the Archipelagoes of Melanesian New Guinea* (New York: Routledge, 2014).
18. Karl Marx, *Capital*, vol. 1, trans. Ben Fowkes (New York: Vintage, 1976), 283.
19. Jürgen Habermas, "Labour and Interaction: Remarks on Hegel's Jena *Philosophy of Mind*," in *Theory and Practice*, trans. John Viertel (Boston: Beacon, 2011), 142–69.
20. See, among others, Jens Beckert, *Beyond the Market: The Social Foundations of Economic Efficiency* (Princeton, NJ: Princeton University Press, 2002). For a philosophical approach, see Honneth, *Freedom's Right*, chapter 6.
21. Jürgen Habermas, *Between Facts and Norms: Contributions to a Discourse Theory of Law and Democracy*, trans. William Rehg (Cambridge, MA: MIT Press, 1998), 39–40. Italics added.
22. Thanks to Anna Katsman for pressing me on this issue.
23. Karl Polanyi, *The Great Transformation: The Political and Economic Origins of our Time* (Boston: Beacon, 1957).
24. Frederick Neuhouser, "Marx: Alienated Social Forces" (unpublished manuscript). Neuhouser discusses an interpretation of capital as an "alienated social force" that is along the lines of the one sketched here.
25. Thanks, again, to Anna Katsman, who insisted on this point.
26. See, for example, Max Weber, *Economy and Society: An Outline of Interpretive Sociology*, 2 vols., ed. Guenther Roth and Claus Wittich (Berkeley: University of California Press, 1987).
27. See Philip Van Parijs, "What Is Intrinsically Wrong with Capitalism" *Philosophica* 34, no. 2 (1984): 85–102; and Rahel Jaeggi, "Alienation, Exploitation, Dysfunction: Three Paths of the Critique of Capitalism," *Southern Journal of Philosophy* (forthcoming).

V

THE END OF PROGRESS IN POSTCOLONIAL TIMES

9

ADORNO, FOUCAULT, AND THE END OF PROGRESS

Critical Theory in Postcolonial Times

AMY ALLEN

PROLOGUE: CRITICAL THEORY IN POSTCOLONIAL TIMES

In the 1993 sequel to his ground-breaking and field-defining book *Orientalism*, Edward Said offers the following searing indictment of Frankfurt School critical theory: "Frankfurt School critical theory, despite its seminal insights into the relationships between domination, modern society, and the opportunities for redemption through art as critique, is stunningly silent on racist theory, anti-imperialist resistance, and oppositional practice in the empire." Moreover, Said argues, this is no mere oversight; on the contrary, it is a motivated silence. Frankfurt School critical theory, like other versions of European theory more generally, espouses what Said calls an invidious and false universalism, a "blithe universalism" that "assume[s] and incorporate[s] the inequality of races, the subordination of inferior cultures, the acquiescence of those who, in Marx's words, cannot represent themselves and therefore must be represented by others."[1] Such "universalism" has, for Said, played a crucial role in connecting (European) culture with (European) imperialism for centuries, for imperialism as a political project cannot sustain itself without the *idea of empire*, and the idea of empire, in turn, is nourished by a philosophical and cultural imaginary that justifies the political subjugation of distant territories and their native populations through claims that such peoples are less advanced, cognitively inferior, and therefore naturally subordinate.[2]

Twenty-plus years after Said made this charge, not enough has changed; contemporary Frankfurt School critical theory, for the most part, remains all too silent on the problem of imperialism.[3] Neither of the major contemporary theorists most closely associated with the legacy of the Frankfurt School, Jürgen Habermas and Axel Honneth, has made systematic reflection on the paradoxes and challenges produced by the waves of decolonization that characterized the latter half of the twentieth century a central focus of his work in critical theory, nor has either theorist engaged seriously with the now substantial body of literature in postcolonial theory or studies.[4]

Like Said, I believe that there is a reason for this silence, and I think the reason is related to the particular role that ideas of historical progress, development, social evolution, and sociocultural learning play in justifying and grounding the normative perspective of contemporary Frankfurt School critical theory.[5] Habermas and Honneth both rely, in different ways, on a (broadly speaking) left-Hegelian strategy for grounding or justifying the normativity of critical theory, in which the claim that our current communicative or recognitional practices represent the outcome of a progressive historical learning or social evolutionary process, and therefore are deserving of our support and allegiance, figures prominently.[6] Although neither thinker subscribes to an old-fashioned, metaphysically loaded philosophy of history with its strong claims to the unity, necessity, and irreversibility of historical progress, both do endorse a postmetaphysical, contingent, disaggregated story about modernity as the result of a process of historical learning or social evolution. Moreover, and more importantly, both *rely* on this story about historical learning or social evolution to justify and ground their own normative perspective. In other words, both Habermas and Honneth ground their forward-looking conception of progress as a moral-political goal—what I call progress as an imperative—in a backward-looking story about the processes of social evolution or historical learning that have led up to "us"—what I call progress as a "fact."[7] For Habermas, this left-Hegelian understanding of modernity is one strand in a larger argument that also consists of a universalist, formal-pragmatic analysis of linguistic communication; for Honneth, it is part of an attempt to work out a thicker, more contextualist account of normativity. These important and substantial differences aside, however, both thinkers are deeply committed to the idea that European, Enlightenment modernity—or, at least, certain aspects or features thereof—represents an advance over premodern, nonmodern, or traditional forms of life. More importantly, this idea plays a crucial role in grounding the normativity of critical theory for each thinker.

But it is precisely this assumption that proves to be a major obstacle in the project of opening Frankfurt School critical theory up to a serious and sustained engagement with postcolonial studies. Perhaps the major lesson of postcolonial scholarship over the past thirty-five years has been that the developmentalist, progressive reading of history—in which Europe or "the West" is viewed as the outcome of a progressive, historical development—is deeply intertwined with the so-called civilizing mission of the West. Both of these ideas have served, historically, to justify colonialism and imperialism, and they continue to underwrite the informal imperialism of the current world economic, legal, and political order.[8] In other words, as James Tully pithily put the point to me, the language of progress and development is the language of oppression and domination for two-thirds of the world's people.

If we accept Nancy Fraser's Marx-inspired definition of critical theory as the "self-clarification of the struggles and wishes of the age,"[9] and if we further assume that struggles around decolonization and postcolonial politics are among the most significant struggles and wishes of our own age,[10] then it seems to follow that, if critical theory wishes to be truly critical, it should frame its research program and its conceptual framework with an eye toward decolonial and anti-imperialist struggles and concerns. In the light of this desideratum, however, Habermas's and Honneth's ongoing commitment to and reliance upon the idea of historical progress raises a deep and difficult challenge for their approach to critical theory: How can their critical theory be truly critical if it relies on an imperialist metanarrative to ground its approach to normativity?

On the other hand, it must be granted that Habermas and Honneth have adopted this left-Hegelian strategy for good reasons. Seeking to ground their normative perspective immanently, within the existing social world, but without collapsing into relativism or conventionalism, they have turned to the idea of social evolution or historical progress as a way of capturing a kind of transcendence from within. Thus, one might justifiably ask how critical theory can be truly critical if it gives up its distinctive, left-Hegelian strategy for grounding normativity.

In what follows, I attempt to chart a way out of this dilemma by sketching an alternative strategy for thinking through the relationship between history and normativity, drawn from the work of Theodor Adorno and Michel Foucault. My overall aim is to show that critical theory can find, within its own theoretical traditions, the resources not only for decolonizing itself by weaning itself off of its progressive reading of history but also for a contextualist, immanent grounding of its own normative perspective. Accomplishing both of these tasks is necessary if critical theory is to remain truly critical in postcolonial times.

CRITIQUE AS HISTORICAL PROBLEMATIZATION: ADORNO AND FOUCAULT

Unlike Habermas and Honneth, the thinkers of the first generation of the Frankfurt School were extremely skeptical about the idea of historical progress, to say the least. Adorno, for example, famously notes that the catastrophe of Auschwitz "makes all talk of progress towards freedom seem ludicrous" and even makes the "affirmative mentality" that engages in such talk look like "the mere assertion of a mind that is incapable of looking horror in the face and that thereby perpetuates it."[11] Importantly, Adorno did not doubt that progress in the future was *possible* but rather doubted that any sense could be made of the claim that progress in the past is *actual*, and he was extremely critical of the ways in which belief in past progress becomes a kind of blind faith or ideological mystification that stands in the way of attempts to achieve progress in the future. In other words, Adorno sought to radically decouple what I have called progress as an imperative from progress as a "fact"; progress as imperative only becomes possible when we rigorously problematize progress as a "fact." This is what motivates his paradoxical-sounding claim that "progress occurs where it ends."[12]

Adorno's skepticism about progress as a "fact" is shared by one of the other great historico-philosophical thinkers of the late twentieth century,

Michel Foucault. Already in his first major philosophical work, *History of Madness*, Foucault announced his intention to write a history that would "remove all chronology and historical succession from the perspective of a 'progress.'"[13] Foucault's skepticism was motivated by a somewhat different moral sensibility than Adorno's. His critique of progress stems not from an awareness of the horrors of the Holocaust but rather from a sensitivity to the ways in which progress in the human sciences is predicated upon the exclusion of madmen, social deviants, homosexuals, and others deemed "abnormals." But both thinkers converged on the philosophical point that conceptions of historical progress proper necessarily presuppose a suprahistorical, atemporal, universal point of view that we now know to be a metaphysical illusion.

In this sense, both Foucault and Adorno can be understood as attempting to break out of—at least, a certain interpretation of—Hegelian philosophy of history and its closely related conception of dialectics. And yet Foucault, like Adorno, remained firmly committed throughout his career to the basically Hegelian thought that philosophy—understood as a project of critique—is a historically situated endeavor, that philosophy consists in a critical reflection on our historical present that makes use of conceptual tools that are themselves the products of history. In this sense, both thinkers can be understood as attempting to think through the possibilities for a thoroughly historicized understanding of critical philosophy, one that also reflexively historicizes itself and its own notion of historicity. In so doing, Adorno and Foucault offer an interesting and compelling alternative to Habermas's and Honneth's left-Hegelianism; Adorno's and Foucault's is a more radical taking up of the Hegelian legacy that preserves and deepens its historicizing impulse while jettisoning its progressive claims.

Precisely because of their skepticism about progress, Adorno and Foucault are often read as offering a negative philosophy of history, a *Verfallsgeschichte*, a conservative story of history as a process of decline and fall. In contrast to this interpretation, I argue that an alternative methodology for thinking history can be found in the work of Adorno and Foucault. Neither progressive nor regressive, this methodology weaves together vindicatory and subversive genealogies—and, as such, it reconstructs history as a story of both progress *and* regress—in the service of a distinctive genealogical aim: a critical problematization of our present historical moment. This problematization is part of a project of immanent critique that aims not at a totalizing refusal or abstract negation of the normative inheritance of modernity but rather at a fuller realization of that inheritance and its ideals of freedom, inclusion, and respect for the Other.

In the remainder of this section, I identify six common themes in the work of Adorno and Foucault, which form the core features of my conception of critique as historical problematization. These themes are reason and power, utopia and utopianism, the historicization of History, genealogy as problematization, critical distance (or philosophizing with a hammer), and problematization and the normative inheritance of modernity. In the final section of the chapter, I will discuss what resources this alternative conception of the relationship between history and normativity offers for a critical theory that seeks to engage in the difficult work of decolonizing itself.

REASON AND POWER

Although Adorno and Foucault are both sharply critical of the idea that history is to be understood as the progressive realization of reason, neither endorses a totalizing critique or an abstract negation of Enlightenment rationality. For Adorno, "what makes the concept of progress dialectical, in a strictly nonmetaphorical sense, is the fact that reason, its organ, is just one thing. That is to say, it does not contain two strata, one that dominates nature and one that conciliates it. Both strata share in all its aspects." In other words, reason is entangled with power, and we cannot, as critical theorists following Habermas have attempted to do, identify a use or a stratum of reason that is not so entangled. Yet Adorno is no advocate of "the denial of reason"; indeed, for him, such a denial would be "certainly not a whit superior to the much derided faith in progress."[14] Rather, the task for philosophy, as Adorno understands it, is to reflect on its own activity as a rational enterprise and, in so doing, to attempt to transcend itself, to transcend the concept, as he says, "by way of the concept."[15]

Similarly, although Foucault's work foregrounds the relationship between reason and power, he does not conclude from this that reason should be put on trial. "To my mind," he writes, "nothing would be more sterile." To say that the entanglement of reason with power justifies putting reason on trial would be to find oneself trapped into "playing the arbitrary and boring part of either the rationalist or the irrationalist,"[16] a trap that Foucault elsewhere refers to as "the 'blackmail' of the Enlightenment." To be sure, unlike Adorno, Foucault is skeptical that " 'dialectical' nuances" can enable us to escape this trap.[17] Moreover, he suggests that his attempt to "analyze specific rationalities rather than always invoking the progress of rationalization in general" distinguishes his approach to the entanglement of rationalities and power relations from that of the Frankfurt School.[18] Nevertheless, like Adorno, he insists that it is the task of philosophy, understood as a mode of critical thought, to reflect on its own rational activity and its entanglements with dangerous relations of power. As he sees it, the central question of critical philosophy is, "How can we exist as rational beings, fortunately committed to practicing a rationality that is unfortunately crisscrossed by intrinsic dangers?"[19]

UTOPIA AND UTOPIANISM

But if the task of philosophy is to reflect on its own rational activity and, in so doing, to attempt to transcend itself, what sense can be made of this notion of transcendence? If the aim of philosophy is to push beyond itself, then what is meant here by "beyond"? One might think that there is an abstract, metaphysically loaded conception of utopia waiting in the wings here. Although Adorno is less hostile than Foucault to the concept of utopia, both are careful to offer only negativistic accounts of utopia or the good life toward which such notions of transcendence might aim.[20] For Adorno, we cannot glimpse the right life from within the wrong one, and the very idea of reconciliation forbids it being posited as a positive concept.[21] This is why utopia can only be glimpsed indirectly and in an anticipatory way through the illumination cast by certain works of modern art.[22] Similarly, for Foucault, we cannot have access to a point of view outside of power relations, which means that any conception of a society that is devoid of power relations will be utopian in the negative sense. Both thinkers are very attuned to the fact that any vision of the good life offered from within a society structured by relations of domination is likely to reproduce those power relations, to be infected by them, so they both eschew utopian speculations about what kind of content "the good life" might have.

However, there is also a sense in which Adorno and Foucault are more radically utopian thinkers than either Habermas or Honneth, for they hold on to the possibility and desirability of radical social change in the direction of an open-ended conception of the future. In other words, Adorno and Foucault envision social transformation not just as the better and fuller realization of our existing normative ideals—for example, a version of liberal democracy that is more transparent and less distorted by power relations, or a recognition order that is more inclusive and egalitarian—but also as the possibility of the radical transformation of those ideals themselves, where that transformation would not necessarily be a regression. The early work of Foucault, in particular, is filled with thought experiments that pose this possibility: someday we might look back on our present preoccupation with mental illness and wonder what all the fuss was about, and from that point of view our current historical a priori may well seem benighted. Although we can't imagine what it would be like to inhabit that future or that point of view, there is a critical value for Foucault in being open to this possibility and to the idea that the creatures who inhabit that point of view will inhabit a different historical a priori and hence a different moral universe.

In order to be genuinely critical, critical theory has to be open to both kinds of social transformation—not just reformism, whether radical or not, but also radical social change. It also has to be careful not to prejudge the outcome of such radical transformations, for to do so would necessarily be to presuppose that our own historical form of life is not only superior to all that came before it but also unsurpassable, that it constitutes the end point of history. Such a presupposition not only is conceptually problematic for a theory that aims to be postmetaphysical, but also, for reasons sketched out in the introduction to this chapter, is politically problematic for a theory that aims to be truly critical.

THE HISTORICIZATION OF HISTORY

Both Adorno and Foucault understood their own critical, historico-philosophical projects as historically situated. In this way, both attempted to think through the logic of the second, historicist Enlightenment, to apply the insights of this historically situated conception of rationality reflexively to the historico-philosophical enterprise itself. This is evident in Foucault's early work, when he makes it clear that history is important for him not because historicity is characteristic of our reason or our existence but rather because History—the Hegelian conception of history as the progressive unfolding of a rationalization process—is central to our modern historical a priori, which is thus both historical and Historical. The point of Foucault's historicization of History in *History of Madness* is to show the historical contingency of this idea of History and to analyze the role that it plays in the exclusion and domination of those who are deemed unreasonable.

Similarly, Adorno, in good dialectical fashion, understood his conception of philosophy as historically situated as itself historically situated. In this way, he too historicized his own conception of historicity.[23] Indeed, Adorno is sharply critical of both Heidegger and Hegel on precisely this point, because they fail, in different ways, to historicize their understandings of historicity.[24] According to Adorno, the proper response to this unhistorical conception in which history becomes "mutation as immutability" is to perform a reverse dialectical "transmutation," this time "of metaphysics into history."[25]

GENEALOGY AS PROBLEMATIZATION

The historicization of History is closely bound up with its problematization, which means two things: first, revealing the historical contingency of our own historically situated point of view; and second, showing how that point of view has been contingently made up and, as such, is bound up with particular relations of power.[26] Because our historically situated point of view is inflected with a certain conception of History, effectively problematizing that point of view demands a distinctive way of taking up while also radically transforming that conception, which I will characterize as a distinctive kind of genealogical method. Following Colin Koopman, who in turn builds on some insights from Bernard Williams, we can distinguish three different modes of genealogical inquiry: subversive, vindicatory, and problematizing.[27]

The common core of these three ways of doing genealogy is their attempt to explicate how specific, contingent historical processes have led human beings to develop and embrace particular values or concepts. However, each of these three modes of genealogical inquiry uses such knowledge for a different end. The subversive mode of genealogy aims not only to raise the question of the historical emergence of our values but also to reject them as lacking value in some other, more important sense. Vindicatory genealogy, by contrast, traces the historical emergence of our values with an eye toward showing those values to be justified and reasonable. The third mode of genealogical inquiry has both subversive and vindicatory features insofar as it aims to reveal both the dangers and the promise contained in the values, concepts, or forms of life whose contingent history it traces, but its aim is neither simply subversive nor vindicatory. Rather, its aim is a critical problematization of our historical present.

In a late interview, Foucault highlights the importance of problematization for his own practice of critique: "It is true that my attitude isn't a result of the form of critique that claims to be a methodical examination in order to reject all possible solutions except for the valid one. It is more on the order of a 'problematization'—which is to say, the development of a domain of acts, practices, and thoughts that seem to me to pose problems for politics."[28] However, the aim of this critical problematization is not, as Foucault's critics have often assumed, to subvert or undermine the acts, practices, and thoughts that are so problematized. Rather, as he put it in an oft-quoted passage from another of his late interviews: "I would like to do the genealogy of problems, of *problématiques*. My point is not that everything is bad but that everything is dangerous, which is not exactly the same as bad. If everything is dangerous, then we always have something to do."[29]

Moreover, although the aim of Foucault's genealogies is clearly not to vindicate our current practices or forms of rationality, there is an important if often underappreciated vindicatory element to his problematizing genealogical method. This element comes out clearly in Foucault's late work on the Enlightenment, when he emphasizes "the extent to which a type of philosophical interrogation—one that simultaneously problematizes man's relation to the present, man's historical mode of being, and the constitution of the self as an autonomous subject—is rooted in the Enlightenment."[30] In other words, Foucault situates his own problematizing critical method within the philosophical ethos of critique that forms the positive normative inheritance of the Enlightenment—an inheritance that demands fidelity not to its doctrinal elements but rather to its critical attitude and that involves reaffirming the legacy of the Enlightenment in and through its radical transformation.

Although Adorno does not use the terms "genealogy" or "problematization"—much less "genealogy as problematization" or "problematizing genealogy"—to describe his approach to history, the outlines of such an approach can nonetheless be found in his work.[31] One of his major criticisms of not only Hegel but also Marx and Engels is that they failed to acknowledge that the antagonism that they saw as the fundamental driving force of history was itself historically contingent, that "it need not have been." Adorno links this recognition to the possibility of a specifically critical social theory: "Only if things might have gone differently; if the totality is recognized as a socially necessary semblance, as the hypostasis of the universal pressed out of individual human beings; if its claim to be absolute is broken—only then will a critical social consciousness retain its freedom to think that things might be different someday."[32]

Moreover, as we have seen, Adorno clearly and emphatically rejects any straightforwardly vindicatory reading of history. However, his aim isn't a straightforward rejection of the values and norms of Enlightenment modernity, either. For example, although Adorno is highly critical of the entanglement of the modern principle of equality with capitalist mechanisms of exchange and bourgeois coldness, and thus with structures of reification and relations of domination, he also regards these principles as important historical achievements that protect individuals from some kinds of injustice.[33] Thus, the aim of Adorno's philosophy of history, like Foucault's, is to chart the simultaneous historical emergence of both the domination and the promise of the ideals of the Enlightenment—the unity, as he says, of discontinuity and continuity.[34] The method for doing so can be understood as a kind of problematizing genealogy, even if Adorno himself doesn't use this term.

CRITICAL DISTANCE, OR PHILOSOPHIZING WITH A HAMMER

However, for it to be possible to problematize our own historically situated point of view and reflect on its entanglements with power relations, we must be able to get enough critical distance on that historically situated point of view to see it *as* a point of view. Adorno and Foucault offer us two tools for gaining such critical distance. First, both make use of an image or a figure that cannot be reconciled into the dialectical unfolding of History; by resisting recuperation into the dialectic, this figure reveals the fragmentary nature of, and opens up lines of fragility or fracture within, our Hegelian Historical modernity, thus making possible our reflection on it. This figure of whatever escapes the reconciling, unifying logic of modernity is, for Adorno, the nonidentical and, for Foucault, unreason.

Although it might be tempting to see Adorno's negative dialectics as rooted in a metaphysical claim about the nonidentical, understood as the ultimate *Ding an sich*, negative dialectics is better understood as a historically situated response to a particular form of social organization and its accompanying worldview. As Adorno puts it, "Dialectical reason's own essence has come to be and will pass, like antagonistic society."[35] In other words, for Adorno, negative dialectics is not a transcendental condition of possibility for thinking but rather a historically situated tool for thinking through our present. It is necessary because of the historically contingent unfolding of the dialectic of Enlightenment; it is a method for jump-starting a historical dialectic that has come to a standstill.

Similarly, Foucault's invocation of unreason should not be thought of as a metaphysical gesture; rather, for Foucault, it is the figure of unreason that opens up lines of fragility and fracture within our historical a priori and allows us to take up critical distance on that historical a priori.[36] For both Adorno and Foucault, tracing the figure of the nonidentical or of unreason through the fragmentary, nonsystematic, and experimental work of critical thought—or through the anticipatory illumination cast by works of art—serves to reveal the fragmentary, fragile, and internally fractured nature of our present historical situation.

However, because our historical a priori sets the historically specific conditions of possibility of thought for us, it forms the backdrop for what "thought . . . silently thinks," as Foucault once put it.[37] Freeing thought up in relation to what it silently thinks is necessary for enabling it to think differently, but freeing oneself up in this way means pulling oneself free of the very conditions of possibility of one's own thinking and acting. The shape and contours of some prior historical epoch can be uncovered through gentle digging, but to see one's own historical a priori as historical, one must "philosophize with a hammer," as Foucault, following Nietzsche, put it. Or, as Adorno puts it, "The dialectic advances by way of extremes, driving thoughts with the utmost consequentiality to the point where they turn back on themselves, instead of qualifying them."[38]

PROBLEMATIZATION AND THE NORMATIVE INHERITANCE OF MODERNITY

Finally, and perhaps most importantly, the problematization of our own point of view can and should be understood not as a rejection or abstract negation of the normative inheritance of modernity but rather as a fuller realization of its central value, namely, freedom.[39] Adorno's account of "second nature" reveals the close link between his philosophy of history and the possibility of freedom. Central to Adorno's complicated account of the relationship between nature and history is the idea that historically constituted objects come, over time, to seem natural and therefore unchangeable. Revealing this second nature to be historically contingent and therefore changeable by uncovering the illusory, congealed history contained within it—an illusion that is reinforced by narratives of historical progress—is a crucial task of critical theory for Adorno.[40] This is very close to Foucault's characterization of genealogy as the attempt to "record the singularity of events outside of any monotonous finality; it must seek them in the most unpromising places, in what we tend to feel is without history."[41] This sort of unmasking of the congealed history contained within what we tend to feel is without history breaks history's illusory and ideological spell, and this is precisely how Adorno understands freedom: "The positive meaning of freedom lies in the potential, in the possibility, of breaking the spell or escaping from it."[42] Breaking or escaping the spell, freeing thought up from what it silently thinks in order to enable it to think differently—these both are ways of, as Foucault once put it, "seeking to give new impetus, as far and wide as possible, to the undefined work of freedom."[43]

So, for both Adorno and Foucault, the problematization of our own point of view has a normative point. It aims not at a debunking of the core normative ideals of Enlightenment modernity but rather at a *fuller realization of the ideal of freedom*. But Adorno's work goes further than this, and in this sense goes beyond Foucault, by also suggesting that the problematization of our own point of view not only enhances our freedom in relation to second nature or to our historical a priori; it also is required if we are to do justice to the Other. This idea comes out in the final lecture of Adorno's lectures on moral philosophy. After spending most of the lecture course offering a detailed and devastating critique of Kantian moral philosophy, Adorno argues, in his final lecture, that moral philosophy can only be possible today as a critique of moral philosophy.[44] Life under modern capitalism is so deformed and distorted that moral philosophy today cannot provide plans or blueprints for living the good life; as Adorno famously laments, "Wrong life cannot be lived rightly."[45] Hence, the goal of moral philosophy should be to uncover this situation and to reflect on—rather than obscure, deny, or ignore—the contradictions to which it leads. The most that one can say about the good life under current conditions is that it "would consist in resistance to the forms of the bad life that have been seen through and critically dissected by the most progressive minds. Other than this negative prescription, no guidance can really be envisaged."[46]

Following on from his critique of Kant, Adorno contends that we have to resist the abstract rigorism of Kantian morality but without giving up on notions of conscience and responsibility without which the idea of the good life is inconceivable. "At this point," Adorno writes, "we find ourselves really and truly in a contradictory situation. We need to hold fast to moral norms, to self-criticism, to the question of right and wrong, and at the same time to a sense of the fallibility of the authority that has the confidence to undertake such self-criticism." In other words, we have to hold fast persistently to the norms that we learned from our experience while at the same time engaging in self-criticism of what presents itself as "unyielding" and "inexorable." Indeed, Adorno continues, it is "by reflecting on our own limitations [that] we can learn to do justice to those who are different," and "true injustice is always to be found at the precise point where you put yourself in the right and other people in the wrong." This is why Adorno claims that, if you were to press him into offering a list of cardinal virtues, he "would probably respond cryptically by saying that I could think of nothing except for modesty," by which he means that "we must have a conscience, but may not insist on our own conscience."[47]

I submit that the best way of achieving the stance of modesty is through a critical, genealogical problematization that combines both vindicatory and subversive, or progressive and regressive, strands but whose aim is neither simply vindication nor subversion. By allowing us to reflexively critique the social institutions and practices, patterns of cultural meaning and subject formation, and normative commitments that have made us who we are, problematizing critique opens up a space of critical distance on those institutions, practices, and so forth, thereby freeing us up in relation to them, and thus also in relation to ourselves. Notice that, for Adorno, this modest stance is motivated not only by the epistemic point that we have a tendency to go wrong in our normative judgments and thus have a duty to call them into question. Although Adorno was enough of a historicist and a practitioner of immanent critique to agree with Foucault that, as far as the project of critique goes, "we are always in this position of beginning again,"[48] Adorno also makes the further claim that the problematization of one's own point of view is *morally* required if we are to do justice to those who are different from ourselves. In other words—and here is a different way of construing the normative point of the method of problematization—such problematization is motivated not merely by epistemic concerns about our inescapable fallibility, given our inability to have access to a god's eye point of view, but also by our commitment to equal respect for the Other, that is, to justice.

ADORNO, FOUCAULT, AND THE "POSTCOLONIAL"

Adorno and Foucault offer a radically different way of thinking about the backward- and forward-looking conceptions of progress in relation to the project of critical theory. Both reject any vindicatory, backward-looking story of historical progress as a "fact" about what has led up to "us," but they do so not in favor of a romantic story of decline and fall but rather in the service of a critical problematization of the present. Moreover, at least Adorno, if not also Foucault,[49] holds on to the forward-looking conception of progress as a moral-political imperative, though he does reconceive progress negativistically as the avoidance of catastrophe and decouples this forward-looking conception from the backward-looking notion of progress as a historical "fact." In stark contrast to Habermas and Honneth, for whom the backward-looking story of historical learning, social evolution, or progress plays a crucial role in grounding their normative visions of what would count as progress in a forward-looking sense, Adorno claims that calling into question the conception of progress as a historical "fact" is necessary for any kind of future progress to be possible.

Thus, even though Adorno doesn't give up on the possibility of progress in the future—in fact, he finds such a resignation to be not only conceptually problematic but also morally repugnant—his understanding of what might count as progress in the future is not rooted in a backward-looking story of progress as what has led up to "us." Progress occurs only where it comes to an end. Although this claim of Adorno's did not seem to be motivated by postcolonial concerns, and although his relationship to postcolonial scholarship—like Foucault's—is rather vexed and complicated, it seems to me that this idea is enormously productive for a critical theory that aims to decolonize itself.

Indeed, despite their well-documented and oft-noted Eurocentrism, both Foucault and Adorno have provided fruitful resources for postcolonial theorizing. Thus, on the one hand, Foucault's work served as an inspiration for a great deal of work in postcolonial theory, including, but certainly not limited to, one of the founding texts of the field, Said's *Orientalism*. Said productively takes up Foucault's notion of discourse, analyzing Orientalism as a discursive construction that dictated how the West understood the East, as a form of "knowledge" that was also a form of colonial power (though it was largely an ideological fantasy of "the Orient" that bore little relation to the actual cultures subsumed under that heading).[50] This analysis proved so productive for postcolonial studies that Ann Laura Stoler could observe, in 1995, that "no single analytic framework has saturated the field of colonial studies so completely over the last decade as that of Foucault."[51]

Yet Foucault's work has also been subjected to harsh critique by postcolonial thinkers—including the later Said, Gayatri Spivak, and Stoler herself.[52] Stoler's important book *Race and the Education of Desire* focuses on Foucault's later work and argues that his historical genealogies of power relations in European modernity systematically ignore issues relating to colonialism, racism, and liberal imperialism. As Stoler puts it, "What is striking is how consistently Foucault's own framing of the European bourgeois order has been exempt from the very sorts of criticism that his insistence on the fused regimes of knowledge/power would seem to encourage and allow."[53] Stoler's critique is motivated by an understandable frustration with Foucault's centrality to postcolonial theorizing, despite his own studied ignorance of the problem of colonialism, an ignorance that is all the more galling considering that Foucault could not have been unaware of this problem. He lived and taught in Tunisia in the late 1960s, and no French person of his generation could have been blind to the Algerian question. As Robert Young has argued, Foucault's "virtual silence" on issues of race and colonialism renders his work "so scrupulously Eurocentric that you begin to wonder whether there isn't a deliberate strategy involved." And yet, Young continues, "The lasting paradox is that despite the absence of explicit discussions of colonialism, Foucault's work has been a central theoretical reference point for postcolonial analysis."[54]

Such issues have played out somewhat differently in the case of Adorno. His oft-noted Eurocentrism makes the usefulness of his work for postcolonial theory seem doubtful, at least at first glance. Thus, Espen Hammer notes that Adorno's "blunt Eurocentrism" is evident in the fact that he was "virtually oblivious to the concerns of postcolonialism, including racism, discrimination, and imperialism," and the editors of *Adorno: A Critical Reader* acknowledge that he was "deeply Eurocentric" and "possessed no knowledge of a world outside of Austria and Germany, let alone Europe."[55] However, despite this deep and blunt Eurocentrism, there has been a wave of attempts in recent years to claim Adorno as a thinker with substantial resources to offer postcolonial theory, focusing particularly on his conception of negative dialectics.[56] Namita Goswami, for example, offers a "radical postcolonial reading of Adorno," arguing that "Adorno's conception of negative dialectics can be understood as postcolonial in its understanding of difference," where "difference," for Adorno, means nonantagonistic heterogeneity. Goswami also turns to Adorno for the kind of "hopeful despair" that she argues is appropriate to our historical moment, particularly in the face of anthropogenic climate change and its differential effects across the globe.[57]

In light of these complex debates, which I cannot even attempt to settle here, I would like to emphasize that my point is not that postcolonial theory can be understood as a simple or straightforward extension of a certain radical strand of European critical theory represented by the likes of Foucault and Adorno. Such a claim would itself be an instance of what Dipesh Chakrabarty calls "historicism," "for such a thought would merely repeat the temporal structure of the statement, 'first in the West, and then elsewhere.'"[58] Nor is it my aim to show that Foucault and Adorno offer important resources for postcolonial theorizing—although I think that this may well be the case. Rather, my point is that Adorno and Foucault—for all of their faults, their own tendencies toward Eurocentrism, and their blindness, willful or not, to issues of colonialism and imperialism—nevertheless offer important resources *within the tradition of critical theory* for the crucially important project of *decolonizing* critical theory. They do so precisely because and to the extent to which they enable us to rethink critical theory's commitment to the idea of historical progress. By historicizing and critically problematizing the very Hegelian notion of History as the progressive unfolding of a rationalization process that progressively rationalizes power relations—on which Habermas and Honneth still implicitly or explicitly rely, even as they seek to recast this idea in more deflationary, pragmatic, and postmetaphysical terms—Adorno and Foucault offer an alternative way of thinking through the relationship between normativity and history, a radically reflexive and historicized critical methodology that understands critique as the wholly immanent and fragmentary practice of opening up lines of fragility and fracture within the social world.

One might object that this approach is too inward looking, too focused on debates and problems internal to critical theory—and to a specific tradition of critical theory, at that. This objection could come in at least two different versions. One version would say that critical theorists should engage with big challenges, such as human rights and international law, the critique of capitalism, the prospects of transnational democracy, and so forth, and that the conception of critical theory sketched here is too inward looking, even navel gazing, to be of much use for such projects. To that critic, my response is that my project is, in a sense, much more modest than she assumes it to be. My aim is not to offer a complete critical theory of society, nor is it to suggest that the reading of Foucault and Adorno that I have sketched here can provide us with such a theory. Rather, my aim is to address a very specific but also quite fundamental and important problem in critical theory, namely, the problem of normative foundations. With respect to that problem, I hope to have shown that the existing strategies for grounding the normativity of critical theory, beholden as they are to ideas of historical progress and sociocultural learning or evolution, are deeply problematic and are ultimately incompatible with a theory that aims to be truly critical, in the sense of aiming at the self-clarification of the struggles and wishes of our postcolonial age. Drawing on my reading of Adorno and Foucault, I have sketched an alternative conception of the relationship among history, normativity, and critique, one that can open critical theory up to a deep and substantial engagement with the challenges of postcolonialism.

A closely related objection has to do with the specific way I have sought to stage the encounter between critical theory and the postcolonial. After all, one might argue, following Terry Eagleton, that it is far from obvious that taking on the insights of "postcolonialism"—understood as a particular theoretical project, prominent in Europe and the United States, heavily influenced by French poststructuralism—is the best way to think through the challenges and injustices of postcolonialism—understood as the current social, economic, and political situation of formally decolonized states, which are still subjected to gross forms of global injustice, largely but not exclusively through the workings of the international financial system.[59] If one wants to think through the challenges of postcolonialism, one might ask, why not turn instead to Marxism, which after all offers ample resources for connecting the critique of capitalism to the critique of imperialism, even if Marx himself never quite connected all of those dots? A longer story needs to be told here, about the ongoing, heated debates between Marxists and postcolonial theorists, and about the not unrelated, and equally heated, debates between Marxists and poststructuralists.[60] But the upshot of that story is that Marx's philosophy of history does not move far enough away from the progressive, developmental reading of history that is rightfully a central target of post- and decolonial critique. This is *not* to say that none of Marx's insights are fruitful, nor is it to say that the critique of capitalism is not important for contemporary critical theory; many of them are, and of course it is. It is just to say that *for the specific project of rethinking the relationship between normativity and history*, we are better off turning to Adorno and Foucault than to Marx.

But here's where the second version of the inwardness objection arises. My approach could be seen as too inward looking in a different sense, too focused on mining the insights of European thinkers to address the legacies of colonialism, and thus too committed to a kind of decolonization from within, when what is needed is a more radical decolonization from without. Why, after all, do I turn to Adorno and Foucault rather than to C. L. R. James, Frantz Fanon, or Enrique Dussel? By keeping the focus on European thinkers, am I not, ultimately, just offering another Eurocentric critique of Eurocentrism, thus repeating the very gesture that I claim to be criticizing?

Following Walter Mignolo, I would say, in response, that although the Eurocentric critique of Eurocentrism may well be insufficient for the project of fully decolonizing critical theory, this does not mean that it is unnecessary. It is true that what I have offered here is largely, though not entirely, an internal critique of European critical theory. This is partly a function of my own social, institutional, and intellectual formation, as someone who was trained in the critical social theory tradition in institutions of higher learning in the United States and Germany—as Richard Rorty never tired of reminding us, we have to start from where we are. But the point of engaging in this kind of internal critique is to show that, even if we start from the tradition of European critical theory, compelling critical theory to decenter its own critical perspective can enable critical theory to become something else.

NOTES

I am grateful to Wendy Brown, Penelope Deutscher, Barnor Hesse, Cristina Lafont, Matthias Lutz-Bachmann, Thomas McCarthy, Charles Mills, Sarah Song, Joshua Cohen, and participants in the Berkeley Political Theory Workshop for helpful comments on an earlier version of this essay.

1. Edward Said, *Culture and Imperialism* (New York: Vintage, 1993), 278–79.
2. Said, *Culture and Imperialism*, 10–11.
3. One prominent exception to this trend is Thomas McCarthy, *Race, Empire, and the Idea of Human Development* (Cambridge: Cambridge University Press, 2009). I discuss some of my criticisms of McCarthy more fully in Amy Allen, review of *Race, Empire, and the Idea of Human Development*, by Thomas McCarthy, *Constellations* 18, no. 3 (September 2011): 487–92.
4. To be sure, in his recent work, Jürgen Habermas has rethought his account of modernity in light of challenges to the secularization thesis and has embraced the concept of multiple modernities. This is a substantial revision to his theory but does not, in my view, go far enough in responding to the challenge sketched here. I discuss this aspect of his recent work in Amy Allen, *The End of Progress: Decolonizing the Normative Foundations of Critical Theory* (New York: Columbia University Press, 2016), chapter 2. Axel Honneth, unlike Habermas, has mostly refrained from discussing how his recognition theory might apply in a global context, with the notable exception of Honneth, "Recognition Between States: On the Moral Substrate of International Relations," in *The I in We: Studies in the Theory of Recognition*, trans. Joseph Ganahl (Cambridge: Polity, 2012), 137–52. Although his chapter offers an interesting extension of his recognition theory to the realm of international politics, it does not engage with issues of postcolonialism, except rather obliquely, nor does it deviate from his basic strategy for grounding his normative project, which is the main focus of my critique.
5. On the importance of the idea of progress for normativity in Habermas's work, see David S. Owen, *Between Reason and History: Habermas and the Idea of Progress* (New York: SUNY Press, 2002). On Habermas and Honneth, see Matthias Iser, *Empörung und Fortschritt: Grundlagen einer kritischen Theorie der Gesellschaft* (Frankfurt: Campus Verlag, 2008).
6. To be sure, a good deal of work needs to be done to back up these interpretive claims, especially in the case of Habermas, who can also be read as a neo-Kantian moral constructivist. For a detailed interpretive argument for the claims summarized here, see Allen, *The End of Progress*, chapters 2 and 3.
7. "Fact" is in scare quotes here because this obviously is also a normative judgment. I borrow the term from McCarthy, though I use it differently than he does. See McCarthy, *Race, Empire, and the Idea of Human Development*, 155–65.
8. The relevant literature in postcolonial theory is too vast to cite in a single endnote, but Said's work could be taken as exemplary in this respect. See Said, *Orientalism* (New York: Vintage, 1994); and Said, *Culture and Imperialism*. For a helpful overview and defense of the idea of informal imperialism as applied to the current global order, see James Tully, "On Law, Democracy and Imperialism," in *Public Philosophy in a New Key*, vol. 2, *Imperialism and Civic Freedom* (Cambridge: Cambridge University Press, 2008), 127–65. I discuss this issue in much greater detail in Allen, *The End of Progress*, chapter 1.

9. Nancy Fraser, "What's Critical About Critical Theory? The Case of Habermas and Gender," in *Unruly Practices: Power, Discourse, and Gender in Contemporary Social Theory* (Minneapolis: University of Minnesota Press, 1989), 113.
10. This is not to say that decolonization *began* in our age, which would be to ignore the very different temporalities and trajectories of decolonization in the Caribbean and the Americas, for example. It is just to say that the waves of formal decolonization in the wake of World War II, and the resulting neocolonial and informally imperialist global political order that has been in place at least since 1970, constitute and are the loci of some of the most significant social and political struggles and wishes of our age.
11. Theodor Adorno, *History and Freedom: Lectures 1964–1965*, ed. Rolf Tiedemann (Cambridge: Polity, 2006), 159.
12. Theodor Adorno, "Progress," in *Critical Models: Interventions and Catchwords*, trans. Henry Pickford (New York: Columbia University Press, 2005), 150.
13. Michel Foucault, *History of Madness*, trans. Jonathan Murphy and Jean Khalfa (New York: Routledge, 2006), 122.
14. Adorno, *History and Freedom*, 157 and 169.
15. Theodor Adorno, *Negative Dialectics*, trans. E. B. Ashton (New York: Continuum, 1973), 15.
16. Michel Foucault, "The Subject and Power," in *Essential Works of Michel Foucault*, vol. 3, *Power*, ed. James D. Faubion (New York: The New Press, 2000), 328.
17. Michel Foucault, "What Is Enlightenment?" in *Essential Works of Michel Foucault*, vol. 1, *Ethics: Subjectivity and Truth*, ed. Paul Rabinow (New York: The New Press, 1997), 312–13.
18. Foucault, "Subject and Power," 328–29.
19. Michel Foucault, "Space, Knowledge, and Power," in *Power*, 358.
20. Unlike Foucault, who prefers to speak of heterotopia rather than utopia, Adorno offers a definition of utopia that is linked to his notion of reconciliation understood as a nonviolent, nontotalizing togetherness of diversity. See Adorno, *Negative Dialectics*, 150. For a compelling defense of Adorno's negativism, see Fabian Freyenhagen, *Adorno's Practical Philosophy: Living Less Wrongly* (Cambridge: Cambridge University Press, 2013).
21. See Adorno, *Negative Dialectics*, 145.
22. See Albrecht Wellmer, *The Persistence of Modernity: Essays on Aesthetics, Ethics, and Postmodernism*, trans. David Midgley (Cambridge, MA: MIT Press, 1991), 63.
23. On this point, see Antonio Vázquez-Arroyo, "Universal History Disavowed," *Postcolonial Studies* 11, no. 4 (2008): 458.
24. For Adorno's critique of Heidegger, see *History and Freedom*, 123; for his critique of Hegel, see *Negative Dialectics*, 356–57.
25. Adorno, *History and Freedom*, 123; *Negative Dialectics*, 360.
26. On the first point, see Raymond Geuss, *Outside Ethics* (Princeton: Princeton University Press, 2005), 153–60; on the second, see Colin Koopman, *Genealogy as Critique: Foucault and the Problems of Modernity* (Indianapolis: Indiana University Press, 2013), chapter 3.

27. Koopman, *Genealogy as Critique*, chapter 3. See also Bernard Williams, *Truth and Truthfulness: An Essay in Genealogy* (Princeton: Princeton University Press, 2002).
28. Michel Foucault, "Polemics, Politics, and Problematizations," in *Ethics*, 114.
29. Michel Foucault, "On the Genealogy of Ethics," in *Ethics*, 256.
30. Foucault, "What Is Enlightenment?," 312.
31. This genealogical element in Adorno should not be too surprising, given the heavy influence of Friedrich Nietzsche on his work. For an insightful discussion of Adorno's relation to Nietzsche, particularly with respect to method, see Christoph Menke, "Genealogy and Critique: Two Forms of Ethical Questioning of Morality," in *The Cambridge Companion to Adorno*, ed. Tom Huhn (Cambridge: Cambridge University Press, 2004), 302–27.
32. Adorno, *Negative Dialectics*, 321 and 323.
33. See, for example, Adorno, *History and Freedom*, 253.
34. Adorno, *Negative Dialectics*, 320.
35. Adorno, *Negative Dialectics*, 141.
36. See Michel Foucault, "Critical Theory/Intellectual History," in *Critique and Power: Recasting the Foucault/Habermas Debate*, ed. Michael Kelly (Cambridge, MA: MIT Press, 1994), 109–37.
37. Michel Foucault, *The History of Sexuality*, vol. 2, *The Use of Pleasure*, trans. Robert Hurley (New York: Vintage, 1985), 9.
38. Theodor Adorno, *Minima Moralia: Reflections from a Damaged Life*, trans. E. F. N. Jephcott (London: Verso, 2005), 86.
39. On this point, see also Freyenhagen, *Adorno's Practical Philosophy*, 82–83.
40. See, for example, Adorno, *History and Freedom*, 135.
41. Michel Foucault, "Nietzsche, Genealogy, History," in *Essential Works of Michel Foucault*, vol. 2, *Aesthetics, Method, and Epistemology*, ed. James D. Faubion (New York: The New Press, 1998), 369.
42. Adorno, *History and Freedom*, 174.
43. Foucault, "What Is Enlightenment?," 315–16.
44. Theodor Adorno, *Problems of Moral Philosophy*, ed. Thomas Schröder, trans. Rodney Livingstone (Stanford, CA: Stanford University Press, 2001), 167.
45. Adorno, *Minima Moralia*, 39.
46. Adorno, *Problems of Moral Philosophy*, 167–68. For insightful discussion, see Freyenhagen, *Adorno's Practical Philosophy*, 133–86.
47. Adorno, *Problems of Moral Philosophy*, 169–70.
48. Foucault, "What Is Enlightenment?," 316–17.
49. Although Foucault would likely be skeptical about the possibility of progress in the future, I am won over by Adorno's argument that to conclude that progress in the future is impossible simply because it has not occurred up to now is to make a false inference. This is, of course, not to settle the extremely thorny question of how we could possibly determine what would count as historical progress in the future.
50. On this point, see Robert Young, "Foucault on Race and Colonialism," *New Formations* 25 (1995): 57–65.

51. Ann Laura Stoler, *Race and the Education of Desire: Foucault's* History of Sexuality *and the Colonial Order of Things* (Durham, NC: Duke University Press, 1995), 1.
52. For a helpful overview, see Robert Nichols, "Postcolonial Studies and the Discourse of Foucault: Survey of a Field of Problematization," *Foucault Studies* 9 (September 2010): 111–44.
53. Stoler, *Race and the Education of Desire*, 5.
54. Young, "Foucault on Race and Colonialism," 57.
55. Espen Hammer, *Adorno and the Political* (London: Routledge, 2006), 5; and Nigel Gibson and Andrew Rubin, "Introduction: Adorno and the Autonomous Intellectual," in *Adorno: A Critical Reader*, ed. Nigel Gibson and Andrew Rubin (Oxford: Blackwell, 2002), 14.
56. See, for example, Paul Gilroy, *Postcolonial Melancholia* (New York: Columbia University Press, 2005); Namita Goswami, "The (M)other of All Posts: Postcolonial Melancholia in the Age of Global Warming," *Critical Philosophy of Race* 1, no. 1 (2013): 104–20; Rajeev Patke, "Adorno and the Postcolonial," *New Formations* 47 (2002): 133–43; Robert Spencer, "Thoughts from Abroad: Theodor Adorno as Postcolonial Theorist," *Culture, Theory and Critique* 51, no. 3 (2010): 207–21; Asha Varadharajan, *Exotic Parodies: Subjectivity in Adorno, Said, and Spivak* (Minneapolis: University of Minnesota Press, 1995); and Antonio Vázquez-Arroyo, "Universal History Disavowed."
57. Goswami, "The (M)other of All Posts," 105–6, 108.
58. Dipesh Chakrabarty, *Provincializing Europe: Postcolonial Thought and Historical Difference*, 2nd ed. (Princeton: Princeton University Press, 2008), 6.
59. Terry Eagleton, "Postcolonialism and 'Postcolonialism'," *Interventions* 1, no. 1 (1998): 24–26.
60. On this point, see Allen, *The End of Progress*, 23–25; and Robert Young, *White Mythologies*, 2nd ed. (New York: Routledge, 2004).

10

"POST-FOUCAULT": THE CRITICAL TIME OF THE PRESENT

PENELOPE DEUTSCHER

> Foucault mapped the contours of the disciplinary society just as the ground was being cut out of it . . . Of course to read Foucault in this way is to problematize his relevance to the present.
>
> NANCY FRASER[1]

In this chapter, I argue for a different understanding of Foucauldian critique[2] and of the possibilities for transformation of the present with which his concept of critique is typically associated. I first ask, What is the Foucauldian present? Michel Foucault's use of "present" is a familiar topic—it was embedded in one of his most-discussed descriptions of his genealogical method as offering a "history of the present."[3] But what is that "present"? The question arises because interpretation of Foucault's history of the present characterizes the *aims* of Foucault's genealogy and his well-known critique of history, more than the meaning of the term "present"—about which we think less frequently. Foucault's present was, however, particularly important to his understanding of critique. His writing on the tradition of critique[4] reinterpreted modernity's newly self-conscious stance in terms of daring to "know knowledge," problematizing the contemporary moment, and deeming the present to be "bursting under the pressure of anticipated possibilities for the future."[5] This chapter will concentrate most on the implications of Foucauldian critique in the second and third senses, revising the way we can associate it with the possibility of contestation.

As part of this argument, I make a case for a "cumulative" understanding of Foucauldian critique. I explore the implications of the diversity of analyses offered by Foucault—and so of his elaboration of the different forms of epistemic conditions, power, governmentality, tacticalization of law and rights, conducts, and subject formation. Foucault clarified that a number of the forms of power he described did not replace each other chronologically in a linear progression.[6] Taking up this point, I attend most to Wendy Brown's revision of Foucault in her analyses of contemporary politics, because of her emphasis on this coincidence of forms of power.

As we press this question still further than Brown or Foucault, there are two fresh outcomes. To think about the politics, bodies, subjects, and times described by Foucault in terms of the intersection of multiple, coinciding forms of power, governmentality, truth, and subjectivity has a certain advantage: it offers a new reason to concentrate on the importance Foucault assigned to the detail of the archive and to an analytic weighting of the *how* over the *that*. I highlight that this *how* can be found not only in the combined effects of tolerance, security, biopower, discipline, and neoliberalism but also in the relations *among* them, which are sometimes conflictual and dissynchronous. Although Jürgen Habermas has suggested that the power of contingency "was ultimately identified [by Foucault] with power as such," we might recall that Foucault, defining critique, emphasized that "no one should ever think there is just one knowledge and one power."[7] Indeed, Foucault's demonstration of their historical multiplicity is sometimes equated with the demonstration of their contingency.

But this chapter attributes a different significance to the multiplicity of coinciding modes of power and the multiple lives of the techniques through which they coalesce. They are most commonly seen as fortuitously coalescing in assemblages and *dispositifs*. But Foucault frequently describes the latter as redeploying elements belonging to other modes—two well-known examples are disciplinary and pastoral techniques, which are differently integrated into feudal, sovereign, and biopolitical contexts. In consequence, assemblages are always incomplete, their elements inevitably able to recombine in new ways while bearing witness to former, different combinations. As forces of possible recombination, such elements are forces of immanent contestation. This phenomenon is heightened by the coexistence of multiple modes of power, the possibility of which Foucault also described. This emphasis is timely when contemporary modes of governmentality (including omnipresent neoliberalism) appear to be particularly intransigent. And, as I will suggest, the proposed alternative also responds to the disagreement between Amy Allen and Charles Mills with regard to Foucauldian critique and its resources.

FOUCAULT'S UNTIMELINESS

Foucault has joined Karl Marx as one of the philosophers whose legacy is being reconsidered by critical theorists for use in contemporary times. Theorists see different kinds of potential in Marx and Foucault. According to Nancy Fraser, to revise Marxist analysis in terms of capitalism's backstory—gender domination, political domination, and the domination of nature—would promise an integrated explanation of society's disparate ills.[8] Wendy Brown finds a different promise in Foucault's work—not of integrated explanation but of attention to history's heterogeneity and discourse's polyvalence.[9]

Such returns to Marx and Foucault as points of reference tend to assess their analyses as still important, even while inadequate, for the analytic needs of the twenty-first century. To Fraser's reflections on the new volumes of *Capital* we would need in order to analyze twenty-first-century capitalism, we can add Brown's reflections on what Foucault's *Birth of Biopolitics* largely failed to address: the disastrous directions taken by neoliberalism.[10] Brown, too, asks how Foucault's analyses would need to be corrected in light of more recent political and economic developments.[11] If, for example, there has been a challenge to the legitimacy of the nation-state and a deficit of political legitimacy attributable to factors ranging from globalization to the state's limited influence over the complex forms of contemporary capitalism, "then this is a fact with which a theory of the imperatives conditioning and organizing governance ought to reckon—and Foucault's theory does not."[12]

For her part, Fraser has argued that some empirical aspects of Foucault's work now have only limited applicability. He did not anticipate post-Fordism: deregulation, postindustrialism, flexibilization, globalization. Moreover, the twentieth-century erosion of social services and the welfare state were, she argues, at the cusp of their decline just when Foucault was theorizing their modes of normalization.[13]

So the first question in these newer debates is whether the social, economic, and political changes of the past two decades have called into question the applicability of Foucault's work to present times. Some have replied that Foucault is idiosyncratic in anticipating such transformations. Responding to Fraser's view that contemporary times are no longer dominated by disciplinary power, Thomas Lemke has recalled that, for Foucault, it was "obvious that we have to say good-bye to the disciplinary society such as it exists today."[14] That the *detail* of his analyses would decline in relevance is consistent with Foucault's understanding that the forms of power and *dispositifs* he described would further mutate.[15] *The Birth of the Clinic* proposed that a new experience of disease was "coming into being," *The Order of Things* anticipated an impending end to the modern man of the human sciences, and *The History of Sexuality* ended with Foucault's suggestion that perhaps "one day," in another economy of bodies and pleasures, the links between sex, truth, identity, confession, and freedom might come to seem, in retrospect, incomprehensible.[16] So thoroughly did Foucault, anticipating such mutation, avail himself of the language of "advent" and "one day" that Derrida diagnosed this language as tending towards the eschatological.[17]

But the complexity of such anticipation of transformation can be understood otherwise. This was not just an anticipation of the currently unimaginable, of radical alterity, but a related view of how the present is interrupted, giving "critique" a distinctive temporal character, which manifested in Foucault's understandings of both archaeology and genealogy. It is true, to turn to some of the best-known understandings of Foucauldian critique, that genealogy has been characterized as "refiguring the present through a past, telling the present's story differently,"[18] and in *The Birth of the Clinic* Foucault describes new formations of things and humans as coalescing to make possible "a historical and a critical understanding of the old experience." But in both cases the "critical aspect" of such coalescence is also understood as making things and humans "endlessly accessible to new discourses and open to the task of transforming them."[19] In other words, critique involves a self-looping and redoubled gesture that makes possible what, in turn, makes it possible.

Thus, Colin Koopman has proposed that "the role of the critical inquirer on this view is therefore not to produce a problematization which does not already have some basis in practice," while emphasizing that these two aspects (problematization as both object of inquiry and practice) presuppose each other.[20]

A second consequence is that the objects that are problematized will not be constants. Nor will the imperatives of the inquirer's practices. Third, Foucault argued, in his early work, that an account of one's own epistemic conditions was more easily accomplished retrospectively. For these three reasons, we might expect such analyses to have the character Fraser observes: a chronically, slightly belated character—a quality of analysis being only just in time, or running a little late.

Thus, the question of how an analytic and contemporary present might be characterizable as post-Foucauldian should be asked in tandem with the analysis of the idiosyncratic status of Foucault's use of the term "present." That critics have wished to correct Foucault's analyses does not itself indicate that our critical times are post-Foucauldian. Nor does it indicate that Foucauldian critique is still viable. But it is a step in reconstructing its specificity so as to reassess its resources.

FOUCAULDIAN CRITIQUE

To these ends, I turn first to Amy Allen, whose emphasis on Foucauldian critique as anticipating transformation leads to her positive assessment of this resource for the project of decolonizing critical theory—a view that need not mean, as she makes clear, minimizing the inadequacies of his brief discussions of race, Orientalism, and colonialism.[21]

For Allen, the point is not simply that we can separate Foucault's contextually dependent content from his flexibly applicable methodologies.[22] Instead, asking which understanding of critique offers the most promise for a decolonizing project, she promotes a creative inheritance of Foucault's understanding of the term, which she also interprets as intensifying Enlightenment critique.

Thus, she returns to Foucault's conversion of an Enlightenment understanding of freedom (in "What Is Enlightenment" and "What Is Critique").

The critical project of "knowing knowledge" would involve disorienting its parameters and shaking its fundamental footholds. Allen adds a further argument. To know, radically, the limits of one's own knowledge could lead us to recognize its Eurocentrism, and this would require us to disorient those occidental parameters. With respect to the Eurocentric norms of reason, communication, and democracy to which many contemporary critical theorists still appeal, the critique of reason one could derive from Foucault would shake up what we take progress to involve. One would have to be ready to be disoriented and undermined by a non-Western perspective. Although Foucault's two "Critique" pieces do not speak specifically to this question, Allen argues that a radical inheritance of Enlightenment ideals would amount to the openness to a postcolonial "other" that is absent from Foucault's own writing.

For Allen, this is also a methodological alternative to normatively grounded critique. It is an immanent form of critique because it requires no external or transhistorical standpoint from which to deem this intensification of the Enlightenment ideal to be the further progress of its progress.[23] On the proposed rereading, Allen argues that Foucault would "allow us to see how we might open ourselves up to postcolonial difference while realizing and accepting that we might be radically transformed in this encounter and that our future selves might well regard that transformation as a kind of progress and we who resisted it as benighted."[24]

Thus, despite Allen's active interest in not doing so, one might say that she does, to some degree, associate the radicalism of this project with the gaining of a secure foothold. Certainly, a radical openness of a Western perspective to an unlearning and to being transformed is associated with pushing critical theory to revise its idea of progress. But Allen counts this openness—its "unlearning"—*as* the progress of progress, though not in so many words.

Allen thinks we cannot anticipate the outcome of this rigorous openness to the other; she does not present this "openness" as a reassuring project. Yet the way she imagines an occidental perspective anticipating a stage beyond its occlusions and resistance seems to involve something less than total disorientation. For this is a vision of Eurocentrism as eventually coming to seem (retrospectively) unprogressed. To anticipate such outcomes may be to open oneself to fundamental challenges to one's suppositions, but in the expectation that the process will produce salutary or differently progressive outcomes for long-standing Eurocentric understandings of progress. Even within radical uncertainty about what this openness would deliver, one can expect to look back, able to see how one had been wrong. Compare Allen's vision with the invitation, at the end of *The History of Sexuality*, to imagine our future selves baffled by the nineteenth- and twentieth-century preoccupations with sexual confession.[25] Here, it is clearer that the anticipated configurations may not constitute progress.

We may compare this with Judith Butler's interpretation of Foucault's account of critique as "an instrument, a means for a future or a truth that it will not know nor happen to be."[26] Also finding that Foucault's radicalization of an Enlightenment heritage of critical practice would amplify what he takes to be its "unthought,"[27] Butler's reading of Foucauldian critique nonetheless offers a differently inflected version of the risk taking:

> Now one might wisely ask, what good is thinking otherwise, if we don't know in advance that thinking otherwise will produce a better world? If we do not have a moral framework in which to decide with knowingness that certain new possibilities or ways of thinking otherwise will bring forth that world whose betterness we can judge by sure and already established standards? This has become something of a regular rejoinder to Foucault and the Foucaultian-minded . . . I think we can assume that the answers that are being proffered do not have reassurance as their aim.[28]

Butler refers to Foucault's evocation of forms of freedom in terms of being governed "less," or otherwise,[29] but she also, and positively, stresses his reluctance to deem that capacity for resistance to be originary. Foucault does not attribute to us a foundational capacity for resistance to being governed. If we resist being governed, it is because we resist being governed "like that." To formulate alternatives and resistance is still to belong to, to be amid, the ways in which one is governed. Thus a different understanding of immanence emerges. Butler sees Foucault as offering "an allegory for a certain risk taking . . . The practice of this kind of speaking posits a value which it does not know how to ground or to secure for itself, but posits . . . anyway."[30]

Similarly, consider Judith Revel's discussion of Foucault's "yet-to-come forms of subjectivization." The problem, Foucault had asked, was whether we must "place ourselves within a 'we'—within any of those 'we's whose consensus, whose values, whose traditions [would] constitute the framework for thought and define the conditions in which it can be validated." In fact, the "we," he proposes, "must not be previous to the question; it can only be the result—and the necessarily temporary result—of the question as it is posed in the terms in which one formulates it."[31]

Understanding Foucauldian critical practice as still more strongly exposed to uncertainty than Allen has allowed, Revel and Butler both see in Foucault's work an image of transforming the environmental norms that will be in play, for freedom emerges *as* exposure to the reformulation of one's own norms.[32] This is to anticipate a more radical risk to frames of intelligibility, according to a model in which Georges Canguilhem would be as much a point of reference as Kant, for Foucault.[33]

In short, there are various ways of understanding the anticipation of alterity immanent to Foucauldian critique. I contend that a further possibility arises from the cumulative aspects of Foucault's archaeological and genealogical analyses.

Consider the challenge put to Allen by Charles Mills: surely the requirements of an analysis of slavery exceed the limits of the concepts of alterity to be found in *History of Madness*'s thematization of unreason.[34] How might the discussion be further modulated, given that, as evidenced in the dialogue between Allen and Mills, unreason was not the only form of alterity considered by Foucault? A multitude of variants emerge from Foucault's analyses, and a diversity of associated conducts. From *History of Madness* through *Birth of the Clinic*; *Order of Things*; *Discipline and Punish*; the *Sexuality* volumes; *Psychiatric Power*; *Abnormal*; *Security, Territory, Population*; and *Society Must Be Defended* he describes modes of alterity found in practices of inclusion, exclusion, confinement, identification, classification, discipline's hierarchization, individuation, scrutinization, standardization, and normalization. He refers to the spectacularization of punishment, to epistemologies ranging from categorization to associations between truth and racial heritage, to the view that populations or political spaces must be defended from the impact (whether understood biologically or in terms of disorder) of certain types of bodies. He describes forms of the biopolitical as overt or covert forms of racism, effecting caesurae within populations between "what must live and what must die,"[35] or forms of indirect murder, to the ends of a defensive management of populations.

Critical race theorists who have responded to Foucault's failure to analyze forms of power appropriate to slavery, plantations, and colonialism, and to his very partial application of genealogy to forms of racism,[36] have sometimes speculated about how Foucault's work could, or ought to, have offered the missing accounts. Epistemologies of race arise from the contingencies of different styles of knowledge and epistemic orders affecting the anthropological gaze. (This question is broached in discussions of *The Order of Things* by Paul Gilroy, Denise Ferreira da Silva, and Achille Mbembe, for example).[37] It has been argued (extensively by Ann Stoler, and also by Hortense Spillers, Marlon B. Ross, and Sharon Holland, among many others) that Foucault's account of sexuality is incomplete and misleading insofar as it does not factor in the intersection of sexuality with race hierarchies, colonialist formations, and formations of slavery.[38] Mbembe has explored the intersections of discipline, sovereignty, and biopolitics in colonialism, plantation, apartheid, and slavery.[39] They call for a new understanding of the relation between biopolitics and thanatopolitics, in which our understanding of their organizing orders must be reversed,[40] while drawing attention to the many conducts Foucault did not consider.[41]

So the disagreement between Allen and Mills concerning the possible contributions of Foucault to projects of decolonization and the theorization of slavery could also be redirected from the question of alterity back to the diverse conducts, epistemologies, spaces, and governmentalities he discusses.[42] We might then ask how the relevant roles of sovereign, biopolitical, disciplinary, psychiatric, and securitizing modes of power intertwine, sometimes coinciding with but sometimes contesting one another's aims—as when the sovereign conduct of geographic expansion coincides with concurrently pursued biopolitical aims of biological defense, or securitizing interest in homogeneity and order.[43] An account of the immanent auto-contestation embedded in these forms could be added to Allen's understanding of immanent critique.

WHAT IS THE MULTIPLICITY OF FOUCAULT'S PRESENT?

What are the implications of this view for understanding the Foucauldian present? Briefly foregrounding the temporal implications of this question,[44] Koopman suggests we should see Foucault's transition from archaeology to genealogy as a concurrent transition from the "singular" temporality of archaeology's epistemic ruptures (alternatives of continuity and discontinuity) to a genealogy expressed in terms of multiple temporalities or temporal multiplicity.[45]

Koopman's interest in complex temporality then becomes distracted as his discussion reorients to apparatuses of power as assembled from a contingent multiplicity of unpredictable elements—from Rose's account of governmentality as a "complex assemblage of diverse forces" through Hacking's account of the niche as "the concatenation of an extraordinarily large number of diverse types of elements which for a moment provide a stable home for certain types of disease," and so on.[46] It's common to focus on Foucault's description of the surprising coalescing of disparate elements into provisionally stable concatenations. Yet Foucault also depicts techniques playing concurrently multiple roles in different apparatuses, whose aims and strategies do not always accord. Among numerous examples, he mentions the death penalty as a classic expression of sovereign power over life, while noting that it may manifest as a technique in biopolitical logics of optimizing collective life.[47] He mentions Franco's body as exemplifying a sovereign right over life and death exercised over forty years, but he notes that this same body will intersect with the biopolitical register of maintaining the dictator's body in life. In this case, Foucault characterizes a *"clash* of two systems of power: that of sovereignty over death, and that of the regularization of life."[48] He describes deployments of atomic power as potentially belonging both to sovereign powers of death and to biopolitical powers of death—powers assumed to optimize life. To be sure, these forms of power could reinforce each other, but it could also happen, as Foucault notes, that these dually unfolding roles and aims undermine each other—most obviously if the pursued aims of the one would entirely annihilate the life managed by the other.[49]

When Foucault added to his various understandings of critique (in terms of the anticipation of radical change, the questioning of authority and of power, the interrogation of the limits and conditions of truth and knowledge, and the identification of the significance of one's present as "contemporary") the well-known interest in multiplicity, he argued that "there is a need for a multiplicity of relationships, a differentiation between different types of relationships, between different forms of necessity among connections, a deciphering of circular interactions and actions taking into account the intersection of heterogeneous processes."[50] But how do heterogeneous processes intersect? How, for example, do techniques and segments come to be redeployed in different modes of power, or belong to them simultaneously, and with what effects? In choosing to foreground the relationship between formations of power, we can foreground the dissonance, in addition to the congruence, between these concurrent registers, though it is not his best-known means of understanding this relationship. A well-known example is that techniques of discipline do not belong to a disciplinary age alone. Redeployed in that context, they also date back to feudal epochs, in which they existed within sovereign organizations of political power, as when instances are found in various monastic orders. But how do they coexist? Foucault argued that they might be "islands" within the contexts of sovereign power. They might reinforce the latter or be tolerated by the latter. Yet monastic disciplines such as the conduct of poverty and asceticism also could serve as a direct challenge to the latter, playing a "critical role of opposition and innovation."[51]

In other words, there may be dissonance among techniques playing a role in forms of power, and a dissonance also among different temporalities to which they belong.[52] A "same" technique might amount concurrently to the coexistence of different functions or forms of power, in which it does or could participate (or has participated). There can be conflicts between the tactics in which these techniques are variously enfolded. I return later to a less well-known example from Foucault's *Psychiatric Power*.

IN TIME FOR FOUCAULT

Further toward this direction of analysis, I turn next to the significance of temporal complexity in Brown's discussion of contemporary governmentalities: tolerance, retroactive biopolitical legitimacy, phantom sovereignty, political rights, and neoliberal common sense. Brown takes it that multiple modes of sovereignty, neoliberal and biopolitical care, and control can be at work today. Thus, Brown's work could be seen as bearing witness to how multiple and contradictory aspects of governmentalities interrelate—particularly in deferred, imaginary, anticipatory modes.

For example, some forms of sovereignty may be undermined by neoliberalism but also provoked into theatrical or reactive display.[53] Declining state power and legitimacy can intertwine with heavy-handed performances of state power, such as the intensified border control described in *Walled States*. These performances could be seen as the lingering of Foucault's "anachronistic" sovereign forms of power, but, more interestingly, Brown discusses forms of state sovereignty that may be vigorously staged in the context of its declining relevance.[54] Although the result might be forms of authority that seem to emanate from centralized, top-down loci, this can nonetheless indicate eviscerated modes of power and politics. In an increasing void of authority and capacity, heavy-handed gestures may stimulate retroactive effects of legitimation. Brown speculates that Foucault overlooked such modes of governmentality because he under-theorized the voids in some formations of power and crises of political legitimacy.

Similarly, Brown invites us to revisit the view that the biopolitical emerges as a new form of governmentality, optimizing health, life expectancy, well-being, quality of life, and civic order. It also can be a new form of political claims *to* legitimacy. Although the state may play its role along with other nodes in its capillary network (experts, the human sciences, parents, and so on), the state also may stand to gain effects of legitimacy as a "good" governmentality associated with the enhancement of quality of life.[55] *Regulating Aversion* similarly takes up tolerance not only as a perverse governmentality but as another retroactive legitimacy-effect. At a time when human rights are undermined, governmental logics of tolerance flourish. Modes of intolerance may be stimulated by mechanisms putatively ensuring tolerance, thus retroactively legitimating the bodies claiming to defend its values. It could be said that, where Foucault identifies governmentalities of efficient optimization, Brown emphasizes even more strongly the dehiscence at their heart, such as the retroactive production of the apparent need for such optimization, and thus the legitimacy of its techniques, agents, states, and subjects.

The dehiscence of the political present might also be seen in the left's ongoing critique of liberalism at a time when neoliberalism and the collapse of liberal values may render this critique redundant. (Perhaps we criticize the welfare state for doing no more than managing poverty, all the while that we criticize neoliberalism for dismantling the welfare state.)[56] As with waning sovereignty, Brown might well ask, What is the "time" of such waning? It can be the time of our greater attachment, either to modes of critique (even as they become less pertinent) or to institutions and values about which one is also ambivalent (normalizing rights that never delivered equality). Seeing us as, today, "at the threshold of a different political formation, one that conducts and legitimates itself on different grounds from liberal democracy even as it does not immediately divest itself of the name," Brown has emphasized the fractured, phantasmatic, melancholic, and imaginary aspects of contemporary politics and their subjects.[57] She also can be seen as thereby exploring the temporal aspects of Foucault's "present," the internal fractures we also should associate with the modes of power he describes.[58]

Foucault presented his analyses as not unrelated to their content. There was more than a jubilant lightness of touch in his mobile and fluctuating self-characterizations of his projects. Even this phenomenon can be thought in terms of a fracturing of a present—his publishing present. His very claim to offer histories of the present was one more step in his sequence of retrospective descriptions of his own projects, the form of which plays a role in the content of what he depicted.

Perhaps his retrospective configurations claimed to provide alternatives to philosophies of history? Perhaps his projects had always been about dividing practices, or contingent truths and practices of truth? Perhaps he had been analyzing *styles* of knowing, in their epistemic conditions of possibility, or in their discontinuities and their possibilities for rupture? Perhaps he had always been interested in different and contingent formations of power? Different contingent modes of subjectivation? Different modes of governmentality? A revised genealogy of ethics? Different formations and conducts of freedom? Revision of the resources of Enlightenment freedom? Perhaps he had rethought the relationship between determination and freedom? Perhaps, from beginning to end, he has been primarily interested in an affirmation of creative force?[59] Perhaps his genealogy of sexuality would become a genealogy of biopolitics or psychiatric power or forms of racism? Or, alternatively, the beginnings of an aesthetics of the conduct of the self, and an associated genealogy of freedom?

As his own reconfigurations of his work unfold chronologically as a sequence of retroactive revisions, they progressively call into question the temporal stability of his own work. His own challenge to the unified character of his work was not just a repudiation of the author function he engaged in the 1960s.[60] In a stylistic congruence with his understanding of *dispositifs*, modes of power, governmentality, subjectivation, truth, and epistemic formations, the more Foucault retrospectively and retroactively reconfigured what he had been undertaking "all along," the more his ongoing projects anticipated further retrospective reconfigurations. The time of Foucault's work, not unlike his understanding of a historical "present," also became the temporality of immanence, anticipation, and retroaction.

We can bring this distinctive match between Foucault's *form* and his *content* into dialogue with Brown's analyses of tolerance, waning sovereignties, rights, and neoliberalism. This prompts greater attention to a second means in which Brown, too, can be understood as interrupting, in a number of ways, the social, political, and analytic "present." This challenge could be found in the relationship between the modes of governmentality she has analyzed in a number of works. In the case of Foucault, I suggested that the better recognized point *that* disciplinary, security, biopolitical, and sovereign modes of power can coexist should lead to closer attention to *how* they do so, beyond his own contributions on this point. Likewise, in the case of Brown, we can respond to the analyses of paradoxes of rights, always incomplete democracy, waning sovereignty, crises of legitimacy, governmentalities of tolerance, and omnipresent neoliberalism with a similar question: How do these interact? I have suggested that Brown's work offers a number of answers to this question, such as when she discusses the interaction of rights and neoliberalism, or waning sovereignty and excessive expressions of sovereignty. This is, in fact, why some of these relationships come to be understood in terms of the phantasmatic, nostalgic, melancholic, and compensatory modes that, I have suggested, particularly manifest an always interrupted social and political "present." This is a direction of interpretation that could be further intensified.

Let's consider two examples from Brown in which the question of how to understand such intersections arises. The first allows us to interconnect a number of discussions of gender equality. While contemporary political times are associated with a progressive and relatively successful recognition of women's civil, social, and political rights, *Undoing the*

Demos makes the case that this progress is less secure within the perspective of neoliberalism. Intensive attention and care (and certain forms of mothering) might come to be understood, instead, as the best investment in one's family, one's children, one's future. Women may possess equal rights and yet still "occupy their old place as unacknowledged props and supplements to masculinist liberal subjects."[61] Women's rights also play a role in the waning sovereignties Brown describes, such as when George W. Bush included respect for women among the values in whose name the United States embarked in a war against Afghanistan, in 2002.[62] We may find women's rights deployed in logics of security: hostility to immigration is sometimes justified through the view that certain cultures and religions deny the equal status of women.[63] Understood as a technique—the appeal to a right—women's rights can be understood as playing conflicting roles in coinciding forms of power and governmentality, particularly if we read "together" those possible intersections as elaborated across a number of Foucault's analyses, and then repeat the gesture with Brown's analyses.

A second example can be found in the intersection of a number of forms of sovereignty, rights, and neoliberalism broached in "Learning to Love Again," in which discussion turned on Christina Colegate's example of Shared Responsibility Agreements, through which the Western Australian state government offered the indigenous community of Mulan such improvements as a gas pump or a swimming pool on the condition that the community agreed to improve disease prevention or school attendance.[64] What is it to think of this as an intersection of modes of governmentality? A state government adopts the biopolitical guise of health optimization. But this role intersects with such traditional forms of sovereignty as appropriation, deprivation, and disposing of or taking life, given that Australian states can only assume biopolitical responsibility by virtue of their colonial history and ongoing forms of sovereign power. Its assumption of a biopolitical role also intersects with the bifurcations of populations described by Foucault, given the differential approach of this form of administered care with respect to indigenous and nonindigenous communities. It relies on the abstractions describing "trends" in populations, communities, ethnicities, but it also serves to individualize and in a specific sense moralize—interpellating "failed" forms of responsibility toward health and well-being.

In addition, biopolitical projects both coincide with and clash with neoliberal models of negotiation, according to which state and indigenous communities are assumed to be sovereign agents negotiating equally at the table for their own interests. Of course, many of the possible moves in such a "negotiation" have been tacitly excluded. Because the very agreement assumes their default irresponsibility, the complex role played by constructions of the "abnormal" in relation to discipline and normalization might also factor. And because indigenous participants cannot negotiate for what will be deemed irresponsible (nor can they entirely decline to negotiate), they are also understood in terms of standardizing modes of docile and submissive subjects requiring the additional analysis, as Brown proposes, of the disciplinary production of identities. Subordination within the register of sovereign power also might amount to what Brown has analyzed as the "wounded" attachments to rights claims (also understood as a stimulated form of subject formations), all the while that these same subjects are reinscribed within the further conflicting neoliberal registers of management, self-management, responsibility, and negotiation.[65] Such analyses intensify but are not entirely foreign to the tenor of some of Foucault's own analyses.

THE TIME OF FOUCAULT'S FAMILIES

Although the most widely cited examples are Foucault's account of how techniques of discipline preceded the "disciplinary," and of pastoral techniques as preceding but integrating with the biopolitical, I turn now to Foucault's less discussed account, in *Psychiatric Power*, of the family as a domain of sovereign power. As such, the family could be seen as a space in which women and children were subordinated to paternal authority—but not just by virtue of a residual, anachronistic sovereign power. Instead, Foucault argued that disciplinary networks were also reinforced by the forms of subordination and obedience ensured by the modes of sovereign power organizing the family space. In consequence—and this is to extrapolate a little further than Foucault, but not beyond the resources of his own material—techniques of parental and particularly maternal "care" participated concurrently in a number of different modes of power and could be understood as, at once, multiple techniques.

A mother's care could belong to the register both of her own subordination within the family nexus, while also participating in the subordination of the child. But because the authority of the expert will come to play a significant role within many families, the mother and father will assume additional and differentiated roles as auxiliaries of expert authority within the family. Paternal and expert authority can both conflict and coincide, the mother becoming the auxiliary of both. As a sovereign space of authority supporting disciplinary societies, Foucault describes the family as eventually also organized by disciplinary modes. Mothers might then be one more nexus of disciplinary power—as with the mothers described in *Abnormal* as embodying good maternity insofar as they scrutinize for signs of masturbation in their children—and of the children's abnormalization and individualization.

At the same time, women themselves will also come to be individualized, normalized, and abnormalized—for example, as "cases" (the potential for hysterical and irresponsible maternity depicted in the first volume of *The History of Sexuality*). And the individualizing problematization of maternal practice deemed potentially harmful to children's health (by virtue of a range of queried practices, including wet-nursing) will intersect with the making of maternal practice into the abstractions of biopolitical interest in populations.[66] But to be understood in terms of trends and rates, from birthrate to maternal risk factors, is also to be newly responsibilized in terms of obligations to values and entities such as health, healthy reproduction, nations, populations, and futures. Moreover, Foucault further added to this picture, in *Birth of Biopolitics*, the reminder that maternal care would *also* become a form of investment in "family capital."[67]

THE TIMES OF WHITE MATERIAL

Foucault's work offers a means of understanding how small daily techniques—I have suggested the example of maternal care—could be understood as participating in a number of modes at once, including subordination to others; the subordination of others; vectors in disciplinary institutions of a number of forms; individualizations; the abstractions of biopolitical optimization; the making of "risk factors"; and the emergence of new, related forms of "responsibilization" and of neoliberal variants of optimization. These may sometimes be coinciding forms of power, such that a simple technique could be understood as at once a multiplicity of techniques, interrupting the "presence" of such formations.

My question is how such a possibility of reading could be further extended. What further questions should we direct at such an interpretation of daily family techniques? Such an analysis could reflect further on the contexts in which such family spaces of care emerge, in ways Foucault did not consider. Most obviously among these: What is the racial and colonial context of the families he described?

I conclude with a discussion of Claire Denis's 2009 film, *White Material*,[68] further opening the analytic possibilities of such a question. In other words, what if the mother in the family is French and white, the inheritor of colonial power, running a plantation in an unnamed African country on the brink of revolution? I turn to *White Material* as a depiction of this scenario and of the states of disorder to which Achille Mbembe has redirected post-Foucauldian biopolitical theory. It offers a means of reflecting on the level of detail called for in analysis of the intersections and cohabitations of multiple modes of power and their techniques.

Here, the character Maria's techniques of domestic management operate concurrently as the colonial assumption of privilege and the means by which she manages her coffee plantation. A complexity of exchanges between multiple forms of sovereign power plays out in the number of senses in which the plantation is not hers. To think in terms of gender subordination, the farm has actually been sold to the local mayor, Cherif, without her knowledge, in a covert negotiation between her ex-husband and her father-in-law (for whom she has been caring in the home). But if the gender subordination replayed in that transaction plays any role in her destitution, it is greatly complicated by the sovereign forms of colonial power securing any claims she might have had, and the unfolding revolutionary temporality according to which the farm ought never to have been theirs.

Maria has a son, who proves to be one of Foucault's disciplinary "abnormals," particularly stimulating Maria's conduct of maternal care and correction. But this is also a participation in the indifference of colonial privilege, as she dismisses the news of his attack on Lucie (the African mother of her ex-husband's second son). Maria's aims also belong to one temporality of neoliberal self-optimization, her bodily habits oriented toward the future in which she has invested, and to whose ends she is attempting to realize value, maximize profit, and manage land, people, and son. But these conducts are no less vectors in the apparatuses of retributive violence and stimulated states of disorder to which Achille Mbembe, in his revision of Foucault, has reoriented analytic attention.[69] We would need one form of power to think about the son's role on the borders of disciplinary norms, another to understand the mode in which he will be attacked by child soldiers, and another to understand the child soldiers' death at the hands of the local militia and the militia's subsequent burning of Maria's crops, farm, and son. Here, techniques of care will participate concurrently in multiple modes of power and in correspondingly multiple temporalities. Maria's concern and her aims at self-realization through various forms of economic and emotional care play out in a time that is shortened and accelerated by its concurrent intersection with and participation in the revolution that is concurrently playing out. Suppositions of futures are playing a role in the distribution of terminated temporalities. These could be understood as unfolding concurrently, relying on one another and challenging one another. The segments of coinciding techniques of power and their complex temporalities give meaning to each other while calling each other into question *because* they participate in each other.

Framed by revised understandings of Foucauldian genealogy as "a way of refiguring the present through a past, telling the present's story differently,"[70] I have proposed a revised understanding of Foucauldian critique and its refiguring of the present. A maximal focus on the conflicting modes of power and governmentality, their techniques, and the complex temporalities in which they participate offers a different means of refiguring the present. This is not to attribute such a reading to *Undoing the Demos*, nor to Foucault's philosophical "presence"—Foucault does manifest a stronger analytic interest in the coalescence than the conflict residing in the coalescing elements of *dispositifs*.[71] Yet the cumulative effects of Brown's and Foucault's analyses could be so deployed.[72]

By the time of *Undoing the Demos*, Brown's discussions of neoliberalism offer a very strong version of the risk to the democratic imaginary earlier depicted in "Learning to Love." When politics is reduced to economic and economized terms, our very ability to appeal critically to democracy's unrealized promise (equality, freedom, and the power of the people) is undermined. The question, then, is how to agree with this analysis of neoliberalism's pervasive, generalized economization while *also* revising our understanding of genealogical critique. This would be to orient genealogical critique toward a maximal emphasis on the concurrently coinciding but also dehiscent elements of power and governmentality, occupying and contesting the political present—relying on each other and contesting each other, and so continuing to contest neoliberalism.

This is a stronger means of identifying the resources for imagining and becoming otherwise than is available from Foucault's understanding of resistance or his references to the polyvalent tactics of power, which also focus on the concurrent role, and temporalities, of the techniques belonging to multiple modes of power.[73] I also take it to be stronger than the definition of critique as imagining "a future . . . that [it] will not know nor happen to be."[74] For these resources are also delivered in the inconsistent and self-contesting relationships between the techniques and governmentalities described by Foucault, just as much as in the unpredictable character of their future combinations. None fully accomplish themselves and none fully belong to one time. It is a more specific understanding of the significance of the multiplicity of modes of power to which Brown's and Foucault's analyses collectively bear witness—by considering the cumulative effects through which the presents to which they belong are interrupted and challenged.

NOTES

Thanks to Amy Allen, Laura Bieger, Max Deutscher, Cristina Lafont, and Helmut Lethen for their very helpful contributions to earlier versions of this chapter, and to participants of the Queer Temporalities and Media Aesthetics project at Ruhr-Universität Bochum, particularly Philipp Hanke and Astrid Deuber-Mankowsky.

1. Nancy Fraser, "From Discipline to Flexibilization: Rereading Foucault in the Shadow of Globalization," *Constellations* 10, no. 2 (2003): 160.
2. A term defined in a number of ways by Michel Foucault, including in "What Is Critique?". Here, it is associated both with a "questioning knowledge on its own limits and impasses" and with "the art of not being governed quite so much." Foucault, "What Is Critique?," in *The Politics of Truth*, ed. Sylvère Lotringer, trans. Lysa Hochroth and Catherine Porter (Los Angeles: Semiotexte, 2007), 45, 68.

3. Michel Foucault, *Discipline and Punish*, trans. Alan Sheridan (New York: Vintage, 1977), 30–31.
4. Essays in which his idiosyncratic response to Kant's "What Is Enlightenment?" plays an important role. Among these, see most obviously Michel Foucault, "What Is Enlightenment?," in *The Foucault Reader*, ed. and trans. Paul Rabinow (New York: Random House, 1984), 32–50. See also Foucault, "Kant on Enlightenment and Revolution," *Economy and Society* 15, no. 1 (1986): 88–96; and Foucault, "What Is Critique?"
5. The formulation is from Jürgen Habermas's reflections on Foucault's understanding of critique. Habermas, "Taking Aim at the Heart of the Present," in *Critique and Power: Recasting the Foucault/Habermas Debate*, ed. Michael Kelly (Cambridge, MA: MIT Press, 1994), 151.
6. "There is not the legal age, the disciplinary age, and then the age of security. Mechanisms of security do not replace disciplinary mechanisms, which would have replaced juridico-legal mechanisms. In reality you have a series of complex edifices in which, of course, the techniques change and are perfected, or anyway become more complicated, but in which what above all changes is the dominant characteristic, or more exactly, the system of correlation between juridico-legal mechanisms, disciplinary mechanisms, and mechanisms of security." Michel Foucault, *Security, Territory, Population: Lectures at the Collège de France, 1977-78*, ed. Michel Sennelart, trans. Graham Burchell (London: Picador, 2007), 8.
7. See Habermas, "Taking Aim," 149; and Foucault, "What Is Critique?," 60. One of the definitions of critique as revealing the "contingency that has made us what we are" is found in Foucault, "What Is Enlightenment?," 46.
8. Nancy Fraser, "Behind Marx's Hidden Abode: For an Expanded Conception of Capitalism," *New Left Review* 86 (2014): 55.
9. Wendy Brown, *Undoing the Demos: Neoliberalism's Stealth Revolution* (Brooklyn, NY: Zone Books, 2015), 92.
10. See Fraser, "Behind Marx's Hidden Abode," 61. Brown does attribute to Foucault an "extraordinary prescience" about the rise and importance of neoliberalism as an art of government. Perhaps there are some developments Foucault could not have anticipated, such as the increasing importance of transnational institutions and the "socialization of risk accompanying the privatization of gain." Nonetheless, Brown queries his inattention to the new permutations of capital, to the importance of political legitimacy and democratic citizenship, in addition to the impact of neoliberalism on the democratic imaginary. See Brown, *Undoing the Demos*, 50, 72–73.
11. See Wendy Brown, *Regulating Aversion: Tolerance in the Age of Identity and Empire* (Princeton: Princeton University Press, 2006), 95. This is another context in which Brown speaks to the need to correct Foucault's neglect of the importance of questions of state legitimacy, as will be discussed further.
12. Brown, *Regulating Aversion*, 82–83.
13. Fraser, "From Discipline to Flexibilization," 160.
14. Thomas Lemke, "Comment on Nancy Fraser: Rereading Foucault in the Shadow of Globalization," *Constellations* 10, 2 (2003): 172–79, 175. See also Michel Foucault, "La

15. société disciplinaire en crise," in *Dits et ècrits*, vol. 3, ed. Daniel Defert and François Ewald (Paris: Gallimard, 1994), 533.
15. For his discussion of this theme of untimeliness, see Lemke, "Comment on Nancy Fraser," 175, 178.
16. Michel Foucault, *The Birth of the Clinic*, trans. A. M. Sheridan Smith (London: Vintage, 1973), xv; Foucault, *The Order of Things: An Archeology of the Human Sciences* (New York: Vintage, 1970), 386–87; Foucault, *The History of Sexuality*, vol. 1, *An Introduction*, trans. Robert Hurley (New York: Vintage, 1980), 159.
17. Jacques Derrida, "To Do Justice to Freud: The History of Madness in the Age of Psychoanalysis," in *Resistances of Psychoanalysis* (Stanford, CA: Stanford University Press, 1998), 127.
18. Wendy Brown et al., "Learning to Love Again: An Interview with Wendy Brown," *Contretemps* 6 (2006): 41.
19. Foucault, *The Birth of the Clinic*, xv, xix.
20. Colin Koopman, *Genealogy as Critique: Foucault and the Problems of Modernity* (Indianapolis: Indiana University Press, 2013), 99. Elaborating on this dual character, Koopman distinguishes between describing how discipline emerges in modernity as a problem and a preoccupation and engaging in that description as a means of actively problematizing discipline.
21. Amy Allen, *The End of Progress: Decolonizing the Normative Foundations of Critical Theory* (New York: Columbia University Press, 2016), 35, 205. See also Allen, "Adorno, Foucault, and the End of Progress: Critical Theory in Postcolonial Times," this volume, chapter 9.
22. See Fraser's proposal that we should distinguish between Foucault's content and his method. Fraser moves on from her diagnosis of the decline of the importance of disciplinary formations to argue that one can, in fact, very profitably draw on Foucauldian critique to analyze the advent of the postdisciplinary modes of governmentality she takes him not to have anticipated. Fraser, "From Discipline to Flexibilization," 166–67. Brown, *Regulating Aversion* also considers the disruptions that can be accomplished by Foucault's genealogical analysis to be no less urgent today. She argues that such analysis continues to be seen as a valuable mechanism for illuminating how we come to understand political imperatives as we do, how such calls are made, to what ends, how they are productive of subjects and objects, and how formations organize what they are supposed to solve.
23. See Allen, *The End of Progress*, 264. "Progress of its progress" is my expression, not used by Allen, who refers only to a "kind of progress" (202).
24. Allen, *The End of Progress*, 202. Allen suggests a similar use of resources from Adorno's legacy.
25. Foucault, *History of Sexuality*, 1:156, 159.
26. Judith Butler, "What Is Critique? An Essay on Foucault's Virtue," in *The Judith Butler Reader*, ed. Sara Salih (Malden, MA: Blackwell, 2004), 308, citing Foucault, "What Is Critique?," 42.
27. Butler, "What Is Critique?," 311.

28. Butler, "What Is Critique?," 307.
29. Foucault, "What Is Critique?," 75.
30. Butler, "What Is Critique?," 319.
31. Judith Revel, "Identity, Nature, Life: Three Biopolitical Deconstructions," in *The Government of Life: Foucault, Biopolitics, and Neoliberalism*, ed. Vanessa Lemm and Miguel Vatter (New York: Fordham University Press, 2014), 124. She is discussing Michel Foucault, "Polemics, Politics, and Problematizations," in *Ethics: Subjectivity and Truth*, ed. Paul Rabinow (New York: The New Press, 1997), 111–19, especially 114.
32. Butler, "What Is Critique?," 313. This offers an alternative to seeing the practice of freedom as itself having a normative status.
33. For example, to read Foucault in the context of his interest in Georges Canguilhem, and so to see a contextual exposure to the "limits of [one's] ordering," would be to see as open to contest such questions as what will count as a life. Butler, "What Is Critique?," 319, 321. For Foucault's discussion of Canguilhem (whose influence on Foucault is to be added to his interest in the Kantian tradition), see Foucault, "Life: Experience and Science," in *Aesthetics, Method, and Epistemology*, ed. James D. Faubion (Harmondsworth: Penguin, 1998), 465–78. On the references to Canguilhem in Foucault's "What Is Critique?" and in Revel's "Identity, Nature, Life," and on the relation of thought between Canguilhem and Foucault, see Maria Muhle, "A Genealogy of Biopolitics: The Notion of Life in Canguilhem and Foucault," in *The Government of Life*, ed. Vanessa Lemm and Miguel Vatter (New York: Fordham University Press, 2014), 95. For a focus on the importance of error and chance in Foucault's turn to resources from Canguilhem, see Astrid Deuber-Mankowsky, "Nothing Is Political, Everything Can Be Politicized," *Telos* 142 (2008): 135–61.
34. Charles Mills, "Criticizing Critical Theory," this volume, chapter 11.
35. Michel Foucault, *Society Must Be Defended: Lectures at the Collège de France 1975–76*, ed. Mauro Bertani and Alessandro Fontana, trans. David Macey (New York: Picador, 2003), 254.
36. On Foucault's very partial application of genealogy to forms of racism, see, in particular, Alex Weheliye, *Habeas Viscus: Racializing Assemblages, Biopolitics, and Black Feminist Theories of the Human* (Durham, NC: Duke University Press, 2014).
37. Among a number of similar references, see Paul Gilroy, *Against Race: Imagining Political Culture Beyond the Color Line* (Cambridge, MA: Belknap Press of Harvard University Press, 2002); Denise Ferreira da Silva, *Toward a Global Idea of Race* (Minneapolis: University of Minnesota Press, 2007); Achille Mbembe, "African Modes of Self-Writing," *Public Culture* 14, no. 1 (2002): 247; and Mbembe, *Critique de la raison nègre* (Paris: La Découverte, 2013). Mbembe's many revisions of Foucault include his challenge to the resources of *The Order of Things*, to emphasize the contingency—and the need for analysis of the epistemic systems—important to the classification of race. For her brief evocation of this potential, see also Hortense Spillers, *Black, White, and in Color: Essays on American Literature and Culture* (Chicago: University of Chicago Press, 2003), 226.

38. See Ann Laura Stoler, *Race and the Education of Desire: Foucault's History of Sexuality and the Colonial Order of Things* (Durham, NC: Duke University Press, 1995); Spillers, *Black, White, and in Color*, 164, 303–8; Sharon Holland, *The Erotic Life of Racism* (Durham, NC: Duke University Press, 2012); and Marlon B. Ross, "Beyond the Closet as a Raceless Paradigm," in *Black Queer Studies*, ed. E. Patrick Johnson (Durham, NC: Duke University Press, 2005), 161–89.
39. See, for example, Mbembe's shift from Foucault's consideration of different spatial relationships, organized by Foucault's emblematic discussions of leprosy, plague, and inoculation, to those with which one could begin to think the organization of plantation, slavery, and apartheid. Mbembe, *Critique de la raison nègre*, 62–63.
40. Otherwise, it may seem, according to Foucault's account, that the thanatopolitical emerges only as a means of accomplishing the ends of biopolitical governmentalities. This is contested by Mbembe in his discussions of colonialism, apartheid, slavery, and decolonial states of disorder.
41. Such conducts include slavery's "pornotroping" (discussed in Spillers, *Black, White, and in Color*, 226) and decolonization's stimulation of states of disorder and terror. See, for example, Achille Mbembe, "On Politics as a Form of Expenditure," in *Law and Disorder in the Postcolony*, ed. J. L. Comaroff and J. Comaroff (Chicago: University of Chicago Press, 2006), 299–336; and Veena Das, *Life and Words: Violence and the Descent into the Ordinary* (Berkeley: University of California Press, 2006).
42. This is also to direct analysis to the archival interests on which Foucault drew in his analyses—an aspect critics have sometimes bypassed. Foucault objected to Derrida's disregard for this aspect of his work. See Michel Foucault, "Reply to Derrida," in *History of Madness*, trans. Jonathan Murphy and Jean Khalfa (London: Routledge, 2006), 575–90.
43. An emphasis of clashing modes of power and their tactics is favored in the analyses of race, considering slavery and colonialism, in Spillers, in Mbembe, and, in particular, in Ferreira da Silva, *Toward a Global Idea of Race*.
44. For his discussion of the temporal aspects and implications of Foucault's work as somewhat deemphasized in Foucault scholarship, and his review of available contributions in the literature in this respect (and for his discussion of the tendency of some scholars to foreground Foucault's emphasis on spatiality over temporality), see Koopman, *Genealogy as Critique*, 33–34 and 41–43.
45. Koopman, *Genealogy as Critique*, 33–34, 131–32. Koopman speculates that there is some shifting of ground from the influence of Canguilhem, seen in Foucault's interest in epistemic ruptures or breaks, to a different inspiration, possibly associable with the French Annales historian Fernand Braudel, who developed an account of concurrent, decomposed, plural time spans. According to Koopman, Foucault would have pushed this direction further, toward a nontotalized, more extreme variant of multiple temporalities—as genealogies.
46. Koopman, *Genealogy as Critique*, 102, citing Nikolas Rose, "Governing Advanced Liberal Democracies," in *Foucault and Political Reason: Liberalism, Neoliberalism, and Rationalities of Government*, ed. Andrew Barrie, Thomas Osbourne, and Niko-

las Rose (Chicago: University of Chicago Press, 1996), 42; and Ian Hacking, *Mad Travelers: Reflections on the Reality of Transient Mental Illnesses* (Cambridge, MA: Harvard University Press, 2002), 13.
47. Foucault, *History of Sexuality*, 1:135–36.
48. Foucault, *Society Must Be Defended*, 248; my emphasis.
49. Foucault, *History of Sexuality*, 1:135. See also Foucault, *Society Must Be Defended*, 253–54.
50. Foucault, "What Is Critique?," 64.
51. Michel Foucault, *Psychiatric Power: Lectures at the Collège de France 1973–74*, trans. Graham Burchell (New York: Picador, 2003), 64.
52. Koopman notes occasional mentions of multiple temporalities in Foucault's work, such as, for example, a reference to history as "not a single time span [*durée*]: it is a multiplicity of time spans that entangle and envelop one another" (Michel Foucault, "Return to History," in *Aesthetics, Method, and Epistemology*, 430).
53. This is to disagree with Koopman's characterization of Brown, who is grouped with a very large number of commentators he takes to focus on the Foucauldian argument *that* there is contingency, not *how* there is contingency. See Koopman, *Critique as Genealogy*, 141–42.
54. In fact, Brown asks whether sovereignty was ever held and wielded, as is sometimes implied when its techniques are taken to have been replaced by those of the biopolitical. Brown counters this view: to describe sovereignty as waning is not to claim that sovereignty was ever fully of its time or that there ever was a "self-present" sovereignty, now eroded. See Wendy Brown, *Walled States, Waning Sovereignty* (Brooklyn, NY: Zone Books, 2010), 22, 57.
55. Which is also, as Foucault argues, an indirect and often undeclared or indirect distribution of death to that putative end. Foucault, *Society Must Be Defended*, 256.
56. Wendy Brown, "Neoliberalism and the End of Liberal Democracy," in *Edgework: Critical Essays on Knowledge and Politics* (Princeton: Princeton University Press, 2005), 53.
57. Brown, "Neoliberalism," 53, 56.
58. Brown directs attention to Foucault's rethinking of the term "present" and to an ontology of the present in the context of his reformulated understanding of critique. Brown, "Politics Without Bannisters," in *Politics Out of History* (Princeton: Princeton University Press, 2005), 91–120. See also her own discussion of critique, in Brown, "Politics Out of History," in *Politics Out of History*, 3–17.
59. These revisitings of his earlier work are to be found continuously throughout Foucault's work. He returned time and again to similar points, figures, institutions, techniques, times, and bodies, reconfiguring these to the ends of alternate yet not unrelated analyses. Thus, *Psychiatric Power* reprises discussions of Philippe Pinel and Samuel Tuke presented in *History of Madness*, without any repudiation of *History of Madness*, while reconfiguring the terms (now disciplinary) in which this material is taken up. *Birth of Biopolitics* refers back to *The Order of Things*. One finds, in "What Is Enlightenment?" (published in 1984) ongoing references to the terms "archaeology" and "genealogy" in his espousing a critical method as "genealogical in

its design and archaeological in its method" (46). In "What Is Critique?," there is a redeployment of some of the terminology used in *Archaeology of Knowledge*, such as "event," and "positivity." For example, Foucault asks, "How can the indivisibility of knowledge and power in the context of interactions and multiple strategies induce both singularities, fixed according to their conditions of acceptability, and a field of possibles, of openings, of indecisions, reversals and possible dislocations which make them fragile, temporary, and which turn these effects into events? In what way can the effects of coercion characteristic of these positivities not be dissipated . . . but instead . . . reversed?" (66).

60. This would be an obvious interpretation, if one reads the introduction to *Archaeology of Knowledge* alongside Foucault, "What Is an Author?" in *Aesthetics, Method, and Epistemology*, 205–21.
61. Brown, *Undoing the Demos*, 89.
62. Brown, *Regulating Aversion*, 172; *Edgework*, 58–59.
63. Brown, *Regulating Aversion*, 76; *Walled States*, 116.
64. Brown et al., "Learning to Love Again," 34.
65. Brown et al., "Learning to Love Again," 35–36.
66. Michel Foucault, "La naissance de la médicine sociale," in *Dits et ècrits*, vol. 2, ed. Daniel Defert and François Ewald (Paris: Gallimard, 2001), 207–28.
67. Michel Foucault, *The Birth of Biopolitics: Lectures at the Collège de France, 1978–79*, trans. Graham Burchell (New York: Picador, 2004), 229, 243.
68. Thanks to the Queer Temporalities and Media Aesthetics project at Ruhr-Universität Bochum, the context that prompted these remarks on its time and objects, and particularly to Philipp Hanke for his excellent introduction of *White Material* in this seminar, organized with Astrid Deuber-Mankowsky.
69. For his analysis of these states in terms of plural and divergent temporalities, see Achille Mbembe, "At the Edge of the World: Boundaries, Territoriality and Sovereignty in Africa," *Public Culture* 12, no. 1 (2000): 259–84.
70. Brown et al., "Learning to Love Again," 41.
71. Brown, *Undoing the Demos*, 53. In what might be a curious parallel to Brown's point that Foucault himself does not emphasize multiplicity of formations in *Birth of Biopolitics*, Brown emphasizes a similar multiplicity least in *Undoing*.
72. This possibility arises in "Learning to Love Again," in response to a question from Christina Colegate. Colegate asks how Brown might approach an analysis of so-called Shared Responsibility Agreements in light of two aspects of her work: Brown's debunking of the fiction of the liberal sovereign subject and her critique of neoliberalism's reduction of human life to economic calculation. Brown's response is enthusiastic: it would, she commented in 2006, require the exploration of the concurrent interrelations of several of her different critiques, although that has not been pursued in *Undoing the Demos*. Brown et al., "Learning to Love Again," 35–36.
73. Foucault, *History of Sexuality*, 1:93–5, 98.
74. Butler, "What Is Critique?," 308, citing Foucault, "What Is Critique?," 42.

11

CRITICIZING CRITICAL THEORY

CHARLES W. MILLS

If self-challenge and self-criticism are definitive of the Western philosophical tradition generally, going all the way back to Socrates, then surely the body of modern philosophical work self-consciously designating itself *as* "critical theory" should be all the more welcoming of the critique of its foundational assumptions. Whether in the individualist Kantian injunction to "persons" to reject heteronomy of reason and think for oneself or in the more sociopolitically informed Marxist call for group demystification from regressive ideologies, a scrutiny of unexamined inherited frameworks is supposed to be programmatically required by critical theory's own commitments. But, as Amy Allen's chapter in the present volume argues, critical theory has yet to rethink its Eurocentrism. In her opinion, more than twenty years after Edward Said's indictment of the biases of Frankfurt School critical theory, outlined in *Culture and Imperialism*, "not enough has changed; contemporary Frankfurt School critical theory, for the most part, remains all too silent on the problem of imperialism."[1]

How could this be, given critical theory's classic pretensions to be advancing an emancipatory project for humanity? Allen's diagnosis locates the problem in the "left-Hegelian strategy" of the two most important living figures in the tradition, Jürgen Habermas and Axel Honneth, which attempts to ground critical theory's normativity in the idea of "progress as a 'fact'" (as against an aspirational ideal). For both thinkers,

Enlightenment modernity "represents an advance over premodern, nonmodern, or traditional forms of life," which for Allen and other postcolonial critics means in effect endorsing "an imperialist metanarrative" that positions Europe as the superior continent over the rest of the world. Thus, it seems to recuperate the traditional civilizing mission in nominally progressive guise. As a corrective, Allen recommends that we return to the less sanguine vision of members of an earlier generation of Frankfurt School thinkers, Walter Benjamin and Theodor Adorno, who were "extremely skeptical about the idea of historical progress." Allen pairs Adorno with Michel Foucault as developing "an alternative methodology for thinking history," and she concludes by emphasizing that she is not saying that postcolonial theory *needs* Foucault or Adorno but that these two thinkers "offer important resources within the tradition of critical theory for the crucially important project of decolonizing critical theory."[2]

I am in sympathy with much of what Allen says—certainly on the silences of critical theory, but also on the desirability of retrieving it. However, I want to bring race more centrally into the conversation, as providing an angle of critique in some ways simultaneously external *and* internal. "Whites" and "nonwhites," after all, do not, as categories and groupings of human beings, predate modernity but are brought into existence and dialectical interrelationship *by* modernity. Moreover, despite what outsiders to the field might expect, much of current postcolonial theory actually marginalizes race thematically (Allen points out Foucault's own ignoring of the relationship), while, on the other hand, many critical race theorists operate with a narrowly US-centric view of race, delinked from global historical processes and comparativist genealogy.

Nonetheless, a significant number of us would argue that they need to be brought together theoretically, and that the most illuminating prism for understanding the emergence of race as a global category is through the history of European expansionism.[3] Indeed, some scholars—such as my former colleague Barnor Hesse—would contend that race is intimately tied up with colonialism because it is, in effect, a structure of colonial governmentality, so that to segregate the two conceptually only makes clear one's misunderstanding of both.[4] If critical theory needs to be decolonized, as Allen suggests, it also arguably needs to be deracialized, and such a deracialization would well exemplify the methodology for which Allen calls, that "reconstructs history as a story of both progress *and* regress."⁵

In this concluding chapter, I will suggest that critical theory's failure to engage seriously with race—whether on the individual level of personhood (as in Kantian ethics) or at the social-systemic level of white supremacy (as in Hegelian/Marxist "world-historical" theorizing)—has blinded it to its own whiteness. As a consequence, it has been handicapped in achieving that self-critical and "estranging" illumination of "the social institutions and practices, patterns of cultural meaning and subject formation, and normative commitments that have made us who we are," which has been an epistemic and ethical goal from the beginnings of Western philosophy.⁶

1

Critical theory needs to start talking to critical race theory. The demand for such a conversation is not at all new, nor is the terminological overlap coincidental. Allen cites Said's critique, but I would highlight an earlier intervention, from 1990, a quarter century ago, by the African American philosopher Lucius Outlaw. In the essay "Toward a Critical Theory of 'Race'," Outlaw criticized the deficiencies on race of *both* Frankfurt School critical theory and party-linked Marxisms.⁷ Generally credited with being one of the first philosophy essays (or maybe *the* first) to make a formal case for a race-sensitive critical theory, Outlaw's article was crucial to the development of what has recently been officially baptized "critical philosophy of race" (as against the more cumbersome "critical race theory in philosophy").⁸ So it is important to appreciate how old this challenge is, even if we restrict ourselves to writings by professional philosophers dialoguing with canonical works. (If we loosen these restrictions, it can be backdated considerably.) The fact that, twenty-five years later, I have to bring this essay to the attention of a critical theory conference and cite it in a subsequent conference volume is itself the clearest possible indication of the extent to which the challenge it raised has been ignored by the field.

Outlaw, addressing both classic Marxism (in its various twentieth-century organized-left versions) and party-independent critical theory, argued at the time that the problem was a social ontology and philosophical anthropology that privileged class membership as real and defining at the expense of other social identities—thus, a race-insensitivity in foundational concepts. It was not necessarily that racism was denied (though that could be a problem also) but that race as a social reality with its own ontology was not acknowledged and was not recognized as central to structuring the modern world. This was, in other words, a class reductionism (race is really class in disguise) or some other kind of racial eliminativism of a distinctively Marxist/critical theoretic variety. These days, of course, contemporary critical theory has moved away from a class ontology to more mainstream liberal conceptions of the self and society. So its eliminativism would now conform to the more familiar, liberal kind, according to which races do not really exist, only individuals.[9] But in neither case is the terrain a welcoming one for critical race theory's insistence on the difference race makes to the interaction of individuals with society, or critical philosophy of race's investigation of the philosophical consequences of this interaction.

Yet over the last three decades, a significant body of work has been produced on such subjects as race and the metaphysics of the self, race and social epistemology, race and the history of philosophy, race and normative theory (ethics, political philosophy, aesthetics), race and existential and phenomenological realities, and race and "whiteness"—work that should surely be relevant to the mission of critical theory.[10] But though this literature has expanded remarkably, it is still largely American, with little influence in European philosophical circles, and even within North America it is generally seen as distinct from critical theory proper.[11] Thus, despite what one would think to be a common agenda of emancipation from social domination, critical theory and critical race theory are not in conversation with each other. The demographic and conceptual segregation of the academy that is routine in other disciplines is no less evident here, with largely white speakers and audiences and largely nonwhite speakers and audiences clustered on different sides of the philosophical color line.

How, then, can this unhappy situation be redressed? We need to begin with an unflinching acknowledgment of the extent to which the need for such decolonization and deracialization is a *general* problem within Western social and political philosophy. In other words, it would be unfair to single out critical theory for critique, even if its pretensions make the gulf between its programmatic ideal and its reality deeper than the corresponding gulf for its mainstream variant. For while the analytic tradition hegemonic in the Anglo-American world (that of Rawls et al.) does not, of course, have the radical emancipatory cachet of critical theory, with its origins (if by now somewhat distant and attenuated) in revolutionary Marxism, it nonetheless is also supposedly committed to the norms of freedom, justice, and respect for the other. After all, Rawls's first and most important book was explicitly titled *A Theory of Justice*, and it is typically credited with reorienting mainstream Anglo-American political philosophy from the goal of the justification of our political obligation to the state to the determination of principles of justice for an ideal "well-ordered" society. In addition, Rawls's resurrection of the contract as a hypothetical "device of representation" is, of course, inspired by Immanuel Kant (for whom respect for our fellow persons is crucial); the blocking of self-knowledge by the veil of ignorance is supposed to be a way of guaranteeing that no one is "othered," or excluded on the grounds of stigmatized identity; and the lexically prior first principle of justice entrenches the basic liberties of all citizens.[12]

So, although it is presented in a very different idiom, analytic political philosophy is supposed to be engaged in a normative enterprise comparable to that of critical theory. Yet as I have documented in various essays, Rawls himself had virtually nothing useful to say about race in any of the two thousand pages of his five books, and he doesn't even *mention* colonialism and imperialism.[13] Nor have his myriad disciples and students done much to remedy this lacuna (Thomas Pogge is the famous exception),[14] as can be seen by looking at the overviews of the secondary literature provided in the numerous companions and guidebooks to Rawls of the last decade.[15] So the problem obviously goes much deeper than the analytic–Continental divide—indeed, it is largely orthogonal to this divide—and needs to be situated, in my opinion, in the reciprocally reinforcing "whitenesses" of the demography of the field and its conceptual architecture.[16]

The underrepresentation of racial minorities in the US academy is a familiar story, but the degree of underrepresentation in philosophy is extreme even by the norms of the white university. No more than 5 percent to 6 percent of professional philosophers are nonwhite (including

Hispanic whites), a degree of disciplinary unrepresentativeness even more exacerbated than its maleness (about 80 percent).[17] Mainstream philosophers may be irked and offended at the invocation of demography, especially in a subject whose pretensions are to leave the (irrelevant) body behind. But for a critical theory with Marxist groundings in materialism and social embeddedness, such a diagnosis should not be found intrinsically problematic, particularly given the nominal commitment to antimonological discursive inclusion.

That people of color, whether liberal or radical, academic or nonacademic, have been the ones who have traditionally raised these questions is no accident. Anybody familiar with the twentieth-century trajectory of the international black radical tradition from the 1920s (post–Russian Revolution) onwards will know of the heated ideological battles between "race" men (and women) and "class" men, black nationalists and black socialists, and the attempt of at least some of the latter to develop a historical materialism—a "black" Marxism—capable of theorizing white racial domination.[18] In W. E. B. Du Bois's *Black Reconstruction*, Richard Wright's stories and nonfiction, C. L. R. James's work on colonialism and race, Frantz Fanon's opposition to a Sartrean subsuming of Negritude under the "universalist" Hegelian dialectic, and his judgment that Marxism has to be "slightly stretched" whenever it comes to the colonial question, there is a long history of black theoretical grappling with white left categories and finding them wanting.[19] Whether in Marxist-Leninist communism or left-liberal social democracy, the unhappy consequence has been, in the title of Michael Dawson's recent book, a history of *Blacks in and out of the Left*.[20] Famous apostates from organized communism—at that distant time when it was still an important political force—would include Richard Wright, Ralph Ellison, George Padmore, and Aimé Césaire. But "reformist" social democracy would be found wanting also. Dawson writes:

> One of the classic questions of American history is why a strong social democratic movement never developed in this country . . . What I want to argue is that a central but understudied aspect of the story is the inability of the organized American left, particularly its social democratic wing, to successfully incorporate black activists, and more generally its refusal to take on questions of racial justice . . . The historical inability of major sectors of the white-dominated left to incorporate these analytical

frameworks led to a more radical and often at least partially separate black radicalism.[21]

Even in the liberal mainstream, then, demands for racial justice have been met with hostility or indifference, requiring black activists to try to reorient to that end a "white" liberalism generally recalcitrant and uncooperative. In sum, across the liberal to radical spectrum, "white" normative political theory has historically proven unsatisfactory. The exclusions in the Western academy—the silences in both Continental critical theory and analytical Anglo-American Rawlsianism—simply mirror, if in somewhat displaced and mediated guise, the exclusions in the self-conceivedly progressive white-dominated political movements of the United States and other Western nations over the course of the twentieth century.

So we need to face the fact that simple demography plays a significant explanatory role in the silences on imperialism and race, not just in philosophical critical theory but in philosophical (left-)liberal theory. As demonstrated by the "second wave" rebirth of feminist philosophy only after the gradual entry of women into the profession in the 1970s, we should not be surprised to find that those actually negatively affected by the injustice in question will be the constituency most reliably interested in theorizing about and addressing it. White privilege materially underwrites the disengagement of white political philosophers, both Continental and analytic, from this issue. Getting more people of color into the profession would itself be an important step toward challenging its dominant frameworks of assumptions and its hierarchy of priorities.

But let me turn now to critical theory, in particular, and its vastly more sophisticated (and thus more blameworthy for its nonfunctioning) theorization of the ways in which structures of domination perniciously shape social cognition and normative diagnosis. (Liberalism, as in Rawls, does emphasize the value of "publicity"/transparency, but—especially given Rawls's and Rawlsianism's ideal-theoretic orientation—provides no analysis of the mechanisms of *social opacity* comparable to that pioneered in the Marxist tradition's analysis of "ideology.") In the same way that class theory (however diluted today) originally sensitized us to—enabling a cognitive distance from—a "bourgeois" point of view, in the same way that feminism has made us self-aware and self-scrutinizingly wary of unconsciously "sexist" and "androcentric" assumptions, so we need to interrogate ourselves—not just whites, but everybody—about tacitly "white" and "Eurocentric" optics of analysis. If race and white racial privilege are *not* acknowledged to be among those key structures of the modern world—if theoretical attention is limited to *racism* (especially if individualistically conceptualized), while "race" as a category is judged to be an atavistic holdover from a discredited biology—then there will be little sense of white domination as a social reality that molds us all, influencing recognized moral standings, civic statuses, doxastic tendencies, patterns of consciousness, opportunities and handicaps, wealth and poverty, or life chances in general.

Hence the need for a dialogue between critical theory and critical philosophy of race to make critical theory more self-conscious of these issues of phenomenology, metaphysics, epistemology, social and political theory, and ethics that critical philosophy of race has been exploring in the past three decades. And the need is particularly urgent not merely because of the relative neglect within philosophy of an emancipatory racially informed perspective but also because, in certain respects, the disruption of "normal" cognition required is more sweeping and subversive than that offered by class and gender rethinkings. After all, class and gender theory in the work of white critical theorists has largely been developed with respect to the *white* working class and *white* women—in other words, to subordination among their white coracials. But critical philosophy of race comes from the *external* perspective of people of color, seeing whites as a group from the *outside*. In disciplines that are a closed book to white critical theorists, in contemporary critical ethnic studies and African American theory, a "critical" body of thought has emerged that takes its starting point from European conquest, African slavery, and the establishment of global white supremacy and that seeks to reorder conventional categories of time, space, and personhood on that basis.

2

Let me illustrate what I mean by turning to the six themes Allen sees as the "core features" of her "conception of critique as historical problematization": "reason and power, utopia and utopianism, the historicization of History, genealogy as problematization, critical distance (or philosophizing with a hammer), and problematization and the normative inheritance of modernity."[22] I will discuss them in an interrelated rather than a linear way, in part to demonstrate how the self-conscious recognition of race and white racial privilege transgresses their boundaries.

Start with reason and power. The operation of philosophical self-critique, the turning of reason (in a putatively more enlightened version) on itself (in a putatively less enlightened version) is, of course, not at all distinctive to critical theory but, as emphasized at the beginning, is general to the Western philosophical tradition as such. From Aristotle's strictures on Plato to Thomas Hobbes's gibes at the medieval "schoolmen" through Karl Marx and Friedrich Engels's derision of the idealism of Hegelianism, the discipline has been marked by a generational score-settling that has often taken place on the terrain of rationality itself. What marks critical theory, at least in its Marxist and Marx-descended versions (as against the earlier Kantian ancestry some would claim), is the linking of this targeted deficient rationality to social structure and group membership. It is not merely a generational blindness that is at work but a supposed propensity some cognizers have for getting things wrong, which is shaped by their societal position, differential experience, and material group interest. The privileged (along a particular axis) live in a "lifeworld" organized by that privilege, so that a subordinated standpoint is required to see its inequities clearly.

But what if the subordinated standpoint in question is largely outside that world altogether? In the idealist tradition, a cognitive Archimedean point aloft from the fray can supposedly be attained, but in the materialist tradition (in its different versions of "materiality"), it is the fray itself that is supposed to generate illuminating norms and insights. The more fundamental the challenge, the less room there is for common ground, the greater the danger of begging the question in the name of a vision of rationality that is itself under scrutiny. If the West itself is under critique (as against a "bourgeois" and "masculinist" rationality *within* the West), how much of "reason" can be uncontroversially taken for granted by both sides?

Moreover, the possibility of such a reciprocally respecting dialogue is further undermined by the fact that one side has historically denied the other's equal capacity to "reason" in the first place. Unlike the intra-Western philosophical disputes of the ancient world, which in modernity become intrawhite philosophical disputes, it is not merely (contingently) bad judgment and dubious assumptions that are being imputed to one's opponents but an inherent incapacity for adequate ratiocination. Aristotle's criticism of Plato's claims about the Forms is different from Aristotle's judgment of the Persians as natural slaves, and, indeed, some theorists of race are now identifying Aristotle as the pioneering Western racist thinker.[23]

In this analysis, the Greek/non-Greek normative hierarchy evolves to become the more general civilized/barbarian normative hierarchy: non-color-coded "races." With the advent of modernity, races as we know them in the modern sense appeared in Western discourse, and philosophers played a crucial role in justifying white Western superiority over the rest of the world, usually on grounds of differential rationality. Hobbes represents Native American "savages" as incapable of taking the prudential steps necessary to exit the state of nature and to create a Leviathan; John Locke depicts them as inefficient appropriators, not among the "industrious" and "rational" who are God's favored humans; David Hume concludes that whites are the only civilized race; Kant is seen by some commentators as the founder of modern "scientific" racism; G. W. F. Hegel denies history to Africans and Amerindians; John Stuart Mill recommends despotism for races in their "nonage"; and even the supposedly revolutionary Marx and Engels limit revolutionary agency to the white Western proletariat.

So the "entanglement" of white Western reason as a whole with white power and white supremacy is arguably much deeper, older, and all-encompassing than that of specific local rationalities. It is tied to a foundational deprecation of nonwhite reason that will make it difficult to come to an agreement on norms of discursive justification that is satisfactory to both sides.

In April 2014, Northwestern University sponsored an event that I was unfortunately unable to attend. But I got hold of a poster after the event was over, and (at an appropriate moment in the talk from which this chapter comes) I displayed this poster to the audience of the critical theory conference. The title of the earlier event was "Settler Common Sense" and, according to the description, the planned agenda was—through an engagement with Thoreau's *Walden*—to answer such questions as "How do varied administrative projects of settler colonialism and accompanying legal categories, geographies, and subjectivities come to serve as the background for ordinary nonnative perception?"

Just think about this question for a moment. "Common sense"—that's recognizable enough as a critical theory category, going back at least to

Antonio Gramsci's work, though with older roots in Marxism's claims about the "phenomenal forms" generated by capitalism as structures shaping everyday ideation and categories that seemingly come "naturally" to us. But *settler* common sense? What's that?

If you move in mainstream critical theory circles, you will, of course, have no clue. You will not be aware of the large literature in history, critical ethnic studies, postcolonial theory, and so forth that talks about white settler colonialism as a particular, important variety of colonialism in general and about how states established on this basis (such as Australia, Canada, New Zealand, South Africa, and—of course—the United States) have crucial commonalities arising out of patterns of indigenous expropriation and the denial to aboriginal peoples of equal (or sometimes any) political status.[24] So all the themes of classic critical theory are here: oppression; domination; and a social structure built around the subordination of a particular group, thereby affecting social cognition, "reason," and common sense, and deeply shaping the identities of the human beings enmeshed (at different locations) in this structure. But for how many white critical theorists in these settler nations will a challenge so radical—undermining the very ground beneath their feet (or at least its moral status), turning it into occupied territory—be admissible into the orthodox apparatus, requiring them, as it does, to see themselves through indigenous eyes as the "nonnative"?

Or consider the black radical tradition, which, though not cognitively disruptive in the same way as the optic of native peoples, has, as discussed, its own disorienting and disquieting consequences for European theory. This is—to abruptly shift metaphors—a formidable "hammer" indeed, since it requires taking up the perspective, the "critical distance," of those who, with the advent of modernity, were deemed a "slave race," the descendants of the accursed Ham, and so were far more thoroughly excluded from the promise of modernity than either the white working class or white women.[25] Can Adorno's negatively dialectical "nonidentical" and Foucault's "unreason" accommodate this figure, or is it too utterly different, too subhumanly irrational, to achieve even this "unrecuperated" status?

What Allen calls "the reconciling, unifying logic of modernity" certainly does not "reconcile" or "unify" enslaved Africans denied what is judged to be modernity's "central value, namely, freedom."[26] Insofar as there is a "unification," it is within a material structure of global oppression, the unpaid black slave labor that a growing body of work (vindicating texts from the 1930s and 1940s by W. E. B. Du Bois and Eric Williams) is arguing needs to be acknowledged as the foundation of the making of American capitalism and, more broadly, the modern world.[27] Thus it is a "unity" of dominant over subordinated, the cognitive costs of which are the impossibility of white recognition of black humanity. In Montesquieu's sardonic judgment: "It is impossible for us to suppose these creatures to be men, because, allowing them to be men, a suspicion would follow that we ourselves are not Christians."[28]

Lewis Gordon has argued that the familiar Continental vocabulary of Self and Other does not actually include blacks, because they are not the Other—they do not even rise to the level of the Other: "Fundamentally, the self–Other dichotomy is across ethnic, class, or gender lines. But what the Black is, is the not-Other and not-self."[29] Blacks are out of the realm of this discourse altogether, and Hegel, in his master/slave dialectic, was not thinking of *African* slaves but the master's co-ethnics, coracials. (Recall Aristotle's dichotomization, and consider its relevance here. Why would you need recognition from "natural slaves"?)

The "problematization of the normative inheritance of modernity," then, would require us to acknowledge that, for those situated on the "darker side" of modernity, especially African Americans and Native Americans (both natural slaves, according to Kant), the problem is not (as in Adorno's critique of Kant) an "abstractly rigorist" ethic of reciprocally recognizing persons unrealizable under capitalism but an ethic *that denies personhood to nonwhites to begin with*.[30] Subpersons rather than persons, their relation to modernity is radically different from those whose inclusion in the scope of these norms is conceded but undercut by material disadvantage. Here, it is not a matter of an equality registered at the level of relations of exchange but undermined at the level of relations of production, as in Marx's famous critique of wage labor, but an inequality that is *itself* formal and thus appropriately manifest in the straightforward brutalities of chattel slavery and colonial forced labor, with their body count in the millions. Failing to attain the threshold of white humanity, these individuals are not protected by norms of Enlightenment equality, because this supposedly generic norm was never intended to cover them in the first place. Hence the recently coined phrase "Afro-modernity" to signify, for blacks, this drastically different perspective and correspondingly dramatically divergent political outlook.[31]

The "historicization of History" that is called for, then, is going to require an engagement with racially informed theory that, in certain respects, will be more challenging and more difficult for mainstream critical theorists to accept and absorb than familiar Marx-inspired revisionism (which, after all, has now been around for more than a century and a half). I am thinking here not merely of critical ethnic studies and African American theory, disciplines already mentioned, but the "new" imperial history, "critical" international relations theory, the "imperial turn" in political theory, and global "whiteness" studies.[32]

Allen cites the familiar left claim, articulated by Adorno, that "historically constituted objects come, over time, to seem natural and therefore unchangeable," thus demanding an estranging realization of the historical contingency of this "second nature."[33] But the radical cognitive estrangement demanded by a race-based theory is even more foundational, not merely revealing, say, capitalism as a contingent economic system but also rewriting the very ("natural") space and time of the polity as themselves "historically constituted," transcending the nation-state not in the way urged by the cosmopolitan but with reference to alternative geographies and chronologies. The political unit for blacks has been not just the nation-state but what could be called, in the language of Paul Gilroy, the White Atlantic, a "slave power" crossing national boundaries, and—by the early twentieth century—a white supremacy that had become global.[34] Jack Goody points out the extent to which overarching Western temporal categories (such as BCE/CE, antiquity, medievalism, and modernity) have become so naturalized that their contingency has been lost sight of, and Eviatar Zerubavel charts the "time maps" that hegemonic mnemonic communities impose on others not permitted to set their own clocks.[35] Could it be that the white time map has become so embedded in Euro thought, liberal and radical, that whites will not be able to struggle free of it, and that the desired historicization would require too profound a self-indictment of the "reason" that charted it to be even intelligible?

Finally, I want to conclude on a seemingly appropriate forward-looking note that is, though not contradictorily, also going to be backward looking, by saying something about normative issues, for which both the "utopia and utopianism" and the "normative inheritance of modernity" themes are relevant. I would submit that, on the question of social justice, there is a strange and problematic convergence between critical theory's origins in Marxism and Rawls's influential development of liberalism. In both cases, arguably, the ideal, the perfect, becomes the enemy of the better.

Marxism, of course, was supposed to be distinguished from utopian socialism in pointing toward a future that could actually be attained, relying on working-class organization and struggle rather than capitalist crises of conscience and philanthropy. But, in the sense of indicating a radically superior social order, even if not adumbrated in detail, it is still broadly in the Western utopian tradition. Similarly, Rawls famously characterizes as our normative target a "well-ordered society" that is "perfectly just" as part of his ideal-theoretic orientation, even if this is supposed to be, following Rousseau, "realistically utopian."[36] In both cases, however, corrective justice is sidelined as a theme. In Rawls's case (his idea of "compensatory justice"), it is deferred to a tomorrow that never comes; in Marxism, it is disparaged in the name of the higher socialist/communist order. (Moreover, Marxism had the additional handicap—even if contemporary critical theory has now severed this particular link—of deprecating justice as an attractive norm in the first place, which Marx saw as tied to a "bourgeois" apparatus of individual rights.)

Racial justice is preeminently a matter of corrective justice—falling under what Rawls would call "non-ideal theory"—the rectification of past racist wrongdoing. But though Rawls emphasizes the importance of partial compliance theory in the opening pages of *Theory of Justice*—"the pressing and urgent matters ... we are faced with in everyday life"—never for the remainder of his career would he get to non-ideal theory as "compensatory justice."[37] (In *Theory of Justice*, his focus is on conscientious objection and civil disobedience, domestically; in *Law of Peoples* he focuses on burdened societies and outlaw states, internationally).[38] As Amartya Sen has pointed out, Rawls gives us very little guidance for correcting the injustices with which we are presently faced.[39]

Similarly, insofar as critical theory is ultimately aimed at the realization of a radically different social system, it may be impatient with "reformist" corrections of present-day injustices that do not challenge the foundations of the existing bourgeois order. But, for people of color, it is precisely these injustices that are most pressing, because these are the wrongs that have most fundamentally shaped not merely their fates as nonwhites but their very identities *as* people of color (and, for that matter, the white identities currently being uncritically taken for granted, too). Liberal democracy, the supposedly uncontroversial achievement of Western modernity, has yet to be achieved for African Americans in the United States, for example, where such basic norms as the right to vote, to not be the victims of discrimination, or to receive equitable treatment from agents of the state, such as the police, continue to be fought over. If racial injustice has indeed been foundational to the existing order, then that order needs to be seen as not merely a bourgeois but also a white-supremacist one.

In her section "Problematization and the Normative Inheritance of Modernity," Allen calls for "uncovering the illusory, congealed history contained within [second nature]."[40] I am suggesting that, for white people, that history is a history of the global establishment of white supremacy and of whiteness itself, categories now naturalized and not even to be found in white critical theory's lexicon. Endorsing Adorno's judgment that "the problematization of one's own point of view is *morally* required if we are to do justice to those who are different from ourselves," Allen challenges her fellow critical theorists to put under scrutiny that which has become "second nature" for them. I applaud these sentiments and suggest that, for white critical theorists in particular, a thorough engagement with critical philosophy of race is imperative, both for the realization of racial justice and for the necessary antiracist transformation of their own unexamined white identities.

NOTES

1. See Edward Said, *Culture and Imperialism* (New York: Vintage, 1993), 278; and Amy Allen, "Adorno, Foucault, and the End of Progress: Critical Theory in Postcolonial Times," this volume, chapter 9.
2. Allen, "Adorno, Foucault, and the End of Progress"; emphasis omitted.
3. See David Theo Goldberg, *Racist Culture: Philosophy and the Politics of Meaning* (Cambridge, MA: Blackwell, 1993); and Charles W. Mills, *The Racial Contract* (Ithaca, NY: Cornell University Press, 1997).
4. Barnor Hesse, "Racialized Modernity: An Analytics of White Mythologies," *Ethnic and Racial Studies* 30, no. 4 (July 2007): 643–63.
5. Allen, "Adorno, Foucault, and the End of Progress."

6. Allen, "Adorno, Foucault, and the End of Progress."
7. Lucius Outlaw, "Toward a Critical Theory of 'Race' " (1990), in *Race and Racism*, ed. Bernard Boxill (New York: Oxford University Press, 2001).
8. See the new (2013) journal *Critical Philosophy of Race*, from the Penn State Philosophy Department. For a collection of reprints of classic articles, see Paul C. Taylor, ed., *The Philosophy of Race: Critical Concepts in Philosophy*, 4 vols. (New York: Routledge, 2012).
9. See, famously, Kwame Anthony Appiah's statement, "The truth is that there are no races." Appiah, *In My Father's House: Africa in the Philosophy of Culture* (New York: Oxford University Press, 1992), 45. One must, of course, distinguish contemporary liberalism's eliminativism from an earlier liberalism whose dominant varieties, far from denying race's reality, emphatically endorsed it.
10. See, for example: Sally Haslanger, *Resisting Reality: Social Construction and Social Critique* (New York: Oxford University Press, 2012); Linda Martín Alcoff, *Visible Identities: Race, Gender, and the Self* (New York: Oxford University Press, 2006); Alcoff, *The Future of Whiteness* (Malden, MA: Polity, 2015); Shannon Sullivan and Nancy Tuana, eds., *Race and Epistemologies of Ignorance* (Albany, NY: SUNY Press, 2007); Andrew Valls, ed., *Race and Racism in Modern Philosophy* (Ithaca, NY: Cornell University Press, 2005); Thomas McCarthy, *Race, Empire, and the Idea of Human Development* (New York: Cambridge University Press, 2009); Derrick Darby, *Rights, Race, and Recognition* (New York: Cambridge University Press, 2009); Robert Gooding-Williams, *In the Shadow of Du Bois: Afro-Modern Political Thought in America* (Cambridge, MA: Harvard University Press, 2009); Elizabeth Anderson, *The Imperative of Integration* (Princeton: Princeton University Press, 2010); Lewis R. Gordon, ed., *Existence in Black: An Anthology of Black Existential Philosophy* (New York: Routledge, 1997); and Emily S. Lee, ed., *Living Alterities: Phenomenology, Embodiment, and Race* (Albany, NY: SUNY Press, 2014).
11. For a self-conscious attempt to expand beyond these national limits, see the forthcoming (as I write) *Critical Philosophy of Race: Beyond the USA*, a special issue of the *Journal of Applied Philosophy*, edited by Albert Atkin and Nathaniel Coleman.
12. John Rawls, *A Theory of Justice*, rev. ed. (Cambridge, MA: Harvard University Press, 1999). Originally published in 1971.
13. See Charles W. Mills, "Rawls on Race/Race in Rawls," in "Race, Racism, and Liberalism in the Twenty-First Century," ed. Bill E. Lawson, supplement, *Southern Journal of Philosophy* 47 (2009): 161–84.
14. Thomas Pogge, *World Poverty and Human Rights: Cosmopolitan Responsibilities and Reform*, 2nd ed. (Malden, MA: Polity, 2008). Originally published in 2002.
15. For the latest bad example, see Jon Mandle and David A. Reidy, eds., *A Companion to Rawls* (Malden, MA: Wiley-Blackwell, 2014). In its nearly six hundred pages, the book includes a grand total of one and a half pages on race.
16. See Charles W. Mills, "Decolonizing Western Political Philosophy," *New Political Science* 37, no. 1 (March 2015): 1–24.

17. As of 2014, minorities (including Hispanic whites) make up about 38 percent of the US population. Thus, non-Hispanic whites make up 62 percent of the population, and non-Hispanic white women are 31 percent of the population. If minority philosophers are about 5 percent to 6 percent of US philosophers, and non-Hispanic white women are about 16 percent to 20 percent, then clearly the degree of underrepresentation of minority philosophers in proportion to the national population is far worse. See Noor Wazwaz, "It's Official: The U.S. Is Becoming a Minority-Majority Nation," *U.S. News & World Report*, July 6, 2015, http://www.usnews.com/news/articles/2015/07/06/its-official-the-us-is-becoming-a-minority-majority-nation; and American Philosophical Association, *Membership Demographic Statistics, FY 2014, FY 2015*, http://c.ymcdn.com/sites/www.apaonline.org/resource/resmgr/Data_on_Profession/Member_Demo_Chart_FY2015_Rev.pdf.
18. See Cedric J. Robinson, *Black Marxism: The Making of the Black Radical Tradition* (Chapel Hill: University of North Carolina Press, 2000). Originally published in 1983.
19. See W. E. B. Du Bois, *Black Reconstruction in America, 1860–1880* (New York: The Free Press, 1998) (first published in 1935); Richard Wright, *Lawd Today!, Uncle Tom's Children, Native Son* (New York: Library of America, 1991); Wright, *Black Boy (American Hunger), The Outsider* (New York: Library of America, 1991); C. L. R. James, *The Black Jacobins: Toussaint L'Ouverture and the San Domingo Revolution*, 2nd ed. (New York: Vintage, 1989) (first published in 1938); Frantz Fanon, *Black Skin, White Masks*, trans. Charles Lam Markmann (New York: Grove, 1991); Fanon, *The Wretched of the Earth*, trans. Constance Farrington (New York: Grove Weidenfeld, 1991).
20. Michael C. Dawson, *Blacks in and out of the Left* (Cambridge, MA: Harvard University Press, 2013).
21. Dawson, *Blacks in and out of the Left*, 13, 15.
22. Allen, "Adorno, Foucault, and the End of Progress."
23. Benjamin Isaac, *The Invention of Racism in Classical Antiquity* (Princeton: Princeton University Press, 2004). Categorizing ancient Athens as "Western" is itself, of course, a contentious point, given the claims some have made about the Afro-Asiatic shaping of the Mediterranean of the time, but I will here assume the conventional narrative.
24. See Carole Pateman, "The Settler Contract," in Carole Pateman and Charles W. Mills, *Contract and Domination* (Malden, MA: Polity, 2007).
25. See David M. Goldenberg, *The Curse on Ham* (Princeton: Princeton University Press, 2004).
26. Allen, "Adorno, Foucault, and the End of Progress."
27. See Du Bois, *Black Reconstruction*; Eric Williams, *Capitalism and Slavery* (Chapel Hill, NC: University of North Carolina Press, 1994) (originally published in 1944); Walter Johnson, *River of Dark Dreams: Slavery and Empire in the Cotton Kingdom* (Cambridge, MA: Belknap Press of Harvard University Press, 2013); Sven Beckert,

Empire of Cotton: A Global History (New York: Knopf, 2014); and Edward E. Baptist, *The Half Has Never Been Told: Slavery and the Making of American Capitalism* (New York: Basic Books, 2014).

28. Montesquieu, *The Spirit of Laws*, ed. David Wallace Carrithers (Berkeley: University of California Press, 1977), 262.
29. Lewis Gordon, interview in *African-American Philosophers: 17 Conversations*, ed. George Yancy (New York: Routledge, 1998), 107.
30. See Walter D. Mignolo, *The Darker Side of European Modernity: Global Futures, Decolonial Options* (Durham, NC: Duke University Press, 2011); and Charles W. Mills, "Kant and Race, Redux," *Graduate Faculty Philosophy Journal* 35, no. 1–2 (2014): 125–57.
31. See Michael Hanchard, "Afro-Modernity: Temporality, Politics, and the African Diaspora," *Public Culture* 11, no. 1 (1999): 245–68; and Gooding-Williams, *In the Shadow of Du Bois*.
32. See Stephen Howe, ed., *The New Imperial Histories Reader* (New York: Routledge, 2010); Marilyn Lake and Henry Reynolds, *Drawing the Global Colour Line: White Men's Countries and the International Challenge of Racial Equality* (New York: Cambridge University Press, 2008); Alexander Anievas, Nivi Manchanda, and Robbie Shilliam, eds., *Race and Racism in International Relations: Confronting the Global Colour Line* (New York: Routledge, 2015); Jacob T. Levy and Iris Marion Young, eds., *Colonialism and Its Legacies* (Lanham, MD: Lexington Books, 2011); and Veronica Watson, Deirdre Howard-Wagner, and Lisa Spanierman, eds., *Unveiling Whiteness in the Twenty-First Century: Global Manifestations, Transdisciplinary Interventions* (Lanham, MD: Lexington Books, 2015).
33. Allen, "Adorno, Foucault, and the End of Progress."
34. See Paul Gilroy, *The Black Atlantic: Modernity and Double Consciousness* (Cambridge, MA: Harvard University Press, 1993).
35. Jack Goody, *The Theft of History* (New York: Cambridge University Press, 2006); and Eviatar Zerubavel, *Time Maps: Collective Memory and the Social Shape of the Past* (Chicago: University of Chicago Press, 2003).
36. Rawls, *Theory of Justice*, 4, 8; and John Rawls, *Justice as Fairness: A Restatement* (Cambridge, MA: Harvard University Press, 2001), 4.
37. Rawls, *Theory of Justice*, 8.
38. See Rawls, *Theory of Justice*, sections 55–59; and John Rawls, *Law of Peoples* (Cambridge, MA: Harvard University Press, 1999), sections 13–16.
39. Amartya Sen, *The Idea of Justice* (Cambridge, MA: Harvard University Press, 2009).
40. Allen, "Adorno, Foucault, and the End of Progress."

BIBLIOGRAPHY

Adorno, Theodor. *History and Freedom: Lectures 1964–1965*. Edited by Rolf Tiedemann. Cambridge: Polity, 2006.
Adorno, Theodor. *Minima Moralia: Reflections from a Damaged Life*. Translated by E. F. N. Jephcott. London: Verso, 2005.
Adorno, Theodor. *Negative Dialectics*. Translated by E. B. Ashton. New York: Continuum, 1973.
Adorno, Theodor. *Problems of Moral Philosophy*. Edited by Thomas Schröder. Translated by Rodney Livingstone. Stanford, CA: Stanford University Press, 2001.
Adorno, Theodor. "Progress." In *Critical Models: Interventions and Catchwords*, translated by Henry Pickford, 143–60. New York: Columbia University Press, 2005.
Alcoff, Linda Martín. *The Future of Whiteness*. Malden, MA: Polity, 2015.
Alcoff, Linda Martín. *Visible Identities: Race, Gender, and the Self*. New York: Oxford University Press, 2006.
Alexy, Robert. *A Theory of Constitutional Rights*. Oxford: Oxford University Press, 2002.
Allen, Amy. *The End of Progress: Decolonizing the Normative Foundations of Critical Theory*. New York: Columbia University Press, 2016.
Allen, Amy. Review of *Race, Empire, and the Idea of Human Development*, by Thomas McCarthy. *Constellations* 18, no. 3 (September 2011): 487–92.
Alston, Philip. "Does the Past Matter? On the Origins of Human Rights." *Harvard Law Review* 126, no. 7 (2013): 2043–81.
American Philosophical Association. *Membership Demographic Statistics, FY 2014, FY 2015*. http://c.ymcdn.com/sites/www.apaonline.org/resource/resmgr/Data_on_Profession/Member_Demo_Chart_FY2015_Rev.pdf.
Anderson, Elizabeth. *The Imperative of Integration*. Princeton: Princeton University Press, 2010.
Anderson, Elizabeth. *Value in Ethics and Economics*. Cambridge, MA: Harvard University Press, 1993.

Anievas, Alexander, Nivi Manchanda, and Robbie Shilliam, eds. *Race and Racism in International Relations: Confronting the Global Colour Line*. New York: Routledge, 2015.

Appiah, Kwame Anthony. *In My Father's House: Africa in the Philosophy of Culture*. New York: Oxford University Press, 1992.

Arrighi, Giovanni. *The Long Twentieth Century: Money, Power and the Origins of Our Times*. London: Verso, 1994.

Balibar, Étienne. "The Basic Concepts of Historical Materialism." In *Reading Capital*, by Louis Althusser and Étienne Balibar, translated by Ben Brewster, 199–308. New York: New Left Books, 1970.

Balibar, Étienne. " 'Possessive Individualism' Reversed: From Locke to Derrida." *Constellations* 9, no. 3 (2002): 299–317.

Baptist, Edward E. *The Half Has Never Been Told: Slavery and the Making of American Capitalism*. New York: Basic Books, 2014.

Beckert, Jens. *Beyond the Market: The Social Foundations of Economic Efficiency*. Princeton: Princeton University Press, 2002.

Beckert, Jens. "Die sittliche Einbettung der Wirtschaft: Von der Effizienz und Differenzierungstheorie zu einer Theorie wirtschaftlicher Felder." *Berliner Journal für Soziologie* 22, no. 2 (2012): 247–66.

Beckert, Sven. *Empire of Cotton: A Global History*. New York: Knopf, 2014.

Beitz, Charles. "Human Rights and the Law of Peoples." In *The Ethics of Assistance: Morality and the Distant Needy*, edited by Deen K. Chatterjee, 193–214. Cambridge: Cambridge University Press, 2004.

Beitz, Charles. "Human Rights as a Common Concern." *American Political Science Review* 95, no. 2 (2001): 269–82.

Beitz, Charles. *The Idea of Human Rights*. Oxford: Oxford University Press, 2009.

Benhabib, Seyla. "Another Universalism: On the Unity and Diversity of Human Rights." In *Dignity in Adversity: Human Rights in Troubled Times*, 57–77. Cambridge: Polity, 2011.

Benhabib, Seyla. "Claiming Rights Across Borders: International Human Rights and Democratic Sovereignty." In *Dignity in Adversity: Human Rights in Troubled Times*, 117–138. Cambridge: Polity, 2011. Originally published in *American Political Science Review* 103, no. 4 (November 2009): 691–704.

Benhabib, Seyla. *The Claims of Culture: Equality and Diversity in the Global Era*. Princeton: Princeton University Press, 2002.

Benhabib, Seyla. "Defending a Cosmopolitanism Without Illusions: Reply to My Critics." *Critical Review of International Social and Political Philosophy* 17, no. 6 (2014): 697–715.

Benhabib, Seyla. "Human Rights, International Law and the Transatlantic Rift." In *The Democratic Disconnect: Citizenship and Accountability in the Transatlantic Community*, by Seyla Benhabib, David Cameron, Anna Dolidze, Gábor Halmai, Gunther Hellmann, Kateryna Pishchikova, and Richard Youngs, 89–96. Washington, DC: Transatlantic Academy, 2013.

Benhabib, Seyla. "Is There a Human Right to Democracy? Beyond Interventionism and Indifference." In *Dignity in Adversity: Human Rights in Troubled Times*, 77–93. Cambridge: Polity, 2011.

Benhabib, Seyla. "Is There a Human Right to Democracy? Beyond Interventionism and Indifference." In *Philosophical Dimensions of Human Rights: Some Contemporary Views*, edited by Claudio Corradetti, 190–213. New York: Springer, 2011.

Benhabib, Seyla. "Moving Beyond False Binarisms: On Samuel Moyn's *The Last Utopia*." *Qui Parle?* 22, no. 1 (Fall/Winter 2013): 81–93.

Benhabib, Seyla. "The New Sovereigntism and Transnational Law: Legal Utopianism, Democratic Skepticism and Statist Realism." *Global Constitutionalism* (forthcoming).

Benhabib, Seyla. "Reason-Giving and Rights-Bearing: Constructing the Subject of Rights." *Constellations: An International Journal of Critical and Democratic Theory* 20, no. 1 (2013): 38–51.

Benhabib, Seyla. Review of *Between Facts and Norms*, by Jürgen Habermas. *American Political Science Review* 91, no. 3 (1997): 725–26.

Benvenisti, Eyal. "Reclaiming Democracy: The Strategic Uses of Foreign and International Law by National Courts." *The American Journal of International Law* 102, no. 2 (2008): 241–74.

Bogdandy, Armin von, and Ingo Venzke. *In wessen Namen? Internationale Gerichte in Zeiten des globalen Regierens*. Berlin: Suhrkamp, 2014.

Bogdandy, Arnim von. "Constitutionalism in International Law: Comment on a Proposal from Germany." *Harvard International Law Journal* 47, no. 1 (2006): 223–42.

Brandom, Robert B. *Making It Explicit: Reasoning, Representing and Discursive Commitment*. Cambridge, MA: Harvard University Press, 1994.

Brown, Wendy. "American Nightmare: Neoconservatism, Neoliberalism, and De-Democratization." *Political Theory* 34, no. 6 (2006): 690–714.

Brown, Wendy. "Neoliberalism and the End of Liberal Democracy." In *Edgework: Critical Essays on Knowledge and Politics*, 37–59. Princeton: Princeton University Press, 2005. Previously published in *Theory and Event* 7, no. 1 (Fall 2003).

Brown, Wendy. "Politics Out of History." In *Politics Out of History*, 3–17. Princeton: Princeton University Press, 2005.

Brown, Wendy. "Politics Without Bannisters." In *Politics Out of History*, 91–120. Princeton: Princeton University Press, 2005.

Brown, Wendy. *Regulating Aversion: Tolerance in the Age of Identity and Empire*. Princeton: Princeton University Press, 2006.

Brown, Wendy. *Undoing the Demos: Neoliberalism's Stealth Revolution*. Brooklyn, NY: Zone, 2015.

Brown, Wendy. *Walled States, Waning Sovereignty*. Brooklyn, NY: Zone Books, 2010.

Brown, Wendy, Christina Colegate, John Dalton, Timothy Rayner, and Cate Thill. "Learning to Love Again: An Interview with Wendy Brown." *Contretemps* 6 (2006): 25–42.

Brownlie, Ian, and Guy Goodwin-Gill, eds. *Basic Documents on Human Rights*. Oxford: Oxford University Press, 2010.

Brunkhorst, Hauke. "Globalizing Democracy Without a State: Weak Public, Strong Public, Global Constitutionalism." *Millennium: Journal of International Studies* 31, no. 3 (2002): 675–90.

Bryde, Brun-Otto. "Konstitutionalisierung des Voelkerrechts und Internationalisierung des Verfassungsbegriffs." *Der Staat* 1 (2003): 61–75.

Buchanan, Allen. *Justice, Legitimacy, and Self-Determination: Moral Foundations for International Law.* Oxford: Oxford University Press, 2004.

Buchanan, Allen, and Roberto O. Keohane. "Precommitment Regimes for Intervention: Supplementing the Security Council." *Ethics & International Affairs* 25, no. 1 (2011): 41–63.

Butler, Judith. "What Is Critique? An Essay on Foucault's Virtue." In *The Judith Butler Reader*, edited by Sara Salih, 302–22. Malden, MA: Blackwell, 2004.

Caliskan, Koray, and Michel Callon. "Economization, Part 1: Shifting Attention from the Economy Towards Processes of Economization." *Economy and Society* 38, no. 3 (2009): 369–98.

Campbell, Jon. "President Obama Syria Speech Transcript Text September 10, 2013: Obama Makes Case for Military Strike on Syria." *Christian Post.* September 10, 2013. http://www.christianpost.com/news/president-obama-syria-speech-transcript-text-september-10-2013-obama-makes-case-for-military-strike-on-syria-104254/#vLqg9HMJsWAszGxG.99.

Chakrabarty, Dipesh. *Provincializing Europe: Postcolonial Thought and Historical Difference.* 2nd ed. Princeton: Princeton University Press, 2008.

Chang, Ailsa. "When Lobbyists Literally Write the Bill." *All Things Considered.* November 11, 2013. http://www.npr.org/blogs/itsallpolitics/2013/11/11/243973620/when-lobbyists-literally-write-the-bill.

Chevenal, Francis. "The Case for Democracy in the European Union." *Journal of Common Market Studies* 51 (2013): 334–50.

Chomsky, Noam. "Statement to the United Nations General Assembly Thematic Dialogue on the Responsibility to Protect." Speech at the United Nations, New York, July 23, 2009. www.un.org/ga/president/63/interactive/protect/noam.pdf.

Christiano, Thomas. "An Instrumental Argument for a Human Right to Democracy." *Philosophy & Public Affairs* 39, no. 2 (2011): 142–76.

Clapham, Andrew. *Human Rights Obligations of Non-State Actors.* Oxford: Oxford University Press, 2006.

Cohen, Jean. *Globalization and Sovereignty: Rethinking Legality, Legitimacy, and Constitutionalism.* Cambridge: Cambridge University Press, 2012.

Cohen, Jean. "Rethinking Human Rights, Democracy, and Sovereignty in the Age of Globalization." *Political Theory* 36, no. 4 (2008): 578–606.

Cohen, Jean. "Whose Sovereignty? Empire Versus International Law." *Ethics & International Affairs* 18, no. 3 (2004): 1–24.

Cohen, Joshua. "Is There a Human Right to Democracy?" In *The Egalitarian Conscience: Essays in Honour of G. A. Cohen*, edited by Christine Sypnowich, 226–48. Oxford: Oxford University Press, 2006.

Cohen, Joshua. "Minimalism About Human Rights: The Most We Can Hope For?" *The Journal of Political Philosophy* 12, no. 2 (2004): 190–213.

Commons, John R. *The Distribution of Wealth.* New York: A. M. Kelley, 1963.

Crouch, Colin. *Post-Democracy.* Cambridge: Polity, 2004.

Darby, Derrick. *Rights, Race, and Recognition.* New York: Cambridge University Press, 2009.

Dardot, Pierre, and Christian Laval. *The New Way of the World: On Neoliberal Society.* Translated by Gregory Elliott. London: Verso, 2013.

Das, Veena. *Life and Words: Violence and the Descent into the Ordinary.* Berkeley: University of California Press, 2006.

Dawson, Michael C. *Blacks in and out of the Left.* Cambridge, MA: Harvard University Press, 2013.

Derrida, Jacques. "To Do Justice to Freud: The History of Madness in the Age of Psychoanalysis." In *Resistances of Psychoanalysis*, 70–118. Stanford, CA: Stanford University Press, 1998.

Deuber-Mankowsky, Astrid. "Nothing Is Political, Everything Can Be Politicized." *Telos* 142 (2008): 135–61.

Du Bois, W. E. B. *Black Reconstruction in America, 1860–1880.* 1935. New York: The Free Press, 1998.

Dworkin, Ronald. "Constitutional Cases." In *Taking Rights Seriously*, 131–49. Cambridge, MA: Harvard University Press, 1978.

Dworkin, Ronald. "Taking Rights Seriously." 1970. In *Taking Rights Seriously*, 184–205. Cambridge, MA: Harvard University Press, 1978.

Eagleton, Terry. "Postcolonialism and 'Postcolonialism.'" *Interventions* 1, no. 1 (1998): 24–26.

Enderlein, Henrick. *Nationale Wirtschaftspolitik in der europäischen Währungsunion.* Frankfurt am Main: Campus, 2014.

Engels, Friedrich, and Karl Kautsky. "Juristensozialismus." In *Marxistische und sozialistische Rechtstheorie*, edited by Norbert Reich. Frankfurt: Athenäum, 1972.

Eppler, Annegret, and Henrik Scheller, eds. *Zur Konzeptionalisierung europäischer Desintegration: Zug- und Gegenkräfte im europäischen Integrationsprozess.* Baden-Baden: Nomos, 2013.

Esposito, Roberto. *Immunitas: The Protection and Negation of Life.* Translated by Zakiya Hanafi. Cambridge: Polity, 2011.

ETO Consortium. *Maastricht Principles on the Extraterritorial Obligations of States in the Area of Economic, Social and Cultural Rights.* February 29, 2012. http://www.etoconsortium.org/nc/en/main-navigation/library/maastricht-principles/?tx_drblob_pi1[downloadUid]=23.

Fanon, Frantz. *Black Skin, White Masks.* Translated by Charles Lam Markmann. New York: Grove, 1991.

Fanon, Frantz. *The Wretched of the Earth.* Translated by Constance Farrington. New York: Grove Weidenfeld, 1991.

Fassbender, Bardo. "The United Nations Charter as Constitution of the International Community." *Columbia Journal of Transnational Law* 36, no. 3 (1998): 529–619.

Fassbender, Bardo. " 'We the Peoples of the United Nations': Constituent Power and Constitutional Form in International Law." In *The Paradox of Constitutionalism: Constituent Power and Constitutional Form*, edited by Martin Loughlin and Neil Walker, 269–90. Oxford: Oxford University Press, 2007.

Feher, Michel. *Rated Agencies: Political Engagements with Our Invested Selves.* Brooklyn, NY: Zone Books (forthcoming).

Feher, Michel. "Self-Appreciation; or, the Aspirations of Human Capital." *Public Culture* 21, no. 1 (2009): 21–41.

Ferguson, Adam. *An Essay on the History of Civil Society*. 1767. Edited by Fania Oz-Salzberger. Cambridge: Cambridge University Press, 1995.

Ferreira da Silva, Denise. *Toward a Global Idea of Race*. Minneapolis: University of Minnesota Press, 2007.

Forst, Rainer. "The Basic Right to Justification: Towards a Constructivist Conception of Human Rights." *Constellations* 6, no. 1 (1999): 35–60.

Forst, Rainer. "The Justification of Human Rights and the Basic Right to Justification: A Reflexive Approach." *Ethics* 120, no. 4 (2010): 711–40.

Forst, Rainer. "The Justification of Justice: Rawls's Political Liberalism and Habermas's Discourse Theory in Dialogue." In *The Right to Justification: Elements of a Constructivist Theory of Justice*, translated by Jeffrey Flynn, 79–121. New York: Columbia University Press, 2012.

Forst, Rainer. *The Right to Justification: Elements of a Constructivist Theory of Justice*. Translated by Jeffrey Flynn. New York: Columbia University Press, 2012.

Forst, Rainer. "The Rule of Reasons: Three Models of Deliberative Democracy." *Ratio Juris* 14, no. 4 (2001): 345–78.

Foster, John Bellamy. "Marx's Theory of Metabolic Rift: Classical Foundations for Environmental Sociology." *American Journal of Sociology* 105, no. 2 (1999): 366–405.

Foucault, Michel. *The Birth of Biopolitics: Lectures at the Collège de France, 1978–79*. Edited by Michel Senellart. Translated by Graham Burchell. New York: Picador, 2004.

Foucault, Michel. *The Birth of Biopolitics: Lectures at the Collège de France, 1978–79*. Edited by Michel Senellart. Translated by Graham Burchell. New York: Palgrave Macmillan, 2008.

Foucault, Michel. *The Birth of the Clinic*. Translated by A. M. Sheridan Smith. London: Vintage, 1973.

Foucault, Michel. "Critical Theory/Intellectual History." In *Critique and Power: Recasting the Foucault/Habermas Debate*, edited by Michael Kelly, 109–37. Cambridge, MA: MIT Press, 1994).

Foucault, Michel. *Discipline and Punish*. Translated by Alan Sheridan. New York: Vintage, 1977.

Foucault, Michel. *History of Madness*. Translated by Jonathan Murphy and Jean Khalfa. New York: Routledge, 2006.

Foucault, Michel. *The History of Sexuality*. Vol. 1, *An Introduction*. Translated by Robert Hurley. New York: Vintage, 1980.

Foucault, Michel. *The History of Sexuality*. Vol. 1, *An Introduction*. Translated by Robert Hurley. New York: Knopf Doubleday, 1986.

Foucault, Michel. *The History of Sexuality*. Vol. 2, *The Use of Pleasure*. Translated by Robert Hurley. New York: Vintage, 1985.

Foucault, Michel. "Kant on Enlightenment and Revolution." *Economy and Society* 15, no. 1 (1986): 88–96.

Foucault, Michel. "La naissance de la médicine sociale." In *Dits et ècrits*, vol. 2, edited by Daniel Defert and François Ewald, 207–28. Paris: Gallimard, 2001.

Foucault, Michel. "La société disciplinaire en crise." In *Dits et ècrits*, vol. 3, edited by Daniel Defert and François Ewald, 532–34. Paris: Gallimard, 1994.

Foucault, Michel. "Life: Experience and Science." In *Aesthetics, Method, and Epistemology*, edited by James D. Faubion, 465–78. New York: The New Press, 1998.
Foucault, Michel. "Nietzsche, Genealogy, History." In *Aesthetics, Method, and Epistemology*, edited by James D. Faubion, 369–91. New York: The New Press, 1998.
Foucault, Michel. "On the Genealogy of Ethics." In *Ethics: Subjectivity and Truth*, edited by Paul Rabinow, 253–80. New York: The New Press, 1997.
Foucault, Michel. *The Order of Things: An Archeology of the Human Sciences*. New York: Vintage, 1970.
Foucault, Michel. "Polemics, Politics, and Problematizations." In *Ethics: Subjectivity and Truth*, edited by Paul Rabinow, 111–19. New York: The New Press, 1997.
Foucault, Michel. *Psychiatric Power: Lectures at the Collège de France, 1973–74*. Translated by Graham Burchell. New York: Picador, 2003.
Foucault, Michel. "Reply to Derrida." In *History of Madness*, translated by Jonathan Murphy and Jean Khalfa, 575–90. London: Routledge, 2006.
Foucault, Michel. "Return to History." In *Aesthetics, Method and Epistemology*, edited by James D. Faubion, 419–32. New York: New Press, 1998.
Foucault, Michel. *Security, Territory, Population: Lectures at the Collège de France, 1977–78*. Edited by Michel Sennelart. Translated by Graham Burchell. London: Picador, 2007.
Foucault, Michel. *Society Must Be Defended: Lectures at the Collège de France, 1975–76*. Edited by Mauro Bertani and Alessandro Fontana. Translated by David Macey. New York: Picador, 2003.
Foucault, Michel. "Space, Knowledge, and Power." In *Power*, edited by James D. Faubion, 349–64. New York: The New Press, 2000.
Foucault, Michel. "The Subject and Power." In *Power*, edited by James D. Faubion, 326–48. New York: The New Press, 2000.
Foucault, Michel. "What Is an Author?" In *Aesthetics, Method, and Epistemology*, edited by James D. Faubion, 205–21. Harmondsworth: Penguin, 1998.
Foucault, Michel. "What Is Critique?" In *The Political*, edited by David Ingram, 191–211. Oxford: Blackwell, 2001.
Foucault, Michel. "What Is Critique?" In *The Politics of Truth*, edited by Sylvère Lotringer, translated by Lysa Hochroth and Catherine Porter, 41–82. Los Angeles: Semiotexte, 2007.
Foucault, Michel. "What Is Enlightenment?" In *Ethics: Subjectivity and Truth*, edited by Paul Rabinow, 303–19. New York: The New Press, 1997.
Foucault, Michel. "What Is Enlightenment?" In *The Foucault Reader*, edited and translated by Paul Rabinow, 32–50. New York: Random House, 1984.
Fox, Gregory, and Brad Roth, eds. *Democratic Governance and International Law* (Cambridge: Cambridge University Press, 2000).
Franzius, Claudio. "Europäisches Vertrauen? Eine Skizze." *Humboldt Forum Recht*, Aufsätze 12 (2010): 159–76.
Fraser, Nancy. "Behind Marx's Hidden Abode: For an Expanded Conception of Capitalism." *New Left Review* 86 (2014): 55–72.
Fraser, Nancy. "Can Society Be Commodities All the Way Down?" *Economy and Society* 43, no. 4 (2014): 541–58.

Fraser, Nancy. "From Discipline to Flexibilization: Rereading Foucault in the Shadow of Globalization." *Constellations* 10, no. 2 (2003): 160–71.
Fraser, Nancy. "Struggle over Needs: Outline of a Socialist-Feminist Critical Theory of Late-Capitalist Political Culture." In *Unruly Practices: Power, Discourse and Gender in Contemporary Social Theory*, 161–87. Minneapolis: University of Minnesota Press, 1989.
Fraser, Nancy. "Transnationalizing the Public Sphere: On the Legitimacy and Efficacy of Public Opinion in a Post-Westphalian World." In *Transnationalizing the Public Sphere*, edited by Kate Nash, 8–42. Cambridge: Polity, 2014.
Fraser, Nancy. "What's Critical About Critical Theory? The Case of Habermas and Gender." In *Unruly Practices: Power, Discourse, and Gender in Contemporary Social Theory*, 113–43. Minneapolis: University of Minnesota Press, 1989.
Freyenhagen, Fabian. *Adorno's Practical Philosophy: Living Less Wrongly*. Cambridge: Cambridge University Press, 2013.
Gaus, Daniel. "Demoi-kratie ohne Demos-kratie: Welche Polity braucht eine demokratische EU?" In *Deliberative Kritik—Kritik der Deliberation: Festschrift für Rainer Schmalz-Bruns*, edited by Oliver Flügel-Martinsen, Daniel Gaus, Tanja Hitzel-Cassagnes, and Franziska Martinsen. Wiesbaden: VS-Verlag, 2014.
Geuss, Raymond. *Outside Ethics*. Princeton: Princeton University Press, 2005.
Gewirth, Alan. *Human Rights: Essays on Justification and Applications*. Chicago: University of Chicago Press, 1982.
Gewirth, Alan. *The Community of Rights*. Chicago: University of Chicago Press, 1996.
Gibson, Nigel, and Andrew Rubin. "Introduction: Adorno and the Autonomous Intellectual." In *Adorno: A Critical Reader*, edited by Nigel Gibson and Andrew Rubin, 1–26. Oxford: Blackwell, 2002.
Gibson-Graham, J. K. *The End of Capitalism (As We Knew It): A Feminist Critique of Political Economy*. Cambridge: Blackwell, 1996.
Gierycz, Dorota. "The Responsibility to Protect: A Legal and Rights-Based Perspective," *Global Responsibility to Protect* 2, no. 3 (2010): 250–66.
Gilabert, Pablo. "Humanist and Political Perspectives on Human Rights." *Political Theory* 39, no. 4 (May 2011): 439–67.
Gilroy, Paul. *The Black Atlantic: Modernity and Double Consciousness*. Cambridge, MA: Harvard University Press, 1993.
Gilroy, Paul. *Against Race: Imagining Political Culture Beyond the Color Line*. Cambridge, MA: Belknap Press of Harvard University Press, 2002.
Gilroy, Paul. *Postcolonial Melancholia*. New York: Columbia University Press, 2005.
Glendon, Mary Ann. *A World Made New: Eleanor Roosevelt and the Universal Declaration of Human Rights*. New York: Random House, 2001.
Goldberg, David Theo. *Racist Culture: Philosophy and the Politics of Meaning*. Cambridge, MA: Blackwell, 1993.
Goldenberg, David M. *The Curse on Ham*. Princeton: Princeton University Press, 2004.
Goodhart, Michael, and Stacy Bondanella Tanichev. "The New Sovereigntist Challenge for Global Governance: Democracy without Sovereignty." *International Quarterly Studies* 55, no. 4 (2011): 1047–68.

Gooding-Williams, Robert. *In the Shadow of Du Bois: Afro-Modern Political Thought in America*. Cambridge, MA: Harvard University Press, 2009.

Goody, Jack. *The Theft of History*. New York: Cambridge University Press, 2006.

Gordon, Lewis. Interview in *African-American Philosophers: 17 Conversations*, edited and with interviews by George Yancy, 95–118. New York: Routledge, 1998.

Gordon, Lewis, ed. *Existence in Black: An Anthology of Black Existential Philosophy*. New York: Routledge, 1997.

Goswami, Namita. "The (M)other of All Posts: Postcolonial Melancholia in the Age of Global Warming." *Critical Philosophy of Race* 1, no. 1 (2013): 104–20.

Graeber, David. *Debt: The First 5,000 Years*. New York: Melville House, 2011.

Griffin, James. "Human Rights: Questions of Aim and Approach." *Ethics* 120, no. 4 (July 2010): 741–60.

Griffin, James. *On Human Rights*. Oxford: Oxford University Press, 2008.

Habermas, Jürgen. "A Political Constitution for the Pluralist World Society?" In *Between Naturalism and Religion*, translated by Ciaran Cronin, 312–52. Cambridge, MA: MIT Press, 2008.

Habermas, Jürgen. *Between Facts and Norms: Contributions to a Discourse Theory of Law and Democracy*. Translated by William Rehg. Cambridge, MA: MIT Press, 1998.

Habermas, Jürgen. *The Crisis of the European Union: A Response*. Translated by Ciaran Cronin. Cambridge: Polity, 2012.

Habermas, Jürgen. "Demokratie oder Kapitalismus? Vom Elend der nationalstaatlichen Fragmentierung in einer kapitalistisch integrierten Weltgesellschaft." Review of *Die gekaufte Zeit*, by Wolfgang Streeck. *Blätter für deutsche und internationale Politik* 5 (May 2013): 59–70. Translated by Ciaran Cronin as "Democracy or Capitalism," http://www.india-seminar.com/2013/649/649_jurgen_habermas.htm.

Habermas, Jürgen. "From the International to the Cosmopolitan Community." In *The Crisis of the European Union: A Response*, translated by Ciaran Cronin, 53–70. Cambridge: Polity, 2012.

Habermas, Jürgen. "Labour and Interaction: Remarks on Hegel's Jena *Philosophy of Mind*." In *Theory and Practice*, translated by John Viertel, 142–69. Boston: Beacon, 2011.

Habermas, Jürgen. "Political Communication in Media Society: Does Democracy Still Have an Epistemic Dimension?" In *Europe: The Faltering Project*, translated by Ciaran Cronin, 138–83. Cambridge: Polity, 2009.

Habermas, Jürgen. "Stichworte zu einer Diskurstheorie des Rechts und des demokratischen Rechtsstaates." In *Im Sog der Technokratie*. Berlin: Suhrkamp, 2013.

Habermas, Jürgen. "Taking Aim at the Heart of the Present." In *Critique and Power: Recasting the Foucault/Habermas Debate*, edited by Michael Kelly, 149–55. Cambridge, MA: MIT Press, 1994.

Habermas, Jürgen. *Theorie des kommunikativen Handelns*. Vol. 2. Frankfurt: Suhrkamp, 1981.

Habermas, Jürgen. *Theory of Communicative Action*. Vol. 2. Translated by Thomas McCarthy. Cambridge: Polity, 1987.

Hacking, Ian. *Mad Travelers: Reflections on the Reality of Transient Mental Illnesses*. Cambridge, MA: Harvard University Press, 2002.

Hakimi, Monica. "State Bystander Responsibility." *The European Journal of International Law* 21, no. 2 (2010): 341–85.
Hammer, Espen. *Adorno and the Political*. London: Routledge, 2006.
Hanchard, Michael. "Afro-Modernity: Temporality, Politics, and the African Diaspora." *Public Culture* 11, no. 1 (1999): 245–68.
Haraway, Donna. "A Cyborg Manifesto: Science, Technology, and Socialist-Feminism in the Late Twentieth Century." In *Simians, Cyborgs, and Women: The Reinvention of Nature*, 149–81. New York: Routledge, 1991.
Harrison, James. *The Human Rights Impact of the World Trade Organization*. Oxford: Hart, 2007.
Hart, H. L. A. *The Concept of Law*. 1961. Oxford: Clarendon, 1975.
Harvey, David. *The New Imperialism*. Oxford: Oxford University Press, 2003.
Haslanger, Sally. *Resisting Reality: Social Construction and Social Critique*. New York: Oxford University Press, 2012.
Hasselbacher, Lee "State Obligations Regarding Domestic Violence: The European Court of Human Rights, Due Diligence, and International Legal Minimums of Protection." *Northwestern Journal of International Human Rights* 8, no. 2 (2010): 190–215.
Hegel, Georg Wilhelm Friedrich. *Elements of the Philosophy of Right*. Edited by Allen W. Wood. Translated by H. B. Nisbet. Cambridge: Cambridge University Press, 1991.
Herstermeyer, Holger. *Human Rights and the WTO: The Case of Patents and Access to Medicines*. Oxford: Oxford University Press, 2007.
Hesse, Barnor. "Racialized Modernity: An Analytics of White Mythologies." *Ethnic and Racial Studies* 30, no. 4 (July 2007): 643–63.
Hirschl, Ran. *Constitutional Theocracy*. Cambridge, MA: Harvard University Press, 2010.
Holland, Sharon. *The Erotic Life of Racism*. Durham, NC: Duke University Press, 2012.
Honneth, Axel. *Freedom's Right: The Social Foundations of Democratic Life*. New York: Columbia University Press, 2014.
Honneth, Axel. "Recognition Between States: On the Moral Substrate of International Relations." In *The I in We: Studies in the Theory of Recognition*, translated by Joseph Ganahl, 137–52. Cambridge: Polity, 2012.
Horkheimer, Max. *Critical Theory: Selected Essays*. New York: Continuum, 1972.
Howe, Stephen, ed. *The New Imperial Histories Reader*. New York: Routledge, 2010.
Ignatieff, Michael. *Human Rights as Politics and Idolatry*. Princeton: Princeton University Press, 2001.
Ihering, Rudolf von. *The Struggle for Law*. Translated by John J. Lalor. Chicago: Callaghan, 1915.
Ingham, Geoffrey. *The Nature of Money*. Cambridge: Polity, 2004.
International Commission of Jurists. *Maastricht Guidelines on Violations of Economic, Social and Cultural Rights*. January 26, 1997. http://www.refworld.org/docid/48abd5730.html.
International Commission on Intervention and State Sovereignty. *The Responsibility to Protect: Report of the International Commission on Intervention and State Sovereignty*. Ottawa: International Development Research Centre, 2001. http//www.iciss.ca/pdf/Commission-Report.pdf.

Isaac, Benjamin. *The Invention of Racism in Classical Antiquity*. Princeton: Princeton University Press, 2004.
Iser, Matthias. *Empörung und Fortschritt: Grundlagen einer kritischen Theorie der Gesellschaft*. Frankfurt: Campus Verlag, 2008.
Isiksel, Turkuler. *Europe's Functional Constitution*. Oxford: Oxford University Press, 2016.
Jaeggi, Rahel. "Alienation, Exploitation, Dysfunction: Three Paths of the Critique of Capitalism." *Southern Journal of Philosophy* (forthcoming).
Jaeggi, Rahel. *Kritik von Lebensformen*. Berlin: Suhrkamp, 2014.
James, C. L. R. *The Black Jacobins: Toussaint L'Ouverture and the San Domingo Revolution*. 2nd ed. New York: Vintage, 1989.
Johnson, Walter. *River of Dark Dreams: Slavery and Empire in the Cotton Kingdom*. Cambridge, MA: Belknap Press of Harvard University Press, 2013.
Jütten, Timo. "Habermas and Markets." *Constellations* 20, no. 4 (2013): 587–603.
Kant, Immanuel. *Critique of Pure Reason*. Unabridged edition. Translated by Norman Kemp Smith. New York: St. Martin's, 1965.
Kant, Immanuel. *The Metaphysics of Morals*. Edited and translated by Mary Gregor. Cambridge: Cambridge University Press, 1996.
Kant, Immanuel. *Religion Within the Boundaries of Mere Reason, and Other Writings*. Edited by Allen Wood and George di Giovanni. Cambridge: Cambridge University Press, 1998.
Kelsen, Hans. *Das Problem der Souveränität und die Theorie des Völkerrechts: Beitrag zu einer reinen Rechtslehre*. 1928. Vienna: Scientia Allen, 1960.
King, Hugh. "The Extraterritorial Human Rights Obligations of States." *Human Rights Law Review* 9, no. 4 (2009): 521–56.
Koh, Harold. "Transnational Legal Process." *Nebraska Law Review* 75, no. 1 (1996): 181–208.
Koh, Harold. "Transnational Public Law Litigation." *Yale Law Journal* 100 (1991): 2347–402.
Koopman, Colin. *Genealogy as Critique: Foucault and the Problems of Modernity*. Indianapolis: Indiana University Press, 2013.
Kuhner, Timothy K. *Capitalism v. Democracy: Money in Politics and the Free Market Constitution*. Stanford, CA: Stanford University Press, 2014.
Kuhner, Timothy K. "*Citizens United* as Neoliberal Jurisprudence: The Resurgence of Economic Theory." *Virginia Journal of Social Policy and the Law* 18, no. 3 (Spring 2011): 395–468.
Lafont, Cristina. "Human Rights, Sovereignty and the Responsibility to Protect." *Constellations* 22, no. 1 (2015): 68–78.
Lake, Marilyn, and Henry Reynolds. *Drawing the Global Colour Line: White Men's Countries and the International Challenge of Racial Equality*. New York: Cambridge University Press, 2008.
Lee, Emily S., ed. *Living Alterities: Phenomenology, Embodiment, and Race*. Albany, NY: SUNY Press, 2014.
Lemke, Thomas. "Comment on Nancy Fraser: Rereading Foucault in the Shadow of Globalization." *Constellations* 10, no. 2 (2003): 172–79.
Levitt, Peggy, and Sally Engle Merry. "Vernacularization on the Ground: Local Uses of Global Women's Rights in Peru, China, India, and the United States." *Global Networks* 9, no. 4 (2009): 441–61.

Levy, Jacob T., and Iris Marion Young, eds. *Colonialism and Its Legacies*. Lanham, MD: Lexington Books, 2011.
Lipton, Eric, and Ben Protess. "Banks' Lobbyists Help in Drafting Bills on Finance." *New York Times*. May 24, 2013. http://dealbook.nytimes.com/2013/05/23/banks-lobbyists-help-in-drafting-financial-bills.
Lukács, Georg. "Reification and the Consciousness of the Proletariat," in *History and Class Consciousness: Studies in Marxist Dialectics*, translated by Rodney Livingstone, 83–222. Cambridge, MA: MIT Press, 1971.
Machiavelli, Niccolo. *The Prince*. Edited by Quentin Skinner and Russell Price. Cambridge: Cambridge University Press, 1988.
Macpherson, C. B. *Democratic Theory: Essays in Retrieval*. Oxford: Clarendon, 1973.
Macpherson, C. B. "Locke on Capitalist Appropriation." *The Western Political Quarterly* 4, no. 4 (December 1951): 550–66.
Malinowski, Bronisław. *The Argonauts of the Western Pacific: An Account of Native Enterprise and Adventure in the Archipelagoes of Melanesian New Guinea*. New York: Routledge, 2014.
Mandle, Jon, and David A. Reidy, eds. *A Companion to Rawls*. Malden, MA: Wiley-Blackwell, 2014.
Marshall, T. H. *Citizenship and Social Class and Other Essays*. Cambridge: Cambridge University Press, 1950.
Marx, Karl. *Capital*. Vol. 1. Translated by Ben Fowkes. London: Penguin Harmondsworth, 1976.
Marx, Karl. *Capital*. Vol. 1. Translated by Ben Fowkes. New York: Vintage, 1976.
Marx, Karl. *Capital*. Vol. 1. Translated by Ben Fowkes. London: Penguin Classics, 1990.
Marx, Karl. *Capital*. Vol. 2. Translated by David Fernbach. London: Penguin Classics, 1992.
Marx, Karl. *Capital*. Vol. 3. Translated by David Fernbach. New York: Random House, 1981.
Marx, Karl. *Capital*. Vol. 3. Translated by David Fernbach. London: Penguin Classics, 1991.
Marx, Karl. *Critique of Hegel's "Philosophy of Right."* Edited by Joseph O'Malley. Translated by Annette Jolin and Joseph O'Malley. Cambridge: Cambridge University Press, 1977.
Marx, Karl. *Das Kapital*. Vol. 1. In *Werke*, vol. 23, by Karl Marx and Friedrich Engels, 11–802. 43 vols. Berlin: Dietz, 1956–90. Translated by Samuel Moore and Edward Aveling as *Capital*. Vol. 1. Moscow: Progress. https://www.marxists.org/archive/marx/works/1867-c1.
Marx, Karl. *Das Kapital*. Vol. 3. In *Werke*, vol. 25, by Karl Marx and Friedrich Engels, 31–893. 43 vols. Berlin: Dietz, 1956–90. Translated as *Capital*. Vol. 3. New York: International Publishers. https://www.marxists.org/archive/marx/works/1894-c3.
Marx, Karl. "Einleitung zur Kritik der Politischen Ökonomie." In *Werke*, vol. 13, by Karl Marx and Friedrich Engels, 615–41. 43 vols. Berlin: Dietz, 1956–90. Translated by S. W. Ryazanskaya as "Introduction to a Contribution to the Critique of Political Economy." Moscow: Progress, 1970. https://www.marxists.org/archive/marx/works/1859/critique-pol-economy/appx1.htm.
Marx, Karl. *The German Ideology*. In *The Marx-Engels Reader*, 2nd ed., edited by Robert C. Tucker, 146–201. New York: Norton, 1978.
Marx, Karl. *Grundrisse der Kritik der Politischen Ökonomie 1857–1858*, 2nd ed. Berlin: Dietz, 1974. Translated by Martin Nicolaus as *Grundrisse: Foundations of the Critique of Political*

Economy. New York: Penguin Books, 1973. https://www.marxists.org/archive/marx/works/1857/grundrisse.

Marx, Karl. "Kritik des Gothaer Programms." In *Werke,* vol. 19, by Karl Marx and Friedrich Engels, 13–32. 43 vols. Berlin: Dietz, 1956–90. Translated as "Critique of the Gotha Programme." Moscow: Progress, 1970. https://www.marxists.org/archive/marx/works/1875/gotha.

Marx, Karl. "On the Jewish Question." In *The Marx-Engels Reader,* 2nd ed., edited by Robert C. Tucker, 26–52. New York: Norton, 1978.

Marx, Karl. "Zur Judenfrage." In *Werke,* vol. 1, by Karl Marx and Friedrich Engels, 347–77. 43 vols. Berlin: Dietz, 1956–90. Translated as "On *The Jewish Question.*" https://www.marxists.org/archive/marx/works/1844/jewish-question.

Marx, Karl. *Zur Kritik der Politischen Ökonomie.* In *Werke,* vol. 13, by Karl Marx and Friedrich Engels, 3–160. 43 vols. Berlin: Dietz, 1956–90. Translated by S. W. Ryazanskaya as *A Contribution to the Critique of Political Economy.* Moscow: Progress, 1970. https://www.marxists.org/archive/marx/works/1859/critique-pol-economy.

Maus, Ingeborg. *Volkssouveränität: Elemente einer Demokratietheorie.* Frankfurt: Suhrkamp, 2011.

Maus, Ingeborg. *Zur Aufklärung der Demokratietheorie.* Frankfurt: Suhrkamp, 1992.

Mauss, Marcel. *Essai sur le don: Forme et raison de l'échange dans les sociétés archaïques.* Paris: Presses Universitaires de France, 2007.

Mazower, Mark. *No Enchanted Palace: The End of Empire and the Ideological Origins of the United Nations.* Princeton: Princeton University Press, 2009.

Mbembe, Achille. "African Modes of Self-Writing." *Public Culture* 14, no. 1 (2002): 239–73.

Mbembe, Achille. "At the Edge of the World: Boundaries, Territoriality, and Sovereignty in Africa." *Public Culture* 12, no. 1 (2000): 259–84.

Mbembe, Achille. *Critique de la raison nègre.* Paris: La Découverte, 2013.

Mbembe, Achille. "On Politics as a Form of Expenditure." In *Law and Disorder in the Postcolony,* edited by J. L. Comaroff and J. Comaroff, 299–336. Chicago: University of Chicago Press, 2006.

McBeth, Adam. "What Do Human Rights Require of the Global Economy? Beyond a Narrow Legal View." In *Human Rights: The Hard Questions,* edited by Cindy Holder and David Reidy, 153–73. Cambridge: Cambridge University Press, 2010.

McCarthy, Thomas. *Race, Empire, and the Idea of Human Development.* Cambridge: Cambridge University Press, 2009.

Meckled-Garcia, Saladin. "What Comes First: Democracy or Human Rights?" *Critical Review of International Social and Political Philosophy* 17, no. 6 (2014): 681–88.

Menke, Christoph. "Genealogy and Critique: Two Forms of Ethical Questioning of Morality." In *The Cambridge Companion to Adorno,* edited by Tom Huhn, 302–27. Cambridge: Cambridge University Press, 2004.

Mignolo, Walter D. *The Darker Side of European Modernity: Global Futures, Decolonial Options.* Durham, NC: Duke University Press, 2011.

Mills, Charles W. "Decolonizing Western Political Philosophy." *New Political Science* 37, no. 1 (March 2015): 1–24.

Mills, Charles W. "Kant and Race, Redux." *Graduate Faculty Philosophy Journal* 35, no. 1–2 (2014): 125–57.
Mills, Charles W. *The Racial Contract*. Ithaca, NY: Cornell University Press, 1997.
Mills, Charles W. "Rawls on Race/Race in Rawls." In "Race, Racism, and Liberalism in the Twenty-First Century," edited by Bill E. Lawson. Supplement, *Southern Journal of Philosophy* 47 (2009): 161–84.
Montesquieu. *The Spirit of Laws*. Edited by David Wallace Carrithers. Berkeley: University of California Press, 1977.
Moravcsik, Andrew. "The Origins of Human Rights Regimes: Democratic Delegation in Postwar Europe." *International Organization* 54, no. 2 (2000): 217–52.
Morsink, Johannes. *The Universal Declaration of Human Rights: Origins, Drafting, and Intent*. Philadelphia: University of Pennsylvania Press, 1999.
Moyn, Samuel. *The Last Utopia: Human Rights in History*. Cambridge, MA: Belknap Press of Harvard University Press, 2010.
Muhle, Maria. "A Genealogy of Biopolitics: The Notion of Life in Canguilhem and Foucault." In *The Government of Life: Foucault, Biopolitics, and Neoliberalism*, edited by Vanessa Lemm and Miguel Vatter, 77–97. New York: Fordham University Press, 2014.
Nagel, Thomas. "The Problem of Global Justice." *Philosophy and Public Affairs* 33, no. 2 (2005): 113–147.
Naujolis, Daniel. *Migration, Citizenship, and Development*. New Delhi: Oxford University Press, 2013.
Negt, Oskar. "10 Thesen zur marxistischen Rechtstheorie." In *Probleme der marxistischen Rechtstheorie*, edited by Hubert Rottleuthner, 46–54. Frankfurt: Suhrkamp, 1975.
Neuhouser, Frederick. "Marx: Alienated Social Forces." Unpublished manuscript.
New York Times. "Wall St. Lobbyists and Financial Regulation." October 28, 2013. http://www.nytimes.com/interactive/2013/10/29/business/dealbook/29lobbyists-documents.html.
Nichols, Robert. "Postcolonial Studies and the Discourse of Foucault: Survey of a Field of Problematization." *Foucault Studies* 9 (September 2010): 111–44.
Nickel, James. "Are Human Rights Mainly Implemented by Intervention?" In *Rawls's Law of Peoples: A Realistic Utopia?*, edited by Rex Martin and David A. Reidy, 263–77. Oxford: Blackwell, 2006.
Nickel, James. *Making Sense of Human Rights*. 2nd ed. Oxford: Blackwell, 2006.
Nietzsche, Friedrich. *On the Genealogy of Morals*. Translated by Douglas Smith. Oxford: Oxford University Press, 1996.
O'Connor, James. "Capitalism, Nature, Socialism: A Theoretical Introduction." *Capitalism, Nature, Socialism* 1, no. 1 (1988): 1–38.
Orford, Anne. *International Authority and the Responsibility to Protect*. Cambridge: Cambridge University Press, 2011.
Outlaw, Lucius. "Toward a Critical Theory of 'Race.'" 1990. In *Race and Racism*, edited by Bernard Boxill, 58–82. New York: Oxford University Press, 2001.
Owen, David S. *Between Reason and History: Habermas and the Idea of Progress*. New York: SUNY Press, 2002.

Pateman, Carole. "The Settler Contract." In *Contract and Domination*, by Carole Pateman and Charles W. Mills. Malden, MA: Polity, 2007.
Patke, Rajeev. "Adorno and the Postcolonial." *New Formations* 47 (2002): 133–43.
Perez, Oren. "Normative Creativity and Global Legal Pluralism: Reflections on the Democratic Critique of Transnational Law." *Indiana Journal of Global Legal Studies* 10, no. 2 (2003): 25–64.
Pogge, Thomas. *World Poverty and Human Rights: Cosmopolitan Responsibilities and Reform*. 2nd ed. Malden, MA: Polity, 2008. Original edition 2002.
Polanyi, Karl. *The Great Transformation*. New York: Farrar and Rinehart, 1944.
Polanyi, Karl. *The Great Transformation: The Political and Economic Origins of Our Time*. Boston: Beacon, 1957.
Polanyi, Karl. *The Great Transformation: The Political and Economic Origins of Our Time*. 2nd ed. Boston: Beacon, 2001.
Post, Robert. "Theorizing Disagreement: Re-conceiving the Relationship Between Law and Politics." *California Law Review* 98, no. 4 (2010): 1319–50.
Post, Robert, and Reva B. Siegel. "Roe Rage: Democratic Constitutionalism and Backlash." *Harvard Civil Rights and Civil Liberties Review* 42, no. 2 (2007), 373–434.
Poulantzas, Nicos. "A propos de la théorie marxiste du Droit." *Archives de philosophie du droit* 12 (1967): 145–62.
Powers, Samantha. *"A Problem from Hell": America and the Age of Genocide*. New York: Basic Books, 2002.
Preuß, Ulrich K. "Europa als politische Gemeinschaft." In *Europawissenschaft*, edited by Gunnar Folke Schuppert, Ingolf Pernice, and Ulrich Haltern, 489–539. Baden-Baden: Nomos, 2005.
Preuß, Ulrich K. *Die Internalisierung des Subjekts: Zur Kritik der Funktionsweise des subjektiven Rechts*. Frankfurt: Suhrkamp, 1979.
Radin, Margaret Jane. *Contested Commodities*. Cambridge, MA: Harvard University Press, 1996.
Rawls, John. "The Domain of the Political and Overlapping Consensus." In *Collected Papers*, edited by Samuel Freeman, 473–98. Cambridge, MA: Harvard University Press, 1999.
Rawls, John. *The Law of Peoples*. Cambridge, MA: Harvard University Press, 1999.
Rawls, John. *Political Liberalism*. New York: Columbia University Press, 1993.
Rawls, John. *A Theory of Justice*. Cambridge, MA: Harvard University Press, 1971.
Rawls, John. *A Theory of Justice*. Rev. ed. Cambridge, MA: Harvard University Press, 1999.
Raz, Joseph. "Human Rights Without Foundations." In *The Philosophy of International Law*, edited by Samantha Besson and John Tasioulas, 321–39. Oxford: Oxford University Press, 2010.
Reckwitz, Andreas. "Toward a Theory of Social Practices: A Development in Culturalist Theorizing." *European Journal of Social Theory* 5, no. 2 (2001): 243–63.
Resnik, Judith. "Comparative (in)equalities: CEDAW, the jurisdiction of gender, and the heterogeneity of transnational law production." *I.CON* 10, no. 2 (2012): 531–50.
Revel, Judith. "Identity, Nature, Life: Three Biopolitical Deconstructions." In *The Government of Life: Foucault, Biopolitics, and Neoliberalism*, edited by Vanessa Lemm and Miguel Vatter, 112–26. New York: Fordham University Press, 2014.

Robespierre, Maximilien. "Draft Declaration of the Rights of Man and of the Citizen." In *Robespierre: Virtue and Terror*, edited by Slavoj Žižek, 66–72. New York: Verso, 2007.

Robinson, Cedric J. *Black Marxism: The Making of the Black Radical Tradition*. 1983. Chapel Hill: University of North Carolina Press, 2000.

Ronge, Bastian. "How to Think Critically about the Economy? Friedrich Pollock and Jürgen Habermas." Conference presentation at Theorizing Crisis: The Economic Thought of the Frankfurt School, Minneapolis, MN, March 28, 2014.

Rose, Nikolas. "Governing Advanced Liberal Democracies." In *Foucault and Political Reason: Liberalism, Neoliberalism, and Rationalities of Government*, edited by Andrew Barrie, Thomas Osbourne, and Nikolas Rose, 37–64. Chicago: University of Chicago Press, 1996.

Ross, Marlon B. "Beyond the Closet as a Raceless Paradigm." In *Black Queer Studies*, edited by E. Patrick Johnson, 161–89. Durham, NC: Duke University Press, 2005.

Rousseau, Jean-Jacques. *"The Social Contract" and Other Late Political Writings*. Edited by Victor Gourevitch. Cambridge: Cambridge University Press, 1997.

Ruddick, Sara. *Maternal Thinking: Towards a Politics of Peace*. London: The Women's Press, 1990.

Said, Edward. *Culture and Imperialism*. New York: Vintage, 1993.

Said, Edward. *Orientalism*. New York: Vintage, 1994.

Salomon, Margot E. *Global Responsibility for Human Rights*. Oxford: Oxford University Press, 2007.

Sandel, Michael J. *Democracy's Discontent: America in Search of a Public Philosophy*. Cambridge, MA: Belknap Press of Harvard University Press, 1996.

Sandel, Michael J. *What Money Can't Buy: The Moral Limits of Markets*. New York: Farrar, Straus and Giroux, 2012.

Sandkühler, Hans Jörg, and Rafael de la Vega, eds. *Marxismus und Ethik: Texte zum neukantianischen Sozialismus*. Frankfurt: Suhrkamp, 1974.

Sassen, Saskia. *Territory, Authority, Rights: From Medieval to Global Assemblages*. Princeton: Princeton University Press, 2006.

Satz, Debra. *Why Some Things Should Not Be for Sale: The Limits of Markets*. Oxford: Oxford University Press, 2010.

Savigny, Friedrich Karl von. *System of the Modern Roman Law*. Vol. 1. Translated by William Holloway. Madras: J. Higginbotham, 1867.

Scharpf, Fritz W. "The Costs of Non-Disintegration: The Case of the European Monetary Union." In *Zur Konzeptionalisierung europäischer Desintegration: Zug- und Gegenkräfte im europäischen Integrationsprozess*, edited by Annegret Eppler and Henrik Scheller, 165–84. Baden-Baden: Nomos, 2013.

Scharpf, Fritz W. "Die Finanzkrise als Krise der ökonomischen und rechtlichen Überintegration." In *Grenzen der europäischen Integration*, edited by Claudio Franzius, Franz C. Mayer, and Jürgen Neyer, 51–60. Baden-Baden: Nomos, 2014.

Scharpf, Fritz W. "Monetary Union, Fiscal Crisis and the Preemption of Democracy." *Zeitschrift für Staats- und Europawissenschaften* 2 (2011): 163–98.

Scheppele, Kim Lane. "A Realpolitik Defense of Social Rights." *Texas Law Review* 82, no. 7 (2004): 1921–61.

Schmitt, Carl. *Der Nomos der Erde im Völkerrecht des* Jus Publicum Europaeum. 4th ed. Berlin: Duncker and Humblot, 1997.

Schmitt, Carl. *The Nomos of the Earth in the International Law of the* Jus Publicum Europaeum. Translated by G. L. Ulmen. New York: Telos, 2003.

Schönberger, Christoph. "Die Europäische Union als Bund." *Archiv des öffentlichen Rechts* 129 (2004): 81–120.

Schönberger, Christoph. "The European Union's Democratic Deficit Between Federal and State Prohibition." *Der Staat* 48 (2009).

Schütze, Robert. "On 'Federal' Ground: The European Union as an (Inter)national Phenomenon." *Common Market Law Review* 46 (2009): 1069–105.

Searle, John. *The Construction of Social Reality*. New York: The Free Press, 1995.

Sellars, Wilfried. *Empiricism and the Philosophy of Mind*. Cambridge, MA: Harvard University Press, 1997.

Sen, Amartya. *The Idea of Justice*. Cambridge, MA: Harvard University Press, 2009.

Sen, Amartya. *Inequality Reexamined*. Cambridge, MA: Harvard University Press, 1992.

Shiffrin, Steven. "The First Amendment and Economic Regulation: Away From a General Theory of the First Amendment." *Northwestern University Law Review* 78, no. 5 (1983): 1212–83.

Shiffrin, Steven. *The First Amendment, Democracy, and Romance*. Princeton: Princeton University Press, 1990.

Shiffrin, Steven, and Jesse Chopper. *First Amendment: Cases, Comments, Questions*. 3rd ed. St. Paul, MN: West Academic, 2001.

Skinner, Quentin. "The Sovereign State: A Genealogy." In *Sovereignty in Fragments: The Past, Present and Future of a Contested Concept*, edited by Hent Kalmo and Quentin Skinner, 26–46. Cambridge: Cambridge University Press, 2010.

Spencer, Robert. "Thoughts from Abroad: Theodor Adorno as Postcolonial Theorist." *Culture, Theory and Critique* 51, no. 3 (2010): 207–21.

Spillers, Hortense. *Black, White, and In Color: Essays on American Literature and Culture*. Chicago: University of Chicago Press, 2003.

Sraffa, Piero. *Production of Commodities by Means of Commodities: Prelude to a Critique of Economic Theory*. Cambridge: Cambridge University Press, 1960.

Stahn, Carsten. "Responsibility to Protect: Political Rhetoric or Emerging Legal Norm?" *American Journal of International Law* 101, no. 1 (2007): 99–120.

Stoler, Ann Laura. *Race and the Education of Desire: Foucault's* History of Sexuality *and the Colonial Order of Things*. Durham, NC: Duke University Press, 1995.

Stone Sweet, Alec. "Constitutionalism, Legal Pluralism, and International Regimes." *Indiana Journal of Global Legal Studies* 16, no. 2 (2009): 621–45.

Streeck, Wolfgang. *Gekaufte Zeit: Die Krise des demokratischen Kapitalismus*. Berlin: Suhrkamp, 2013.

Sullivan, Shannon, and Nancy Tuana, eds. *Race and Epistemologies of Ignorance*. Albany, NY: SUNY Press, 2007.

Tasioulas, John. "Are Human Rights Essentially Triggers for Intervention?" *Philosophy Compass* 4, no. 6 (2009): 938–50.

Tasioulas, John. "The Moral Reality of Human Rights." In *Freedom from Poverty as a Human Right*, edited by Thomas Pogge, 75–101. Oxford: Oxford University Press, 2007.

Tasioulas, John. "Taking Rights Out of Human Rights." *Ethics* 120, no. 4 (2010): 647–78.

Taylor, Paul C., ed. *The Philosophy of Race*. 4 vols. Critical Concepts in Philosophy. New York: Routledge, 2012.

Teubner, Günther. "Global Bukovina." In *Global Law Without a State*, edited by Günther Teubner, 3–28. Aldershot: Dartmouth, 1997.

Teubner, Günther. "Societal Constitutionalism: Alternatives to State-Centered Constitutional Theory." In *Transnational Governance and Constitutionalism*, edited by Christian Joerges, Inger-Johanne Sand, and Günther Teubner, 3–29. Oxford: Hart, 2004.

Tronto, Joan. *Moral Boundaries: A Political Argument for an Ethic of Care*. New York: Routledge, 1993.

Tully, James. "On Law, Democracy and Imperialism." In *Public Philosophy in a New Key*. Vol. 2, *Imperialism and Civic Freedom*, 127–65. Cambridge: Cambridge University Press, 2008.

Tushnet, Mark. "The Inevitable Globalization of Constitutional Law." Paper no. 0906, presented at the Public Law and Legal Theory Working Paper Series, Harvard Law School.

Tushnet, Mark. "The Inevitable Globalization of Constitutional Law." *Virginia Journal of International Law* 49 (2009): 985–1006.

United Nations Committee on Economic, Social and Cultural Rights. *Substantive Issues Arising in the Implementation of the International Covenant on Economic, Social and Cultural Rights*. E/C.12/2001/15. December 14, 2001. http://www2.ohchr.org/english/bodies/cescr/docs/statements/E.C.12.2001.15HRIntel-property.pdf.

United Nations High-Level Panel on Threats, Challenges and Change. *A More Secure World: Our Shared Responsibility*. UN Doc. A/59/565. December 2, 2004. https://documents-dds-ny.un.org/doc/UNDOC/GEN/N04/602/31/PDF/N0460231.pdf?OpenElement.

United Nations Human Rights Council. *Promotion of All Human Rights, Civil, Political, Economic, Social and Cultural Rights, Including the Right to Development*. A/HRC/11/13. April 22, 2009. http://www2.ohchr.org/english/bodies/hrcouncil/docs/11session/A.HRC.11.13.pdf.

United Nations Office of the High Commissioner for Human Rights. *Guiding Principles on Business and Human Rights: Implementing the United Nations "Protect, Respect and Remedy" Framework*. New York: United Nations, 2011. http://www.ohchr.org/Documents/Publications/GuidingPrinciplesBusinessHR_EN.pdf.

United Nations Office of the High Commissioner for Human Rights. "Human Rights Bodies—Complaints Procedures." Accessed June 23, 2016. http://www.ohchr.org/EN/HRBodies/TBPetitions/Pages/HRTBPetitions.aspx.

United Nations Trust Fund for Human Security. "Human Security Approach." Accessed June 23, 2016. http://www.un.org/humansecurity/human-security-unit/human-security-approach.

Valls, Andrew, ed. *Race and Racism in Modern Philosophy*. Ithaca, NY: Cornell University Press, 2005.

Van Parijs, Philippe. "What (if Anything) Is Intrinsically Wrong with Capitalism?" *Philosophica* 34, no. 2 (1984): 85–102.

Varadharajan, Asha. *Exotic Parodies: Subjectivity in Adorno, Said, and Spivak*. Minneapolis: University of Minnesota Press, 1995.

Vásquez-Arroyo, Antonio. "Universal History Disavowed: On Critical Theory and Postcolonialism." *Postcolonial Studies* 11, no. 4 (2008): 451–73.
Verdross, Alfred. *Die Verfassung der Völkerrechtsgemeinschaft* (Vienna: J. Springer, 1926).
Vincent, R. J. *Human Rights and International Relations*. Cambridge: Cambridge University Press, 1986.
Waldron, Jeremy. *"Partly Laws Common to All Mankind": Foreign Law in American Courts*. New Haven, CT: Yale University Press, 2012.
Waldron, Jeremy. *The Right to Private Property*. Oxford: Clarendon, 1988.
Waldron, Jeremy. "The Supreme Court, 2004 Term-Comment: Foreign Law and the Modern Ius Gentium." *Harvard Law Review* 119, no. 1 (2005): 129–47.
Walker, Neil. "Constitutionalism and the Incompleteness of Democracy: An Iterative Relationship." *Rechtsfilosofie & Rechtstheorie* 39, no. 3 (2010): 206–33.
Walker, Neil. "Constitutionalism and the Incompleteness of Democracy: A Reply to Four Critics." *Rechtsfilosofie & Rechtstheorie* 39, no. 3 (2010): 276–88.
Wallerstein, Immanuel. *Historical Capitalism*. London: Verso, 1983.
Walzer, Michael. "The Moral Standing of States: A Response to Four Critics." *Philosophy & Public Affairs* 9, no. 3 (1980): 209–29.
Walzer, Michael. *Spheres of Justice: A Defense of Pluralism and Equality*. New York: Basic Books, 1983.
Watson, Veronica, Deirdre Howard-Wagner, and Lisa Spanierman, eds. *Unveiling Whiteness in the Twenty-First Century: Global Manifestations, Transdisciplinary Interventions*. Lanham, MD: Lexington Books, 2015.
Wazwaz, Noor. "It's Official: The US Is Becoming a Minority-Majority Nation." *U.S. News & World Report*. July 6, 2015. http://www.usnews.com/news/articles/2015/07/06/its-official-the-us-is-becoming-a-minority-majority-nation.
Weber, Max. *Economy and Society: An Outline of Interpretive Sociology*. 2 vols. Edited by Guenther Roth and Claus Wittich. Berkeley: University of California Press, 1978.
Weheliye, Alex. *Habeas Viscus: Racializing Assemblages, Biopolitics, and Black Feminist Theories of the Human*. Durham, NC: Duke University Press, 2014.
Wellmer, Albrecht. *The Persistence of Modernity: Essays on Aesthetics, Ethics, and Postmodernism*. Translated by David Midgley. Cambridge, MA: MIT Press, 1991.
Wheeler, Nicholas, and Frazer Egerton. "The Responsibility to Protect: 'Precious Commitment' or a Promise Unfulfilled?" *Global Responsibility to Protect* 1, no. 1 (2009): 114–32.
Williams, Bernard. *Truth and Truthfulness: An Essay in Genealogy*. Princeton: Princeton University Press, 2002.
Williams, Eric. *Capitalism and Slavery*. 1944. Reprint, with a new introduction, Chapel Hill: University of North Carolina Press, 1994.
Winter, Jay. *Dreams of Peace and Freedom: Utopian Movements in the Twentieth Century*. New Haven, CT: Yale University Press, 2006.
Wood, Ellen Meiksins. *Empire of Capital*. London: Verso, 2003.
World Trade Organization. "Doha Declaration on the TRIPS Agreement and Public Health." WT/MIN(01)/DEC/2. November 20, 2001. http://www.wto.org/english/thewto_e/minist_e/min01_e/mindecl_trips_e.htm.

World Trade Organization. "Draft Ministerial Declaration: Proposal from a Group of Developing Countries." October 4, 2001. http://www.wto.org/english/tratop_e/trips_e/mindecdraft_w312_e.htm.

World Trade Organization. *Final Act Embodying the Results of the Uruguay Round of Multilateral Trade Negotiations.* Annex 1C, "Agreement on Trade-Related Aspects of Intellectual Property Rights," 319–51. April 15, 1994. http://www.wto.org/english/docs_e/legal_e/legal_e.htm#TRIPs.

Wright, Richard. *Black Boy (American Hunger), The Outsider.* New York: Library of America, 1991.

Wright, Richard. *Lawd Today!, Uncle Tom's Children, Native Son.* New York: Library of America, 1991.

Young, Katharine. *Constituting Economic and Social Rights.* Oxford: Oxford University Press, 2012.

Young, Robert. "Foucault on Race and Colonialism." *New Formations* 25 (1995): 57–65.

Young, Robert. *White Mythologies.* 2nd ed. New York: Routledge, 2004.

Zerubavel, Eviatar. *Time Maps: Collective Memory and the Social Shape of the Past.* Chicago: University of Chicago Press, 2003.

ABOUT THE CONTRIBUTORS

AMY ALLEN is Liberal Arts Research Professor of Philosophy and Women's, Gender, and Sexuality Studies at the Pennsylvania State University. Her research interests are in twentieth-century Continental philosophy, with a particular emphasis on the intersection of critical social theory, poststructuralism, and feminist theory. Her current research project focuses on the relationship between psychoanalysis and critical theory. She is the author of *The End of Progress: Decolonizing the Normative Foundations of Critical Theory* (Columbia University Press, 2016); *The Politics of Our Selves: Power, Autonomy, and Gender in Contemporary Critical Theory* (Columbia University Press, 2008); and *The Power of Feminist Theory: Domination, Resistance, Solidarity* (Westview, 1999). Her recent publications include "Psychoanalysis and the Methodology of Critique," *Constellations* 23, no. 2 (2016): 244–54; "History, Critique, and Freedom: The Historical A Priori in Husserl and Foucault," with Andreea Smaranda Aldea, *Continental Philosophy Review* 49, no. 1 (2016): 1–11; "Progress, Philosophical and Otherwise," *Journal of Speculative Philosophy* (SPEP Supplement) 28, no. 3 (2015): 265–82; and "Are We Driven? Critical Theory and Psychoanalysis Reconsidered," *Critical Horizons* 16, no. 4 (2015), 311–28.

SEYLA BENHABIB is the Eugene Meyer Professor of Political Science and Philosophy at Yale University. She specializes in nineteenth- and twentieth-century Continental social and political thought, feminist theory, and the history of modern political theory. Her recent research focuses on issues relating to refugees, exile, asylum, citizenship, cultural conflict, multiculturalism, and nationality. She is the author of *Dignity in Adversity: Human Rights in Troubled Times* (Polity, 2011); *Politics in Dark Times: Encounters with Hannah Arendt* (Cambridge University Press, 2010); *Another Cosmopolitanism: Hospitality, Sovereignty and Democratic Iterations* (Oxford University

Press, 2006); *The Rights of Others: Aliens, Citizens and Residents* (Cambridge University Press, 2004); *The Claims of Culture: Equality and Diversity in the Global Era* (Princeton University Press, 2002); *The Reluctant Modernism of Hannah Arendt* (Sage, 1996); *Feminist Contentions: A Philosophical Exchange* (Routledge, 1994), with Judith Butler, Drucilla Cornell, and Nancy Fraser; *Feminism as Critique* (Polity, 1986), with Drucilla Cornell; *Situating the Self: Gender, Community and Postmodernism in Contemporary Ethics* (Polity, 1992); and *Critique, Norm and Utopia: A Study of the Normative Foundations of Critical Theory* (Columbia University Press, 1986). Her recent publications include "The New Legitimation Crises of Arab States and Turkey," *Philosophy & Social Criticism* 40, no. 4–5 (May 2014): 349–58; and "Transnational Legal Sites and Democracy-Building: Reconfiguring Political Geographies," *Philosophy & Social Criticism* 39, no. 4–5 (May 2013): 471–86.

WENDY BROWN is the Class of 1936 First Professor of Political Science at the University of California, Berkeley. Her research interests include the history of political theory, nineteenth- and twentieth-century Continental theory, critical theory, and theories of contemporary capitalism. She is the author of *Undoing the Demos: Neoliberalism's Stealth Revolution* (Zone, 2015); *Walled States, Waning Sovereignty* (Zone, 2010); *Regulating Aversion: Tolerance in the Age of Empire and Identity* (Princeton University Press, 2006); *Edgework: Essays on Knowledge and Politics* (Princeton University Press, 2005); *Politics Out of History* (Princeton University Press, 2001); *States of Injury: Power and Freedom in Late Modernity* (Princeton University Press, 1995); and *Manhood and Politics: A Feminist Reading in Political Theory* (Rowman and Littlefield, 1988). She is coauthor of *The Power of Tolerance: A Debate* (Columbia University Press, 2014), with Rainer Forst; and *Is Critique Secular? Injury, Blasphemy and Free Speech* (University of California Press, 2009), with Judith Butler, Saba Mahmood, and Talal Asad; and is coeditor of *Left Legalism/Left Critique* (Duke University Press, 2002), with Janet Halley. Her recent publications include "Sacrificial Citizenship: Neoliberalism, Human Capital, and Austerity Politics," *Constellations* 23, no. 1 (2016): 3–14; and "Marxism for Tomorrow," *Dissent* 62, no. 4 (2015): 91–94.

PENELOPE DEUTSCHER is the Joan and Sarepta Harrison Professor of Philosophy at Northwestern University. Her current research focuses on the intersections of biopolitics, reproductive futurism, and the genealogy of gendered rights claims. She is the author of *Foucault's Futures: A Critique of Reproductive Reason* (Columbia University Press, forthcoming); *The Philosophy of Simone de Beauvoir: Ambiguity, Conversion, Resistance* (Cambridge University Press, 2008); *How to Read Derrida* (Granta, 2005); *A Politics of Impossible Difference: The Later Work of Luce Irigaray* (Cornell University Press, 2002); and *Yielding Gender: Feminism, Deconstruction and the History of Philosophy* (Routledge, 1997). Her coedited volumes include *Foucault/Derrida Fifty Years Later: The Futures of Deconstruction, Genealogy, and Politics* (Columbia University Press, 2016), with Olivia Custer and Sam Haddad; and *Repenser le politique: l'apport du féminisme* (Campagne première, 2004), with Françoise Collina. Her recent publications include " 'On the Whole We Don't': Michel Foucault, Veena Das and Sexual Violence," *Critical Horizons* 17, no. 2 (2016): 186–206; " 'Foucault for Psychoanalysis': Monique David-Menard's Kind of Blue," *Philosophia* 5, no. 1 (2015): 111–27; "Fraternal Politics and Maternal Auto-Immunity: Derrida, Feminism, and Ethnocentrism," in *A Companion to Derrida*, ed. Zeynep Direk and Leonard Lawlor (Wiley-Blackwell, 2014), 362–77; and "The Membrane and the Diaphragm: Derrida and Esposito on Immunity, Community, and Birth," *Angelaki* 18, no. 3 (2013): 49–68.

RAINER FORST is Professor of Political Theory and Philosophy at the Goethe University Frankfurt. He is Co-Director of the Excellence Cluster on "The Formation of Normative Orders" and of the Center for Advanced Studies, "Justitia Amplificata." He is also Director of the Leibniz Research Group, "Transnational Justice," and Member of the Directorate of the Institute for Advanced Study in the Humanities in Bad Homburg. His research focuses on questions of practical reason and the foundation of morality as well as on basic concepts of normative political theory, especially justice, toleration, and democracy. He is the author of *Justification and Critique* (Polity, 2013); *Toleration in Conflict* (Cambridge University Press, 2013); *The Right to Justification* (Columbia University Press, 2012); and *Contexts of Justice* (University of California Press, 2002). He is coauthor of *The Power of Tolerance: A Debate* (Columbia University Press, 2014), with Wendy Brown; and *Justice, Democracy and the Right to Justification: Rainer Forst in Dialogue* (Bloomsbury, 2014). His recent publications include "Noumenal Power," *Journal of Political Philosophy* 23, no. 2 (2015): 111–27; and "A Critical Theory of Politics: Grounds, Method, and Aims," *Philosophy and Social Criticism* 41, no. 3 (2015): 225–34.

NANCY FRASER is the Henry A. and Louise Loeb Professor of Political and Social Science at The New School for Social Research. Her research focuses on social and political theory, feminist theory, and contemporary French and German thought. She is the author of *Fortunes of Feminism: From State-Managed Capitalism to Neoliberal Crisis* (Verso, 2013); *Scales of Justice: Reimagining Political Space in a Globalizing World* (Columbia University Press, 2008); *Redistribution or Recognition? A Political-Philosophical Exchange* (Verso, 2003), with Axel Honneth; *Justice Interruptus: Critical Reflections on the "Postsocialist" Condition* (Routledge, 1997); and *Unruly Practices: Power, Discourse, and Gender in Contemporary Social Theory* (University of Minnesota Press, 1989). She is coeditor of *Pragmatism, Critique, Judgment: Essays for Richard J. Bernstein* (MIT Press, 2004), with Seyla Benhabib; and *Revaluing French Feminism: Critical Essays on Difference, Agency, and Culture* (Indiana University Press, 1992), with Sandra Bartky. Her recent publications include "Legitimation Crisis? On the Political Contradictions of Financialized Capitalism," *Critical Historical Studies* 2, no. 2 (Fall 2015): 157–89; "Can Society Be Commodities All the Way Down?" *Economy and Society* 43, no. 4 (2014): 541–58; and "Transnationalizing the Public Sphere: On the Legitimacy and Efficacy of Public Opinion in a Post-Westphalian World," in *Transnationalizing the Public Sphere*, ed. Kate Nash (Cambridge: Polity, 2014), 8–42.

JÜRGEN HABERMAS is Emeritus Professor of Philosophy at Goethe University Frankfurt. He is one of the most influential living philosophers in the world. His work addresses topics stretching from social-political theory to legal theory, aesthetics, epistemology, philosophy of language, and philosophy of religion. He is the author of more than thirty books, including *The Lure of Technocracy* (Polity, 2015); *The Crisis of the European Union: A Response* (Polity, 2012); *Europe: The Faltering Project* (Polity, 2009); *Between Naturalism and Religion* (Polity, 2008); *Truth and Justification* (MIT Press, 2003); *The Postnational Constellation* (MIT Press, 2001); *The Inclusion of the Other: Studies in Political Theory* (MIT Press, 1998); *Between Facts and Norms: Contributions to a Discourse Theory of Law and Democracy* (MIT Press, 1996); *Justification and Application* (MIT Press, 1993); *Moral Consciousness and Communicative Action* (MIT Press, 1990); *The Structural Transformation of the Public Sphere* (MIT Press, 1987); and *The Theory of Communicative Action* (Beacon, 1987). He is the recipient of numerous prestigious awards, including the Kluge Prize (2015), the Erasmus Prize (2013), the Holberg Prize (2005), the Kyoto Prize (2004), the Prince of Asturias Award (2003), and the Peace Prize of the German Book Trade (2001).

RAHEL JAEGGI is Professor of Practical Philosophy with emphasis on Social Philosophy and Political Philosophy at the Humboldt University, Berlin. Her research focuses on social, legal, and political philosophy, philosophical ethics, anthropology, and social ontology. She is the author of *Kritik von Lebensformen* (Suhrkamp, 2014; English translation forthcoming); *Alienation* (Columbia University Press, 2014); and *Welt und Person: Zum anthropologischen Hintergrund der Gesellschaftskritik Hannah Arendts* (Lukas Verlag, 1997). Her coedited volumes include *Karl Marx: Perspektiven der Gesellschaftskritik* (Akademieverlag, 2013), with Daniel Loick; *Nach Marx: Philosophie, Kritik, Praxis* (Suhrkamp, 2013), with Daniel Loick; and *Sozialphilosophie und Kritik* (Suhrkamp, 2009), with Rainer Forst, Martin Hartmann, and Martin Saar. Her recent publications include "Alienation, Exploitation, Dysfunction: Three Paths of the Critique of Capitalism," *Southern Journal of Philosophy* (forthcoming); "Towards an Immanent Critique of Forms of Life," *Raisons Politiques* 57 (2015): 13–29; and "Philosophy as Criticism," *Deutsche Zeitschrift für Philosophie* 63, no. 3 (2015): 569–76.

CRISTINA LAFONT is the Wender-Lewis Research and Teaching Professor of Philosophy at Northwestern University. Her current research focuses on issues in contemporary political philosophy such as deliberative democracy, human rights and global governance, and religion and politics. She is the author of *Global Governance and Human Rights* (Spinoza Lecture Series) (van Gorcum, 2012); *Heidegger, Language, and World-Disclosure* (Cambridge University Press, 2000); and *The Linguistic Turn in Hermeneutic Philosophy* (MIT Press, 1999). She is coeditor of the *Habermas Handbuch* (Metzler Verlag, 2012). Her recent publications include "Should We Take the Human out of Human Rights? Human Rights and Human Dignity in a Corporate World," *Ethics & International Affairs* 30, no. 2 (2016): 233–52; "Deliberation, Participation and Democratic Legitimacy," *The Journal of Political Philosophy* 23, no. 1 (2015): 40–63;

"Religious Pluralism in a Deliberative Democracy," in *Secular or Post-Secular Democracies in Europe? The Challenge of Religious Pluralism in the 21st Century*, ed. Ferran Requejo and Camil Ungureanu (London: Routledge, 2015), 46–60; and "Accountability and Global Governance: Challenging the State-Centric Conception of Human Rights," in *Ethics & Global Politics* 3, no. 3 (2010): 193–215.

CHRISTOPH MENKE is Professor of Philosophy at the Goethe University Frankfurt. His research focuses on political and legal theory, theories of subjectivity, ethics, and aesthetics. He is author of *Kritik der Rechte* (Suhrkamp, 2015; English translation forthcoming); *Force: A Fundamental Concept of Aesthetic Anthropology* (Fordham University Press, 2012); *Recht und Gewalt* (August Verlag, 2011); *Tragic Play: Irony and Theater from Sophocles to Beckett* (Columbia University Press, 2009); *Reflections of Equality* (Stanford University Press, 2006); *The Sovereignty of Art: Aesthetic Negativity in Adorno and Derrida* (MIT Press, 1999); and *Tragödie im Sittlichen: Gerechtigkeit und Freiheit nach Hegel* (Suhrkamp, 1996). His recent coedited volumes include *Kreation und Depression: Freiheit im gegenwärtigen Kapitalismus* (Kulturverlag Kadmos, 2012), with Juliane Rebentisch; *Paradoxien der Autonomie* (August Verlag, 2011), with Thomas Khurana; and *Der Mensch als Person und Rechtsperson: Grundlage der Freiheit* (Berliner Wissenschafts-Verlag, 2011), with Eckart Klein. His recent publications include "Back to Hannah Arendt: The Refugees and the Crisis of Human Rights," *Merkur* 70 (July 2016): 49–58; "The Possibility of the Standards: About a Practice Beyond Morality and Causality," *Deutsche Zeitschrift für Philosophie* 64, no. 2 (2016): 299–306; and "At the Brink of Law: Hannah Arendt's Revision of the Judgment on Eichmann," *Social Research* 81, no. 3 (2014): 585–611.

CHARLES W. MILLS is a Distinguished Professor at the City University of New York Graduate Center. His work in recent years has looked at the challenge of theorizing race, racism, and racial justice within a liberal framework, with a particular focus on the adequacy (or lack thereof) of Rawlsianism. He is the author of *Black Rights/White Wrongs: The Critique of Racial Liberalism* (Oxford University Press, forthcoming); *The Racial Contract* (Cornell University Press, 1997); *Blackness Visible: Essays on Philosophy and Race* (Cornell University Press, 1998); *From Class to Race: Essays in White Marxism and Black Radicalism* (Rowman & Littlefield, 2003); *Contract and Domination* (Polity, 2007), with Carole Pateman; and *Radical Theory, Caribbean Reality: Race, Class and Social Domination* (University of the West Indies Press, 2010). His recent publications include "White Time: The Chronic Injustice of Ideal Theory," *Du Bois Review* 11, no. 1 (2014): 27–42; "Kant and Race, Redux," *Graduate Faculty Philosophy Journal* 35, no. 1–2 (2014): 125–57; "Decolonizing Western Political Philosophy," *New Political Science* 37, no. 1 (2015): 1–24; and "Racial Equality," in *The Equal Society: Essays on Equality in Theory and Practice*, ed. George Hull (London: Lexington, 2015), 43–71.

INDEX

abnormal, constructions of, 187, 222–24
acceptable political society, 78, 80, 85
accumulation, xx, 144, 145–47, 151, 157, 175–76; expropriation, 146–47, 149–50, 243
Adorno, Theodor, xxii–xxiii, 186–88; critical distance, 188, 194–95; Eurocentrism, 198–200; genealogy as problematization, 191–93; historicization of History, 190–91; negative dialectics, 194, 199–200; nonidentical, 194, 243; postcolonial studies and, 198–202; problematization and normative inheritance of modernity, 188, 195–97, 241, 247; reason, view of, 188–89; utopia and utopianism, 189–90
Adorno: A Critical Reader (ed. Gibson and Rubin), 199
African Americans, 235, 240, 244–45, 247
Afro-modernity, 244–45
agency, 27, 52, 75–76, 86, 242
Agreement on Trade-Related Aspects of Intellectual Property Rights (TRIPS), 57–59
Alexy, Robert, 28
Alien Tort Statute (ATS), 21

Allen, Amy, xvii–xxiv, 209, 233–35, 247; critical distance, 188, 194–95, 240–41; Foucauldian critique, view of, 211–15; genealogy as problematization, 188, 191–93, 240; historicization of History, 188, 190–91, 245; reason and power, 188–89, 240–44; reconciling, unifying logic of modernity, 194, 243–44; utopia and utopianism, 188–90, 204n20, 240, 245–46
Alston, Philip, 69n8
alterity, xxiii, 210, 214–15
American exceptionalism, 21–24
American exemptionalism, 22
American Revolution, 31–32
analytic tradition, 237–39
Anthropocene, 149
anticapitalism, 142, 156, 158
antidistortion rationale, 103
archaeology, 210, 214, 216, 231, 232n59
archive, 208
Aristotle, 36, 241, 242
Arrighi, Giovanni, 151
assemblages, 208–9
assets, 133–34

Australian states, 221
authority, xv–xvi, 134, 196; biopolitical, 218, 222–23; decision-making, 3, 7, 9–17; human rights and sovereignty, 32–34, 55, 59–60; legitimate political, 80, 83–84
authorship model of democratic legitimacy, 32–34, 45n36
autonomy, 75, 79, 86

banking sector, 4–6, 16, 17n3, 108
basic rights: justification, right to, 74–75, 83–85; socialist, xix, 121–23
Beckert, Jens, 163
Beitz, Charles, 27, 30, 76, 77, 80, 87n20
Benhabib, Seyla, xv–xvi, 69n9, 87n26, 88n29
Benjamin, Walter, 234
binding claims, 76–78, 83–85
biopolitics/biopower, xix, 214–15, 220–24; legitimacy, 217–18
The Birth of Biopolitics (Foucault), 91, 209, 223
The Birth of the Clinic (Foucault), 210
black radical tradition, 238, 243
Blacks in and Out of the Left (Dawson), 238–39
boundaries, 38, 154–56, 173
bourgeois private law, xix, 91, 119–21; circle of, 127–29, *129*; dialectical unity of, *129*, 129–36; double formation, 117, 126, 127–28, 131–34; empowerment, 130–31; sale of labor power as commodity, 120–21; social law and, 123–28; socialist basic rights and, 121–23; subjective rights, 118, 130–36
Brandom, Robert, 46n45
Brazil, 37, 58
Brown, Wendy, xviii, xxiii, 58, 207, 217–19, 225, 228n22, 231nn54
Buckley v. Valeo, 96, 103, 109
Bush, George W., 221
Butler, Judith, 213

campaign finance regulations, 96–98. *See also Citizens United v. Federal Election Commission*

Canguilhem, Georges, 214, 229n33
capital: accumulation, xx, 144–47; family, 223; human, 95; self-expansion, 144, 145, 151; speech as, 98–103, 112
Capital (Marx), 146–47, 157–58
capitalism: background conditions of possibility, xx–xxi, 143, 146–48; boundary struggles, 154–56, 157; bourgeois law and, 119–21; breakup of previous world, 143, 148–51; contradictions of, 156–58; core features, xx–xxi, 143–46; crisis of, 142, 148, 157; divisions, xxi, 143, 148–53; as economico-juridical complex, 91–92; expanded conception of, 141–59; as form of life, 175–77; hidden abodes, xx–xxi, 143, 146–49, 155; institutionalized social order, 152–54; legal status of free market, 143, 150; natural vs. economic realm, 149–52; noneconomic phenomena and, xxi, 92, 94, 142, 145–46, 151–58; polity vs. economy, 150–53; production, relations of, 121–23; as reified form of ethical life, 152–53; renewed interest in, 141–42, 162–63; romantic view, 155–56; slavery as foundation of, 244; social reproduction, xx, 147–48, 152–53, 157–58. *See also* economization of rights; free labor market
capitalist society, xxi, 144–46, 152–54, 175–76
care, techniques of, 221–25
censorship, as government interference, 98–101
Chakrabarty, Dipesh, 200
children, abnormalization of, 223–24
citizenry, 5, 7, 9–11
Citizens United v. Federal Election Commission, xviii–xix, 96–112; corruption and influence, 107–11; disavowal of stratification, 101–2; dissenting opinion, 107–8; inversions of democratic meaning, 111–12; multiplication of marketplaces, 103–4;

strict scrutiny, 104–6. *See also* economization of rights
civil rights discourse, 31, 104–7
civil society, global, 25–26
class division, 143, 157, 235–36
classical economic liberalism, 95
club-law, 118
Cohen, Jean, 24, 38, 50–56, 70n23
Cohen, Joshua, 51–52, 77–78, 82
Colegate, Christina, 221
colonialism, 150–51, 161, 242–43
commodification, xxi, 120–21, 132; exchange, 169–70, 176; of nature, 149; noncommodification, xxi, 144, 152–53
commodity form, 152, 160–61
common sense, 242–43
communicative freedom, 27
companies, human rights due diligence standards, 61, 72–73n43
compensatory justice, 246
concept, xv, 24, 28–29, 32–33
conditions of possibility, xx, 143, 146–53; nature and power; 149–52 political, 150–51
confederations, 7–8
consensus, 14, 24, 36, 38, 47, 77
Constitution, US, 111, 150, 151; First Amendment, 97–98, 101–3
constitutional monism, 23, 26
constitutional revolutions, 7, 16
constitutional rights, xiv–xv, 27–33, 34–35
constitutions: France, 7, 16; United States, 8–10, 15–16
constructivism, political and moral, 83–85, 91
contestation, 208
contingency, 208, 231n53
contract, 237
Contribution to the Critique of Political Economy (Marx), 117, 118
Convention Against Torture and Other Cruel, Inhuman or Degrading Treatment or Punishment, 26
core values, 75–76, 77

corporate speech, 102, 105, 111–12. *See also Citizens United v. Federal Election Commission*
corporations: "as associations of citizens," 100, 102, 104; as disadvantaged class, 105–6; strict scrutiny, 104–6
corruption and influence, 107–11, 115n37
cosmopolitanism. *See* legal cosmopolitanism
courts: democratic iterations and, 34–35; international, 54. *See also* Supreme Court
criminal acts, 52–53
crisis, practices and, 167, 172
critical distance, 188, 194–95, 240–41
critical ethnic studies, 240, 243
critical race studies, xxiv, 215, 234–35, 240. *See also* race
critical theory, xiii–xiv, 74–88; Adorno and Foucault and, 183–205; as approach to human rights, 75; critique of, 233–50; decolonization and deracialization required, xxiv–xxv, 200, 211, 234–37; Eurocentrism, xxiv, 198–200, 202, 212–13, 233; inwardness objection, 200–2; narrow understanding of economy, 160–61; normative, 184–85, 200–2; postcolonial studies and, 183–86, 200–1; reason and power, 188–89, 240–44
critique, 207, 210; political critique of law, 117–18, 126–27; social critique of law, 117–18, 124–25, 128–30. *See also* critical theory
Culture and Imperialism (Said), 183–84, 233
customary use rights, 143–44

Dawson, Michael, 238–39
decent hierarchical regimes, 30–31, 71n26, 76, 81–82
Declaration of the Rights of Man and the Citizen, 47
Declaration on the Human Rights of Individuals Who Are Not Nationals of the Country in Which They Live, 42n13

decolonization, 184, 185, 204n10; of critical theory, xxiv–xxv, 200, 211, 234–37
de-democratization, 96, 99
democracy, xiv–xv; definitions, 7–8; historical connection with capitalism, 162; justification for, 12, 15; meanings shaped by neoliberalism, 92–93, 96; not achieved for people of color, 247; representative, shift away from, 109, 111–12; right to, 48, 78, 82
democratic iterations, xvi, 24, 30–31, 32; recursive, 34, 36–37; sites of, 34–35
democratic legitimacy, 3–4, 6, 7; authorship model, 32–34; international human rights principles and, 33–38
Denis, Clare, 224–25
Derrida, Jacques, 22, 210
Deutscher, Penelope, xxiii
developing countries, pharmaceutical patents and, 57–60
development, right to, 64–65
dialectical reversal, 128–29
dialectical unity, 129–36
dialectics, 187–89, 191; negative, 194, 199–200
difference, 199–200
difference principle, 36
differentiation-theoretical approach, 161–62
dignity, 83
disciplinary techniques, xix, xxiii, 208, 210, 217, 221–22, 227n6
discourse, 36, 198
discretion, 132–34
disposal rights, 120, 131–34, 169
dispositifs, 208, 210
dispossession perspective, 147
division of powers, 7, 9
Doha round of trade negotiations, 58–59
domination, xix, xxii, 82, 117–38, 175–76; bourgeois private law and capitalism, 119–21; capitalist relations of production, 121–23; corporate, 111; "different form" of law and, 118–19, 121, 123, 125–26; human rights as weapon against, 74; labor power as commodity, 120–21; legal equality required for, 119, 121, 123, 127; social law and normalization, 123–25; socialist basic rights, 121–23; struggle for law, 125–29, 134; two forms of, 127–28
Du Bois, W. E. B., 244
duty to cooperate, 64

Eagleton, Terry, 201
ecological commons, 150
ecological perspectives, 152, 154
economic practices, 167–68; economic social practices, 163–64; as failed social practices, xxi, 164, 176–77; human rights and, 60, 63–64; practice character of, 171–73, 176
economism, 160–61
economization of rights, xviii–xix, 4, 91–116; civil rights discourse, 104–6, 107; as conversion of political processes, 99, 111–12; corruption and influence, 107–11; few drown out many, 107–8; law shaped by neoliberalism, 91–93; process of, 93–94; self-investment, 94–95; speech as capital, 98–100. *See also* Citizens United v. Federal Election Commission; *Citizens United v. Federal Election Commission;* neoliberalism
economy, xxi–xxii; as autonomous sphere, 161–62; narrow concept, 160–61; polity vs, 150–53; as set of economic social practices, 163–64; as social practice, 163–64; wide concept, 160–61, 163–64, 173–75
ecosocialist thinkers, 149–52
electoral contests: as political marketplaces, 99, 101, 103; voters equated with financial contributors, 109, 110–11
empire, 183–84
empiricism/positivism, 134–36
empowerment, 130–31
enclosures, 149–50

end point of history, 190
Engels, Friedrich, 242
Enlightenment, xxii, 189, 191–92, 211–12, 233–34
entitlements, 52
entrepreneurialism, 94–95
environmentalism, marketizing of, 149–50
equality: bourgeois society, 120, 122; "different form" of law and, 118–19, 123, 125–27; rights' distribution, 104; social law and, 123–25
equality of persons, 29, 78–84
equalization, marketplaces free of, 103–4
equal participation, 124–26
equiprimordiality, 88n30
ethical life, xxi, 152–53, 173
ethnocentrism, xviii, xxii, 75, 79, 81–82
ethos, xxi–xxii, 176
Eurocentrism, xxiv, 198–200, 202, 212–13
European Central Bank, 5, 6
European citizenry, 5, 12–17
European Commission, 6, 13
European Council, 6, 13, 55
European Court of Human Rights (ECHR), 44n25, 54–55
European Parliament, 6, 13
European peoples, 5, 12–17
European Union, xiv–xv, 3–7, 10–18; crisis, 4–5, 16, 17n3; decision-making authority, 3, 7, 9–17; double sovereign, 12–13; eurozone, 3–18; public spheres, 11–12; right of exit and review, 14; trust issue, 5, 10–12. *See also* federation, supranational
exchange, 169–70, 176
expert, role of, 223
exploitation, 146–47
expropriation, 146–47, 149–50, 243

faded cosmologies, 168, 178n15
family, 222–23
Federal Election Commission, 96–103, 98–99

Federalist Papers, 8, 15
federation, supranational, 12–15. *See also* European Union
federations, 3, 7–10
Feher, Michel, 95
feminist theory, 148, 152, 239
Ferguson, Adam, 167
feudalism, 119, 143, 151, 153, 217
fictitious (corporate) persons, 97
First Amendment, 97–98, 101–3
First National Bank of Boston v. Bellotti, 96, 103
Fordism, 145
foreign law, 21–23
forms of life, 164, 166–67
Forst, Rainer, xvii–xviii, xxii, 36
Foucault, Michel, xix, xxii–xxiii, 91–92, 93, 186–88, 207–32; Allen's view, 211–15; anticipating transformation, 207, 209–20; applicability of, 209–10, 227n10; assemblages, 208–9; bifurcations of populations, 221; critical distance, 188, 194–95; Eurocentrism, 198–200, 212; genealogical method, 191–93, 207, 228n22; historicization of History, 190–91; multiplicity of present, 215–17; normalization, 124–25; oppression, lack of attention to, 214–15; postcolonial studies and, 198–202; "present, "use of, 207–32; problematization and normative inheritance of modernity, 188, 195–97; reason, view of, 188–89; reconfigurations of projects, 219–20; right to participation, 124–25; uncertainty, 212–14; unreason, xxiii, 193, 214, 243; utopia and utopianism, 189–90
—Works: 187, 191; *Abnormal,* 223; *Birth of Biopolitics,* 91, 208, 223; *The Birth of the Clinic,* 210; "Critique" pieces, 212; *History of Madness,* 187, 191, 214; *The History of Sexuality,* 210, 213, 223; *The Order of Things,* 210; *Psychiatric Power,* 217, 222–23; *Volonté de savoir,* xix

"four E's" (mass extermination, expulsion, ethnic cleansing, and enslavement), 52–53, 70n23
Frankfurt School, 183–85, 186, 233
Fraser, Nancy, xx–xxi, xxiii, 207, 209–10, 228n22
free labor market, xx; core feature of capitalism, 143; legal status, 143, 150; state role in, 91. *See also* capitalism; markets
free speech rights, 97; equated with capital, 99; government as enemy of, 100–2
freedom, xxiii, 120, 214; communicative, 27; problematization of, 195–96
French Revolution, 7, 31–32
functionalist approaches, 27, 48–49, 76, 79–80

gendered division of labor, 148, 153
gender equality, 29, 220–21
genealogical critique, 207; Foucault, 188, 191–93, 210, 216, 231–32n59; Marx, 130–31; problematization, 188, 191–93, 240; three modes of, 191–92
generality, xvii, 79, 83–84, 86
Geneva Convention, 22
German government, 6
Gewirth, Alan, 27
Gilroy, Paul, 245
global constitutionalism, 23, 38
global warming, 142, 150, 200
globalization, xiv–xv, 4, 49, 67
Globalization and Sovereignty (Cohen), 50–52
good life, 76–78, 83, 177; utopian thinking, 188, 189–90
Goody, Jack, 245
Goswami, Namita, 199–200
governance, global (supranational institutions), xiv–xv, xviii, 33–34, 57–60, 63, 84–85, 151; attempts to entrench human rights law in, 60–62; international action and, 65–66

government, as enemy of free speech, 100–2, 104–5, 112
governmentality, 91, 96, 213; biopolitical legitimacy, 217–18; Shared Responsibility Agreements, 221; temporality and, 217–19
Gramsci, Antonio, 243
Greek/non-Greek normative hierarchy, 241–42
Griffin, James, 27, 75–76

Habermas, Jürgen, xiv–xv, xxii, 44n26, 70n20, 88n30, 188, 198, 200, 203n4; on Foucault, 208; left-Hegelian approach, 184–85; progress as fact, 233–34; wide concept of economy and, 161, 173
Hammer, Espen, 199
Haraway, Donna, 150
Harvey, David, 146
Hegel, G. W. F., 117, 119, 176, 191, 242, 244
Hesse, Barnor, 234
Hirschl, Ran, 30
historical a priori, 194–95
historical learning approach, 184–85
historicism, 200
historicization of History, 188, 190–91, 245
history: problematization of, 187–88, 191–93
History of Madness (Foucault), 187, 191, 214
The History of Sexuality (Foucault), 210, 213, 223
HIV/AIDS, 58
Hobbes, Thomas, 242
Holocaust, 186, 187
homo oeconomicus, 94–95, 96, 97
homo politicus, 96, 97
Honneth, Axel, xxii, 162, 184–85, 198, 200, 203n4, 233–34
hopeful despair, 200
Horkheimer, Max, 160, 161, 175
human capital, 95
human interests, 75–78, 84–85
human rights: accountability of governments, 51; bifurcation strategy, 50–53; as class of

INDEX 283

moral rights, 27; constitutional rights and, 27–33; as core of legal cosmopolitanism, 27; de-internationalization, 52, 53–54, 61; demanding standards, xvii, 49–50, 52, 54, 55, 56–57, 60–66; democratic legitimacy and, 33–38; ethical justification, 75–76, 78; foreign doctrine and US Constitution, 21–22; "four E's," 52–53, 70n23; fulfillment of obligations, 62–64; historiography, 42–43n14; human security rights, 51–54, 56; "institutionalized and enforceable," 51, 53–57, 61–62; interpretation, xv–xvi, 24, 26, 28–29; lack secure access to any rights at all, 53; legal life, 74–75; minimalism, xvii, 48–49, 50–52, 61; moral justification of, 27, 77–79, 83; moral life of, 74–75; narrow list, 48–49, 50, 52–53; nongovernmental organizations, 35; normative gap, 32, 36, 39; philosophical account, xvii, 27; political life, 74–75; primary responsibility, 63–67; procedural aspect, 75; require justiciable form, 27, 29, 33; respect for, 30, 50, 61–63, 78–84; self-government and, xv–xvi, 29–30, 33; social aspect, 74–75; structural approach, 64; substantive aspect, 75, 85–86; third parties and, 62–65; tripartite model of obligations, 62–64. *See also* intervention, coercive; Responsibility to Protect (R2P) doctrine
human rights conventions, xv, 25–28, 37, 47–50, 54
human rights due diligence standard, 61, 72–73n43
human rights norms, 49, 54; strengthening of sovereignty, 24, 55–57, 59–60, 65
human rights proper, 51, 67, 71n26
human security rights, 51–54, 56
Hume, David, 242

ideal-theoretic orientation, 246
Ignatieff, Michael, 22, 77
immanent critique, xxii, 188, 197, 212, 213, 215
immigrants, 18n11, 42n13
imperialist metanarrative, xxiv, 151, 183–85, 233–34
inclusion, 77–78
indigenous communities, 221–22
individual, 30–31, 236; legal person, 24, 25, 31, 119–20; moral, 25, 31
injury, 131
Institute for Social Research, 161. *See also* Frankfurt School
intellectual property, 57–60
interests, 132–34
internal legitimacy, 80–81
International Convention on the Elimination of All Forms of Racial Discrimination, 26
International Covenant on Civil and Political Rights, 25, 48
International Covenant on Economic, Social and Cultural Rights (ICESCR), 25, 58–59
international law: customary, 25; human rights conventions, xv, 25–28, 37, 47–50, 54; local iterations, 37; as main function of human rights, 76; state equality, 8–9, 50, 56. *See also* governance, global (supranational institutions); Responsibility to Protect (R2P) doctrine
International Monetary Fund (IMF), 57
international treaty law, 22–23, 48–49; covenants, 25–26; level of interpretation, 54
interpretation: democratic iterations, 34; level of, 54; range of, 28–29, 32, 35, 39; of social practices, 165–66, 168–72
intervention, coercive, xvi–xvii, 30–31, 47–54, 69n13; justification of, 47–54, 77; "prodemocratic," 48, 66–67; primary actors disabled, 66–67; revisited, 66–68. *See also* Responsibility to Protect (R2P) doctrine
invisible hand, 114n17, 173
Isiksel, Turkuler, 33

Jaeggi, Rahel, xxi-xxii
justice: compensatory, 246; corrective, 244; fundamental, 84–85; maximal, 85
justification, right to, xvii–xviii, 74–88; as basic right, 74–75, 83–85; for democracy, 12, 15; discourse model, 36; discursive constructivism, 83–85; ethical, 75–76, 78; ethnocentrism and, 79; moral, 27, 77–79, 83
justificatory minimalism, 77

Kant, Immanuel, 237, 242, 244
Kennedy, Anthony, 96–111; corporations "as associations of citizens," 100, 102, 104; electoral campaigns as marketplace, 103–4; government as enemy of free speech, 100–2; on markets vs. rights, 107–8; on mistrust of government, 101
Kiobel et al. v. Royal Dutch Petroleum, 21
Koopman, Colin, 191, 211, 215–16, 230n45, 231n52

labor, 170–71
labor power, as commodity, 120–21
Lafont, Cristina, xvi, 44n29
law: bourgeois, 91; "different form," 118–19, 121, 123, 125–26; natural, 118; as "necessary function" for domination, 119, 123; neoliberal mobilization of, 91–93, 96; normative content, 117–18, 127; struggle for, 125–29, 134. *See also* bourgeois private law
The Law of Peoples (Rawls), 27, 30, 48–49, 69n13, 71n26, 76, 77, 81, 246
"Learning to Love" (Brown), 225
"Learning to Love Again" (Colegate), 221
left-Hegelian approach, 184–86, 233
legal cosmopolitanism, xv, xvi, 23–27, 38
legal person, 24, 25, 31, 119–20
legal pluralism, 24, 26, 38
legislative branch, 7, 9

legitimacy, 32–33; biopolitical, 217–18; internal, 80–81; recognitional, 80; threshold for, 51. *See also* democratic legitimacy
legitimate use of force, 3, 14
Lemke, Thomas, 210
Levitt, Peggy, 34
liberalism, 134, 135, 239; left critique of, 218–19; white, 239–40. *See also* neoliberalism
lifeworld, 161, 173–74, 241
Locke, John, 242
lowest common denominator approach, 77, 81
Lukács, Georg, 152, 160

Maastricht Principles, 61, 65
margin of appreciation, 37–38, 43n25, 54
marketization, xviii–xix, 4, 94, 145–46, 150
marketplace: of ideas, xviii, 98–100; speech as property right, 104, 112
markets, xx; exchange, 169–70, 176; multiplied, 103–4; rights vs., 107–8; role of in capitalist society, 144–45. *See also* free labor market
Marshall, T. H., 31
Marx, Karl, xix, 91–92, 121, 241, 242; bourgeois private law and capitalism, 119–21; context of contextlessness, 176; core features of capitalism, 143–46; critical theory of law, 117; Foucault's critique of, 192; genealogical critique, 130–31; general conceptual resources, 142–43; metabolic rift, 149; postcolonial studies and, 201–2; socialist basic rights, 121–23; socialist law, view of, 122–26
—Works: *Capital*, 146–47, 157–58; *Contribution to the Critique of Political Economy*, 117, 118
Marxism, 91–92, 246; "black," 238; racial eliminativism, 235–36, 241
master/slave dialectic, 244
material conditions of life, 91, 117
material structures, 167

maximizing preferences, 170, 171
Mbembe, Achille, 224, 225, 229n37, 230n39
McConnell v. Federal Election Commission, 108–9
McCutcheon v. Federal Election Commission, 96, 115n37
meaning, 92–96
medicines, access to, 57–60
membership principle, 52, 53, 70n23, 77–78
Menke, Christoph, xix, xxiii, 205n31
Merry, Sally Engle, 34
Mignolo, Walter, 202
military interventions, "prodemocratic," 48, 66–67
Mill, John Stuart, 242
Mills, Charles, xxiii–xxv, 209, 214–15
minimalism, xvii, 48–49, 50–52, 61, 77, 81
modernity: left-Hegelian approach, 184–85; nonwhite relationship to, 244–45; problematization and normative inheritance of, 188, 195–97, 241, 245–47; problematization of history, 187–88; racial categories, 234
modes of production, 91, 119, 125
modesty, stance of, 197
monastic disciplines, 217
monetization, xxi, 94, 95, 145, 152
money, 169–70
Monroe Doctrine, 22
Montesquieu, 244
moral contemporaneity, 31
moral individual, 24, 25
moral philosophy, 196
moral rights, xvii, 27, 52, 75, 84–85
mothers, 222–23
Moyn, Samuel, 24, 38

Nagel, Thomas, 23, 24, 38
national consciousness, 10–11
nationalism, 10
nation-states, 3–5, 9–16, 245
Native Americans, 244

naturalism, 135
natural law, 118
nature, capitalism and, 149–54
neoliberalism, xviii–xix, 91–116; democracy's meanings shaped by, 92–93, 96; homo oeconomicus, concept of, 94–95; legal reasoning, 91–93, 96; nature and, 149–52; negotiation models, 222; as order of normative reason, 94; persons, construction of, 97; public interest, elimination of, 108, 111, 115–16n37; rationality, political, 91–92, 94, 96; Supreme Court decisions, 96–112. *See also* economization of rights; liberalism
Nickel, James, 49, 76
Nigeria, 21
"no demos" thesis, 12
noncommodification, xxi, 144, 152–53
nondomination, 74, 78–79, 84
noneconomic sphere: capitalism dependent on, xxi, 92, 94, 142, 145–46, 151–58; commodity form, 160–61; normativity, xxi–xxii, 154–55; other social practices and, 168, 172–74
"non-ideal theory," 246
nonidentical, 194, 243
nonretrogression principle, 58
normalization, xix, xxiii, 123–25
normative gap, 32, 36, 39
normativity, xxi–xxii; critical theory, 184–85; of economic practices, 173; history and, 200–2; inheritance of modernity, 188, 195–97, 241, 245–47; noneconomic, 154–55
norms, xv, xvii, 28, 32; international, 33–34, 51; limits specified, 48–49; practices regulated by, 165, 172

Obama, Barack, 66–67
On Human Rights (Griffin), 75–76
openness, 212–13
opinion-formation, 35–36

Optional Protocol to the International Covenant on Economic, Social and Cultural Rights, 54
The Order of Things (Foucault), 210
ordoliberals, 91
Orientalism (Said), 183, 198
Other: blacks excluded from, 244; justice to, 196–97; openness to, 212–13
Outlaw, Lucius, 235–36

parité, 29
parliamentary deliberation, 7
participation, right to, xvii–xix, 9, 36, 38, 124–25; assets, 133–34; will of subject, 133–34
pastoral techniques, 208, 222
Perez, Oren, 40n6
persons: as consumers of speech, 100; fictitious (corporate), 97; legal, 24, 25, 31, 119–20; natural (human), 97; neoliberal construction of, 97
perspective taking, 81–82
philosophers of color, xxiv, 237–38
philosophy: as historically situated, 187, 190–91; as mode of critical thought, 189
pluralism, reasonable, 30–31, 76–77, 82
political action committees (PACs), 99, 110–11, 113n16
political critique of law, 117–18, 126–27
political-legal approach, xiv–xv, 75–76, 79–81, 84
Political Liberalism (Rawls), 28
political logic, 117, 126–28, 216
political rights, xix, 31–32, 52, 55, 138n32; exclusion of from human rights, 61–62
politics, economization of, 97, 104, 107, 115–16, 225–26
polity vs. economy, 150–53
Post, Robert, 35
postcolonial studies, xxiv, 183–85, 197–202; critical theory and, 183–86; race marginalized, 234

postdemocracy, 33
post-Fordism, 209–10
postmetaphysical theory, 184, 190, 200
poststructuralism, 201
power, 188–89; coinciding techniques of, 221–25; of contingency, 208, 231n53; forms, 207; multiple modes, 208–9, 215–17, 221–26
practical conception of human rights, 77, 80
practice character, 171–73, 176
practices, 163–66; economic, 167–68; ensembles of, 166–68; regulated by norms, 165. *See also* social practices
practice-theoretical approach, 163–64, 173–74
present, xxiii, 207–10; multiplicity of, 215–17; reconfiguration in Foucault's work, 219–20. *See also* temporality
principles, 28, 32–38
private law. *See* bourgeois private law
private property, xx, 91, 131; arbitrary disposal rights, 120, 131–34, 169; in means of production, 143; proprietary principle, 131–32
private sphere, 31, 131, 132–33, 148
privileges, 30
problematization, 187–88, 211; genealogy as, 188, 191–93, 240; of maternal practice, 223
"prodemocratic" interventions, 48, 66–67
production, 170–71; conditions of possibility, xx, 143, 146, 150; dispossession perspective, 147; hidden abode, xx–xxi, 143, 146–49, 155; inputs, 144; modes of, 91, 119, 125; social reproduction required for, 147–48; speech like capital, 100–1
progress, xxii–xxiii; as "fact," 186–87, 233–34; in future, 186, 190, 198, 205n49; as imperative, 184, 186; postcolonial and, 197–98; present and, 212; skepticism about, 186; Western-centric approach, 184–85

property rights, xix; assets, 133; bourgeois redefinition of, 131–32; free speech as, 104, 112; social practice, 168–69
proprietary principle, 131–32
protection of human rights. *See* Responsibility to Protect (R2P) doctrine
Psychiatric Power (Foucault), 217, 222–23
public reason, 27, 78

quid pro quo arguments, 108, 111, 115*n*37, 132

Race and the Education of Desire (Stoler), 199
race, xxiv–xxv; eliminativism, 235–36, 241, 248*n*9; European expansionism and, 234; nonwhite professional philosophers, 237–39, 249*n*17; silence of left on, 236–39; white privilege, 239–40. *See also* critical race studies
racism, 183, 214–15, 241–42
rationality, political, 91–92, 94, 96
Rawls, John, 28, 36, 51, 80; decent hierarchical regimes, 30–31, 71*n*26
—Works: *The Law of Peoples*, 27, 30, 48–49, 69*n*13, 71*n*26, 81, 246; *Political Liberalism*, 28; *A Theory of Justice*, 236, 246
Raz, Joseph, 30, 76, 80
reason, xxii, 188–89, 240–44; denied to nonwhite thinkers, 241–42
reasonable pluralism, 30–31, 76–77, 82
reciprocity, xvii, 11, 31, 38, 51, 79, 83–84
recognitional legitimacy, 80
reflective adjustment, 33
reflexive argument, 75, 79, 85, 86
regional human rights bodies, 54–55
Regulating Aversion (Brown), 218
reification, 152–53, 160
"Reification and the Consciousness of the Proletariat" (Lukács), 152
Report of the International Commission on Intervention and State Sovereignty, 47
representation, 237

resistance, 213
Resnik, Judith, 37–38
respect for human rights, 30, 50, 61–64, 78–84; external vs. internal, 80–81
Responsibility to Protect (R2P) doctrine, xvi–xvii, 47–73; coercive intervention revisited, 66–68; demanding interpretation of, 62–66; as emergent norm, 47–48; public standards of critique, 51; revisionary approach, 48–49; sovereignty and human rights not mutually exclusive, 50–56; as threat to sovereignty, 47–50; tripartite model of human rights obligations, 62–65. *See also* human rights
responsibilization, 222, 223–24
Revel, Judith, 213–14
revisionism, 245
right to have rights, 27, 53, 87*n*26
rights: to development, 64–65; to health, 58; legitimate range of legal variation, 28–29, 32, 35, 39; markets vs., 107–8; moral, xvii, 27, 52, 75, 84–85; political/functional conception, 27; political, social, and economic, xix, 31–32, 54–56; to self-government, xv–xvi, 29–30, 33; subjective, 118, 130–36; "the right to have rights," 27. *See also* human rights
risk taking, 213
Roberts, John G. Jr., 21, 23, 98
Roman law, 119–20
Rorty, Richard, 202
Ruggie, John, 61
rules, 28

Said, Edward, 183–84, 198, 199, 233
Sandel, Michael, 41*n*11
Sassen, Saskia, 37
Savigny, Friedrich, 119
Schmitt, Carl, 22
second nature, xxv, 172, 195–96, 245, 247
self-criticism, 196–97, 233, 239–41

self-determination, 7, 38–39, 82; Westphalian understanding, 23–24, 32–33
self-government: human rights and, xv–xvi, 29–30, 33
self-interest, 162, 163
self-investment, 94–95
self–Other, 244
semiproletarianization, 145
Sen, Amartya, 246
Senate, 9
settler colonialism, 242–43
settler common sense, 243
sexuality, 215
Shared Responsibility Agreements, 221
Shiffrin, Steven, 114n17
skills, 170–71
slavery, xxiii, 214–15; foundation of capitalism, 244
Smith, Adam, 94
social critique of law, 117–18, 124–25, 128–30
social democracy, 238–39
social forces, 176
social justice, 246
social law, 122–23; counterhypothesis, 126–27; normalization and, 123–25
social logic of law, 117–18
social opacity, 239
social order, institutionalized, 152–54
social practices: economic practices as, 167–68; economy as, 163–64; forms of life and, 164–67; interpretations, 165–66, 168–72; labor and production, 170–71; market and exchange, 169–70, 176; property as, 168–69; results, 174, 177. *See also* practices
social reproduction, xx, 147–48, 152–53; contradictions, 157–58; institutionalized, 152–54; noncommodification, 152–53
social structure of justification, xvii, 85
socialist basic rights, xix, 121–23
solidarity, 10
South Africa, 58

sovereignty, xiv–xv; American exceptionalism, 21–24; corporate speech and, 101–2, 105; democratic, 21–46; doubled, 12–13; equality of states, 8–9, 50, 56; family as domain of, 222–23; human rights not mutually exclusive, 50–56; over death, 216; phantom/waning, 217, 219, 220, 231n54; popular, 7–10; R2P as threat to, 25–26, 47–50; strengthened by human rights norms, 24, 55–57, 59–60, 65; waning, 217, 219; of weak states, xvi–xvii; Westphalian understanding, 21, 23, 32–33
speech: as capital, 98–103, 112; citizen right to know, 100, 102, 105, 106; corporate, 102, 105, 111–12; government as enemy of, 100–2, 104–5, 112; as public good, 99–101, 108
Spivak, Gayatri, 199
Sraffa, Piero, 144
state: alliances, 8; bourgeois constitutional, 118; capitalism and, 91, 150; primary responsibility for human rights, 63–67; sovereignty, xvi–xvii, 8–9, 50, 56; systemic relationships and, 3–4
"state of the understanding," 122
Stevens, John Paul, 106, 107–8
Stoler, Ann Laura, 198, 199
strict scrutiny, 104–6
structural approach, 64
subjective rights, 118, 130–36; dualism of, 131–34; empiricism/positivism of, 134–36
subjectivization, xix, xxii, 213–14
subordination, 148, 241; of women in families, 222–23
subpersons, nonwhites as, 244
substantive minimalism, 77
subversion, 191–92, 197
supranational democracy, 3, 9
supranational institutions. *See* governance, global (supranational institutions)
Supreme Court, xviii, 22, 96–112; *Buckley v. Valeo*, 96, 103, 109; *Citizens United v.*

Federal Election Commission, 96–112;
First National Bank of Boston v. Bellotti,
96, 103; *Kiobel et al. v. Royal Dutch
Petroleum*, 21; *McConnell v. Federal
Election Commission*, 108–9;
*McCutcheon v. Federal Election
Commission*, 96; *United States v.
Automobile Workers*, 111
surplus capacities, 144–45
Switzerland, 8
system-theoretic approach, 173

Tasioulas, John, 76
technologies, 170–71
temporality, xxiii–xxiv, 215–16;
contemporary governmentalities and,
217–19; daily techniques, 223–25; white
time map, 245. *See also* present
Teubner, Günther, 23
A Theory of Justice (Rawls), 236, 246. *See also*
difference principle
time maps, 245
toleration argument, 82
"Toward a Critical Theory of 'Race'"
(Outlaw), 235–36
"Traditional and Critical Theory"
(Horkheimer), 160
transcendence, 186, 189, 194
transnational democratization, xiv–xv, 3–18
transnational law, 3, 21–46; American
exceptionalism, 21–24; democratic
legitimacy, 33–38; heterarchical
practices, 33; human rights and
constitutional rights, 27–33; legal
cosmopolitanism, xv–xvi, 23–27, 38
treaty regimes, 4, 14, 54–55
trust, 5, 10–12
Tully, James, 185

UN Charter, 25, 47
UN Committee on Economic, Social and
Cultural Rights, 54, 58–59
UN General Assembly, 47

UN General Assembly Declaration on the
Right to Development, 64–65
UN Global Compact initiative, 65
UN High Commissioner for Human
Rights, 61
UN Human Rights Council, 61
UN human security approach, 52–53
UN Security Council, 68n6
UN treaty-monitoring bodies, 53–54
Undoing the Demos (Brown), 220–21,
225–26
unification movements, 10
United Nations Convention on Refugees, 25
United Nations Convention on the
Prevention and Punishment of the
Crime of Genocide, 25
United Nations Convention to Eliminate of
All Forms of Discrimination Against
Women (CEDAW), 25–26, 37
United Nations Protocol of 1967, 25
United States, 7–9, 18n10; constitution, 8,
9–10, 15, 16
United States v. Automobile Workers, 111
Universal Declaration of Human Rights, 25,
37, 47, 55, 82
universalism, xvi, xviii, 78, 106, 183; false,
79, 183
unreason, xxiii, 194, 214, 243
US Constitution, 9–10, 18n10, 21–22
use value, 120
utopia and utopianism, 188–90, 204n20,
240, 245–46

veto rights, 36, 79
vindication, 191–93, 197

Walden (Thoreau), 242
Waldron, Jeremy, 23
Walker, Neil, 36, 46n44
Walled States (Brown), 218
Wallerstein, Immanuel, 145
Walzer, Michael, 23, 24, 38
weak states, xvi–xvii

Weber, Max, 130, 177
welfare state, 122, 125, 210, 218–19
well-ordered society, 237, 246
Western philosophical tradition, 241–42
White Atlantic, 245
White Material (Denis), 224–25
white privilege, 239–40
white supremacy, 235; global, 235, 240, 242, 245, 247
white-dominated political movements, 238–39
will, individual, 131–34, 132

will-formation, 8, 11, 14, 16, 35–36
Williams, Bernard, 191
women's work, 147–48
Wood, Ellen, 151
working-class consumerism, 145
World Bank, 57
world society, xiv–xv, 3, 30
World Trade Organization (WTO), 57–60

Young, Robert, 199

Zerubavel, Eviatar, 245

GPSR Authorized Representative: Easy Access System Europe, Mustamäe tee 50, 10621 Tallinn, Estonia, gpsr.requests@easproject.com